THE INTELLIGENT PORTFOLIO

Practical Wisdom on Personal Investing from Financial Engines

CHRISTOPHER L. JONES

John Wiley & Sons, Inc.

Published by John Wiley & Sons, Inc., Hoboken, New Jersey.
Published simultaneously in Canada.

For general information on our other products and services or for technical support, please contact our Customer Care Department within the United States at (800) 762-2974, outside the United States at (317) 572-3993 or fax (317) 572-4002.

Wiley also publishes its books in a variety of electronic formats. Some content that appears in print may not be available in electronic books. For more information about Wiley products, visit our web site at www.wiley.com.

Library of Congress Cataloging-in-Publication Data:

Jones, Christopher L., 1967–
The intelligent portfolio : practical wisdom on personal investing from Financial Engines / Christopher L. Jones.
p. cm.
Includes bibliographical references and index.
ISBN 978-0-470-22804-3 (cloth)
1. Investments. 2. Portfolio management. 3. Investment analysis. 4. Risk management. I. Financial Engines (Firm) II. Title.
HG4521.J6632 2008
332.6–dc22 2007052402

Printed in the United States of America.

10 9 8 7 6 5 4 3 2 1

For Barbara and our two wonderful kids
(the best investments I've ever made), and
to my parents for always providing a steady tailwind.

Contents

Foreword

When the idea of a personal investment book based on Financial Engines' ideas and experience was first broached, the reaction was enthusiastic but guarded. Who could do the project justice? And who could find the time to produce a book that would be practical, approachable and sufficiently broad?

There was no question concerning the best choice. Christopher Jones has been the leader of the finance team at Financial Engines since the firm was founded. His ability to explain the most complex investment ideas and bring them down to earth was well-established. But what about the time required to complete such a project? "Not to worry," he said. "That is the reason that we have evenings and weekends."

The result—*The Intelligent Portfolio*— is before you now. And I am sure that the effort required many late nights.

His style is engaging. His thoughts are richly practical but firmly based in financial economic theory and rigorous empirical work. And most importantly, Chris dives deeply into the lessons learned over more than a decade by a large group of talented people dedicated to helping individuals make better financial decisions.

The investment world has changed—and keeps evolving—in a way that makes more and more people responsible for their own financial destiny. While defined benefit plans (DBs) once managed retirement savings for you, the new reality is that defined contribution plans (DCs) such as 401(k) are rapidly becoming our primary savings vehicles. The decisions you make with your DC plan can thus have a profound impact on your life.

Fortunately for you, the reader, this is not a book written by committee. Nor does it reflect a singular "official" position of Financial Engines. Rather it is the work of an experienced and talented investment professional, distilling his views of the key ideas and facts that any intelligent investor should know in order to invest and save sensibly. And is it a great read! Chris has managed to convey the essence of financial economics with nary an equation and to make the experience both fun and educational.

The Intelligent Portfolio emphasizes the lessons learned over decades based on financial research in both academic institutions and financial firms. But there is so much more here. The book draws heavily on insights gained by working with hundreds of thousands of individual investors struggling with important lifetime financial decisions. Financial Engines was founded to serve literally millions of people at a small fraction of the cost of existing comprehensive approaches. This ruled out consideration of any process in which key investment decisions are made by highly paid advisors based on instincts or gut feelings. Instead, it required a new and systematic approach to investment advice–one in which expertise is captured in algorithms used to generate personalized recommendations for investors. In pursuing this goal, tens of thousands of mutual funds and stocks have been analyzed in great detail, millions of portfolios have been simulated, and investment performance over time analyzed in exquisite detail. The book capitalizes on all this experience, bringing to the reader much that is new as well as much that is old.

Alright. But do you need to use the Financial Engines service to gain from reading this book? Of course not. The lessons it contains are fundamental principles of personal investing. One way or another, either you or your financial advisor need to know them, and there is a great deal to be said for plenty of overlap. It is, after all, your financial life.

If you are inclined to use the Financial Engines' service, this book will equip you to get far more from the experience. It will explain why Financial Engines recommends diversification, lower cost investments, adequate savings rates, and how it offers you a personalized approach to reaching your own financial goals. It will also illustrate the tradeoffs between risk and return, the importance of making long-term financial decisions taking both risk and return into account, and the nature of the opportunities available to investors in financial markets. Finally, it will insulate you from those in the financial community who are eager to take your hard-earned money in return for promises that are literally too good to be true.

Read on and you will certainly become a more realistic and intelligent investor. Then you can get back to enjoying the rest of your life.

William F. Sharpe
Palo Alto, California
February 13, 2008

Preface

Investors should start with a view of skepticism.

—Arthur Levitt, former Chairman of the United States Securities and Exchange Commission (SEC)

When I was in high school, I had a rather colorful American history teacher. A compact man with closely cropped gray hair and a decidedly Hemingway-esque demeanor, Mr. Ryan was, in the best sense of the word, a skeptic. In our classroom discussions, he quickly established a reputation for questioning assumptions and challenging conventional wisdom. He pushed us to expose sloppy thinking—especially our own—and not be afraid of challenging views that were widely held and espoused. Though I picked up a good bit of history in that class, the most vivid lesson had nothing to do with the Founding Fathers or the Louisiana Purchase. Mr. Ryan's passionate belief was that the most important skill in life you can develop is the ability to *think critically,* though in truth he had a slightly less genteel way of phrasing the point.

Mr. Ryan's lesson has stuck with me through the years and remains one of the most important things I learned in school. Time and time again in my career I have been reminded of the merits of a healthy dose of skepticism when it comes to evaluating financial decisions. Whether in the boardroom or around the kitchen table, being willing to question assumptions and not be distracted by irrelevant or misleading information is a highly valuable skill, and sadly one that is not developed often enough in our schools. Far too often, we fall prey to having our attention focused on the inconsequential rather than the essential. Through modern media and advertising, we face a veritable blizzard of useless information vying for our attention. Keeping track of the truth through such a haze of falsehoods, minutia, pretensions, and misdirection requires considerable energy and diligence. And nowhere is the impact of critical thinking more pronounced than in the investing world, where it can make the difference between success and outright disaster.

Since most of us do not try to become self-educated authorities in every aspect of our lives, we seek advice from experts. In working with such experts, including those who fix our teeth, service our cars, and prepare our taxes, we walk the fine line between knowing enough to stay out of trouble, and wasting time and energy on things that we don't really need to learn. However, the perils of making big mistakes or being led astray by phony wisdom are particularly vivid when dealing with decisions about your money.

If you spend any time at all on the subject of personal finance, your skeptical eye will have noticed the deluge of claims that you can beat the market, generate millions of dollars in quick rewards, impress friends, and look better in a bathing suit, all by following a few simple investing rules. Most would correctly view such claims with a healthy dose of doubt, if not outright derision. Putting it mildly, there is a lot of dumb advice out there when it comes to investing. If fact, many of the most important ideas from financial economics, promoted by popular media and advertised by financial services firms, are distorted or misused in order to sell more products and services. Things that you hear about the most (such as past performance) are often among the least important factors in making good investment decisions, while aspects that are crucially important (like fees and expenses) are often hidden from view.

As with many things in life, a good strategy to use when you lack experience is imitation. Want to learn how to make better investment decisions? Look at how the most skilled and experienced professionals invest the billions of dollars in their care. Methods used by multibillion-dollar institutional investors are directly applicable to the decisions faced by individual investors (albeit with differences in the way the problems are framed). Moreover, so are the results. Today the technology exists to perform the same analyses on your investments that institutional investors used to pay hundreds of thousands of dollars to carry out—and accomplish the task in a few minutes. What does this analysis do for you? It helps you understand how different decisions affect possible future outcomes and how to structure portfolios that will improve your odds of success. So-called *outcomes-based* investing can be a revelation for those faced with difficult choices. The key to good investment decisions is making informed choices. Life is unpredictable. That might sound like a cliché tagline from an insurance commercial, but it really is true. We do not get to pick which future we will live through, but we can structure investment strategies that contemplate the full range of possible outcomes.

For the past 11 years, as a founding employee and head of investment management for Financial Engines, I have been in the unique position to both witness and participate in the migration of institutional investing techniques to the world of individual investors. Financial Engines has been a pioneer in bringing the best of financial economics and institutional money management to everyday investors through independent and personalized advisory and investment management services. The creation of these services required significant insights into how the best practices from academic and institutional finance could be applied to the needs of individual investors—insights that I will now share with you.

What you need to know to make good investment decisions can be distilled down into 10 basic concepts:

- Recognize the linkage between risk and reward
- Avoid being deceived by history
- Leverage the wisdom of the market
- Select an appropriate risk level
- Avoid the perils of stock picking
- Don't spend too much on investment fees
- Diversify intelligently
- Select funds using relevant forward-looking criteria
- Understand how to realistically fund financial goals
- Invest tax-efficiently

Each of these concepts is explored in the chapters that follow. Some of these ideas will seem like common sense, some will seem counterintuitive and surprising; all of them are important in making good investment decisions. This book builds from some basic intuition on how financial markets function, to practical tips on evaluating trade-offs, to real-world advice on selecting investments, building portfolios, and maximizing the chance of reaching your financial goals. If you learn and follow these principles, you will become a better investor as well as a better judge of whether you are getting good advice. The half-truths, shoddy thinking, and bad advice you regularly encounter in the investing world will become that much more apparent—and that much easier to avoid.

I first began mentioning to friends and family that I was considering writing a book on personal investing in the winter of 2006. The reaction was usually an enthusiastic thumbs up, but I could not help wondering if they were secretly harboring thoughts more along the lines of "Oh boy, another personal finance book . . ." By my informal count, there have been about a million books published on the topic of investing. Second only to cooking and getting men and women talking to each other, few subjects seem to enthrall prospective authors like investing. When I began my research for this book, I went out to my local bookstores and surveyed the genre. With a few notable exceptions, what I found was that most personal finance books come in one of three basic flavors. First there are the engaging *concept* books—filled with witty anecdotes about people using the concept (such as value investing, commodities trading, or real estate speculation) to get rich and achieve Zen-like peace. While this category of book can be a fun read, like a meal of stir-fry vegetables, you often find yourself hungry again after only a few hours. When you are done, there remains that disquieting feeling of "what did I really get from this?"

Next are the personal finance *potpourri* books, filled with every manner of charts, tables, statistics, and investing minutia you can imagine. These volumes take a throw-the-spaghetti-against-the-wall-and-see-what-sticks approach to financial education. The appeal here is to the hard-core do-it-yourself investors; those who find comfort in memorizing IRS contribution limits and understanding the finer points of municipal bond credit ratings. Although chock full of information, drawing actionable advice from the pages of such books is left as an exercise for the reader.

Finally there are the *academic* books, which contain interesting and valuable information, but where the use of advanced math and financial jargon put the conclusions out of reach for all but the most determined readers. Reminiscent of a formal 10-course French dinner, it takes an adventurous palette, a big appetite, and considerable endurance to get the most from the experience. Unless financial economics is your passion, chances are most of these books never make it to your nightstand.

What seemed to be missing from the personal investing genre was a book that distilled the most important intuition from modern financial economics down to a few key ideas and then combined it with practical advice on how to make better investment decisions. How do you identify the most important factors in determining investment success? How do you judge what is valuable advice and what is pure baloney? And how do you come up with a successful investment strategy when the future is uncertain?

Another profound frustration with the personal finance genre is that all too often the material stops just short of giving people the information they need to make actual decisions. Generalities are all good and fine, but *what should you actually do?* Investment advice, like finding your significant other, is a highly personal affair. Differences between individuals matter a lot. With this truism in mind, Financial Engines has agreed to waive the fees for a 12-month subscription to its award-winning *Personal Online Advisor* service for purchasers of this book, so that you can apply the ideas presented here to your own personal circumstances. Any book, with its limited length and static content, can only go so far, but an interactive investment advisory service can provide that final crucial step of connecting abstract ideas with real-world circumstances. While you don't need to use the *Personal Online Advisor* service to get value from this book, I hope that you will find it to be a helpful and enlightening resource.

My goal in writing this book was to provide you with the literary equivalent of meatloaf—a compact, but rewarding meal that sticks to your ribs (apologies to vegetarians for the choice of metaphor). I will illustrate what really counts in making personal investment decisions through simple explanation of powerful ideas and bringing them to life with real-world examples from my experience with Financial Engines clients. I'll introduce you to some of the secrets that institutional investors have known for decades, but where most individual investors are still in the dark. Consider it a crash course in financial critical thinking.

Writing a book that imparts useful knowledge in an easily digested manner is difficult. Accomplishing this goal while creating an engaging read that you would not be embarrassed to be seen reading on the beach is a daunting goal indeed. I hope that you find this book to be interesting, enlightening, provocative, and at least occasionally entertaining.

To paraphrase the famous satirist Ambrose Bierce, I trust that you will not find that the "covers of this book are too far apart."

Acknowledgments

With any project of this magnitude, the list of people who contributed in meaningful ways becomes rather lengthy. Certainly this book was no exception. I could not have completed this work without the noteworthy efforts and support of many friends and colleagues.

I owe a great debt of gratitude to William Sharpe, whose mentorship over the last 11 years has been a profound learning experience. Bill's insights and practical wisdom are well represented throughout the pages of this book, though I must take sole responsibility for any errors or omissions. In addition to Bill, I have had the good fortune to work with an amazing team of colleagues who have helped build Financial Engines over the last decade. I owe special thanks to the Financial Engines Executive and Investment Management teams for providing me with the flexibility to complete the book in a timely manner, despite the many demands of a challenging day job.

Many people contributed their time, analysis, suggestions, and ideas to the material found here. In particular I would like to single out Brenda Ayres, Geert Bekaert, Scott Campbell, John Choi, Peter Cohn, Melinda Deutch, Asma Emneina, Kenneth Fine, Tim Gallagher, Irene Gitin, Steven Grenadier, Joseph Grundfest, Michael Hahn, Garry Hallee, Wei Hu, Brandon Kirkham, Helen Kuo, Sylvia Kwan, Richard Lipes, Jeff Maggioncalda, Gavin Noronha, Greg Pallas, David Ramirez, Jason Scott, Jim Shearer, Ray Sims, Gregory Stein, Anne Tuttle, Patricia Wang, John Watson, Robert Young, and my parents Douglas and Jerilyn Jones for their contributions, counsel, encouragement, and assistance of many kinds.

I would also like to thank Bill Falloon and the team at John Wiley & Sons, including Emilie Herman, Kevin Holm, and Michelle Fitzgerald, for their help in making this book a reality. Bill's persistence and energy in bringing the project to fruition were extremely helpful, and his good-natured badgering to keep things clear and simple was sound advice (hopefully largely successful). Caroline Pincus also provided very helpful copyediting assistance throughout the project.

Finally, I would like to thank my wife Barbara and our two incredible kids for putting up with the enormous amount of time and energy devoted to this project. Their unending support and generous patience made this book possible. And my wife's careful and diligent editing made it a much better book than it would have otherwise been.

I hope that this book provides a measure of illumination to those who find themselves traveling the often poorly lit road to financial security.

Introduction to Financial Engines

Spring comes suddenly to the campus of Stanford University, located about 30 miles south of San Francisco, as the lingering rains and chill of winter suddenly give way to a seemingly unending string of sunny warm days. The spring of 1996 was a particularly auspicious time in the Silicon Valley. Just six months earlier, a little-known start-up company named Netscape had burst into the public consciousness with a record-setting initial public offering, igniting a digital gold rush like the world had never seen. Everywhere new Internet companies and business plans were sprouting like weeds. Where previously students at Stanford competed for high-paying consulting and investment banking jobs, attention now focused on which Internet start-up to join. The arrival of the Internet, it seemed, had changed everything. In the midst of all this frenetic commotion, two friends met, as they often did, in the faculty lounge on the Stanford campus. Bill Sharpe is a kindly, some say grandfatherly man with a trademark goatee and lively eyes. Bill won the Nobel Prize in economics in 1990 for his pioneering work on the theory of financial economics, including how prices of financial assets are determined and the link between risk and return. Unlike a number of similarly accomplished Nobel laureates, Bill gracefully avoids the problem of too much ego for one person. But Bill's ability to intuit simple solutions to complex problems and then explain them in plain language is unparalleled in financial economics. Far from being unapproachable, Bill has always worked hard to make sure his ideas are both practical and useful in the real world. In the spring of 1996, Bill was looking for a way to apply his ideas, developed over decades of working with institutional investors, to the increasingly large group of individual investors in need of help with their retirement investments. The catalyst for moving these ideas from the academic world to the realm of individual investors came in the form of a one-man dynamo named Joseph Grundfest. Joe is a good friend of Bill's, a professor of law at Stanford University and a former commissioner of the Securities Exchange Commission (SEC). Joe is also widely regarded as one of the nation's top experts on securities law. He is also one of the most energetic guys you will ever meet—ideas don't just trickle out of Joe, they burst forth like a broken fire hydrant.

The topics of conversation that morning were some tools that Bill had recently posted to his personal web site. Bill, a lifelong computer enthusiast, had immediately been struck by the opportunities afforded by the Internet to make information easily available to people all over the world. In the spirit of helping teach others about his passion, he had recently been adapting programs from his work in helping pension funds with their asset allocation decisions to allow individuals to experiment with the techniques on his personal web site. As Bill related the capabilities of these simple but powerful programs, it became clear that many people could benefit from access to such financial tools. Bill was initially planning to put the models up on a free web site where anyone could access them. The problem was that few people were comfortable enough with the technology to get very far on their own. Reaching a broader audience would require a different approach.

Rather than being content to pursue the project as a purely academic exercise, Joe began to sell Bill on the idea of starting a company to develop and promote the tools so that they could be used by average investors to make better investment decisions. At first, Bill was reluctant to seriously consider the idea, as his passion is academic research, not the grind of daily business management. But Joe is a very persuasive guy, and soon convinced Bill to meet with another friend, Craig Johnson, a well-known lawyer and venture capitalist to discuss the possibility. Craig immediately perceived the opportunity to leverage Bill's work to help the growing tens of millions of individual investors who were struggling with investment decisions in corporate retirement plans.

In the conversations that followed, the three men decided that a company was needed to take the best practices from the institutional world and academic finance and make them widely available to individual investors facing the ever-increasing burdens of managing their own investments. A few months later, in May of 1996, a new company was born—Financial Engines—with the goal of bringing the benefits of modern financial economics through personalized advisory and management services to everyone, regardless of their wealth. Soon the three cofounders hired a CEO for the new firm in the form of an energetic Stanford MBA graduate named Jeff Maggioncalda. A couple of months later, Jeff hired me to build and manage the team of financial experts needed to develop Bill's ideas into tangible products. Delivering on Bill's vision would take the enormous efforts of hundreds of talented employees in the years that followed.

Today, Financial Engines is a leading provider of independent investment advice and portfolio management services to millions of individual investors at hundreds of America's largest companies. The company provides services to more than 6.8 million employees, including workers at more than a hundred Fortune 500 companies. In addition, as of December 31, 2007, Financial Engines managed more than $16 billion in defined contribution assets on a discretionary basis for individual investors in defined contribution plans. The company works with many of the nation's largest 401(k) providers, including Vanguard, Fidelity, JPMorgan, T. Rowe Price, ACS, Mercer, Hewitt, and CitiStreet.

Financial Engines pioneered the use of sophisticated Monte Carlo simulation with individual investors by building advanced financial expertise into software so that high-quality, personalized analysis could be provided to individual investors at a tiny fraction of the costs that institutional investors pay. The company was also the first to offer comprehensive taxable investment advice online to individual investors. Through its award-winning *Personal Online Advisor* service, the company has brought institutional-quality investment advice to investors of all wealth levels. Beginning in late 2004, Financial Engines introduced a discretionary portfolio management service, the *Personal Asset Manager* program, for those investors who wish to delegate the responsibility for managing their 401(k) plan to an independent expert. As of the end of 2007, the company managed portfolios for more than 225,000 investors representing more than $16 billion in assets.

From its inception, Financial Engines has been an independent, federally Registered Investment Adviser and does not receive compensation based on the investments it recommends. The company only receives fees from the advice it renders, and is free from conflicts of interest with the customers it serves. This independence ensures that its recommendations are in the best interests of each investor. Today, more than a decade after the founding of Financial Engines, Bill Sharpe's vision of providing independent, high-quality investment advice and portfolio management to millions of investors is well on its way to being fully realized.

CHAPTER 1

Now It's Personal

The future ain't what it used to be.

—Yogi Berra (1925–)

Over the last few decades, there has been a profound shift in investment responsibility – away from the professional institutions that traditionally manage financial assets and right into your lap. Today, tens of millions of people are faced with making personal investment decisions that will have a big impact on their future quality of life – but only a few feel like they know what they are doing. This shift in responsibility is not simply the result of some cyclical government policy change or a conspiracy among big corporations to avoid funding retirement for their employees, but rather it is a necessary response to a global population that is rapidly aging. In the future, whether you like it or not, you are going to be responsible for managing your retirement investments. The good news is that within the last 10 years, changes in technology have opened the door to the widespread use of modern financial economic methods in personal investing. For the first time, it is possible to apply the same rigorous techniques used by the largest institutional investors to personal investment choices. In this chapter I explore these techniques, how they became available to individual investors, and how they enable a powerful new way of looking at personal investment decisions—outcomes-based investing.

How the heck did we end up here?

Since when did it become accepted that truck drivers, marketing analysts, lawyers, bakers, computer programmers, dentists, and teachers should all become expert investment managers? Who decided that we all need to become well-versed in mutual fund selection and dealing with the impact of investment risk? I don't recall voting on this, do you?

If you are reading this book, chances are that you have at least a passing interest in becoming a better investor. For some people, the subject of investing is a passion or a hobby, for others it is more of a reluctant obligation – like cleaning the house. The reality is that we now live in a world that expects everyday people to understand a great deal about investing. Expectations go far beyond how to balance a checkbook or apply for a credit card. Today, virtually everyone over the age of 18 is expected to understand concepts such as the value of compounding, progressive tax rates, the differences between equities and bonds, and the benefits of tax-deferred savings. Those who do not bother to acquire this knowledge are roundly criticized by TV commentators, newspaper editors, and personal finance gurus for being dangerously out of touch. The era of the self-directed investor has truly arrived – even if most of us were not ready for it.

Unfortunately, investing is a sprawling and complicated subject, rich with intimidating jargon and numerous conflicts of interest thrown in for good measure. It is no surprise that many people approach investing decisions with a sense of dread, or at least acute anxiety. Why do *I* have to make all these investment decisions? Generally speaking, I am not expected to diagnose the strange knocking sound coming from the hood of my car on my own, nor am I presumed to figure out the origin of a blotchy rash on my son's back without expert help. Somehow, when it comes to investing, the prevailing opinion seems to be that you need to be educated enough to make good decisions on your own. But most people have better things to do with their lives than to become self-educated investment experts. And so, here we are, with tens of millions of individual investors directing how trillions of dollars of retirement money is invested, and bearing the consequences of those decisions for better or worse.

But why? Is this really the best way to make sure that we retire comfortably? It turns out that the dramatic movement towards more individual responsibility in retirement investing has its roots in a more fundamental and irreversible trend – we are all living quite a bit longer than we used to.

A CHANGING WORLD

Sixty years ago in the United States, things were a bit different. Back then, there were fewer decisions left to individuals. Mostly such choices were out of your hands. In the past, retirement was based on the concept of a three-legged stool, represented by family, government, and the employer. For much of recorded history, the most important leg of the stool (and often the only one) was your family. It was generally accepted that when you got old, your kids or extended family would take care of you (assuming you had any and that you had been nice to them). This was generally not an undue burden, as families were larger and most relatives tended to live in close proximity to one another. Moreover, retired people did not typically live that long after they stopped working. You might find it hard to believe, but for a male born in 1900, the National Center for Health Statistics reports that the average expected life span was only 48 years. Often, people would simply work until they were no longer able to continue on. Of course, things are a bit different today. Families are smaller and often spread out across large geographic distances. We are also living much longer. By 2003, the average 65 year-old woman in the United States could expect to live an *additional* 20 years. Moreover, steady advances in medical technology continue to increase average life spans. With earlier retirement dates, and longer life spans, retirement is now often measured in terms of several decades, not years.

In the summer of 1935, another leg of the stool was added—*Social Security*. With Franklin Roosevelt's signing of the *Social Security Act*, the U.S. government would provide a safety net for those in retirement of a lifetime guarantee of income. Social Security was a monumental change in public policy, and is one of the enduring legacies of the modern welfare state. When the system was created, however, there was a large working population paying into the system to support a relatively small retired population. Now, with the aging of the baby boomer population, the system's finances are under strain. Under current course and speed, either benefits will have to be reduced or payroll taxes will have to be significantly increased (or both) in order to fund the promised benefits, due to the growing population of retirees. Reaching such a political compromise has proven to be a difficult task in recent years, and so the magnitude of the funding problem continues to grow. Of course, this stalemate has potential serious consequences for taxpayers like you and me.

The third leg of the retirement security stool (at least in the last 50 years or so) was the employer. For those lucky enough to work for large companies, *defined benefit* (DB) plans often provided generous guarantees of retirement income, if you stuck with your employer sufficiently long. A DB plan provided employees with a guarantee of future retirement income funded from a pool of assets managed by the employer (usually without any input from the employees). The money was professionally managed on the employees' behalf, and if the markets went down, the company made contributions to the plan to insure the benefits were appropriately funded. If you were part of such a plan, all you had to do was show up to work each day for 30 years or so, and you were often comfortably set for retirement.

However, even in their heyday, defined benefit plans were not available to everyone. It is estimated that only about a third of people over the age of 55 receive any form of pension income.[1] In many situations, employees failed to qualify for any DB income because they changed jobs before they became eligible for the plan, or the companies they worked for simply did not offer such pension benefits. In the most recent generations, the availability of DB pension plans for new employees has declined dramatically.

Why are DB plans going away? One significant factor is the fact that people in today's economy tend to change jobs frequently. Under a traditional defined benefit plan (which provides guaranteed benefits), an employee must stay with a single employer for more than 10 years or more to accumulate significant retirement benefits. When the concept of "employment for life" was more popular, these restrictions were not as big a problem. However, today, most people change jobs multiple times during their careers, and hence would not accumulate significant benefits under the traditional defined benefit structure. But the biggest reason for the demise of DB plans is cost. It is increasingly expensive to run a defined benefit plan.

Most companies invest their defined benefit plan assets in a broadly diversified portfolio of stocks and bonds that is used to pay the future income of retired workers. If the market goes down, the company is obligated to make additional payments into the plan to ensure that it can pay out its promised retirement benefits. However, this creates a potential problem for companies such as General Motors and Ford, with large retired populations relative to their current workforce. With a DB plan, the company may have to come up with more money to fund the plan at precisely the time when money is scarce. When stock market returns are poor, chances are that the company is also feeling the pinch from a downturn in its business. The need to make payments into the plan when markets are down and when the cost of those payments to the company is highest (more on this concept later) makes DB plans a potentially expensive and risky proposition.

The magnitude of this cost problem is further accentuated when we take into account the impact of an aging population. Because we are all living longer, on average, the number of older retired people has grown dramatically over time, while, at the same time, birth rates have declined significantly. The following figure is an example of a *population pyramid chart* using 1950 data from the United States Census Bureau.[2] Such graphics are called pyramid charts due to their distinctive shape, consistent with the distribution of age groups in a growing population. Historically, in most societies, there have been a large number of young people relative to the population of older persons. If the age of the population is plotted on the

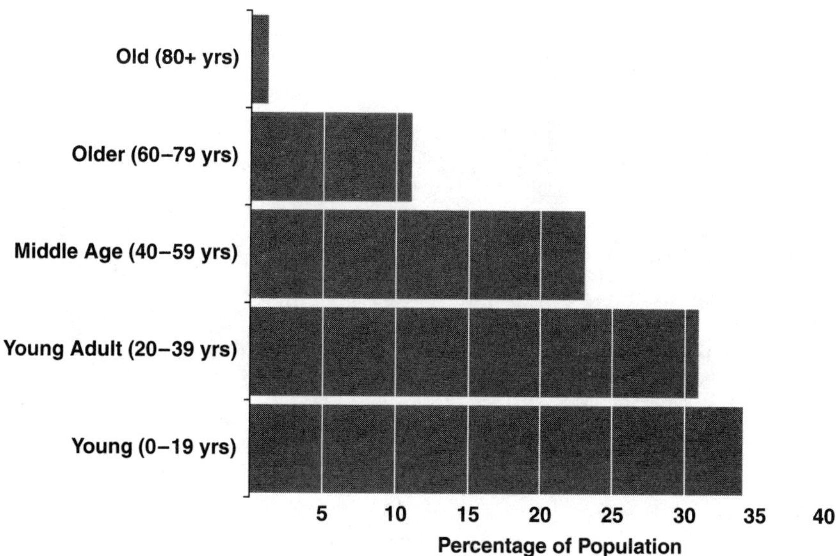

FIGURE 1.1 U.S. Population by Age Group in 1950

Source: U.S. Census Bureau.

vertical axis, and the length of the bars represent the proportion of the population in that age group, you get a distinctive triangle shape. In the United States of 1950, this pattern was clearly evident, as shown in Figure 1.1.

In 1950, the U.S. population was growing fast, and while life spans were gradually increasing, the proportion of older people had not yet begun to grow disproportionately. Now contrast this with the picture in 2006 (Figure 1.2).

The combination of lower average birth rates and greatly increased longevity has dramatically changed the relative proportions of active workers supporting retirees. For instance, in 1950, there were 47 people in their prime working years (between the ages of 20 and 59) for every person age 80 or older. By 2006, this ratio dropped to only 15—a decline of 68 percent. By 2050, there will be only 6 employees in their prime working years for every person age 80 or older. This implies a very different division of resources between generations than what has been historically observed.

The net effect of this demographic shift is that companies (and many governments) are increasingly unable to afford guaranteed income for life to the growing retiree population. If you guarantee income for retirees, it means working employees must fund this income with increasingly high taxes, or they must be willing to assume the financial risk of pension assets

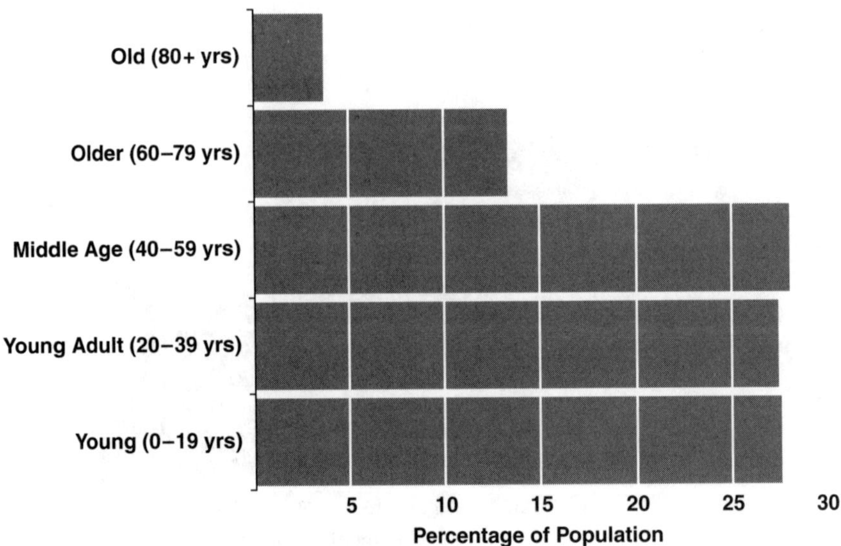

FIGURE 1.2 U.S. Population by Age Group in 2006

Source: U.S. Census Bureau.

falling short when markets turn sour. When there are only a small number of retirees for each worker, as was historically the case, this is not such a big problem. But when the retiree population gets large, look out. The burden on the working population becomes too onerous. Just as a company that takes on too much debt greatly increases the risk to stockholders and employees, guaranteeing retirement income for an ever-increasing retiree population is not an economically sustainable proposition. If retirees don't have any risk in their retirement income, then existing workers must assume all the risk. But now there are simply too many retirees to support—something has to give. The only way out of this predicament is to have the retired population share the risk of market downturns with the working population—that is, to make individual retirement income dependent on market performance. Enter the 401(k).

THE GRAND SOCIAL EXPERIMENT: 401(k)

In the last 20 years, the United States has seen enormous growth in *Defined Contribution* (DC) plans such as the *401(k)*. What was once an obscure part of the tax code, the 401(k) plan is now the primary retirement vehicle for most U.S. workers. In fact, DC plan assets now exceed the total value of DB plans by a wide margin. In 2006, according to the Federal Reserve, DB plans totaled $2.3 trillion, while DC plan assets totaled more than $3.3 trillion.[3] Defined contribution plans differ from DB plans in that the *individual* is responsible for making the investment decisions and for bearing investment risk, not the employer. With the rising prevalence of 401(k) plans, *Individual Retirement Accounts* (*IRAs*), *Health Savings Accounts* (*HSAs*), *529 Plans*, and other plans where individuals must manage their assets, more and more financial responsibility is being placed squarely on the shoulders of everyday people.

In many ways this is a grand social experiment—never before has so much financial responsibility been in the hands of so many nonexperts. We do not yet know what the results of the experiment will be for the United States. If financial markets perform well in the coming decades, people save aggressively and invest prudently, the experiment will likely be successful. However, if this rosy state of the world does not come to pass—there are going to be a lot of grumpy and cash-strapped retirees wondering how all this came to be.

The rise of defined contribution plans like the 401(k) has dramatically altered the landscape for individual investors. As of 2006, there are now more than 55 million individuals managing trillions of dollars of defined contribution assets.[4] For most employees hired in the last decade or so, the defined contribution plan is their principal (and often only) retirement benefit. In fact, DC assets now account for 61 percent of overall retirement assets in the United States. *Importantly, there is no turning back from this trend.* Since the economic need for defined contribution plans like the 401(k) is based on long-term demographic trends, there is no going back to the days of guaranteed retirement benefits. In the future, your retirement paycheck will depend to some extent on market performance and how you choose to allocate your investments. Put another way, if markets decline, you will be the one holding the bag—not your employer.

THE KNOWLEDGE GAP

Sadly, our educational system has been woefully behind the curve in preparing people for the heavy new financial responsibilities of a self-directed investment world. Unless you happen to work in financial services, what you know about these subjects is likely to have come from friends, family, and the media, not from high school or college coursework in economics and finance. Relatively few people have any significant exposure to academic finance or economics, and hence many of the important concepts that govern good decision-making are unknown to those who could benefit from them. Much of what we do learn is incomplete and reduced to three bullet-point sound bites on talk radio or cable TV shows. Most people rely on a haphazard mix of conventional wisdom, rules of thumb, and outright dart-throwing to manage their personal investments. The predictable result is that most investors are not doing a very good job of managing their assets. Unfortunately, most of us are flying by the seat of our pants.

To successfully navigate the waters of modern financial life, you have to make a basic choice. You can educate yourself so that you are able to make informed decisions on your own, or you can hire a competent and objective financial professional to help you (the third option of avoiding the subject, though immensely popular, is generally ill advised). The do-it-yourself approach has several advantages. You are in control, you do not have to delegate decisions to other parties, and you develop first-hand experience with the process of portfolio management. The downside is that it takes a lot of time and energy to become well educated on investments, and a comparable amount of time to monitor your portfolio on an ongoing basis. Also, if things go wrong, you have no one to blame but yourself (don't laugh; this is a major element of stress for many investors). In fact, most surveys on the subject, including those conducted by Financial Engines, estimate that only 10 to 20 percent of the population is truly comfortable with the do-it-yourself approach. The vast majority of people are looking for help, either to validate their own decisions, or to delegate the responsibilities to a professional who they can trust. Of course, finding an honest, qualified, and reasonably priced investment advisor can be a challenge.

THE TRADITIONAL ADVICE MODEL

It is true that many, if not most, individuals can use help with making investment decisions. What is less clear is how to get objective, personalized advice at a reasonable cost. If you are lucky enough to be wealthy—say, financial assets of a few million dollars or more—there are thousands of advisors eager to work with you. Of course, not all of these eager advisors know what they are doing, but nonetheless, there is a big pool to choose from. If your means are more modest, sources for high quality and objective investment advice can be particularly difficult to find. Like many aspects of life, the *caveat emptor* proverb applies to investment advice as well. As we will see, a big part of being an informed consumer of investment advice is being able to detect when your advisor may be making claims that don't stand up to scrutiny.

Up until a few decades ago, people with modest assets generally did not have a need for personalized investment advice. Most personal savings were simply kept in the bank. Few middle class individuals had reason to own mutual funds or even individual stocks until the early 1980s, with the rise of 401(k) plans. Since most clients for investment advice were wealthy, the advice model that developed was based on the concept of one or more expert advisors personally interacting with each client and developing a customized investment strategy. Generally advisors were expected to have high levels of expertise (often across multiple domains), and as a part of their services spent substantial time interacting with each client. The costs of providing such investment advisory services are considerable, typically paid as an annual percentage of client's assets. Fees for traditional investment advisory services generally range from 75 basis points (0.75 percent) to more than 200 basis points (2.00 percent) of assets under management, depending on the types of services provided and the size of the client account. For the process to be profitable for the advisor, the client account must generate sufficient fees to cover the overhead and compensation for the experts, who are typically paid handsomely. This model works well for high-net-worth individuals or families with big assets who can afford to pay for the personalized attention. But the reality of the advice business is that people with a limited number of zeros at the end of their account balance are simply left out. It is not economically feasible for well-paid experts to spend tens of hours putting together a financial plan for an individual investor with only $50,000 in financial assets.

To service the needs of investors who fall short of the high-net-worth benchmark, financial services firms have typically relied upon the structure of product-based compensation, or *commissions*. Rather than charging an explicit hourly or asset-based fee for advice, the compensation of the advisor or broker is structured in the form of commissions on the sales of investment products. However, this approach suffers from a big conflict of interest, as some products invariably result in larger commissions for the broker or advisor than others. The result is that the advisor may have a vested interest in selling certain products (such as the funds of their own firm), even if it is not necessarily in your best interests. This fundamental conflict of interest between commission-based brokers or advisors and the clients they serve is at the heart of many lawsuits and arbitrations that occur in the industry each year. Actually, it gets a little worse. Since commission-based compensation is triggered by transactions (buying and selling of products), the commission model also creates incentives for excessive trading. All of a sudden you find out from your broker that the great fund you bought 18 months ago no longer makes the cut.

Fundamentally, the commission-based structure does not alter the basic economics of providing advice—it merely changes (and conceals) the form of payment. Since the costs of the commissions are often built into the financial products (through *expense ratios* and *loads*), they are not as visible to the investor as in the case of an explicit advisory fee. However, the impact is the same—lower overall investment returns for the investor, and higher compensation for the broker or advisor. As we will see in Chapter 7, it is critically important to understand how fees impact the value of your investments.

INSTITUTIONAL TOOLS OF THE TRADE

Successfully addressing the needs of average investors requires a different type of advice model—one that leverages technology to change the economics of providing personalized investment advice. By using technology to automate much of the investment analysis process, it is now possible to provide high-quality advice at a much lower cost than was historically the case. The basic idea behind Financial Engines' advisory services is to emulate how the big guys manage investments using state of the art financial technology, but do it for millions of individual investors instead of a handful of giant funds. Want to know how to best invest your money? Apply the same techniques used by the largest institutional investors investing hundreds of billions of dollars.

For instance, consider the problems faced by pension funds. Putting together well-structured portfolios to fund future pension liabilities is not a particularly easy task, and usually requires significant expertise and analysis. Pension funds use advanced techniques to evaluate risk, forecast possible investment outcomes, value future liabilities, structure portfolios, and evaluate the performance of investment managers. While such techniques might seem intimidating to most investors, these same ideas are directly relevant for your personal retirement investing.

Albeit on a smaller scale, individuals face many of the same problems as institutional money managers like pension funds and university endowments. The biggest difference is that institutional money managers are able to apply much greater resources in evaluating these questions than most individuals (unless your last name happens to be Buffett or Gates). Large institutional investors such as the General Motors pension plan and the Stanford University endowment fund have benefited from the tools of modern financial economics for decades. But it has been only recently that comparable techniques have been applied to the needs of average individual investors. The reasons for this are myriad, but the biggest factor has been cost. Up until the last ten years or so, it has simply been too expensive to rigorously apply the techniques of modern financial economics to individual investment problems. In the mid-1990's, contemporaneous with the rise of the Internet, technology began to make possible a new approach to personal investment advice. A key development in this process was giving individual investors the ability to realistically view how their investments might perform in the future.

To understand how such techniques can be used to make better investment decisions, it is helpful to introduce some of the most important tools used by institutional investors. In later chapters, I will use these tools to illustrate important concepts with some real-world examples. It is not crucial that you understand the details of such methods, but having some basic understanding of what they are and how they work is very useful, whether you make your own decisions, or use the services of an investment advisor.

As a first step, when choosing an investment strategy, you want to develop a realistic view of the potential future outcomes associated with your investment choices. With knowledge of the possible range of outcomes, you can make an informed choice about the appropriate level of risk and savings to construct an investment strategy that will have a high probability of success. The methods for making such financial projections run the gamut from simplistic calculations based on a constant rate of return to sophisticated simulations that take into account the complex relationships among economic variables and asset returns. Among institutional investors, the most utilized method for understanding the range of possible investment outcomes is a technique called *Monte Carlo simulation*.

What Might the Future Hold?: Monte Carlo Simulation

Monte Carlo simulation provides a powerful way to analyze problems that involve uncertainty. The formal development of the Monte Carlo method dates from the Manhattan Project to develop the atom bomb during World War II and is based on the work of two famous mathematicians, Stanislaus

Ulam and John von Neumann. At the time, they were focused on random neutron diffusion in fissile material—how far little atomic particles, called *neutrons*, could penetrate into various types of metal. Solving this problem experimentally was expensive and dangerous (neutrons can give you cancer by damaging your DNA, not to mention they make your eyebrows fall out). While they had developed good theoretical models for the behavior of a single neutron, summarizing the interactions between large numbers of neutrons was so complex that it was analytically intractable (they could not even write down the equations, much less solve them). Their solution was to perform a large number of random hypothetical experiments simulating the paths of individual neutrons through various materials and then add them up. By averaging the behavior of individual particles over enough such simulations, the mathematicians could accurately estimate how far neutrons would penetrate different types of materials (they purportedly chose the name *Monte Carlo* after its namesake in Monaco in honor of Stanislaus's gambler uncle).

From its early use in nuclear physics, Monte Carlo simulation made its way into other fields of study and is now used in a wide range of domains, including weather forecasting, traffic analysis, chemistry, genetics, statistics, and investment analysis. The method is particularly useful in solving problems where the probabilistic behavior of a system is very complex. The probabilistic behavior of an investment portfolio consisting of a mix of different securities represents one such complex system. That is why institutional investors such as defined benefit pension managers have used Monte Carlo simulation for more than two decades to evaluate the likelihood of meeting future liabilities. More recently, Monte Carlo simulation has rapidly evolved from a mathematical curiosity into something of a marketing buzzword in the financial services industry. The purpose of Monte Carlo investment simulation is to provide a better understanding of the *range* of possible outcomes when the future values of the assets in the portfolio are uncertain. That is, Monte Carlo simulation can't help you predict the future (unfortunately no one can do that), but it can show you the range of possible future outcomes you might expect with different market performance.

These simulation tools provide important benefits for investors, including the ability to:

- Calculate the probability of reaching investment objectives
- Provide forward-looking measures of investment risk
- Test drive investment strategies prior to implementation

Virtually all types of financial assets have some degree of uncertainty in their future values. For instance, the future value of a portfolio of stocks may be worth more or less than its current value based on whether the stock market moves up or down. Even guaranteed securities like bank CDs, which are advertised as being very low (or no) risk, have some uncertainty in their future values. While the rate of interest may be guaranteed at the end of the period (say, one year), the actual value of the assets is dependent on how inflation behaves over the holding period. If inflation is low, the value of the CD account will be worth correspondingly more; if inflation spikes up unexpectedly, the value of the CD will be lower (in today's dollars), since the value of the accumulated returns will have been eroded by inflation.

The simulation of investment portfolios provides a powerful tool for investors. It allows the evaluation of different decisions (such as how much risk to take, how much to save, etc.) and how they affect the range of possible investment outcomes. Rather than evaluating such choices in the dark, we can directly observe how different decisions impact the outcomes that you ultimately care about. For instance, you can calculate how additional savings of $100 per month influences the probability of reaching your desired retirement income goal. Such simulations can be quite realistic, taking into consideration the impact of market performance, fees, specific security risks, taxes, account distribution rules, and even uncertainty in how long you might live.

The mechanics of Monte Carlo simulation are straightforward in principle but often complex in implementation. The Monte Carlo method is predicated on repeated randomized experiments of a statistic of interest (for instance, the future value of an investment portfolio). The idea is to model the random behavior of a complex system (such as a portfolio of investments) by repeatedly sampling different possible random values of the variables that drive the outcomes of the system (such as the future values of each security in the portfolio).

A Simple Simulation Example: Coin Flipping To illustrate some intuition behind how such models work, let's examine a very simple Monte Carlo simulation. As an example, consider the range of possible values for flipping a coin 10 times in a row and counting up the number of heads observed. The statistic of interest (the number of heads observed in 10 coin flips) can take on values ranging from 0 to 10. However, values in the middle of the range (4, 5, and 6) are much more likely to be observed than values at the extremes (0 or 10). To understand what the range of possible values and their associated probabilities looks like, one can simply simulate the flipping of the coin a thousand times or so on a computer and tabulate the results (you could try this by hand, but you would likely expire from boredom).

To create a single observation, a computer program generates random numbers to simulate 10 flips of a coin with a 50/50 probability of heads or tails in each flip. After the 10 simulated coin flips, the number of heads is counted and stored as one possible value of the statistic (let's say the first count comes up with six heads). Next, the process is repeated to calculate a different possible value for the variable (say, four heads). By running this simple experiment a thousand times, one derives a thousand possible values for the experiment—a distribution of outcomes for the number of heads in 10 coin flips.

Figure 1.3 shows the distribution of outcomes from a thousand random trials of this simple experiment.

This chart is called a *histogram,* and shows not only the range of possible values (0 to 10), but also how often each value is observed—the frequency of occurrence. As you can see, the most frequently observed number is five heads (as we would expect for a fair coin flip); however, there are many observations that are above or below five heads. In fact, for this sample of 1,000 trials, only 24 percent of the time did the number

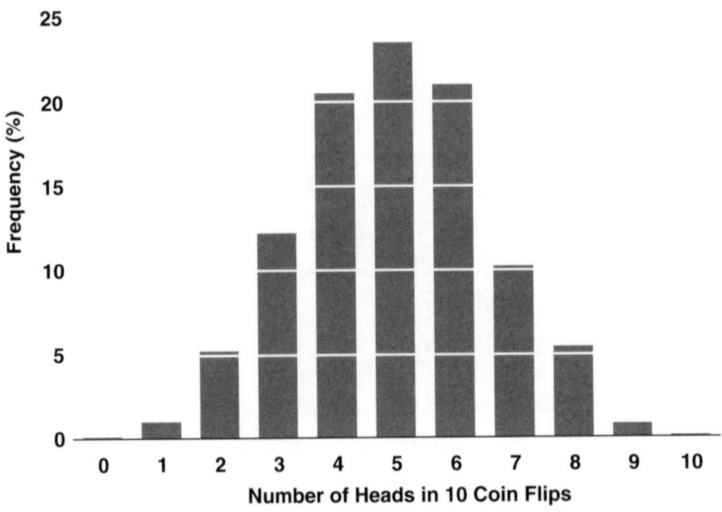

FIGURE 1.3 Plot of the Total Number of Heads Occurring in 10 Coin Flips, Based on 1,000 Trials.

of heads match the expected number of five. The chance of observing a very small or large number of heads is much less common. For instance, in this sample of a thousand trials, there were only eight observations of nine heads (less than 1 percent of all the experiments). In all of the 1,000 simulated trials, there was only one observation of zero heads in ten flips, and only one observation of ten heads in a row. Generally speaking, the further away the value is from the expected value, the lower its probability of being observed. If we were to run this experiment another 1,000 times, we would see a similar, but different set of observations. To get an increasingly accurate estimate of the true probability for each observed number of heads, we would need to run more and more simulations.[5]

Immediately we see that the statistic in this simple experiment (the number of heads in ten coin flips) has *volatility*. It can range over a number of different values, depending on the randomness of the individual coin flips. As human beings, we like to think of outcomes in terms of the typical result. It is important to realize, however, that most of what we experience is not the expected case, but one of many other possibilities. In this experiment, we observe a different number of heads that is different from the expected case (five heads) about 75 percent of the time. This means that you only see the "expected" result about 25 percent of the time. As we will see in later chapters, investment returns have a very similar property—their range of possible outcomes can and often does vary dramatically from the expected value. Making good investment decisions means recognizing that you will more often than not, end up with a different outcome than the expected result.

Simulating Investments Simulating a portfolio of investments is considerably more complex than modeling coin flips (and a lot more interesting, for that matter). A thorough explanation of how modern investment simulation models work would fill a book or two, which thankfully, I won't attempt here. For those that are interested, I provide a brief overview of how such models work, but it is not necessary that you understand all the details in order to benefit from investment simulation.

The hard part in developing a realistic investment simulation is specifying a model for how the returns of investment securities vary over time in response to different realistic economic conditions. This is where financial economics comes into play. Once you have a robust model for the investments, then you can apply the well-known techniques of Monte Carlo simulation to generate results rather easily. But if you have a poor economic model, even a large number of simulations and the fastest computers in the world won't get you good results. Investment simulation is a classic example of garbage in, garbage out. Getting the economic model right is the most difficult part of the process.

While specific simulation models for investments differ in their implementation details, the general process for creating portfolio scenarios is reasonably straightforward. The idea is to generate possible future paths that the economy might take and then determine how a particular portfolio might perform in each set of market circumstances. By generating thousands of such scenarios, one can accurately describe the range of portfolio outcomes that might be experienced and determine the relative probability of observing each outcome.

Generally, investment simulation models are built in layers. At the bottom layer is a model for estimating the joint behavior of key economic variables like inflation and interest rates. The process is complicated by the fact that interactions between economic variables are not purely random, but are partially governed by relationships between them. For example, when inflation unexpectedly increases, this has a predictable impact on current interest rates (they tend to go up). Because of this complexity, simulation models differ in their ability to capture the observed properties of economic and investment variables, and in their consistency with accepted financial economic theory. More sophisticated models use a combination of structural relationships (such as the link between today's inflation and inflation in the previous period) along with random noise to generate possible future values of economic variables. This way the future scenarios have randomness but still abide by theoretical constraints based on the linkage between different types of economic variables.

In the middle layer of most investment simulation models is something called a *factor model*, which generates possible returns for various types of asset classes (for instance, large capitalization stocks, corporate bonds, or international equities) given the values of the key economic variables determined in the first layer. The factor model may be simple, dividing the investment world into as few as three categories: stocks, bonds, and cash, or it may be more complex considering a dozen or more classes of investments. In the case of the Financial Engines simulation model, the investment world is divided into fifteen different asset classes spanning domestic and international equities and bonds.[6]

The top layer of the simulation model captures the linkage between specific securities and the returns in the underlying asset classes. In some models, a specific security may be related to one or more of the underlying asset classes. For instance, a balanced mutual fund might have investments in both bond and equity asset classes. Depending on the mix of assets classes in the specific security, its returns will tend to move with different segments of the market. A given security inherits its *expected return*, the level of return that you can expect, on average, from its underlying investments. For instance, a bond fund will tend to have similar expected returns to bond asset classes, while an equity fund will tend to have similar expected returns to various equity asset classes.

In addition, it is often necessary to adjust the expected returns of a specific security to capture characteristics that make its returns different from those of its underlying investments. For instance, a mutual fund charges fees in the form of an *expense ratio,* which lowers its expected return relative to the assets in its underlying portfolio.

To make the process more concrete, let us examine what it takes to create scenarios for a simple portfolio consisting of a single hypothetical equity mutual fund. At a high level, the simulation process consists of several steps that are repeated many times:

1. Start with current values of key economic variables (interest rates, inflation, etc.).
2. Generate possible values for the economic variables in the next period based on a random draw from an economic model with the current values as inputs.
3. Derive returns for each asset class for that period.
4. Derive returns for the mutual fund based on the underlying asset class returns.
5. Repeat steps 2 through 4 until you have a complete scenario.
6. Repeat steps 1 through 5 to generate multiple scenarios.

For instance, if we start with an initial $10,000, one possible future scenario for an equity mutual fund over a 40-year period might look like Figure 1.4 (assuming no taxes).

This is but just one possible path for how this fund might perform over the next 40 years. Depending on the economic environment and the performance of the securities held by the fund, the outcomes could be very different. This becomes evident as we add additional possible scenarios to the chart, as shown in Figure 1.5.

As you can see, there is already quite a wide range of potential outcomes from the mutual fund portfolio with only five scenarios. With just five scenarios, the $10,000 initial investment outcomes range from as little

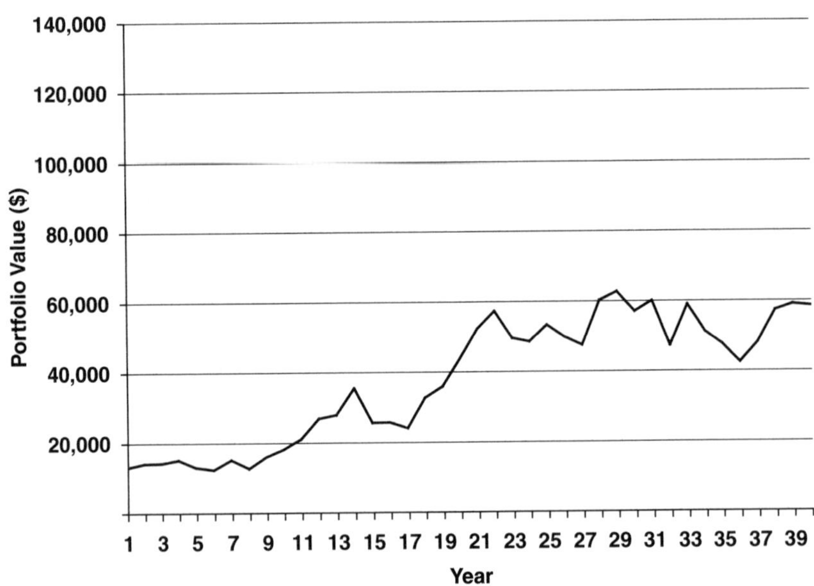

FIGURE 1.4 One Possible 40-year Scenario for an Equity Mutual Fund with a $10,000 Initial Investment.

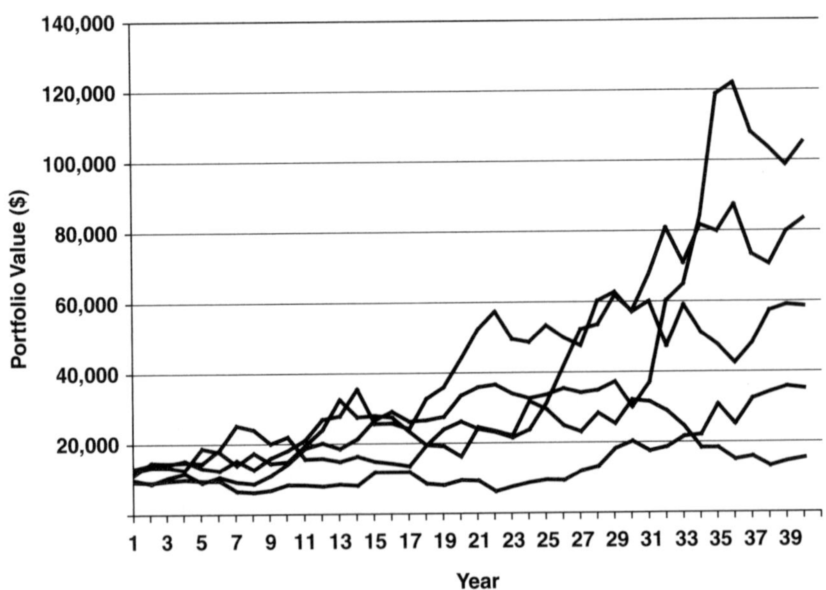

FIGURE 1.5 Five Possible 40-year Scenarios for an Equity Mutual Fund with a $10,000 Initial Investment.

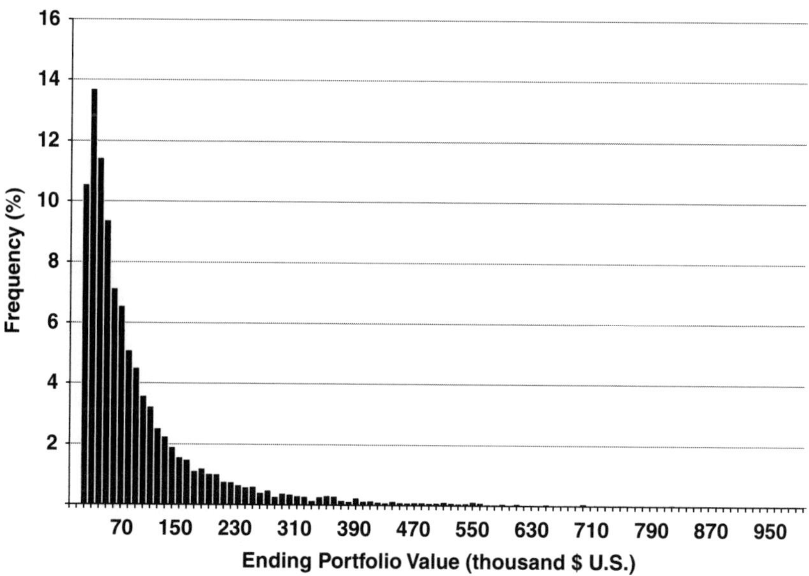

FIGURE 1.6 Histogram of 10,000 Simulations of an Initial $10,000 Investment in a Hypothetical Mutual Fund over 40 Years.

as $15,000 to as much as $105,000 depending on how the market and specific securities held by the fund performed over the 40-year period. If you have ever daydreamed how your life would have been different had you married your high school sweetheart, taken that job in New York years ago, or decided to become an artist in Paris, you have a feel for the simulation concept. With simulation, we let our investments live through many *possible* futures to see how things might play out. By generating thousands of such scenarios, we get a distribution of possible outcomes from which we can calculate many useful statistics. Figure 1.6 shows what the distribution of final wealth outcomes after 40 years looks like for our hypothetical mutual fund after 10,000 simulated scenarios.

The shape of this distribution of portfolio outcomes is very typical for investments with higher levels of volatility (like a stock mutual fund). The minimum outcome is bounded by zero (unless you borrow money to buy the fund, you can't lose more than you started with). About two-thirds of the outcomes lie between zero and $75,000. However, there are a significant number of observations that greatly exceed the expected value. This is called a *skewed distribution,* and is characteristic of portfolio distributions when holding volatile assets like equities over long time periods. Note that there are small probabilities of some very good outcomes. Even though 50 percent of the outcomes are below $46,700 (the *median* or middle value), the average outcome is over $89,000. The reason for the difference is that the very good outcomes drive up the average, yet they do not affect the median case very much since their probabilities are small. The higher the volatility of the asset, the more skewed the distribution will become, and the bigger the difference between the median value and the average value. You can play around with this type of investment simulation and see the results for different kinds of portfolios on the Financial Engines *Personal Online Advisor* service. This service allows you to input the investments in your portfolio and perform simulations of how they might perform over different time horizons. It can be a very enlightening exercise to see the range of possible investment outcomes.

The goal of the preceding analysis is not to create pretty charts, but to calculate statistics that are useful for making decisions. For instance, we can calculate the probability that our investments will exceed a certain target goal. We can also calculate how much we might lose if markets perform poorly over the period. We can calculate the range of possible outcomes, including the downside, median, and upside cases. Of course, knowledge of the distribution of outcomes is very valuable in making informed investment decisions.

In the following chapters, we will use the Financial Engines simulation engine to illustrate and quantify the tradeoffs that exist when developing an investment strategy.

Which Investments Are Best?: Investment Analysis

Another prominent technique in the institutional investor toolkit is the use of analytic methods to determine how specific investments are related to market returns, and how they have performed relative to what we would expect given the type of investment. When selecting investments for a portfolio, it is very useful to know what their expected risk and return characteristics are and how they have performed compared to other similar assets. Financial Engines has adopted these methods used by institutional investors to help individual investors do a better job of investment selection. One important technique for determining what an investment acts like is *investment style analysis*.

Investment style analysis, or *returns-based style analysis,* was developed by William F. Sharpe, a 1990 Nobel laureate and cofounder of Financial

Engines, for use in assessing and measuring the performance of investment managers for pension funds and other institutional money managers. The technique was first published in a paper by Sharpe in 1988.[7] Since then, the method has gained widespread use throughout the investing world due to its unique ability to look through a fund's underlying investments to understand how it behaves.

The key to the technique is to recognize that the performance of a fund is actually driven by a combination of exposures to different parts of the economy. For instance, a large-capitalization growth equity mutual fund may have exposures to growth stocks with large capitalizations. However, most funds have exposures to other parts of the market as well. Perhaps some of the stocks held by the fund may be from small or midsized companies, or from value-oriented stocks. If the fund is actively managed (as opposed to an index fund), it may keep a small percentage of assets in cash in order to better handle daily inflows and outflows. Style analysis of such a fund would yield exposures to large-cap growth equity, and perhaps various other equity exposures, or a small percentage in cash. The important point is that most funds are not easily categorized into a single asset class. In the real world, funds have several exposures and often behave significantly different from their stated investment objective. It's kind of like the difference between the name on the label and the list of ingredients on the back of the can (for instance, check out the ingredients listed on a can of Cheez Whiz).

Style analysis works by examining how a fund's returns move with various asset classes in the market. For example, some funds might move more closely with changes in the value of smaller company stocks, while other funds might be more related to movements in corporate bonds. Sharpe discovered that by setting up the problem a particular way, one could derive accurate estimates of a fund's investment exposures with a relatively small amount of data on historical returns. This opened up a whole new window of analysis of funds and their investment behavior. Instead of relying on a single designated *benchmark* like the S&P 500 Index, one could construct a custom benchmark for each fund that was representative of types of investments selected by their investment strategy. A manager who mostly invested in value stocks but held 20 percent of the portfolio in growth stocks could be measured against the performance of a benchmark based on 20 percent growth equity and 80 percent value equity. With the use of such custom benchmarks, it is possible to more accurately ascertain the extent an investment manager is actually adding value. The use of style analysis techniques among professional investors has greatly expanded in recent years due to its flexibility and utility.

Knowledge of a fund's investment style, as we shall see, is critical in building effective portfolios that maximize the expected return for a given level of risk.

How Do You Construct a Good Portfolio?: Optimization

A third major tool of the institutional investor is *portfolio optimization.* Optimization is a mathematical technique for figuring out the best solution to a particular problem, given a range of possible alternatives. In the context of investing, the purpose of optimization is to select investments that do the best job of meeting a set of objectives. These objectives may be fairly simple (give me the combination of funds with the highest expected return for a desired level of risk), or they may be very complex, with numerous competing goals and constraints.

In the institutional world of pension funds and university endowments, portfolio optimization is used to create alternative investment strategies. Data on each of the investment options, along with information about desired risk levels and other constraints, are fed into an optimization algorithm to yield a recommended portfolio allocation. The most popular forms of portfolio optimization are based on the concept of *mean-variance* portfolio theory. Very simply, this means an optimization where the goal is to maximize the expected return of the portfolio for a given level of variance (volatility). The optimizer takes information on each of the securities available to you and determines the portfolio that offers the highest expected return for the level of risk that you are willing to assume.

Of course, there are many ways to measure risk other than looking at just the volatility of returns. More complex optimization methods are able to accommodate different measures for risk, and the inclusion of various types of constraints. For instance, a given investment may have a minimum investment amount, or you may wish to impose a maximum percentage allocation to a particular security. Moreover, there may be factors other than expected return that you may wish to optimize. For instance, capital gains taxes can impact the desirability of buying or selling certain securities. There may also be preferences for the number of securities in the portfolio, or for concentration in a single security. Each of these constraints or preferences can add significant complexity to the optimization algorithm. Modern portfolio optimization engines are able to handle a wide variety of such real-world complexities. The bottom line is that optimization engines are able to help you build portfolios that achieve desired objectives while abiding by constraints and preferences that you believe are important. They are an invaluable tool for modern portfolio management, both for institutions and for individual investors.

TAKE-AWAYS

- The world has changed—and you had better get used to it. You *will* have personal responsibility for managing retirement assets in the future. There is no going back to the days where your employer or the government took care of your retirement income needs.
- Make a fundamental choice: either educate yourself enough to make informed decisions or admit that you need some help. If you choose to get help, make sure that it comes at a reasonable cost and from a competent and objective expert that you can trust. Be realistic about your ability and interest in managing your investments on your own. But most importantly, don't make the mistake of doing nothing.
- If you do work with an advisor, learn enough to spot obviously bad advice when you see it. Also, be careful of how your advisor gets paid—conflicts of interest can yield advice that is not in your best interest.
- Monte Carlo simulation is a powerful technique for understanding the range of possible investment outcomes you might experience. Remember that the expected outcome is only one possibility. It is more likely that you will experience an outcome that is different from the expected one.
- Leveraging tools from the institutional world provide important insights for making informed decisions. Try out the *Personal Online Advisor* service to see how your own investments might perform at www.financialengines.com/intelligentportfolio.[8]

CHAPTER 2

No Free Lunch

There ain't no such thing as a free lunch.
—Robert Heinlein (1907–1988), *The Moon is a Harsh Mistress* (1966)

Understanding the fundamental link between risk and return is critical to intelligent investing. But the intuition for how the two relate is not often explained. How are prices set for risky assets? Why should the return of an asset be related to risk? Should you be able to find assets with high rates of return and little risk? What do the trade-offs look like for typical investments? In the investing world, risk and return are always related. This chapter will show you how to understand, quantify, and evaluate investment risk. It will also help you recognize unrealistic advice and financial projections when you see them.

Now I have nothing against complimentary mid-day meals, but as with most things in life, the concept of getting something for nothing is rarely realized. This is particularly true in the investing world. Whenever you seek higher rates of return, risk always comes along for the ride. The risk may not be visible, nor will it necessarily be realized, but it is always there, lurking in the shadows. Investing without recognizing and accounting for risk can be disastrous, a truism for both individual and institutional investors. History is littered with examples where financial firms have lost billions of dollars by forgetting this reality. For instance, in late 2007 and early 2008, Citigroup, Merrill Lynch, and UBS had to collectively write-off losses of more than $50 billion due to bad bets on the U.S. mortgage market. The golden rule with investments is to take on risk that you get paid for and avoid risk that comes with no expected reward. In addition, you should be careful to expose yourself to only those risks for which you are willing to bear the consequences if things do not go your way.

Institutional investors generally spend a great deal of time and effort analyzing the amount and types of investment risk in their portfolios (for very good reasons). In fact, some of the most important contributions from financial economics have to do with the role of risk in markets, especially how to evaluate risk and mitigate its impact. Surprisingly, in the deliberations of many individual investors, it is not obvious that risk enters into the decision at all.

I'LL TAKE THE ONE WITH THE HIGHEST RETURN...

If you have ever visited an advisor, broker, or used one of the many online investing tools on the Web, you have no doubt encountered the mythical "return-return" trade-off. Typically, the interaction goes something like this: You are shown three to five colorful pie charts representing different potential asset allocations for your portfolio, each with a different *expected return* The expected return is simply an estimate of the average future rate of return for the investment. The Conservative portfolio might have an expected return of 5 percent per year, the Moderate portfolio an expected return of 7 percent per year, and the Aggressive portfolio an expected return of 10 percent per year. Usually, historical returns for the asset classes represented in each pie are used to estimate the expected returns. Next, you are shown a series of charts illustrating the future value of your portfolio if you achieve the average rate of return each year for the next 25 years as shown in Figure 2.1. In the chart, the portfolios dutifully deliver the average expected return each year, resulting in a nice smooth ramp to the final value at the end of the investment period. Of course there is some fine print below the graphs stating that the average historical returns may not be representative of the future, but this is usually brushed aside as mere legal boilerplate. Then the $64,000 question is posed: Which portfolio do you prefer?

Unless you are not paying attention, the answer seems pretty obvious, right? Of course, the 10 percent portfolio looks the best. After all, it provides the largest expected account balance in 25 years. What's wrong with this picture? Plenty.

This chart should certainly give you pause as a skeptical investor. Until very recently, most individual financial planning exercises assumed a constant rate of return for investments (and unfortunately, many still do). The problem is that the simplified constant rate of return assumption is not a realistic model for how markets actually behave. The probability of observing a scenario where the market return is equal to the average expected return each year for 25 years is essentially zero—it will never happen. The issue with *deterministic* models—those that do not consider uncertainty

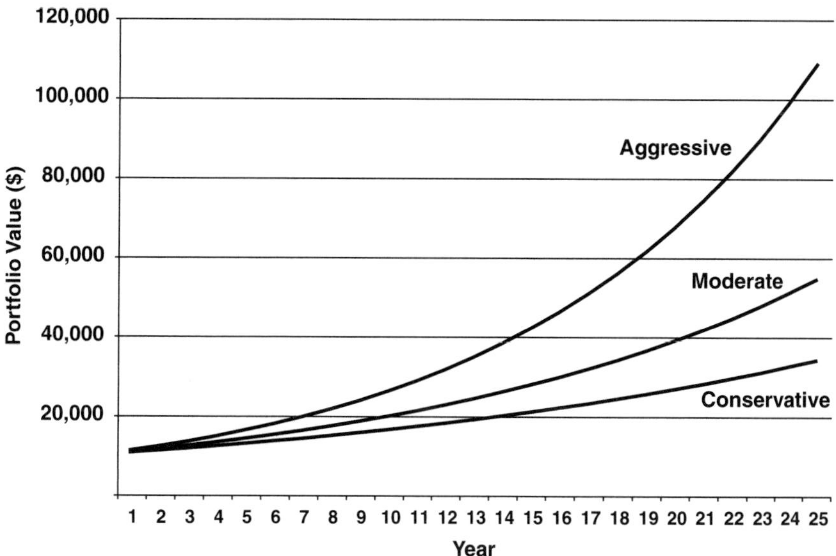

FIGURE 2.1 Hypothetical Portfolio Values for $10,000 Invested over 25 Years: Conservative, Moderate, and Aggressive Allocations

at all—is that they answer the wrong question, specifically: How much money will I have if I receive 10 percent per year? Anybody with a calculator or spreadsheet can easily answer that one. Because it assumes a constant rate of return, a deterministic model does not answer the more important and relevant question: What is the chance that I will achieve 10 percent per year? This is a much more interesting and important question, albeit more difficult to answer.

Ignoring the relevant question exposes the deterministic model's Achilles heel: it focuses exclusively on return without accounting for the consequences of investment risk. This shortcoming leads to a false "*return-return tradeoff*." In fact it is not a trade-off at all, but merely an exercise in selecting the highest expected return asset. Because the question focuses only on return, and not on how deep or frequent possible losses may be, higher expected-return strategies *always* appear superior to lower-return strategies. After all, who would prefer to have less money in the future? This misleading tradeoff is a hallmark of deterministic financial planning models.

Luckily, thanks to the efforts of companies such as Financial Engines, the use of deterministic forecasts in financial planning is on the decline. Many advisors now have access to forecast results (often based on Monte Carlo simulations) that explicitly illustrate a range of possible outcomes.

These models are not a panacea, but they do provide critical insights into how investment risk impacts the chance of reaching financial goals. As we will demonstrate in later sections, the higher the volatility of the portfolio assets, the wider the range of portfolio outcomes that may be observed in the future. Knowledge of the tradeoff between expected returns and the range of possible outcomes is not only useful but essential in making informed investment decisions. If your advisor still insists on using deterministic projections for financial planning, tell him or her to get with the program (or go shop for a new advisor). It is time to consider risk and return as they really are, inextricably linked.

A LITTLE BIT OF LATIN: EX-ANTE AND EX-POST

I promised myself when I started writing this book that I would avoid the use of economic jargon where it might obscure the meaning of important ideas. However, sometimes a little bit of Latin is warranted, and here is one of those times, so I ask for your indulgence. The Latin word for "beforehand" is *ex-ante*. When economists talk about ex-ante risk, they mean uncertainty that is yet to be resolved. For instance, if I were to put on a blindfold and leisurely stroll across a busy freeway, I would be taking on a huge amount of ex-ante risk (not to mention exposing other drivers to great risk and potential psychological trauma). The opposite of ex-ante is *ex-post*, which means "after the fact." If I were to make it to the other side of the street unscathed, then the ex-ante risk of me becoming a permanent hood ornament was not realized (luckily for me). Obviously, I was still an idiot for taking on such risks ex-ante, even though things worked out okay for me in the end.

The distinction between ex-ante risk and ex-post outcomes is an important one. Much of the time, risks that are present ex-ante do not actually show up in the observed outcomes. Going back to our example, just because I made it across the road does not imply that the risk was not there, but merely that I experienced a good outcome from the set comprised of mostly lousy outcomes. If I only paid attention to the observed outcome, I could be making a huge mistake in underestimating the potential risk. But if I were to try this experiment 10 more times, chances are I would soon realize just how much risk I was taking. Odds are I would end up as road kill more times than not.

In the investing world, we have to make decisions based on our best assessment of ex-ante risk. Many times, investors or advisors will point to a historical track record with good performance and low volatility to suggest that the risk of the investment going forward is minimal. This can be very misleading. Just because bad outcomes were not observed in the historical results does not imply that risk was not there ex-ante. Maybe you just happened to miss stepping in front of that speeding semi. *Most of the possible outcomes for an investment decision will not actually be observed.* Put another way, there are an infinite number of futures we might experience, but ex-post *we will live through just one.* This implies that the measure of a prudent decision is not whether it leads to a good outcome, but whether the choice was prudent given the ex-ante risk and potential rewards.

If you went to Vegas and put all your retirement savings down on number seven on a roulette wheel, you might be really lucky and win a fantastic retirement. But even if you did win, it was still a stupid decision because the odds were against you. You might get lucky and be bailed out of a bad investment decision by having things break your way, but you are much better off making informed decisions based on the best possible assessment of ex-ante risks. *Good decisions do not always result in good outcomes and bad decisions do not always result in bad outcomes.* Sometimes you make the best decision you can but the forces of fate simply work against you. Don't confuse good decision making with good outcomes, and vice versa.

So why is investment risk and expected return related? That turns out to be a very interesting question.

HOW ARE THE PRICES OF RISKY ASSETS SET?

The relationship between risk and expected return or the prices of assets is one of the most studied and complex questions in financial economics. Most people have little to no experience with *asset pricing theory*, the area of economics that focuses on such questions. Unfortunately, modern asset pricing theory makes heavy use of sophisticated mathematics to understand how investors' buying and selling actions assign values to risky securities. Because of this barrier, the basic intuition behind why risk and return are related is often inaccessible to the non-economist. Here is an attempt at breaking through jargon and complexity to explain the most important ideas.

Asset pricing theory seeks to explain the values of securities with uncertain future payoffs—for instance, a stock with uncertain future dividend payments. There are two basic factors at work in valuing an asset: the *time* elapsed until the expected payoff, and the *risk* associated with the payoff. Time matters because a dollar today is worth more than a dollar in the future (economists call this the *time value* of money). If I offered to pay you $100 today, or give you the money 3 months from now, you would clearly prefer the more immediate payoff. The degree to which you would be willing to accept a smaller payment now in lieu of a larger payment later measures the time value of money. Of the two factors, the risk dimension is the most complex and interesting. The basic idea behind asset pricing theory is that the value of a security today is *related to the timing and probability of possible future payoffs.*

The time component is relatively straightforward to compute. The value of the future payoff is discounted by a factor dependent upon the amount of time elapsed, just like a compound interest rate calculation, but dividing instead of multiplying. The factor used to adjust for the time delay is called a *discount rate.* It measures the degree to which dollars in the future are worth less than dollars now. For instance, if I deposit $100 into a bank (i.e., loan it $100) for a year, and they pay me an interest rate of 5 percent, I will receive $105 at the end of the year. Put another way, the value today of receiving $105 one year from now is $100 if the discount rate is 5 percent. The higher the discount rate, the less valuable future dollars are relative to current dollars. The discount rate is determined in the market by how much people prefer to have money now as opposed to in the future. Or correspondingly, how much you have to pay in the form of interest in order to borrow money for later repayment.

The expected payoffs are also discounted by how likely they are to occur in the future. This part of the computation is more complex, as it depends on your assessment of the future probabilities of different payoff events. The more likely the future payoff, the more valuable the asset is today. If everyone agreed on the probabilities of the different payoffs and their amounts, pricing the asset would be easy. However, different people will often have different beliefs about these probabilities, leading to differences in the estimated values for the asset. Ultimately, investors who assign different values to an asset trade with one another until the price adjusts such that nobody wants to buy or sell any more. Exactly how different beliefs about future payoffs among investors are resolved into a single price in the marketplace is a vibrant area of financial economics research.[1]

One can use these basic ideas to price a wide variety of different types of assets, including stocks, bonds, apartment buildings, oil rigs, gold mines, options, and even pork-belly futures. Because the value of an asset today is a discounted function of its future potential payoffs, this implies a simple relationship between the price and expected returns. When the asset price is lower (assuming nothing else has changed), the expected return is higher. Similarly, if the price of the asset is higher, then the expected return must be lower. Thus asset pricing theory explains both the current value of assets and their expected returns.

It was estimated by McKinsey & Company in 2005 that the global economy encompasses some $140 trillion dollars of financial assets, a roiling sea of capital ebbing and flowing with the fears and desires of global investors, big and small. Within this maelstrom of global capital, investors make bets on the future value of the securities they choose to buy and sell. There is a tremendous amount of information embedded in these trades, as they represent the consensus value estimates of thousands or even millions of investors. For many financial assets such as widely held stocks and bonds, there will be large amounts of money willing to trade on either side of the current price. The current price reflects the balance between those investors who would like to sell their holdings and those who would like to purchase more of the asset. The desire to buy or sell for a given investor is based on a variety of factors, including preferences for risk, expectations of the probabilities of future market conditions, access to capital, investment horizon, costs of trading, current portfolio holdings, regulatory restrictions, tax rates, and many other factors.

It is really quite amazing that all this information—the hopes and doubts of millions of investors—can be boiled down into a single number—the market price of an asset. The price of an asset at any point in time reflects the complex dance between buyers and sellers reacting to information about the economy and the future prospects of different payoffs. In reality, prices change continuously to account for the arrival of new information, making the dynamics of markets quite complex. However, at any point in time, the price will generally reflect all publicly available information about the asset.

THE LINK BETWEEN RISK AND RETURN

What does asset pricing theory suggest about the relationship between risk and expected return for financial securities? Some securities, like U.S. government bonds, have comparatively little risk associated with them (their value, if held to maturity, is guaranteed by the federal government). Others, like the stocks of a struggling company with high levels of debt, have a great deal of risk. Generally speaking, if expected returns were the same, people would prefer to hold less risky assets rather than those with more risk and uncertainty.

If I offered you $9,000 outright or the chance to play in a lottery with a 95 percent chance that you win $10,000 and a 5 percent chance that you owe me $10,000, I bet that you would take the guaranteed $9,000. After all, both propositions have the same expected value ($10,000 × 95 percent – \$10,000 × 5 percent = \$9,000), but the guaranteed \$9,000 comes with no risk. A preference for the guaranteed proposition shows that you are *risk averse*. If the expected value is the same, you would prefer the less risky version. Almost everyone shows some amount of risk aversion, though some people are more risk averse than others.

So if most people are risk averse, why don't they just hold the less risky securities? In the global market economy, not everyone can choose to hold the less risky securities even if they wanted to. Why? Because there are not enough low-risk assets to go around. Not everyone can hold their assets in U.S. government bonds (or similar securities), because the supply of such bonds is limited. What this means is that some investors will have to hold the riskier securities in order for markets to function. But why would they choose to hold the riskier securities if they are risk averse? *Because investors holding such risky securities expect higher returns as compensation for taking on the additional risk.* Okay, why should they expect higher returns from riskier assets? We need to introduce one more idea to answer this question.

If you were to starve yourself for 24 hours, and then I offered you a handful of M&Ms, you would probably greedily devour them (hey, watch the fingers!). When you are very hungry, that little bit of food is really desirable. However, if I offered you a handful of M&Ms right after you had just finished eating an entire 16-ounce bag of them, your reaction would likely be quite different (unless you happen to be a three-year-old). When you have plenty to eat, a little bit of extra food is not all that appetizing. It turns out that we think about money much the same way. When you have very little money, a few extra dollars feels really important. However, if you are very rich, the value of a few extra dollars does not mean much at all (this is why one can find things like gold-plated commodes). This simple intuitive idea of diminishing preferences for wealth or consumption has big implications for the kinds of investment risk that we are willing to assume.

As an example, let's say we live in a very simple world where there are only two, equally probable things that can happen next year. One possibility is that you will be fired and lose your job (along with everyone else). The other possibility is that you will be promoted and have your salary doubled (along with everyone else). Now, let's assume that there are two different kinds of assets in this world. The first asset, called a "safety net," pays off \$10,000 next year only if you lose your job. The other asset, called a "bonus," pays off \$10,000 next year only if you are promoted and see your salary double. In one sense, both of these assets are equally risky, as the probability of a payoff is the same—50 percent in each case. See Figure 2.2 for a diagram of the payoffs for each possible outcome next year.

	Lose Your Job Outcome	Double Your Salary Outcome
Safety Net Asset	+ $10,000	$0
Bonus Asset	$0	+ $10,000

FIGURE 2.2 Payoffs from Safety net and Bonus Assets for Each Outcome

Now which asset has the higher expected return?

Assume that you can buy and sell the safety net and bonus assets with other investors in the market. If investors in the market are risk averse (they prefer less risk to more) and have diminishing preferences for wealth (remember the M&Ms), then the prices of the assets will adjust such that the expected return of the safety net will be *lower* than that of the bonus asset. Why?

Even though the payoffs for each asset are the same and have the same probability of occurrence, the payoffs from the two assets occur under different circumstances that impact how you feel about that extra $10,000. If you just lost your job, the $10,000 from holding the safety net asset feels really good, but if your salary doubled, you don't need the extra money very much anyway. The $10,000 payoff from the bonus asset is not as valuable, since it only happens when your salary doubles and you are wealthier. Because everyone shares these basic preferences to some degree, the price of the more desirable safety net asset will be bid up in the market relative to the price of the less desirable bonus asset. If I have to pay a higher price for an asset, that makes the expected return of the payoff lower, all other things held equal. On the other hand, the price of the bonus asset will fall to such a point that the expected return becomes high enough such that people are willing to hold it, even though the payoff is not as valuable as the safety net asset. The lower the price, the higher the expected return from holding the asset, since the payoff ($10,000) is fixed. Of course, the real world is much more complicated than our simple example, but the basic principles illustrated here still apply. When times are bad (you lose your job), a little extra wealth is highly valuable, but when times are good (your salary doubles), the extra money is less valuable.

In the real world, the proxy for good times and bad times is the performance of the overall market, the aggregate of all stocks and bonds traded on world exchanges. When times are good (the market is up), the ability to consume is relatively cheap, since there is more money to go around and everyone is wealthier. Correspondingly, when times are bad (the market is down), consumption is expensive because there is less money to go around. *People are willing to give up expected return in order to have money in bad times*. Similarly, they are not willing to pay as much for the ability to have additional money when times are good. This depresses the prices of the securities that have risk related to the overall market performance and increases their expected returns. At a fundamental level, this implies that the expected returns of securities in the open market will be related to the degree their payoffs vary with the overall market return. Securities such as government bonds that pay off whether the market is up or down will have lower expected returns than securities that pay off well only when the market is up (such as stocks). The fundamental link between expected return and the chance of doing badly in bad times is a fixture of market economies. The more the value of the security is related to the value of the overall market, the higher its expected returns.

The bottom line here is that high expected-return assets will have lots of risk that is closely related to overall market performance, while low expected-return assets will have less risky payoffs that are not as correlated with market performance. In general, only the portion of the risk that is correlated with the overall market will be rewarded with higher expected returns. However, not all risk is correlated with the overall market. This implies something interesting. *Not all risky assets have high expected returns.*

WHEN HIGH RISK DOES NOT MEAN HIGH RETURN

To see why higher risk does not always correlate with higher expected returns, let us add some other kinds of assets to our simple market example. This first asset is a bond. The bond asset has a $5,000 payoff next year no matter what. Obviously, it has no risk, as you always receive $5,000 a year from now irrespective of what happens with your job. On average this bond has the same payoff as the safety net and bonus assets, but it has no risk.[2] Since the safety of a guaranteed payoff is highly desirable to risk-averse investors, this asset will have a very low expected return, reflecting only the time value of money.

Now consider two additional assets—we'll call them *coin flip shares*—one for heads and one for tails. The heads shares pay off $10,000 next year if a simulated coin flip comes up heads, and nothing if it comes up tails. Similarly, the tails share pays $10,000 if the simulated coin flip comes up tails, and nothing if it comes up heads. In both cases the payoffs are purely random and not related to whether you get fired or get a raise. Note that on average you get the same payoffs as the safety net, bonus, and bond assets, but in this case the payoffs are based on purely random coin flip events. Obviously, these securities have lots of risk, since you either get $10,000 or nothing, depending on the flip of a coin. Since they are riskier than the bond, should they have a higher expected return? The answer turns out to be no.

The reason is that the payoffs of the coin flip shares are not correlated with anything. Therefore, you can eliminate their risk by holding half your money in the heads shares and half in the tails shares. If the simulated coin flip comes up heads, you win on half your investment and lose everything on the other half. The same is true if the coin flip comes up tails. In the end, you get the same return as holding the bond ($5,000) no matter how the coin flip turns out. This implies that the portfolio of the two coin flip shares must have the same low expected return as the bond share; otherwise no one would want to buy the bond, since they could get a higher return from putting half their money into each coin flip share. While risky by themselves, the coin flip shares do not earn any higher expected return, since the risk can be completely diversified away by holding half of each type of share.

Now even though the payoffs of these two shares perfectly complement each other, this principle holds even if the payoffs only cancel each other out on average. As long as the additional risk is not correlated with the overall market, you should not expect any additional expected return. You can eliminate risks not correlated with the market by holding lots of different kinds of assets. On average, the *nonmarket* risks—those risks that are not correlated with the overall market—will cancel out. So while high expected return assets always come with risk, not all high-risk assets come with high expected returns. As we will see in later chapters, this argument explains why you don't want to put all your money into a single stock, since much of the risk of a single company is not related to the market, but to company-specific factors that can be eliminated by holding a broadly diversified portfolio. The bottom line is that all risk is not equal. You are only compensated for risks that are related to overall market outcomes.

This theory explains why there is no free lunch when it comes to investing. To get higher expected returns, you must be willing to assume certain kinds of risk. However, sometimes the risks that you assume with an investment are not so obvious.

HIDDEN RISKS AND THE PESO PROBLEM

Ex-ante risk is what drives economic prices and expected returns. As we shall see, investment decisions are all about forward-looking expectations. The prices and expected returns of investments are based on what the future is likely to hold, not how things have played out in the past. In some cases, the observed range of historical outcomes can provide reasonable estimates of ex-ante risk. For instance, if you analyzed a decade's worth of daily returns for IBM common stock, you would have a reasonable estimate of what the future distribution of one-day returns might look like. Much, but not all, of what is possible in single-day returns is likely to have been observed at some point in the last 10 years. Where the analysis becomes more problematic is when there are risks associated with high impact but low-probability events—especially events that are possible, but have never before been observed.

In financial economics, there exists a class of risk known as the *peso problem*. The term was first popularized by the famous economist Milton Friedman in studying the exchange rate between the United States and Mexico in the early 1970s. At that time, the exchange rate between the U.S. dollar and Mexican peso was fixed by law and had been stable for decades. However, during the early 1970s, interest rates in Mexico were significantly higher than those in the United States. This provided an opportunity for people to make money by borrowing in the United States at a low interest rate, investing the proceeds in Mexican bonds with high interest rates, and then paying back the loan later with the proceeds from redemption of the bonds. Economists call this type of scheme an *arbitrage* or free-money strategy. Assuming there was no restriction on your ability to borrow money in the United States or a limit on the amount of Mexican bonds you could purchase, you could make an arbitrarily large amount of money with this technique. In a properly operating market, true arbitrage opportunities tend not to stick around for very long. If you want to see why, try tossing a $20 bill onto a busy sidewalk and watch how long it takes for someone to pick it up. Usually when "free money" opportunities exist, they are quickly exploited, resulting in the elimination of the conditions that created the arbitrage opportunity in the first place.

So why were the U.S. and Mexican interest rates so different? Friedman postulated that the reason was the market expected the peso to be devalued relative to the U.S. dollar at some point in the future. That is, there was a risk that the fixed exchange rate policy would not continue indefinitely. In 1976 that is exactly what happened, when the exchange rate between the peso and dollar was allowed to float, resulting in a sudden and dramatic 45 percent devaluation of the peso. Had you been unlucky enough to have borrowed lots of money in the United States to buy Mexican bonds, the abrupt change in exchange rate would have likely resulted in a considerable financial loss. You would have received fewer dollars for your redeemed Mexican bonds, but would have still owed the same amount in dollars to the U.S. lenders. In hindsight, the higher relative interest rates observed in Mexico prior to 1976 were required to compensate investors for the potential risk of the devaluation in the peso. Otherwise, there would not have been many investors willing to hold the Mexican bonds. What appeared to be an arbitrage opportunity actually involved speculation on the future longevity of the fixed exchange rate policy. There have been many examples of such "peso problems" over the years. Sometimes the risks inherent in an investment strategy are not so obvious.

Why is the "peso problem" relevant for individual investors? *Because the market is always anticipating risks that may occur in the future, regardless of whether they have been observed in the past*. Unprecedented events, like the 1976 peso devaluation, can lead to very bad outcomes and hence can impact prices and expected returns. At the heart of the no-free-lunch hypothesis is the notion that observed high returns for a security implies that there is considerable potential future risk, even if the risk factors have not been observed in the historical record. So-called "peso problem" risks are among the most difficult types of risk to guard against. By definition they occur very infrequently, but when they do they can pack a wallop. Small risks of doing very poorly in bad times can drive expected returns as much as the more visible kinds of volatility observed in past returns. Often, the infrequent but catastrophic risks are created when the investment decision involves leverage (borrowing to increase the size of your position). Borrowing money to increase exposure to the market can greatly increase the potential damage from infrequent but very bad market outcomes. For instance, if I invest in the market and the market drops by 20 percent over several months, I have lost a significant, but not catastrophic chunk of my assets. But if I use my money as collateral to borrow five times my original stake and then invest the proceeds into the market, I have magnified my exposure to the market by a factor of five (this is easily done with financial instruments called *futures contracts*). If the market then fell by 20 percent I would have lost everything, since the drop in the value of my larger stake would have wiped out the collateral that I put up (20 percent loss times 5 equals a 100 percent loss). Leverage can turn small risks into potentially catastrophic risks, as many a hedge fund manager has discovered in the last few decades.

Even without leverage, you should be highly skeptical of investments with records of high returns but seemingly low risk. Often strategies that generate such return patterns are subject to the kinds of "peso problem" risks that can cause infrequent but very painful periods of exceptionally poor performance. Often, it is not obvious where this risk comes from until after the fact. Be aware that high returns almost always come with substantial risk exposure, even when it may not be visible in the historical record. This applies to real estate, hedge funds, commodities, market-neutral funds, and many other forms of so-called alternative investments. That is not to say that such investments might not be reasonable as part of a diversified strategy, but if it looks too good to be true, there is likely more to the story.

HOW MUCH RISK AM I TAKING?

Now that we have established some basic intuition around the relationship between risk and return, let us examine some actual analysis of real investments. In the following sections, we will use the Financial Engines simulation engine to illustrate the kinds of risk/return tradeoffs that you see with common types of investments. For each class of investment, we will show how the range of possible outcomes varies with the time horizon. Also, we will demonstrate how the various types of assets relate to one another in both risk and expected return. Note that these estimates are *projected* values of what might happen in the future, not what has been observed historically. Since we are considering investments for the future, it is much more informative to consider the range of possible forward-looking outcomes than it is to focus too much attention on the observed historical performance of the last few decades. Comparing the simulation results across different types of assets allows us to quantify how outcomes vary with different levels of expected return and volatility.

In the simulation examples presented in the following, we will focus on returns that are adjusted for the impact of inflation. Economists call such inflation-adjusted numbers *real* returns. The opposite of real returns are *nominal* returns, which are not adjusted for the impact of inflation. For instance, if an investment has a nominal return of 5 percent and the rate of inflation is 2 percent, this implies that the real return of the investment is 3 percent. If I invest $1 in the investment, in one year I would have $1.05 in future dollars, but only $1.03 in the equivalent of today's dollars (because of the adjustment for inflation). In these examples, the dollar values for future time periods will always be expressed in the equivalent to today's dollars. This makes it easier to determine the value of future payoffs in terms of today's purchasing power.

Different types of investment securities have different levels of risk. While risk can be measured in a number of ways, the most common measure used by institutional investors is the volatility of returns, typically expressed on an annual basis. The least-risky assets are those with low volatilities, and the highest-risk assets are those that expose investors to high levels of returns' volatility.

For most individual investors, the range of investable securities is broadly divided into two categories: *fixed income*, or bonds, and *equities*, or stocks. Bonds are securities that involve one or more periodic payments at specific times in the future by a government or corporate entity. Unlike stocks, bonds do not imply any ownership of an entity, but rather represent a loan of money. When you purchase a bond you are in effect loaning money to that organization in return for interest payments. Equities or stocks, on the other hand, represent ownership shares of a corporation. While some companies pay regular payments to stockholders in the form of *dividends*, many stocks have no regular payments at all. The prices of stocks vary with the outlook for the overall market and the fortunes of that specific company.

The reason that we divide investable securities into categories is that different types of assets have very different risk and return characteristics. For example, bonds tend to have less correlation with the overall market and thus have lower expected returns than equities.

Within the categories of fixed income and equities, assets are often broken down into subcategories called *asset classes*. For fixed-income asset classes, the categorization is usually based on how far out the payments extend (the maturity of the bond), and who is guaranteeing the payments (usually a bank, corporation, or government). Fixed-income assets include cash, money market funds, government bonds of various maturities, corporate bonds, municipal bonds, mortgage bonds, and foreign government bonds.

For equities, the division into asset classes is typically based on the size of the company (in terms of its market value), the market value of the company relative to the accounting value of its assets, and whether the equity is foreign or domestic. In the case of the Financial Engines asset class model, domestic equities are divided into six asset classes: large, medium, and small capitalization stocks (often referred to as large-cap, mid-cap, and small-cap, respectively) in both value and growth dimensions. Growth stocks have relatively high prices compared to the value of their corporate assets, while value stocks have relatively low prices compared to their assets. Since the prices of growth stocks imply a higher ability to generate future profits from their assets, their returns tend to be more sensitive to the performance of the overall market. Value stocks tend to be a bit less sensitive to the movements in the overall market. For foreign equities, the Financial Engine model divides the world into asset classes for Europe, Pacific Rim countries, and emerging markets.

As we will see in later chapters, the risk of any overall portfolio depends on the specific combination of assets and their relative proportions. However, it is also helpful to understand the risk of different asset classes in isolation. Table 2.1 provides an approximate ordering of different types of asset classes, ranked by volatility. Note that the ordering is not exact, as some asset classes have similar volatilities and thus may be somewhat higher or lower within a specific time period (as an example, small and mid-growth U.S. equities have very similar volatilities). Nonetheless, this ordering lays out the general ordering of the volatility of real returns for various types of asset classes. Of course, specific individual investments from each asset class can vary dramatically in terms of risk (for instance, Google and General Electric have very different risk levels, even though they are both large capitalization stocks). The ranking in Table 2.1 pertains to the volatility of the asset class (or perhaps an index fund that tracks the asset class).

A few things are notable about this list. First, the volatility of fixed-income asset classes (bonds) is mostly a function of their maturity. Short-term instruments generally have lower volatility than longer-maturity instruments. Second, the risk of equities is generally dependent on capitalization (larger capitalization stocks are less volatile than smaller ones) and whether they are defined as value equities (lower market-value to book-value ratios) or growth equities (higher market-value to book-value ratios). Third, foreign equities and bonds tend to be more volatile than domestic assets, though there is overlap with some of the domestic asset classes. As we will see in the next section, the different levels of volatility imply significantly different outcomes over various time horizons.

TABLE 2.1 Ranking of Different Asset Classes from Least Volatile to Most Volatile

Asset Class	Description
Cash/short-term U.S. government bonds	High-quality fixed-income securities, such as a money market fund, with a duration of less than a year
Intermediate-term U.S. government bonds	Bonds issued by the U.S. Treasury with maturities of between 2 and 10 years
Corporate bonds	Bonds issued by corporations, typically involving higher levels of risk than U.S. government bonds, with maturities of 1 to 30 years
Mortgage bonds	Bonds secured by mortgages on property (real estate or physical equipment). Due to the possibility of default, these bonds tend to pay higher yields than government bonds
Long-term U.S. government bonds	Bonds issued by the U.S. Treasury with durations of greater than 10 years
Foreign bonds	Bonds issued by the governments and corporations of foreign countries
Large-capitalization value U.S. equities	Stocks of large (measured by market value) U.S. companies with relatively low prices compared to the value of their assets
Mid-capitalization value U.S. equities	Stocks of medium-size U.S. companies with relatively low prices compared to the value of their assets
Small-capitalization value U.S. equities	Stocks of small-size U.S. companies with relatively low prices compared to the value of their assets
Large-capitalization growth U.S. equities	Stocks of large (measured by market value) U.S. companies with relatively high prices compared to the value of their assets
Mid-capitalization growth U.S. equities	Stocks of medium-size U.S. companies with relatively high prices compared to the value of their assets
Small-capitalization growth U.S. equities	Stocks of small-size U.S. companies with relatively high prices compared to the value of their assets
Pacific Rim equities (including Japan)	Stocks from countries bordering the Pacific Ocean, including Japan, China, Taiwan, Australia, and others
European equities	Stocks from companies in Europe
Emerging market equities	Stocks from developing countries, usually smaller countries with limited stock market histories

RISKS AND RETURNS OF DIFFERENT ASSETS

Different assets have varying levels of risk. But how does one characterize the level of risk? For instance, many advisors recommend a basic 60/40 mix of stocks and bonds as a typical portfolio allocation. But what does a 60/40 allocation mean to me? What does it imply about the possible future dollars that I may end up with? The distribution of possible outcomes for an investment can be summarized by a variety of statistics, some quite simple while others are more complex. Four basic statistics are commonly used by Financial Engines to communicate portfolio forecasts. While these are not the only statistics that may be useful, they are representative of measures that will be relevant for most individual investors.

Median: The median outcome for a portfolio forecast represents the value when 50 percent of the outcomes are above that amount, and 50 percent of the outcomes fall below. The median forecast represents the middle of the distribution of outcomes. That is, there is an equal chance of being above or below the median estimate. It is often characterized as the "typical" outcome for a distribution of possible outcomes.

Downside: The downside forecast is represented by the 5th percentile of the distribution of outcomes. The 5th percentile indicates that only 5 percent of the outcomes were below this amount, and correspondingly 95 percent were higher than this amount. Put another way, you would expect to exceed the downside value about 95 percent of the time.

Upside: The upside forecast is represented by the 95th percentile of the distribution of outcomes. The 95th percentile indicates that only 5 percent of the outcomes were above this amount, and correspondingly, 95 percent were lower than this amount. You would expect to exceed the upside value only 5 percent of the time.

Short-Term Risk: The short-term risk measure provides an indication of how large a loss the portfolio may experience in the next 12 months if the financial markets perform poorly. It is calibrated to show the loss associated with a 1-in-20 bad market outcome. In other words, one could expect to lose this amount or more with a 5 percent probability over the next year.

Let us look at some actual examples to see how these numbers play out for some typical portfolios. Note that these examples assume investments in different types of assets without the imposition of any fees or taxes. As we will see in Chapter 6, investment management fees and expenses can make a significant difference in expected returns and forecast values. Also, remember that the portfolio outcomes shown in the following will change when multiple types of assets, such as stocks and bonds, are combined into a single portfolio (e.g., a portfolio of mutual funds).

Cash One of the most common investment vehicles in investor portfolios is cash. Typically, cash is a generic term for a broad range of very short-term (one year or less) fixed-income products. Examples of such assets include interest-bearing checking accounts, money market funds, treasury bills, short-term CDs, and other fixed income positions. Currency, the kind of cash you keep in your wallet, is typically not included in this definition. Cash assets are often the default investment for brokerage accounts when you do not specify a desired holding. Within this category, interest rates can vary depending on the service provider and specific instrument. As a proxy for cash instruments, the following discussion looks at the behavior of a portfolio based on U.S. government bonds with a one-year maturity (1-Year Treasury Bills).

As you might expect, the relatively low volatility of cash creates a narrow range of possible future portfolio outcomes. Table 2.2 provides the upside, median, and downside forecasts (in today's dollars) for a $10,000 initial investment over different time horizons.[3]

The one-year results imply that the median outcome for a cash investment is about the same amount of money as the initial investment, adjusted for inflation. By keeping your money invested in cash, you can expect to approximately keep up with inflation, but not much more. You are not likely to see real returns substantially in excess of the initial investment. Ninety percent of the time, you would expect to get between 97.2 percent

TABLE 2.2 Simulation Results for a Portfolio of Cash

	Value of $10,000 Initial Investment in Cash (in today's dollars)			
	At 1 Year	At 5 Years	At 10 Years	At 20 Years
Upside	$10,400	$11,200	$12,100	$14,000
Median	$10,000	$10,500	$11,100	$12,200
Downside	$9,720	$9,410	$9,430	$9,760

Source: Financial Engines calculations.

and 104 percent of your initial investment back in today's dollars after one year. Of course, there could be scenarios with less than a 5 percent chance of occurrence that could generate values below the downside. Similarly, there is a 5 percent chance that you would reap more than the 104 percent upside for your investment.

Why is there a range of outcomes for a cash investment? The variation in the outcomes is due to uncertainty in future interest rates changes and unanticipated inflation. A sharp increase in unanticipated inflation could cause the purchasing power of your investment to diminish if the nominal return on your cash holdings did not fully adjust.

For a five-year horizon, the median outcome is a small gain, even in today's dollars. Similarly, the upside and downside cases are more spread out. As the length of the investment horizon increases, the spread of the distribution of outcomes becomes larger. At 10 years, the median is again a bit higher at $11,100, but the implied annualized real return over 10 years is only 1.05 percent. Also note that the 5 percent downside case is basically indifferent to time horizon. The amount of money that you could lose due to unfavorable inflation rate changes is limited, even over longer horizons.

What can we learn from these simulation examples? Well, for starters, the range of outcomes with a cash investment is quite narrow, even going out to a 10-year investment horizon. About 90 percent of the time, you can expect to receive between 97.3 percent and 121 percent of your initial investment over 10 years. In one sense, this implies that cash is a safe investment, as the probability of a significant loss relative to your starting principal is low. However, it is also true that you are unlikely to see returns that significantly out-perform inflation—particularly over longer time horizons. By investing in short-term fixed-income securities, you are getting the benefit of low volatility, but you are unlikely to end up with much return after adjusting for the impact of inflation.

Long-Term U.S. Government Bonds Now let us examine the risk/return tradeoffs for a more volatile class of assets—long-term U.S. government bonds. Long-term bonds (assumed to have maturities of 10 years in this example) are considerably more volatile than cash. The investment results in Table 2.3 illustrate a portfolio consisting entirely of long-term U.S. treasury bonds. As the bonds in the portfolio mature a year, the 9-year maturity bonds are assumed to be replaced with new bonds of the full 10-year maturity. This allows the portfolio to consist entirely of bonds with 9–10-year maturities. A constant-maturity long-term government bond mutual fund would provide a similar portfolio composition.

TABLE 2.3 Simulation Results for a Portfolio of Long-Term U.S. Government Bonds

	Value of $10,000 Initial Investment in Long-Term Treasury Bonds Index (in today's dollars)			
	At 1 Year	At 5 Years	At 10 Years	At 20 Years
Upside	$11,500	$14,500	$18,600	$29,700
Median	$10,200	$12,000	$14,300	$19,600
Downside	$8,990	$7,850	$7,560	$8,260

Source: Financial Engines calculations.

Notice two things about the distribution of outcomes for the long-term bond portfolios: The range of possible outcomes is significantly wider, and the median and upside scenarios are higher, implying a larger expected rate of return. At a 10-year horizon, the range of likely outcomes is between 76 percent and 186 percent of the starting portfolio value.[4] In dollar terms, this is more than four times the size of the range of outcomes in the cash investment simulation. At 20 years, the range is more than five times as large. However, the median outcome for long-term bonds is 29 percent higher than cash at 10 years, and 61 percent higher at the 20-year horizon. At the 10-year horizon, the median outcome for long-term bonds has an implied annualized real return of 3.6 percent (more than three times higher than that of cash).

U.S. Large-Capitalization Stocks With equity assets, the range of possible portfolio outcomes is even wider than long-term U.S. government bonds. This additional volatility creates distributions of portfolio values that differ significantly from fixed-income portfolios such cash or bonds. To get a feel for the risk of equities, consider a portfolio invested in large-capitalization U.S. stocks represented by the S&P 500 index. This index is an asset-weighted index of 500 large-capitalization stocks from U.S. exchanges. Again, we assume that there are no fees or taxes paid on the realized returns. Table 2.4 shows the results for different investment horizons.

At one year, the outcomes for the stock portfolio are modestly more volatile than that observed for bonds; however, the volatility is much more pronounced over longer horizons.[5] Compared to the fixed-income portfolios of cash or bonds, the stock portfolio has both a higher expected return and a wider range of potential outcomes (volatility). At 10 years, the range of typical outcomes is between 69 percent and 401 percent of the starting

TABLE 2.4 Simulation Results for a Portfolio Large-Capitalization U.S. Stocks

	Value of $10,000 Initial Investment in the S&P500 Index (in today's dollars)			
	At 1 Year	At 5 Years	At 10 Years	At 20 Years
Upside	$13,200	$23,600	$40,100	$100,000
Median	$10,400	$13,100	$17,400	$30,500
Downside	$8,170	$6,880	$6,890	$8,070

Source: Financial Engines calculations.

portfolio value. In dollar terms this is more than 12 times the size of the range of outcomes of the cash portfolio, and three times the range of the bonds. At the 20-year horizon, the range of outcomes is even more pronounced, at 22 times the results for cash, and more than four times the spread for long-term bonds. Over 20 years the $10,000 initial investment could be worth between $8,070 and $100,000 in today's dollars. This is an enormous range of potential outcomes, with the upside performance representing more than 10 times the value of the downside case. Notice how the gap between the median and the upside scenarios greatly increases with the investment horizon. At one year, the ratio is 1.3, at 10 years it is 2.3, and at 20 years it grows to 3.3. Also note that the downside scenario (the 5th percentile case) is relatively constant over the different horizons, differing by only a few thousand dollars. However, the more extreme downside values, such as the 1st percentile of the distribution (not shown), continue to drop the longer the investment horizon.

The median estimates for the stock portfolio are significantly above both the cash and bond portfolio estimates at all horizons, except at the one-year mark. Here we can directly observe the benefits and costs of seeking higher expected returns through higher equity exposure. For many scenarios, the higher expected return asset will do better, particularly as the time horizon lengthens. However, the penalty of the higher volatility is a much wider range of potential outcomes and a lower downside if markets perform poorly. Of course, the results for other asset classes are somewhat different from the previous three examples. I will explore the risk and return tradeoffs of other asset classes in subsequent chapters.

Again, we run into the no-free-lunch rule. If you want the chance at higher expected returns, you should expect to endure higher risk as well. Longer time horizons do not remove the risk of holding equities, but they do increase the probability that the higher-equity portfolio will outperform portfolios consisting of fixed-income securities. However, in those scenarios where the equity portfolio underperforms the fixed-income assets, the degree of underperformance can be dramatic.

DOES IT PASS THE BLUSH TEST?

With the information presented in this chapter, I have armed you with the critical intuition for why risk and expected returns are inherently linked. This intuition should improve your ability to spot dubious investment advice. If you are presented with an investment proposal or product that promises high expected returns, with little or no risk, you are most likely being taken for a ride. I have often heard individual investors confidently state that they expect returns of 15 percent, 20 percent, or even 25 percent per year from their investment portfolio. While it possible to achieve such returns in a given year, there are no standard financial instruments with expected returns of more than about 15 percent per year (unless you are willing to assume significant leverage). They simply do not exist. Your expectations should be reasonable, even if you are willing to assume large amounts of equity risk. A claim that you can expect returns of 15 percent or more per year is not credible. The notion that you can expect 20 percent annual returns from a diversified portfolio is simply preposterous. If it sounds too good to be true, it usually is.

Investments with high expected returns are almost always exposed to high levels of market risk (the kind of risk that cannot be diversified away). Sometimes that risk may not be visible in the historical performance charts (remember the Peso Problem), but it is always there if expected returns are truly high. Certain investment strategies, such those used by some hedge funds, have risk profiles that only become apparent in times of economic volatility (for instance, when the cost of borrowing suddenly increases). Despite showing multiyear track records of consistent returns, such strategies can suddenly lose large amounts of money when illiquid positions cannot be sold and suddenly drop in value. For instance, a hedge fund complex called Sowood Capital Management lost more than $1 billion in just a month, representing more than half the assets of their two flagship funds, due to turmoil in the credit and mortgage markets in July 2007. Complex investments like hedge funds can blow up spectacularly and without warning when market conditions turn sour.

Don't allow yourself to be misled based on a slick presentation and fancy charts. If you want higher expected returns, you must be willing to assume higher levels of risk. Similarly, don't purchase risky securities unless the expected returns are higher than those of less risky assets. There is no reason to take on investment risk unless you are being compensated for it. *Risk and expected return are the yin and yang of investing and you will not find one without the other.*

TAKE-AWAYS

- There is no free lunch—risk always accompanies expected returns.
- Higher expected return assets like equities will have higher ex-ante risk associated with them. However, the corollary is not true. Not all high-risk investments come with higher expected returns.
- Not all risk comes with expected reward. Only risks that are correlated with the overall market are compensated with higher expected returns. Other forms of risk can be easily diversified away.
- Be careful about investment strategies that expose you to small probabilities of very negative outcomes (doing very badly in bad times). With such strategies, the historical record can be a poor guide to the potential risks.
- For cash investments (with no fees), expect to see portfolio values in the range of 95 percent to 105 percent of the initial investment over one year (adjusting for inflation). Over a five-year horizon, you can expect values in the range of 95 percent to 115 percent of the initial investment.
- For long-term bond investments (with no fees), expect to see portfolio values in the range of 90 percent to 115 percent of the initial investment over one year (adjusted for inflation). Over a five-year horizon, you can expect values in the range of 80 percent to 145 percent of the initial investment.
- For large-capitalization U.S. equity investments (with no fees), expect to see portfolio values in the range of 80 percent to 135 percent of the initial investment over one year (adjusting for inflation). Over a five-year horizon, you can expect values in the range of 70 percent to 235 percent of the initial investment.

CHAPTER 3

History Is Bunk

History is more or less bunk.

—Henry Ford (1863–1947)

It is human nature to look to the past for an idea of what might happen in the future. However, one of the biggest mistakes that investors make is relying too much on history and past performance in making decisions. This chapter explores some of the subtle and not-so-subtle problems of using historical data to generate financial forecasts and evaluate investment choices. Many of these issues are not well recognized among individual investors and even their advisors. Advice and financial projections based solely on history can be misleading and can ultimately lead to poor investment decisions. Moreover, too much emphasis on past performance often leads to mistaking luck for investment skill.

How many times have you seen the disclosure "past performance is no guarantee of future returns" on financial statements and investment advertisements? In the pantheon of marketing boilerplate, this one ranks right up there with "your mileage may vary" and "sealed for your protection." While commonly used, these phrases have ceased to have any real meaning to consumers. Pick up nearly any financial magazine, newspaper, or popular self-help book on investments and you are likely to find endless pages devoted to trumpeting the historical performance of mutual funds and investment managers. But what does historical performance have to say about selecting good investments? Not nearly as much as you might think.

This chapter is all about history—no, not the birth of civilization, Founding Fathers, and Industrial Revolution kind of history—but the performance history of financial assets. Why is it important to talk about history? Because we are programmed at birth to pay a lot of attention to history—humans are pattern-recognition machines. In fact, our ability to recognize patterns and predict future events is one of our most remarkable and important skills.

Even today, while computers can beat grandmasters at chess, predict hurricanes with increasing accuracy, and search billions of web pages in fractions of a second, they still have trouble with simple pattern recognition tasks that even small children find trivial. Our ability to spot patterns and make predictions about what will happen next is a key evolutionary advantage that helped make *Homo sapiens* the dominant species on this planet. For instance, when our ancestors learned to predict the behavior of herd animals based on the season and grazing habits, it became much easier to keep their children fed. Unfortunately, our ability to spot patterns is also often the source of our undoing when it comes to financial decisions. *The problem is that we often find patterns even when there are no patterns to be found.*

It turns out that our intuition of how to evaluate historical data and how to weight its importance is flawed—we are wired to believe that the past will repeat itself. The marketers of financial products recognize this weakness and spend hundreds of millions of dollars reinforcing our natural inclination to focus on historical trends to sell more investment products. Somehow it seems intuitively obvious that a fund manager with a few years of great performance must be a better bet than one with a poor track record. And yet, that intuition is often dead wrong. There are numerous studies that show investors tend to chase past winners, though there is scant evidence that such behavior has any value.[1]

We tend to radically underestimate the variation in investment performance that is due solely to chance, and thus mistakenly attribute good performance to skill rather than the more plausible explanation of simple luck. *The presence of a good track investment record does not imply the existence of skill.* Even if all investment performance were perfectly random (no managers had any investment skill), we would still expect to see examples of long winning streaks by investment funds. When we look backward, we *always* find some winners, but the winners in one period are rarely the winners in the next. Accordingly, the process of distinguishing luck from investment skill is a very difficult task.

Now let us explore some of the myths and misunderstandings about historical performance and what it means for personal investing. I will show how historical returns are a poor guide to the future, why past performance is so easy to manipulate, why it does not mean as much as you might think, and why you must be very careful about extrapolating from the past to predict the future—especially when selecting investment managers. In Chapter 4, we will explore some alternative methods of generating expected return forecasts that do not suffer from the same problems as extrapolating from history.

HISTORY AND EXPECTED RETURNS

History is an extremely poor guide to future expected returns for financial assets. While it might seem reasonable that the average stock market return over the last 50 years is a logical estimate for what the next 50 years may hold, there is a large range of error in the historical average. The reason is that stock returns are very volatile relative to their average value. If a variable is very consistent, then only a relatively few observations are needed to accurately estimate its expected value. However, if the uncertainty in the number is large relative to its average value, then a much larger number of observations are required to accurately estimate its expected value.

For example, if U.S. stock market returns (adjusted for inflation) have a true long-run annualized average of 7.5 percent with a volatility of only 1 percent, then a small number of years would need to be observed to estimate the average expected return to within plus or minus 1 percent. In fact, with only four years of data you could be quite sure that your estimate of the expected return was within plus or minus 1 percent of the true value.[2] In this example, the uncertainty of stock returns (volatility) is about one-eighth as large as the average value. While the long-run historical annualized average for inflation-adjusted U.S. equity returns may be in the range of 7.5 percent, the volatility of these returns is approximately 20 percent—or roughly two-and-a-half times larger than the average value. This means you need *a lot* more data to accurately estimate the average value with any confidence.[3]

Here is an interesting question that I have sometimes posed in conference presentations: *How many years of U.S. stock returns would you need to observe in order to estimate the expected return on stocks to within plus or minus 1 percent with high confidence?* Ask this question of most individual investors or even financial advisors, and you will typically get numbers in the range of 50–100 years of data. But if you believe that the actual volatility of stock returns is about 20 percent per year (consistent with historical estimates), then you would need an astounding *1,500 years* of historical stock returns in order to estimate the expected return on stocks to within plus or minus 1 percent accuracy.[4] Obviously we don't have stock return histories going back to the end of the Roman Empire, and even if we did, it is doubtful that the returns on the stocks of chariot makers in 400 A.D. would have any relevance to today's modern market.

Accordingly, historical equity returns are not a very valuable guide to future expected returns. With the 100 years or so of data we are able to observe for stock returns in the United States, the historical average is only accurate to within plus or minus about 4 percent of the long-term expected value.[5] This is a huge range of possible expected returns when doing future wealth projections. The consequence of overestimating or underestimating expected returns on stocks by 4 percent, over a 25-year investment horizon, results in about a factor of six. That is, the high-end return estimate would yield wealth that is over six times more than the low-end estimate (adjusted for inflation). Clearly any forecast that could be off by this magnitude is going to be problematic—hence the futility of generating accurate forward-looking returns estimates solely from historical averages. Remember this the next time you are presented with a chart of historical stock returns and told that they represent the best forecast of what might happen in the future. In reality, there is a great deal of uncertainty about the level of returns we can expect to see in the future.

THE PAST IS NOT THE FUTURE

For the same reasons that our estimates of future returns are highly uncertain, historical average rates of return are very sensitive to the time period selected. Say you wanted an estimate of the long-term expected return for U.S. stocks to use in forecasting the value of a portfolio over the next 30 years. One way of coming up with such an estimate is to calculate the average return from history. For instance, in Table 3.1, measured over the period 1950–1994, the annualized cumulative return on U.S. large capitalization stocks was 7.6 percent per year (with dividends reinvested and not adjusting for inflation). However, by 1999, just five years later, the average annualized rate of return had increased to 9.3 percent, a jump of 1.7 percent per year.

While 1.7 percent may not sound like a lot, compounded over 30 years that additional return would yield approximately 61 percent more wealth than the earlier estimate. Consider this result for a minute. You might think that after observing nearly 50 years of data, you would have a pretty darn

TABLE 3.1 Average Compound Rates of Return on U.S. Large-Capitalization Stocks

	Large-Capitalization U.S. Stock Returns	
	1950–1994	1950–1999
Compound Annualized Return	7.6%	9.3%
Value of $10,000 invested for 30 years using average annualized return	$89,859	$144,952

Sources: Yahoo! Finance, S&P 500 historical prices adjusted for dividends.

good handle on the long-term average rate of return for stocks. But just five years go by, and kablooey, your long-term average increased enough to change your 30-year projection by more than 60 percent! This huge difference in the estimated return averages resulted from just *five years* of good equity performance, despite using historical returns going all the way back to 1950. Even periods of a few years of unusually good or bad stock market performance can significantly alter our estimate of the historical average return. Given how much the average can move around with a few more years of data, we need to be very cautious about assuming that the observed average return on stocks is a good predictor of the future.

Another interesting observation is that there is nothing unique about the historical returns that we have observed in the United States compared to what we *might* have observed. If we had the ability to go back in time and observe other possible (but unrealized) returns histories we would expect to see a range of potentially very different outcomes. It is like those science fiction stories where there are multiple parallel universes where things are a bit different from our own. The history we lived through was just one of many possible scenarios. It could have been better or worse than what it was. Looking forward, it is difficult to know whether we will live through a particularly good historical period or just an average one. And if we don't know how to characterize the past, it is hard to know what to expect in the future.

In fact, there are other countries whose financial markets did not even survive to the present. If we include these failures in our survey of history we get a less rosy view of expected returns. The United States enjoyed many advantages in the last hundred years, including no major political upheavals, no significant damage to our infrastructure due to war, and no collapse of our financial system (though we came close in the Great Depression). Many countries were not so fortunate, and some of those failed economies are not even around anymore. Only the survivors are around to observe their historical returns.

This is a key difference between ex-ante (forward-looking) forecasts of returns and ex-post (historical returns). Ex-ante, future returns might be better or worse than what was actually observed, but they would undoubtedly be different from history—often by a large margin. Given the limited data we have to observe, it will be hundreds of years before we can know whether the historical experience of the U.S. investor was better than expected, worse than expected, or just typical.

Just how different could the future be from history? Very. To better understand just how much uncertainty there is in future stock market returns,

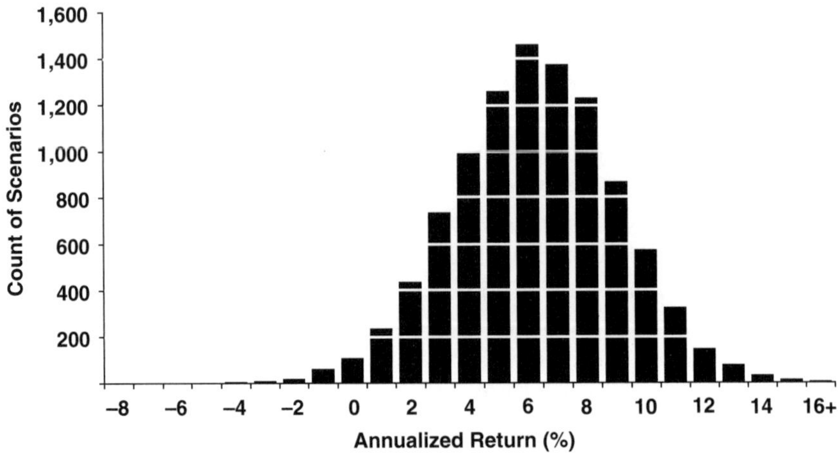

FIGURE 3.1 Histogram of Compound Annualized S&P 500 Real Returns for 10,000 Simulated 40-year Periods

Source: Financial Engines calculations.

let's take a look at the distribution of possible real returns on the S&P 500 index over the next 40 years. Using data from the Financial Engines simulation engine, we can generate 10,000 possible 40-year scenarios for how large-capitalization U.S. stock returns might perform in the future, adjusted for inflation. Over the last 40 years, the S&P 500 index had an annualized compound return of 6.0 percent adjusted for inflation.[6] This is the historical average, but how different could an investor's experience be over the next 40 years? For each of the 10,000 scenarios, each lasting 40 years, we can calculate the real cumulative rate of return of the simulated S&P 500 (Figure 3.1).

The results of this analysis show that realized stock returns can vary widely over a period of 40 years, even if the expected average is constant. The graph in Figure 3.1 shows the number of scenarios in the simulation with different levels of annualized cumulative returns. As you can see, the spread of annualized returns is quite wide. Half of the 10,000 simulated scenarios had annualized rates of return that were below 3.9 percent per year or were above 7.6 percent. Think about how differently we would feel if for the last 40 years, we had observed annualized real S&P 500 returns of only 3.9 percent (a very possible outcome given the volatility of returns) versus an annualized rate of 7.6 percent per year adjusted for inflation. Both of these average rates of return were equally probable in the range of results shown in Figure 3.1. In this simulation, every one of the 10,000 scenarios had *exactly the same expected return*, yet the range of *realized* 40-year cumulative returns varied widely due to the volatility of returns.[7] The bottom 5th percentile of the 40-year simulations had an annualized return of only 1.2 percent, while the top 5th percentile experienced average annualized returns of 10.3 percent. If you started with an initial investment of $10,000, this range of returns over 40 years corresponds to projected portfolio values that vary between $15,800 and $503,000 in today's dollars—quite a spread of outcomes. Given the wide variation in returns that is possible, there is little information about the long-run average expected return on equities based on any observed 40-year period.

It is also obvious from this discussion that focusing too much on historical returns can blind you to events that could happen, but have not happened before. For instance, prior to September, 2001, we had never seen terrorist events impact global stock markets in such a dramatic fashion. Such events are inherently unpredictable, but are a major part of the uncertainty in future scenarios. Just because we have never experienced a particular outcome does not mean that the outcome is impossible. For instance, since 1950 we have never seen the S&P 500 index drop by more than 44 percent in a single 12-month period (unadjusted for inflation). But of course, such an outcome is certainly possible. Within the constraints imposed by financial theory and market structures, there are a nearly infinite range of possibilities, only a small fraction of which have actually occurred. *It is critically important to remember that investment decisions should be based on what is possible, not just on what has transpired in the past.*

The bottom line with this analysis is that our historical experience with stock market returns may bear little relation to what we might experience in the future. While it seems intuitive and comfortable to simply extrapolate the experience of the last few decades to the years ahead, the chance that we will be wrong is substantial. One must take this uncertainty into account when making financial projections and structuring investment portfolios.

HISTORY IS SOMETIMES NOT WHAT IT SEEMS

Not only is history often a poor guide to the future, sometimes it is not even an accurate reflection of the past. Let's say I was interested in starting an investment newsletter business where I would select stocks for my subscribers to invest in. If you were evaluating such a newsletter, chances are you would assess the value of my newsletter based on how well I did picking stocks historically. But what if I did not really have any stock picking ability? Could I still generate an impressive track record to generate business?

One way to create such a track record would be to send out 10,000 copies of a newsletter via e-mail to potential subscribers one month, each with a different random stock pick. One month later, if the markets were relatively flat, one would expect that about half of the 10,000 stock picks would have increased in price, and about half would have decreased in price simply due to random variations.[8] Now I would have about 5,000 potential subscribers who have seen me pick a stock that subsequently went up that month. One-for-one, not too bad.

Next I e-mail 5,000 newsletters, each with a different random stock pick only to those subscribers who received predications in the first month that turned out to be correct. Again, we would expect that on average about half of the stocks would go up over the next month and about half would go down. However, now I have a population of about 2,500 potential subscribers who have seen me pick stocks two months in a row that subsequently went up. Two-for-two—perhaps now I am getting their attention.

Of course, I can keep going. By sending out another 2,500 e-mails, each with a different random stock pick, I can generate a group of about 1,250 potential subscribers who have seen three straight months of good stock picks. After four months, I might have 625 potential subscribers who have witnessed four straight months of stock picks that subsequently went up—which some might regard as an impressive track record. Now I suggest that I will send them the next issue of the newsletter if they subscribe for the modest price of $1,000 per year. Do you think I would get any takers?

What I have described above is a classic example of an investment newsletter fraud. There are many such variations on this particular swindle. Even though I was picking stocks purely at random, I would be able to convince 625 prospective customers that I could pick winning stocks four months in a row. The problem, of course, is that the 625 prospective customers only saw the winning picks by construction. They did not see all the other picks that did not turn out, and hence could not make an accurate assessment of my stock-picking prowess. In reality, I had no stock-picking ability at all, but by cleverly setting up the process I could (illegally) shield that information from a group of potential subscribers to my potential benefit.

Now usually you don't run into such blatant examples of fraud being perpetrated on investors (though the number of e-mails I receive from scammers posing as third-world bankers makes me wonder). But the idea that the historical track records of investments may not be unbiased is a real concern. One example practice in financial services that can lead to such a bias is called *fund incubation*. Under this practice, which is currently legal, a number of new funds are set up as private investments (not available to the public) with modest amounts of seed money. After two or three years, those funds that perform well are turned into publicly available mutual funds and advertised with their impressive track records. Those funds that did not perform well are quietly terminated or merged into existing funds and not offered to the public, never to be heard from again. When incubation techniques are being used, there is a *selection bias* in the observed returns of new mutual funds that are brought to market. A selection bias occurs when the process used to create a sample (new mutual funds) results in a biased group of observations (only winners survive). The result is a population that has a disproportionate number of winners.

The problem here is that even if the fund managers have no investment skill at all, the fund incubation process practically guarantees that there will be one or more funds with positive track records. An investor evaluating such funds may be impressed with the two- or three-year history of good performance and invest in the fund, even though there is no reason to believe that the performance was due to anything other than luck. If they observed all the funds that were started, they might be able to correctly deduce the managerial ability of the firm, but since they only see winners, they come away with an unbalanced impression. This, of course, is the same technique used by casinos on the Las Vegas strip. From the number of pictures of smiling people holding million-dollar checks, you would get the impression that every third person is hitting the jackpot at the slot machines. The reality is far less exciting.

If such practices as fund incubation are used in the fund industry, then one would expect to see a positive bias in the returns of new investment funds. And there is significant evidence for just such a bias.[9] New mutual funds in various sectors appear to have upwardly biased returns for their first year or so relative to more seasoned mutual funds with similar characteristics. Fund incubation is just one of many ways that historical performance information can be used to entice prospective investors.

INVESTING WITH PERFECT HINDSIGHT

Another common practice in the investment industry is to illustrate the performance history of investments based on *backtested* results, in addition to or in lieu of actual trading histories. Though regulations exist to make it clear to investors which performance results are based on actual trading histories and which are hypothetical, sometimes the presentations of the results are not so obvious. Backtesting is the process of seeing how an investment strategy would have performed over different historical time periods if that strategy had been employed during that time. Often, when investment managers devise a new strategy, they will test the performance of the method across various historical time periods to see how it would have fared. If you came up with an idea, and then tested it once on relevant historical data, you might expect that the test could be informative as to whether the strategy had any promise. A problem occurs, however, when you test not one, but *many* possible strategies over historical data to see which one works best. By doing so, you create a potential bias in the results. The performance of a single tested strategy over 30 years might be informative of its future expected performance (though not as much as you might think). *But the historical performance of the best of 100 tested strategies says very little about its future performance.* Why? The more models you test, the more likely you are to find a spurious fit to the historical data. For any historical period, there exist some strategies that would have worked well for that period. If you look long and hard enough, you are sure to find one. However, just because you find one that works for one period does not mean that it is likely to work for any future period.

For instance, a common example of getting silly results from backtesting investment strategies is the apparent correlation of the Dow Jones Industrial Average index with the height of women's hemlines.[10] Every year or so you will see articles in the press talking about the correlation of the stock market with the length of skirts. Apparently shorter skirts are correlated with higher stock prices. Alternate goofy stock market theories include correlations with whether the AFC or NFC wins the Superbowl, and the prevalence of sunspots. In any of these results, it is highly likely that the observed correlations are simply spurious and of little use in predicting the stock market. There is certainly no plausible reason why such variables should explain future stock returns. Drawing conclusions from a small number of data observations is highly speculative, particularly when you test not one, but many potential strategies. It is pretty easy to find *some* factor that is historically correlated with the stock market. But it is much more difficult to find something that is truly predictive of the future.

Of course, very few investment managers test just one strategy. Often the selected investment methodology is based on the evaluation of sometimes thousands of candidate models with thousands of variables. The backtested historical performance of such strategies is often highly biased (in the positive direction) as a result. Worse, when the investment product or strategy is promoted, the results of the backtested historical data are often shown in addition to the actual investment results. While there are performance-reporting regulations designed to make it clear which is which, you sometimes have to carefully read the fine print to figure it out.

Obviously this can distort the evaluation of the performance of a new fund. You are not looking at the results of testing the strategy against a random sample of historical data, but rather the performance of a strategy that performed best out of perhaps thousands of candidate strategies tested over that period. Given that one can almost always find some strategy that performed well over a given period of time if you look long enough, the value of the historical track record in such cases is dubious at best.

Another common problem with backtested models is their failure to take transaction costs into consideration. A strategy might look good on paper, but if you can't implement it, the profits are illusory. Many managers have been fooled by strategies that involve high levels of trading in thinly traded securities. Often the apparent profits from such strategies disappear when the costs of trading are incorporated into the model.

Yet another example of the use of backtesting is in the reporting of the performance for mutual funds that are comprised of other mutual funds, such as *fund-of-funds* or *lifecycle funds*. Such funds invest across a number of submanagers, each with potentially different asset allocation strategies. Lifecycle funds allocate their assets across a number of submanagers in ways that decrease the risk of the investment allocation as the fund matures. These funds are marketed as diversified solutions for investors who do not wish to choose their own allocations. When such funds are new, they often include backtested performance histories that show how the fund would have behaved had the fund-of-fund allocation strategy been used historically. Of course such performance histories are likely to be positively biased since the allocation strategy was determined with knowledge of what actually happened (this is often referred to as *20/20 hindsight*). It is no surprise that such allocations would have done well historically, since the same historical data was used to determine the allocation strategy in the first place. The manager would not have likely picked an allocation strategy that performed poorly historically. A lesson here is to be sure the performance history you are evaluating is an *actual* trading history, not a backtested hypothetical track record. Sometimes you have to read the footnotes carefully to figure this out.

As in the fund incubation example described previously, the rampant use of backtesting to devise new investment strategies should make you skeptical about the historical performance of newly created mutual funds, hedge funds, fund-of-funds, or exchange-traded funds. Often the historical performance track record of such products will be heavily biased in favor of good performance, regardless of whether there is credible evidence that such performance will persist in the future.

THE LUCKY AND THE SKILLFUL

In the world of investment management, there is a vigorous and continuing debate on the evidence for investment management skill in financial markets. The difficulty is that given the degree of uncertainty in investment returns, it is very hard to definitively separate the effects of luck and skill. An unskilled manager can have good performance due to luck, while a skilled manager may have poor performance due to bad luck. Given the nature of the randomness in the data, we cannot *prove* that a manager has skill, nor can we *prove* that an investment track record was entirely due to luck. However, we can assess how likely a particular track record is given the uncertainties in returns, and thus make judgments about the chance that the observed performance was due to random luck. If an investment track record is likely to occur simply due to random variation in returns, then we might be less likely to attribute the results solely to skill. Correspondingly, if a performance record were so wildly improbable that it was very unlikely to have happened randomly, we might be more inclined to believe that investment skill had something to do with it. While it is true that the presence of investment skill makes good performance results more likely, the mere presence of a good track record does not imply that skill must have been the cause.

Ultimately, the decision of whether luck or skill is the most likely explanation depends on your prior beliefs, and for some, these beliefs border on religious conviction. Many investment managers and practitioners in the industry start with the assumption that some managers have skill, and thus strong performance track records are indicative of more skillful management. Many economists take a more skeptical view, noting that the range of performance that one would expect to observe, even in the absence of investment skill (i.e., the assumption that nobody can beat the market) is quite wide and that it takes extraordinary observed performance over long time periods to provide reliable evidence of investment skill. As we will see in this section, it is easy to underestimate the impact of random variation in market returns and thus put too much emphasis on the explanation that investment skill must have been responsible for the observed performance.

If you are an aficionado of personal investing books and magazines, you have no doubt been well indoctrinated in the phenomenon of the "hot manager." Popular financial media devotes endless pages to profiling the performance of investment managers with strong performance records. Sometimes the accolades showered on these star managers border on a celebrity cult of personality. For instance, the financial media might have us believe that beating the S&P 500 index for 15 years straight must be incontrovertible evidence of superior investment skill. But is this really the case?

As we will see, the mere presence of long winning streaks does not prove the existence of managers with superior skill. *Even in a world populated by managers with no investment skill, we would still expect to see examples of long streaks of outperformance purely due to chance.* Going back to our coin-flipping examples in the first chapter, the odds of a single person picking up a coin and flipping eight heads in a row are low (1 in 256 to be precise). But the odds of someone in a group of 100 such coin flippers getting eight heads in eight coin flips are not so bad (about 1 in 3).[11] Note that the probability of seeing eight heads in a row does not depend on the skill of the coin flipper, but only on the number of people trying. If you saw someone pick up a coin and flip eight heads in a row, you might be impressed (or perhaps a bit suspicious of the coin). But if you saw one person out of 100 coin flippers accomplish the feat, you probably would not think it was such a big deal, and you would be right.

The investing world is filled with *tens of thousands* of investment managers competing to create good performance track records. Even if we take the extreme position that *none* of them have any investment skill, quite a few are bound to get lucky and post impressive winning streaks. To provide compelling evidence of investment skill, we need evidence of track records that are so improbable that it would be highly unlikely that chance alone could explain the results. It turns out that this is a pretty high bar. With the large number of investment managers and the relatively high volatility of their strategies, the range of possible outcomes due to chance is quite wide—much more than you might think. It is simply being lazy to blindly attribute good investment track records solely to investment skill alone without taking into account the role played by chance. Ignoring this effect can lead to poor assessments of funds and bad investment decisions.

Naturally, the media like to focus on the gaudy track records of hot managers. One mutual fund in particular, the Legg Mason Value Trust fund (LMVTX), has been held up as an illustration of remarkable investment acumen by the media in recent years.[12] To provide some insight into how randomness might impact our assessment of a particular investment track record, we will use the Legg Mason Value Trust fund as a case study. It is important to note that nothing in this analysis proves that the performance results of this fund were not due to superior skill on the part of the investment manager. The Legg Mason Value Trust fund may very well be run by managers of considerable skill, and you certainly cannot fault them for publicizing their good performance to market their services. My only point with this exercise is that our intuition about such performance results is often flawed, and that the press often makes unfounded assumptions about the root cause of good historical performance.

First let's look at some data. Over 15 calendar years, from 1991–2005, the Legg Mason Value Trust fund generated average annual returns of 16.5 percent. Over the same period, the S&P 500 index had annualized returns of 9.4 percent. On its face, this seems like a pretty impressive track record over a relatively long period of time. Figure 3.2 shows that a $10,000 investment in the fund would have grown to $98,283 by the end of the 15-year period (assuming you did not have to pay any taxes along the way and not adjusting for inflation). In comparison, a similar investment in the S&P 500 over the same period would have yielded only $37,802—a substantial discount to the wealth generated by the investment in the Value Trust fund.

The Legg Mason Value Trust fund also had the notable distinction of beating the performance of the S&P 500 index (its declared benchmark) each and every calendar year from 1991 through 2005. In isolation, this track record sounds particularly impressive. And the press certainly thought so. By my count, there were no fewer than 506 articles in major publications during the period 2001–2006 discussing the Legg Mason Value Trust fund

FIGURE 3.2 Growth of a $10,000 Initial Investment in the LMVTX Fund over the Period 1991-2005

and its remarkable winning streak.[13] However, the real question is how unusual is such a performance track record for a fund like the Legg Mason Value Trust fund? To analyze such a question, we need to better understand the investment style of the fund.

According to its fact sheet, the Legg Mason Value Trust "follows a value discipline of investing by purchasing primarily large-capitalization stocks at large discounts to the manager's assessment of their intrinsic value."[14] While this might sound like a fund that tends to invest in large-cap value stocks, in reality, the story is a bit more complex. If you evaluate the average investment style of the Legg Mason Value Trust fund over this period using Financial Engines' methodology, you discover that the manager does not have an investment style that focuses exclusively on large-capitalization stocks, nor does the style always center on value stocks. Over this period, the average investment style of the fund was about 54 percent large-cap value stocks, 30 percent large-cap growth, and 16 percent mid-cap growth. Different fund-rating services variously categorize the fund as large-cap growth, value, or blend. In short, it is not an easy fund to categorize into a single investment style, because it holds both value and growth stocks in its portfolio at various times.

In addition to the exposures to multiple-asset classes, the fund holds relatively concentrated positions in a modest number of securities. This concentration leads to additional volatility in the returns of the fund relative to an index fund with similar but more broadly diversified investment exposures (like the S&P 500). Called *fund-specific risk*, this portion of the fund's total risk is due to the active investment choices made by the manager, above and beyond the risk of the underlying investment style. All actively managed funds have some degree of fund-specific risk associated with their strategy. The more active the management style, the more fund-specific risk there will be. Only passively managed index funds are able to avoid the additional volatility, since they are designed to closely track a particular asset class index. The Legg Mason Value Trust fund had a fund-specific volatility of about 7.5 percent over this period. This is pretty high for a fund that largely invests in large-capitalization companies. As a point of reference, other funds with similar investment exposures as the Legg Mason Value Trust fund had an average fund-specific risk of about 3.8 percent over this period. So the Value Trust fund had almost double the fund-specific risk of funds with similar investment styles. Higher levels of fund-specific risk imply more volatile and less predictable future returns. Of course, this risk can play out in the good direction (as in the case of the Legg Mason Value Trust fund during this period), or in the bad, when a fund substantially underperforms its investment style.

To evaluate the question of whether the Legg Mason Value Trust fund's performance over 1991–2005 was particularly unusual we need the ability to model the typical range of performance expected for similar funds. However, there is a problem. We have only one history of the Legg Mason Value Trust fund to examine. How can we tell whether the observed performance was typical or unusual with a sample of one?

Fortunately this question can be examined through the use of Monte Carlo simulation. We can generate thousands of possible 15-year histories of funds with a similar investment style and volatility as the Legg Mason Value Trust fund (but with no manager skill by construction) and see how often they demonstrate performance comparable to that generated by the fund itself over the period 1991–2005. That is, we can calculate how unusual the observed performance history is for this kind of investment fund. If the observed performance of the real fund was in excess of all 10,000 simulated histories, then we might be inclined to believe that the track record of the Legg Mason Value Trust fund was reflective of investment skill, since the odds of seeing such an event due to chance were very low. But if our simulated funds routinely beat the observed performance of the Legg Mason Value Trust fund due to chance, we would be more likely to consider the possibility that the track record involved good luck.

For our comparison we create synthetic versions of the Legg Mason Value Trust fund with no ability to beat the market at all. Each synthetic fund is designed to have the same average investment style as the original Legg Mason fund. Fund returns are modeled as having the same returns as their underlying average asset class exposures adjusted for fund expenses and fund-specific risk, but with no adjustment for manager skill. You can think of these funds as blind versions of the original Legg Mason fund, since they have the same average investment style, but randomly select the specific investments in that style. Now we can simulate thousands of possible scenarios for a fund with the same risk level and investment style of the Legg Mason Value Trust fund, but where there is no management skill by construction.

So how do our unskilled versions of the Legg Mason Value Trust fund do compared to the real thing?

First we estimate how likely our synthetic funds are to beat an annualized return benchmark of 16.5 percent over a 15-year holding period. Out of 10,000 15-year scenarios analyzed, 318 of our synthetic funds exceeded a 16.5 percent annualized rate of return purely due to chance. That is, we would expect a fund with a similar investment style as the Value Trust fund to beat annual returns of 16.5 percent over a 15-year period about 3.2 percent of the time. Clearly the Legg Mason Value Trust fund performed well over the period 1991–2005, based on this analysis, beating more than 96 percent of the simulated unskilled hypothetical funds. But was it skill or simply good luck that led to the result?

Remember that our synthetic funds were set up to have no investment skill at all. In effect, the funds were managed by throwing darts at a dartboard. While demonstrating performance in the top 4 percent of simulated 15-year performance results might sound impressive, keep in mind that *someone* has to be in the top percentiles of performance, even if the result was completely random. If we took 1,000 fund managers with this investment style, but no skill whatsoever, we would expect about 32 of them to demonstrate performance of at least 16.5 percent over a 15-year period. Moreover, *we are virtually guaranteed to see at least one fund* out of 1,000 beating this benchmark return even if each individual fund had only a 3.2 percent chance of success.

Even if the world was populated entirely by unskilled investment managers, we would still be likely to observe such performance by a significant minority of them. Does this imply that there are no managers with investment skill? Of course not. But the bottom line is that when we look at the historical performance results of the best of a large population of managers, it is not unusual to see some pretty impressive track records. *In fact, we would be surprised not to see such results.* Just like someone has to win the lottery, no matter how unlikely the odds of winning, some investment managers are bound to get lucky. This is not to take away anything from the impressive results posted by the Legg Mason team. But just because the results were very good does not mean that the only explanation was superior investment skill.

But what about the result of beating the S&P 500 index for 15 years in a row? Surely the odds of such an occurrence happening by chance are infinitesimal. In the recent book, *More Than You Know: Finding Financial Wisdom in Unconventional Places,* author (and Chief Investment Strategist at Legg Mason Capital Management) Michael Mauboussin portrays this result as a "one in a 2.3 million" event.[15] Given the extraordinarily low odds, he argues that the 15-year winning streak of the Legg Mason Value Trust fund clearly implies investment skill as opposed to chance occurrence. Indeed, if the odds of such a result occurring randomly were truly one in 2.3 million, it would suggest that investment skill is likely to have played a role.

Before analyzing the probability of such an event, it is useful to remind ourselves that what really matters in investment performance is the cumulative return, not the number of time periods that a fund beats its benchmark. Would you rather have a fund that beats the S&P 500 each year by a penny, or one that delivers double the cumulative return of the index with a few down periods? The answer is obvious—cumulative returns are what create wealth, not arbitrary comparisons with benchmarks. Nonetheless, the record of beating the S&P 500 on a calendar-year basis is what attracted the attention of the financial press, so let's take a look at this achievement in more detail.

It turns out that the 15-year winning streak against the S&P 500, while uncommon, is far from a one-in-2.3-million event. Again, we can estimate the probability of such an event using Monte Carlo simulation. This time we create 10,000 different scenarios for both the synthetic versions of the Value Trust fund and for the S&P 500 index, using the same initial market conditions and underlying asset class returns. This provides a realistic way to compare the year-by-year performance of the two investments and allows us to count how many times we see 15 consecutive years where the simulated unskilled Value Trust funds outperform the S&P 500.

Of our 10,000 simulated scenarios, we find precisely one scenario where the synthetic Legg Mason Value Trust fund beats the simulated S&P 500 index for 15 years in a row. So clearly this is a much less probable event than beating annualized returns of 16.5 percent for a 15-year period.[16] Interestingly, it turns out that the Legg Mason Value Trust fund was the only equity mutual fund to beat the S&P 500 index each calendar year over the period 1991–2005 and was the only equity fund to do so in the last 40 years.

Unfortunately, this particular simulation does not allow us to accurately resolve the probability of such a rare event with only 10,000 scenarios. It does, however, provide proof that such an event is possible due to chance alone. To more accurately assess the probability that we would observe such performance by a fund like the Legg Mason Value Trust fund, we need to estimate how many times we would observe a 15-year track record of beating the S&P 500 by an equity fund over a 40 year period of observation.

A fund with the same average investment style, level of fund-specific risk, and fees as the Value Trust fund has about a 42 percent chance of beating the S&P 500 in any given year due to random variation in returns (again assuming no investment skill by the manager).[17] Through simulation, we can estimate that the corresponding chance of seeing a 15-year winning streak within a period of 40 years for similar funds is about 1 in 29,400. This is very uncommon, but *much* more probable than one in 2.3 million. But the real question is not the chance of seeing a single fund accomplish the feat, but the chance that *at least one fund out of thousands of equity mutual funds* could post a 15-year winning streak versus the S&P 500 index. After all, the Legg Mason Value Trust fund was the *only* equity mutual fund in the last 40 years to post such a record.

During the period 1995–2007, there were an average of 6,817 equity mutual funds in the Financial Engines database. If we assume that each of these funds had a similar 42 percent chance of beating the S&P 500 in a given year, and that all the funds were devoid of any investment management skill, then we would expect to see a 15-year winning streak versus the S&P 500 within a 40-year period by at least one of these funds about 1 in 5 times. So much for the 1-in-2.3-million miracle. Of course you can argue that the number of equity funds was substantially smaller in the early 1990s than it is now, as the fund population has grown substantially in recent years. In 1995, there were about 1,500 equity mutual funds in the United States. Getting a precise estimate of the number of funds in existence over long periods is challenging, as funds are discontinued and merged into other funds over time. Even with a population of only 1,500 equity funds, we would still expect to see a 15-year winning streak versus the S&P 500 within a 40-year period about 1 in 20 times, due entirely to chance.

Interestingly, in our sample of 10,000 scenarios, there were no scenarios where the simulated Value Trust funds beat the S&P 500 16 years running. Indeed, this would be a significantly less probable event (about 1 in 63,300). Coincidently, the Legg Mason Value Trust fund underperformed the S&P 500 index by significant margins in both 2006 and 2007.

So was it luck or skill that allowed the Legg Mason Value Trust fund to post a 15-year winning streak against the S&P 500? Certainly the fund posted an impressive track record that would be uncommon under the assumption of no investment skill. It is impossible to know for sure, but even track records as impressive and historically unprecedented as that posted by the Legg Mason Value Trust fund may still be artifacts of random variation, as opposed to convincing demonstrations of investment skill. It does not prove a lack of skill, but it does raise doubts that skill alone is the only reasonable explanation for the observed performance.

This example was intended to help you develop some intuition in evaluating the importance of historical track records when analyzing investment funds. What may seem like extraordinary displays of investment skill are not as unusual as they might seem when viewed in the context of expected random variation, particularly when we are observing a large population of managers. When there are many managers to choose from, a significant number will generate great track records purely due to chance, given the volatility of their investment strategies.

Maintaining a skeptical mindset is good prudence when it comes to selecting investment managers. After all, you can easily achieve the market performance by purchasing a low cost index fund. When selecting an active fund manager, you are making a bet that they have skills that will allow them to beat the market in the future. At best, they will only have some chance of beating the market (since nobody wins all the time). Because the natural alternative is achieving market returns with an index fund, it makes sense to be a skeptic when making assessments of whether the observed track record is due to skill or luck. Even if skill is present, there is still a significant possibility that the fund will underperform due to random variation in returns. To properly put past performance into perspective in predicting future performance, it is critical to adjust for the random variation expected in a population of investment managers. This is a topic that will be addressed in more detail in Chapter 9. There may very well be managers who are expected to beat the market (at least some of the time) due to superior skill or access to information. A challenge for investors in actively managed funds is to identify such managers *before* they demonstrate such performance. This makes the job of selecting good active managers much more difficult.

EVALUATING FUND PERFORMANCE

The fund analysis described earlier required access to sophisticated analytics to determine the investment exposures of a fund, how well it did relative to an appropriate benchmark, and how well it might perform in the future. Luckily, you don't need to invent your own tools in order to apply these ideas to your own portfolio. The Financial Engines' *Personal Online Advisor* service includes easy access to fund scorecards with just this type of information.

The Financial Engines' investment database includes over 17,000 mutual funds at the time of this writing (including multiple share classes of each fund). Each one of those funds has an associated scorecard that ranks the fund on several measures relative to its peer group (defined by funds with similar investment styles). Each fund is ranked on four separate measures:

- Fund-specific risk (risk in addition to its investment style)
- Expenses (the total cost of the fund)
- Turnover (how often the fund manager trades)
- Historical alpha (the degree to which the fund over- or underperformed relative to its investment style)

For each of these measures, the fund's ranking relative to its peer group is charted in terms of 20 percent increments (represented by five yellow dots). A rating of one out of five dots indicates that the fund ranks below 80 percent of its peers for this measure, while a rating of four dots indicates that the fund is in the top 40 percent of its peer group. A rating of five dots indicates that the fund is in the top 20 percent of its peer group.

The *fund-specific risk* measure evaluates how much active management, concentration, or investment style rotation the fund displays. Actively managed funds have more fund-specific risk than index- or passively managed funds, sometimes much more. Funds have higher fund-specific risk when they concentrate their investments into a small number of stocks, or when they frequently change their investment style over time.

The *expenses* metric evaluates the cost of owning the fund. Higher expenses paid to the fund manager imply less money that you get to keep. As we will see in Chapter 7, expenses are an extremely important factor in selecting good investments.

The *turnover* metric evaluates how often the fund buys and sells securities in its portfolio. This is important because any time a fund manager purchases or sells a position in its portfolio, he or she incurs costs in the form of brokerage commissions and market spreads (the difference between the price that you can buy and sell a security in the stock market). While these costs are generally small for a given transaction, they can add up quickly for an actively managed fund that is doing lots of trading. Furthermore, a fund that trades often is less tax efficient than one that trades infrequently, due to the fact that the manager must distribute capital gains to its shareholders. This can be an important consideration for funds held in a taxable account.

Finally, the *historical alpha* metric evaluates the historical performance of the fund relative to its specific investment style. The alpha measure can be positive or negative depending on whether the manager showed performance above or below the returns of its investment style benchmark. The historical alpha measures the difference between the returns of the funds and the returns of the underlying investment style benchmark.

In addition, Financial Engines provides an overall rating (on a scale of 1 to 10) that describes the expected performance of the fund relative to other peer funds with similar investment styles. This measure incorporates a number of different analyses to estimate how well this fund is expected to do relative to its investment style benchmark and relative to its peers. It takes into consideration the investment style of the fund, expenses, historical performance, and fund-specific risk to estimate the forward-looking expected performance. A rating of 10 indicates that the fund is in the top 5 percent of expected performance relative to its peer group, while a rating of 9.5 indicates that it is in the top 10 percent of expected performance. A fund with a rating of 5.5 would be expected to outperform 50 percent of its peer group in the future. Figure 3.3 shows a scorecard for the Legg Mason Value Trust fund as of November 2007.

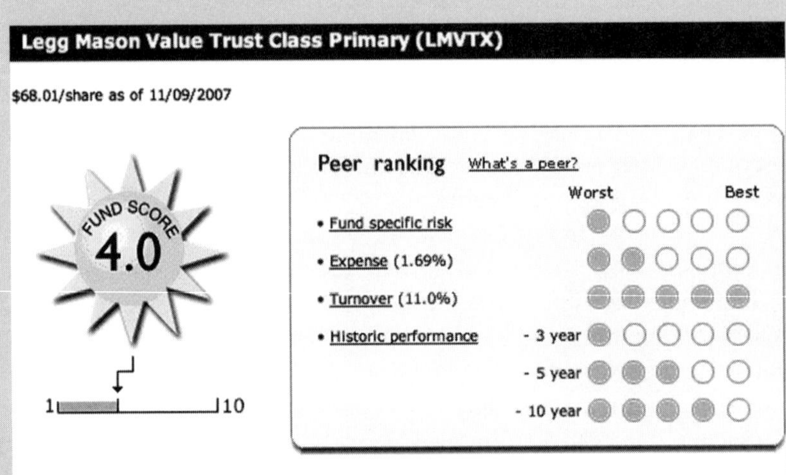

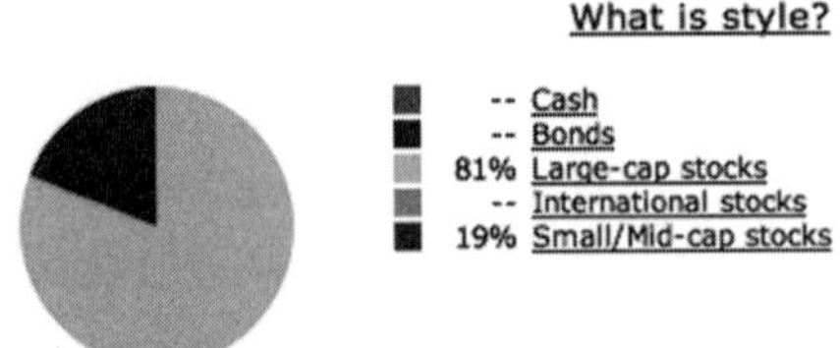

FIGURE 3.3 Example Fund Scorecard for the Legg Mason Value Trust Fund

Source: Financial Engines.

It is important to note that the fund score is not a sufficient metric on which to select funds for a portfolio. As will be illustrated in subsequent chapters, you must take into consideration additional information including the risk and correlations of the fund in combination with other funds in order to build high-quality portfolios. Chapters 8 and 9 will provide more detail on how to analyze funds and build efficient portfolios, but the scorecards can be a convenient source for information on how a fund's performance measures up against its peers.

Now that may have been a bit more analysis than some of you were counting on. But the core ideas in this chapter are really pretty simple. Unlike most endeavors, the link between observed performance and skill in investing is very noisy. When someone hits 50 home runs during a major league season, you can be reasonably sure that they must have some uncommon skill in hitting baseballs to have accomplished such a feat. But a person who randomly flips eight heads in a row is no more skilled at coin flipping than anyone else. They just got lucky. Given the amount of uncertainty in the performance of investment managers, it is very difficult to separate out the good from the lucky (or the bad from the unlucky, for that matter). Wall Street knows that a good track record is a big selling point for investment funds. They put a lot more marketing muscle behind those products with the gaudy performance records than those with only average returns. *Very* few investment performance histories fall outside of what can be attributed to random variation. Make sure you consider this carefully before committing your hard-earned dollars to a speculative bet on future performance matching that of the past.

TAKE-AWAYS

- Past performance is a poor guide for future expected returns, either for assets classes or investment funds.
- Historical data can be useful for understanding volatility and correlations, but be aware that some risks may not have been observed in the past.

(Continued)

- Don't be misled by the appearance of a strong historical track record, particularly for newer investment products (those less than five years old). There are many reasons why such historical track records may not be representative of the future. Be skeptical.
- The predictive value of manager track records is weak. Even great track records can often be attributed to random variation in performance. There is nothing wrong with selecting active managers, but don't make big bets on managers with strong track records being able to maintain that performance in the future, as it is likely that chance played a significant role in their success.
- Base your fund selection on factors that are predictive of future performance. Chapter 9 provides additional information on this point.

CHAPTER 4

The Wisdom of the Market

To make no mistakes is not in the power of man; but from their errors and mistakes the wise and good learn wisdom for the future.

—Plutarch (46–120 AD)

Building high-quality investment portfolios requires accurate information about the future risk and returns of assets. When it comes to predicting the future, the market is usually smarter than any one person, no matter how astute or educated. The global market portfolio represents the consensus view—the expectations of all investors taken together—and is a potent source of information about the future. Despite its obvious value, it remains one of the less used methods of estimating future expected returns, especially among individual investors. Using the wisdom of the market can help you build better portfolios, avoid unintended market bets, and help you more easily detect bad investment advice.

In the previous chapter, we saw how relying on historical returns to predict the future can be a really bad idea. But what is an intelligent investor to do? Where can we get reasonable information about the expected returns of different types of assets? The answer lies in using the wisdom of the market. The market speaks with dollars—investors big and small investing their money based on their own individual predictions about the future. There is tremendously valuable information embedded in the market values of the assets held by investors. In a broad sense, the aggregate market value of different asset classes reflects consensus expectations about the future. Over time, these market consensus estimates turn out to be more reliable than the estimates from any single investor. Ignoring this information is throwing away some of the most important data about what the future holds for different types of assets.

What is the intuition behind the idea that averaging many opinions tends to outperform the views of a single individual? The basic idea goes back quite some time. Remember the expression that "two heads are better than one"? It has long been recognized that you can cancel out the errors of individual predictions by averaging across a number of individuals. The process of averaging across estimates reduces errors by averaging away the errors of each individual making a prediction. In fact, a paper on this phenomenon was published one hundred years ago. In the March 1907 edition of the journal *Nature,* a paper, titled *Vox Populi,* noted the results of a weight-judging competition involving estimates of some 787 people trying to guess the weight of a particular ox. The "middlemost" or median estimate of the crowd was 1,207 pounds, with individual estimates ranging from less than 1,074 to more than 1,293 pounds. The ox actually turned out to weigh 1,198 pounds, only 0.75 percent off the median estimate of the crowd. The paper noted the amazing ability of a population of people to accurately estimate the weight of the ox. Depending on your point of view, this concept also underlies the remarkable resiliency of the democratic process in selecting a political leader. Individual votes may be wacky, but on average the population consensus will often reflect a good choice. It turns out that the same idea applies to financial markets as well.

In the financial market, the prices of traded assets reflect the future value predictions of millions of market participants. It is not surprising, then, that these prices are an excellent source of information about the future prices and expected returns of financial assets. Even if you have opinions that differ from the expectations of the market, you are still better off understanding the market consensus perspective so that you can make educated bets about future asset returns. Using the wisdom of the market does not mean that you must follow the market's views in lockstep, but if you are going to make a market bet, you had better understand the bet you are making, which implies first determining what the market thinks.

THE EFFICIENT MARKET?

No self-respecting author of a book on personal investing could fail to address the concept of *market efficiency*. Perhaps no topic in finance generates more controversy and emotion among investors, advisors, and financial economists. At times, this debate takes on an almost religious fervor, with those who believe you can beat the market on one side of the divide, and those that regard such efforts as a foolish waste of time on the other.

An *efficient market* is one that incorporates all relevant information about the future payoffs of assets into the prices of those assets. In a perfectly efficient market, the future returns of financial assets are entirely unpredictable. This implies that the future prices of assets are simply random deviations from the current price. The strongest proponents of market efficiency argue that the market takes into account *all* information that is relevant to the valuation of assets when setting the price (such as earnings estimates, management team skill, industry conditions, estimated demand, etc.), and thus it is nothing but a big waste of time and money to try to outsmart the market. This point of view, first expressed in the 1960s in academic circles, claims that prices are perfectly efficient and the only reasonable investment strategy is to index your wealth to the performance of the overall market. If the market already incorporates everything that is knowable into the prices of assets, then there is no point in seeking an edge through superior research or analysis. You are simply wasting your time and increasing your costs with no expected gain. Naturally, folks expressing this point of view aren't much fun at a cocktail party of active mutual fund managers. If they are right, or even just mostly right, there are an awful lot of people in the financial services industry wasting their time and money chasing illusory profit opportunities. And despite decades of research by economists, it has been quite difficult to shoot glaring holes in the basic market efficiency argument.

On the opposite side of the efficiency debate are those who proclaim that the market is subject to all kinds of biases, fads, and judgment errors that regularly skew the prices of individual assets and even entire asset class sectors in predictable ways. An *inefficient market* is one that does not properly consider all available information in setting the price of financial assets, and thus the future returns of financial assets are at least partially predictable if you do enough research. In fact, the "market is inefficient" view is probably closer to the conventional wisdom regularly expressed in the popular media and among many financial professionals than the efficient market view held by most economists. These investors believe that careful analysis and street smarts can pay off by allowing you to beat the market with some consistency. Some of these market inefficiency evangelists base their arguments on the madness of crowds, the existence of apparent speculative bubbles, and the evidence for systematic biases in how we make decisions under uncertainty to suggest why the market may often get it wrong. They point to all kinds of situations where it appears that humans systematically make mistakes in reacting to new information about possible future outcomes. Of course, it is easier to point out situations where the market appeared to get it wrong with 20/20 hindsight. But it is much more difficult to establish that the market made an obvious mistake in valuation based on information that was actually available at the time.

The obvious problem with the market inefficiency argument is that there is very little evidence that such biases, if they do in fact exist, result in consistently profitable trading opportunities. For instance, it is one thing to say that people tend to overreact to events with small probabilities of occurrence. It is quite another to demonstrate that the market as a whole systematically overacts to such events in a way that can be easily exploited to make money. It is not good enough to have insights that beat the average market participant; you have to beat all the really smart and rich ones, too, in order to profit. It only takes one well capitalized and observant investor to eliminate a discrepancy in the price of a traded security by exploiting the incorrect price with a large purchase or sale. If all these opportunities to beat the market exist, they seem to be difficult to document in a rigorous way, despite the energetic efforts of thousands of financial economists and statisticians. While difficult to categorically rule out, the evidence for widespread and exploitable market inefficiency appears decidedly weak.

In its starkest terms, the argument over market efficiency is really kind of silly. Of course the market *is* efficient (or I suppose, inefficient, depending on your point of view); the real debate revolves around the *degree of efficiency*. The overwhelming consensus among financial economists and most institutional investors is that the market is very good at incorporating public information into prices, usually within very short periods of time. There is little doubt that prices react quickly to new information about the future value of assets and that there are few obvious opportunities to make easy money with little or no risk. The more interesting debate involves just what kinds of information are incorporated into prices by the trading process, and just how that information impacts the value of assets. This remains an active and ongoing area of research among financial economists.

A slightly less austere view of the market efficiency theory is that the market is very good at assimilating information into prices, making it quite difficult to spot and exploit erroneous valuations placed on assets. Adherents to this point of view make the obvious observation that if the market were widely and predictably making mistakes about the value of assets, then there would be informed traders ready to exploit their superior knowledge to make money from these errors. However, in so doing, these informed traders would eliminate the very errors that created the profit opportunity in the first place. For instance, if you believe a stock is priced too low by the market, then you would buy the stock. But purchasing the stock drives its price up, and if you purchase enough of it, you eliminate any opportunity for further gain. Given the literally hundreds of billions of dollars chasing profit opportunities globally on a second-by-second basis, it seems likely that if such pricing inefficiencies exist they are going to be difficult and perhaps costly to find and exploit. And if they do exist, they sure won't stick around for very long.

My own point of view is that markets are highly efficient, particularly at the aggregate level of overall asset classes. While there may be examples of individual securities that have prices that are too high or too low for short periods of time, it is highly unlikely that the market is making consistent mistakes that result in predictable and easy-to-exploit profit opportunities. There is an active debate among economists over the precise degree of market efficiency, but few would argue that there are a large number of figurative $20 bills lying around on the sidewalk just waiting to be picked up by observant investors. It is much more likely that if such market inefficiencies exist, they are costly to find and fleeting in nature. Trying to beat the market is a very difficult game and perhaps only worth pursuing if you have substantial resources and uncommon access to information (for instance, the ability to directly observe trading activity in real time at a high level of detail, or superior information about nonpublic companies and the value of their assets). It is no exaggeration to say that there are hundreds of billions of dollars and thousands of the world's brightest minds devoted to finding just such market inefficiencies. As a consequence, it is highly unlikely that individual investors on their own will be able to find consistently profitable opportunities to beat the market. While this view may be at odds with hundreds of personal investing books out there pushing various investing systems, it is a much more realistic and pragmatic view of the investing world—one that is far more likely to result in good outcomes for your investments.

Even if you admit the possibility that there may be inefficiencies in the market, it may be the case that the cost of finding and exploiting such opportunities may just offset the expected profit. Perhaps the transaction costs to exploit such an inefficiency eat up most of the potential profit. Or those with access to valuable insights about future asset values may charge an amount that offsets some or all of the potential for excess gains. In any event, there is strong evidence that reliably beating the market is a very tough thing to do.

Furthermore, with the rapid development and application of technology and computing to financial trading, markets are almost certainly becoming more efficient over time. Information that once took days to be disseminated is now globally transmitted in microseconds, with near instantaneous impact on market prices. I would not argue that markets are perfectly efficient at all times, but merely that the prices for traded financial assets reflect relevant public information about their future value under the vast majority of circumstances. Perhaps intelligent traders with superior knowledge and analytic tools can find opportunities for excess profit beyond market returns, but it is not easy for the every-day investor to do this. And the strategies that are employed to exploit such opportunities almost always incorporate significant additional investment risks and transaction costs. It pays to be skeptical when considering the claims of someone who says he or she has a sure-fire way to beat the market. The market is a very tough competitor and the playing field is littered with those who, to their own detriment, underestimated its remarkable wisdom.

WHAT IS THE MARKET PORTFOLIO?

If you believe that the market is mostly efficient, at least at the level of asset classes such as large-cap stocks or corporate bonds, then there is significant information in the market's consensus view of the future embedded in the prices of traded assets. One way of getting at that information about the future is to add up what all investors hold in their investment portfolios. The *market portfolio* consists of the aggregation of all the assets in the world, weighted in proportion to their total market values. For instance, at a high level, the market portfolio consists of all the bonds and stocks in the world, with the portfolio allocations determined by the current total market value of stocks and bonds, respectively. Of course, you can specify the composition of the market portfolio in a greater degree of detail by splitting up the various asset classes into finer categories (for instance into large-, medium-, and small-capitalization stocks, value and growth stocks, or different types of bonds).

You can also think of the market portfolio as representing the average portfolio allocation of all investors, since it reflects the average portfolio held by all investors. In principle, the market portfolio should consist of all financial assets, though usually approximations are made using indexes that track the most widely held asset classes. Standard financial economic theory dictates that the *market portfolio* is efficient and that it has the highest expected return of any portfolio for that level of volatility. You can achieve higher expected return portfolios, but only if you are willing to assume more market volatility. As we will see, this is an important characteristic of the market portfolio.

Another aspect of the market portfolio is that it represents an efficient allocation of asset classes for an investor with an average tolerance for risk.

Investors often ask me what a "typical" efficient investment allocation looks like. If you have risk tolerance similar to the average investor, you have the ability to invest in all asset classes at a reasonable cost, and you are not forced to hold any particular assets or positions (for instance, holding restricted positions in your employer's stock), then the market portfolio is a natural benchmark for an efficient allocation to the various asset classes. Of course, your circumstances may be different and you may require something other than what is appropriate for the average investor.

Furthermore, the market portfolio is based on market consensus expectations about the future risk and return of each asset class. Since it represents the combined expectations of all market participants, it embeds an enormous amount of information about the future. Accordingly, any investment methodology that ignores this important source of information is likely to be flawed. What is surprising is how many investors, even experienced professional ones, completely ignore this important source of information about future expected returns. The value of this information does not depend on you adhering strictly to the market consensus view. Even if you wish to make bets that differ from the overall market consensus, it is still highly valuable to understand what the market consensus is projecting so that you can know how to act upon your predictions based on how they differ from the market's perspective.

In this chapter, we will examine efficient allocations of different asset classes for various levels of risk. Note that we still are not taking into consideration the characteristics of specific investments (like mutual funds or individual stocks) at this point. The impact of information about specific investments on investment decisions will be considered in Chapter 9. These next sections focus only on efficient allocations at the asset class level. It is important to recognize that such efficient allocations would be suitable if you were investing in low-cost index funds, but they may not be appropriate if you are using actively managed mutual funds or building portfolios of individual stocks, due to the differences in the risk-and-return characteristics of those investments (we will cover these topics in later chapters.)

WHAT DOES THE MARKET PORTFOLIO LOOK LIKE?

The market portfolio consists of the market proportions of each asset class. Market proportions are estimated from the market valuation of broad-based indexes that represent the vast majority of the securities in each asset class. Financial Engines uses estimates of the market portfolio to establish asset class expected returns for its forecast and advisory services. Such estimates

TABLE 4.1 Market Portfolio Proportions (January 2007)

Asset Class	Market Proportion
Cash	2.6%
Intermediate Government Bonds	5.3%
Long-Term Government Bonds	1.1%
Corporate Bonds	3.4%
Mortgage Bonds	6.2%
Foreign Bonds	18.0%
Large-Value U.S. Equities	13.1%
Large-Growth U.S. Equities	13.1%
Mid-Value U.S. Equities	3.7%
Mid-Growth U.S. Equities	3.7%
Small-Value U.S. Equities	1.8%
Small-Growth U.S. Equities	1.8%
Europe	15.8%
Pacific	8.1%
Emerging Equities	2.4%

Source: Financial Engines calculations.

Note: Financial Engines uses the following indexes to calculate the market values of each asset class in the market portfolio: U.S. Lehman Brothers 1–3 yr. Treasury Index, Lehman Brothers Intermediate Government Bond Index, Lehman Brothers Long-Term Government Bond Index, Lehman Brothers Corporate Bond Index, Lehman Brothers Mortgage Bond Index, Salomon Brothers Non-U.S. Government Bond Index, S&P/Citigroup 500 Value Index, S&P/Citigroup 500 Growth Index, S&P/Citigroup Mid Cap 400 Value Index, S&P/Citigroup Mid Cap 400 Growth Index, S&P/Citigroup Small Cap 600 Value Index, S&P/Citigroup Small Cap 600 Growth Index, MSCI Europe, MSCI Pacific, IFCI Emerging Market Index.

of the market allocations are updated monthly by Financial Engines' systems. For each asset class in the market portfolio, the allocation represents the total holdings by all investors based on the consensus view of future risk and return.

Table 4.1 illustrates an estimate of the market portfolio using data from Financial Engines as of January 2007.

The market portfolio has a few salient characteristics. First, it is mostly composed of equities. Typically the market portfolio consists of approximately 60 percent to 70 percent equities (stocks) and about 30 percent to 40 percent fixed income securities (bonds). Of the equity exposure, about 60 percent of it is invested in U.S. stocks, and about 40 percent of it is invested in foreign stocks, with large-capitalization U.S. stocks representing almost 40 percent of the total global equity exposure. Of the non-U.S. equities, most of the allocation comes from European companies, with the remaining portions coming from Pacific Rim countries (including Japan) and a smaller amount from emerging markets (developing countries like China, India, and Chile).

THERE'S NO PLACE LIKE HOME

Note an interesting fact about the market portfolio—a significant proportion of the portfolio is in foreign bonds. Since not many U.S. investors hold a large proportion of their portfolio in foreign bonds, who is holding these securities? Foreign investors are. This reveals the presence of something called the *home country bias*. The home country bias is a measure of the preference to hold assets denominated in your own currency (dollars for U.S.-based investors) versus those in the rest of the world. The stronger the home country bias, the more likely you are to hold assets denominated in your home currency. The measurement and desirability of a home country bias is a bit controversial, but in examining the behavior of investors, even large institutional money managers, there is a clear preference shown for U.S.-based assets relative to the overall global allocation among U.S. investors. Explanations for the observed home country bias in investor portfolios include the desire to hold assets in the same currency as their liabilities (the currency you pay your bills with), difficulties in measuring the risk of foreign assets, transaction costs, incentives due to taxes and market structure, potential political instability, investment restrictions on money flows between countries, and even outright patriotism. Regardless of the explanation, the empirical evidence shows that investors tend to show a preference for overweighting their own country's assets relative to the overall global market portfolio.

One way to measure the home country bias is to look at the behavior of very large sophisticated investors, namely the largest U.S. pension funds. In general, pension funds among large companies tend to underweight foreign bonds significantly, and also reduce their holdings of foreign equities to a lesser degree. As of September 2006, large U.S. institutional investors held about 33 percent of their overall equity in foreign stocks, compared to an overall global mix of about 40 percent foreign equity, showing a modest preference for holding domestic equity. For foreign bonds, the home bias appears to be stronger. However, this home bias effect is waning over the years as global markets become more integrated and U.S. investors become

TABLE 4.2 Market Portfolio Proportions for a U.S.-Based Investor (January 2007)

Asset Class	Adjusted Market Proportion
Cash	4.4%
Intermediate Government Bonds	9.1%
Long-Term Government Bonds	1.9%
Corporate Bonds	5.9%
Mortgage Bonds	10.8%
Foreign Bonds	1.0%
Large-Value U.S. Equities	15.7%
Large-Growth U.S. Equities	15.7%
Mid-Value U.S. Equities	4.4%
Mid-Growth U.S. Equities	4.4%
Small-Value U.S. Equities	2.2%
Small-Growth U.S. Equities	2.2%
Europe	13.4%
Pacific	6.8%
Emerging Equities	2.1%

more accustomed to holding non-U.S. financial assets. U.S.-based investors have been steadily increasing the proportions of foreign securities they hold as the United States becomes a smaller proportion of the overall global market portfolio, and at least for equities, the bias seems to be going away.

Table 4.2 shows what the market portfolio looks like as of January 2007 after adjusting for the home country bias using Financial Engines' methodology.

Notice how the proportion of foreign bonds in the adjusted market portfolio is substantially lower than in the unadjusted global mix shown in Table 4.1. Also note that the foreign equity proportions are lower, but to a lesser degree than is true for bonds. However, the overall characteristics of the portfolio are very similar. The adjusted market portfolio is still predominantly equities (about 2/3 of the portfolio as of January 2007). And large-capitalization U.S. stocks make up about half of the total equity exposure. As the global market becomes more integrated and U.S. markets become a smaller proportion of the overall global mix, we can expect that the home country bias will decrease. Over time, the adjusted market portfolio is likely to move toward the unadjusted global portfolio mix for U.S.-based investors.

HISTORY OF THE MARKET PORTFOLIO

The market portfolio is not a static mix. As investors react to new information and economic developments, the market proportions of each asset class vary over time. The asset class market value proportions react according to changes in the supplies, expected returns, volatilities, and the extent to which different assets move together. If the market believes the expected return for an asset class increases, this makes it more desirable to hold and its overall proportion in the market portfolio will get larger. Similarly, increases in the risk of an asset class make it less desirable to hold (assuming nothing else changes at the same time). One interesting point about portfolios is that the desirability of an asset class also depends on how correlated it is with the other assets in your portfolio.

Correlation is a measure of how much the returns of two different assets move together. It is a number that varies between –1.0 and +1.0. If two assets move together in nearly lockstep (say, two large-cap mutual funds with the same investment style), their correlation measure is positive and has a value near one. If two assets are completely independent of each other and have no relationship at all, their correlation value will be near zero. Finally if two assets move exactly opposite one another—one goes up when the other goes down—their correlation would have a value of –1.0. Most financial assets have positive correlations with one another. In a portfolio it is desirable to mix assets whose correlations are less than one, since it allows you to lower the overall risk of the portfolio. Why? Because you offset the movements of individual assets by holding multiple assets that don't move in lockstep in the same portfolio. When one asset goes up, the other may often go down or vice versa, thus offsetting the movements of the first asset. This reduces the overall volatility of the portfolio. As we will see in later chapters, mixing assets that are somewhat uncorrelated with one another is a key objective in building diversified investment portfolios.

Changes in any one of the values of expected returns, volatility, or correlations can result in updated proportions of each asset class in the market portfolio. For instance, if new information becomes available that reduces the future expectations around economic growth in the United States relative to the rest of the world, the market may react by reducing the market value of U.S. equities versus the rest of the world. Of course, such information could also impact the expected volatility of U.S. equities as well as their correlations with international equities. It might even have an impact on the expected returns of other countries, to the extent that they are dependent on the U.S. economy for their own economic growth. Finally, a change in

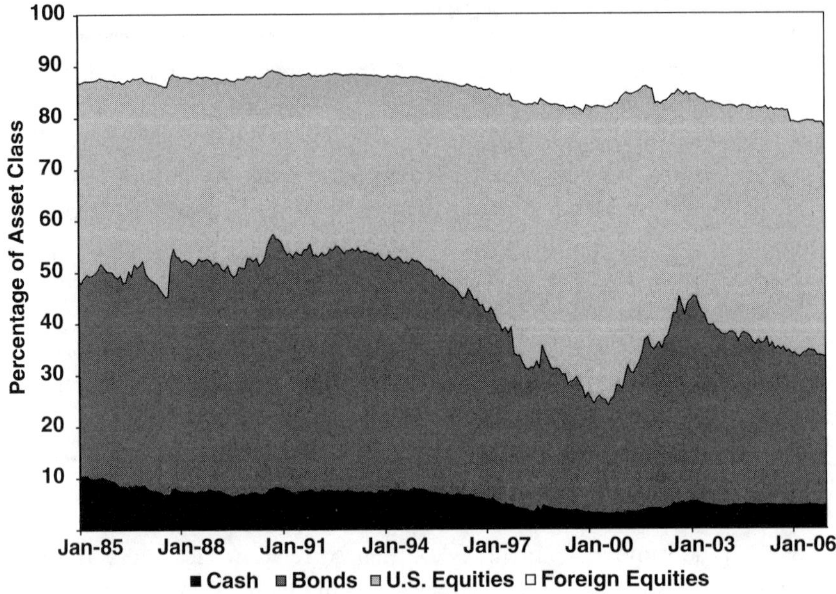

FIGURE 4.1 Adjusted Market Portfolio: 1985–2006

Source: Financial Engines.

expected returns for U.S. equities may have a corresponding impact on fixed income expected returns. As you can see, the relationships between all the asset classes can become very complex. However, at any point in time, the market portfolio proportions represent the dynamic consensus assessment of the expected returns, volatilities, and correlations of each asset class. The market is constantly assimilating new information about the future into the prices of traded assets. As an investor, if you totally ignore this information, you do so at your own peril.

Figure 4.1 shows how the market portfolio (adjusted for the home country bias) has changed over time since 1985. To keep the chart simple, I have combined the 15 asset classes into four major asset classes: cash, bonds, U.S. equities, and foreign equities.

As you can see, the proportions of different asset classes in the market portfolio change over time. Note that the proportion of foreign equity has been steadily increasing over the years. This is due to two factors: the value of U.S. assets has been shrinking as a proportion of the overall global market as the world economy has grown (the rest of the world has been growing faster than the United States), and U.S. investors have been steadily increasing their preferences for holding foreign assets. It is also striking to note the period beginning in the mid-1990s, when the proportion of equity in the overall market portfolio increased dramatically, only to readjust during the period 2001–2003. For those investors who experienced this adjustment firsthand, this turbulent period is not likely to be soon forgotten. Generally, we have seen a trend toward the market portfolio having greater allocation toward both domestic and foreign equities over time.

BETTING AGAINST THE MARKET

There are a few characteristics of the market portfolio that have some interesting implications. First of all, every asset class is included in the portfolio in some proportion. While that might seem eminently obvious, it implies something important: *it makes sense for the aggregate of all investors to hold each of the asset classes in their respective market proportions.* Thus the expected returns, correlations, and volatilities of each asset class are such that, taken together, investors would want to hold the assets in an amount equal to their actual market valuation at any point in time. If this were not the case, then the market value of the assets would change until this was true. If you believe that the market is functioning well (i.e., it is mostly efficient), then there are no asset classes that should be skipped over by *all* investors. Particular investors may choose not to hold an asset class in their portfolio due to risk preferences, available investments, or other constraints, *but it will make sense for some investors to hold a proportion of their wealth in each one of the asset classes.* If nobody wanted to hold a particular asset class under any conditions, then it would not show up in the market portfolio. The fact that an asset class exists in the market portfolio implies that it makes sense for someone to hold it.

A few years ago when interest rates in the United States were near historic lows, you often heard market prognosticators on TV suggesting things like "you should avoid long-term bonds in your portfolio" since "interest rates are at historical lows and are clearly going up." These kinds of predictions are called *market timing bets*. In effect, statements like this suggest that certain asset classes are over- or undervalued relative to other asset classes based on current market conditions. However, the market portfolio tells us otherwise. Since the market proportions of each asset class represent the consensus expectations about the risk and returns of each asset class, the market already takes into account current conditions and expectations about the future. Even if interest rates are at historic lows, the market value of long-term bonds already reflects this information. Investors, in assigning values to the prices of long-term bonds, are taking into consideration the probability of future interest rate movements and their impact on the prices of long-term bonds. The information is already incorporated into the prices of the bonds.

While the market timing advice may sound reasonable on its face, what people are really saying with predictions like this one is that *everyone who currently holds long-term bonds is stupid*. Given that there are literally hundreds of billions of dollars invested in an asset class, this is a pretty bold assertion. You might be right, but for the market timing bet to be correct all those hundreds of billions of dollars invested in long-term U.S. bonds by individual and institutional investors have got to be wrong. You have to ask yourself, why do I (or my broker or advisor, for that matter) have information that is beyond that which is already incorporated into the market? It is not enough to recognize that interest rates are near historic lows—you have to have special knowledge that *is not understood by the market that impacts the future expected returns*. While this may not be impossible, it certainly creates a high hurdle for a successful market timing bet. It is easy to fall into the trap of thinking that you have some important insight about where the market is headed. Remember that it is highly unlikely that you are the only one with this insight. There are many investors all over the globe making bets with their money about the value of financial assets. Consequently, the overall market consensus view is likely to be a very good predictor of future values.

Another major problem with market timing strategies is that they reduce the amount of diversification in your portfolio. By trying to time the market, you are excluding certain asset classes for certain periods of time. The purpose of diversification is to reduce your exposure to unforeseen events by spreading your wealth across assets that behave differently in reaction to economic events. When you engage in market timing, you remove certain asset classes from your portfolio, under the assumption that they will perform differentially poorly relative to the other asset classes. However, the cost of making this bet is that you reduce your diversification and increase your exposure to economic events that impact asset classes remaining in your portfolio. This often creates a riskier portfolio, or at least one more susceptible to certain types of risk. If you turn out to be wrong about the market timing bet, or if something bad happens that dramatically impacts your remaining portfolio, you have paid a steep price for trying to time the market.

Market timing is a very hard game to play. While many individual investors engage in such activity, most do poorly relative to what they could achieve with a more stable and diversified portfolio strategy. For instance, examining the flows into and out of mutual funds for the last 20 years, a study of investor behavior by the research firm DALBAR found that market timers in stock mutual funds lost 3.29 percent per year on average relative to investors who pursued a consistent strategy.[1] It is extremely difficult to consistently identify times when the market consensus has got it wrong and make bets that pay off accordingly. And it only takes being out of the market on a few big days to wreck your overall performance.

For example, if you invested $10,000 in the S&P 500 index on January 2, 2002, and held the investment until December 29, 2006, you would have ended up with a respectable $12,283. But if you happened to miss being out of the S&P 500 index for just the top 5 days out of the 1,259 trading days during this period, you would have ended up with a much less impressive $9,729 after the five-year period. Just 0.4 percent of all the trading days made the difference between a cumulative return of +22.8 percent and one of −2.7 percent over the five-year period. Just five days separate a loss from a sizable gain, even over a period as long as five years. Obviously, it is hard to be right all the time. More often than not, the pursuit of market timing increases your risk and results in poorer performance than what you could achieve with a longer-term efficient allocation. The bottom line as an individual investor is that you are much better off spending your energy elsewhere. Figure out what kind of portfolio you want and stick with that strategy. Getting cute with jumping in and out of the market rarely pays off.

AVOIDING UNINTENTIONAL BETS

What does the market portfolio say about the advice you are getting from your advisor? An interesting test that can be applied to investment advice is whether the recommended allocations vary with the market proportions of different asset classes. The reason that this is important is that if the target recommendations don't vary with market portfolio, then you are implicitly *making market timing bets whether you realize it or not.* Let's say your advisor is recommending a portfolio that is fixed at 70 percent equities and 30 percent bonds and that you rebalance to these proportions on a quarterly basis. When you rebalance to fixed proportions, you are engaging in a *contrarian* strategy. A contrarian strategy is one that sells off assets that go up and buys assets that fall in value. If you invest in a portfolio of 70 percent equities and 30 percent bonds, and equities go up in value, you have to sell equities to purchase more bonds in order to maintain the fixed proportions. Similarly, if equities go down, you need to sell off bonds to purchase more equities in order to keep the original proportions.

The problem here is that not everyone can be a contrarian. When you sell off the equities that increase in value in order to purchase more bonds, there has to be someone on the other side of the trade willing to purchase the equities when they go up in value. These types of investors are called *momentum* traders, since they tend to follow trends—buy more of things that go up in value, and sell more of those that go down in value. In order for contrarian investors to exist, there have to be momentum investors around with whom they can trade.

Since the market proportions represent the market's consensus view of the value of each asset class, a fixed-proportion strategy like the 70 percent equity and 30 percent bond portfolio is inherently a market timing bet. If you believe in the market consensus, then when equities go up in proportion relative to bonds, you should be willing to hold a little higher proportion of equities. If you sell the equities to maintain the original 70 percent proportion, then you are implicitly stating that you believe equities to be overvalued and bonds to be undervalued. By pursuing the contrarian strategy of rebalancing to fixed proportions you are actually making market timing bets on the relative value of asset classes that are different than the market consensus expectations. While there may be times when you intend to make such bets, in general most advisors and individual investors are *not even aware that such strategies imply a market timing bet*. Making a bet on the relative value of an asset class that is different from the market consensus may be ill-advised, but making an *unintended* bet is clearly a bad idea. Of course the momentum strategy also involves making market timing bets, but the direction of the bets is reversed from the contrarian strategy. Many popular investment strategies, including those promoted by advisors and fund companies, rely on the concept of rebalancing to fixed proportions. Be aware that such strategies are inherently market timing bets that are at odds with the overall market consensus expectations.

In contrast to the contrarian or momentum strategies, an investment strategy that was consistent with observed market portfolio would avoid any market timing bets. If equities were to increase as a proportion of the market portfolio, then all other things being equal, the average investor would desire to hold a bit more equity, negating the need for rebalancing back to a previous allocation. Such an investment approach is known as a *macroconsistent* strategy. The test for such strategies is that if you added up all the recommendations for all the different levels of risk, you should end up with a portfolio that approximates the market portfolio. A nice feature of this approach is that if everyone took the advice being offered, investors would have preferences for the holdings of assets that match up with their relative availability. Unlike the contrarian and momentum approaches, it is possible for everyone to use a macroconsistent investment strategy. There would be no unwanted asset classes, nor excess demand for assets that exceeds their supply in the market. By definition, such strategies avoid the possibility of market timing bets, since they are based on the consensus expectations of the market itself. For these reasons, Financial Engines employs such a macroconsistent approach in its advisory and investment management services. This approach is also used by some institutional investors like pension funds and endowments to avoid market timing biases in their investment strategies. Using this approach, you also avoid the need for frequent rebalancing of your portfolio since when the market moves, your preferences tend to move in the same direction.

The bottom line: be careful about making unintended bets on the relative value of asset classes. The advice you receive from your advisor should ideally be related to the changing proportions of the market portfolio. If your investment strategy is based on rebalancing to fixed proportions, be aware that you may be making some unintended bets on the market.

RISK AND THE MARKET PORTFOLIO

Another useful thing you can do with the market portfolio is to express the risk of your investment portfolio in terms of the volatility of the market portfolio. Most of the time in finance, the risk of a portfolio is expressed in terms of the *standard deviation* of annual returns. However, this measure is rather abstract and has little meaning to most individual investors. A more intuitive way of expressing the volatility of a portfolio is to rescale this number as a proportion of the volatility of the overall market portfolio. A portfolio with a risk of 1.0 on this scale then has the same investment volatility as that of the overall market portfolio. A value of 1.0 says that your risk level is the same as the average investor (or equivalently an investor who invests in the market portfolio). A value lower than 1.0 signifies that the risk of your portfolio is lower than the average investor. For instance, a portfolio consisting of nothing but cash or very short-term bonds has a risk of about 0.2 on this scale, or about 20 percent of the volatility of the market portfolio. A number higher than 1.0 indicates a portfolio with more volatility than the average investor's portfolio. One nice thing about this risk measure is that it provides a comparison to a natural benchmark, the overall market allocation. It also provides an immediate answer to the question "Am I taking on more risk than the average investor?" Values above 1.0 imply portfolio allocations with more risk than the average investor. The number itself

TABLE 4.3 Risk Levels in Terms of Market Risk for Various Assets (1.0 = Market Risk)

Asset Type	Risk Level (1.0 = Market)
Money Market fund	0.2
Long-term bond fund	0.7
Market portfolio	1.0
S&P 500 Index fund	1.5
Small-capitalization stock index fund	1.8
Typical large-capitalization stock	3.0+
Typical small-capitalization stock	4.0+

Source: Financial Engines calculations.

provides a sense of where your volatility lies on the continuum of different types of portfolio allocations. In general, this measure is a more intuitive way to express volatility, rather than the more traditional measure of standard deviation of returns. Financial Engines uses this measure throughout its services to communicate the risk level of investor portfolios.

Table 4.3 shows the risk levels of different types of portfolios in units of market risk.

As you can see from Table 4.3, different asset types have a wide range of risk levels. It is also important to note that these risk values can vary over time as the composition of the market portfolio changes. A portfolio that consists of a broadly diversified portfolio of equities such as the S&P 500 index has about 50 percent more risk than the market portfolio. Even more risky is an index of small capitalization stocks. An index of smaller company stocks tends to be riskier than an index of larger capitalization stocks because the constituent stocks are more susceptible to economic downturns and hence more volatile than larger, more established companies. If you have ever dabbled with investments in penny stocks (those with very low share prices), you probably have a good sense of this.

By far, the most risky assets typically held by everyday investors are individual stocks themselves. Most of the risk of a single stock is due not to the overall market, but to factors that are specific to that company alone. A typical stock in the S&P 500 index might have more than twice the risk of the index itself. When such stocks are combined together in an index, the company-specific risks that account for the majority of the volatility of each individual stock are diversified away. Events that impact the stock of one company are likely to be offset by events that impact the price of another company in the opposite direction. The ups and downs of individual stocks tend to average out and reduce the volatility of the overall stock index, which might consist of hundreds or even thousands of stocks. The risk that is left over is the risk that is common to each stock—namely, the risk of the overall market. No matter how many stocks you choose to hold, you cannot get rid of market risk. Of course, as we learned in the previous chapter, this is precisely the type of risk that you get compensated to bear.

THE MARKET'S VIEW OF FUTURE RETURNS

As discussed previously, information about the market portfolio is very useful in estimating expected returns. Indeed, Financial Engines and many institutional investors use the market portfolio to estimate expected returns for different asset classes. In the case of Financial Engines, this expected return information is updated monthly. The resulting estimates are thus consistent with the market portfolio allocations. The investment philosophy of the firm is that the market is a likely better judge of expected returns than the subjective opinion of any investment expert (including me). By incorporating the market consensus information into the asset class expected returns, Financial Engines' methodology explicitly avoids any market timing. Since the recommendations are consistent with the observed market portfolio, there are no subjective bets on the relative value of different asset classes. This helps prevent unnecessary portfolio turnover and results in more stable estimates of expected returns over time.

How does it work? There are a few different ways of using the market portfolio to generate estimates of asset class expected returns. One of the simplest is through the use of a technique called *reverse optimization*. William Sharpe shared the 1990 Nobel Prize in Economics with Harry Markowitz and Merton Miller for his contributions to the field of financial economics, and in part for his work on the underlying concepts motivating what is known as *modern portfolio theory*. The basic idea of portfolio theory, whose concepts were first developed and published by Harry Markowitz in 1952, is that you want to combine risky assets in a portfolio in such a way that the overall expected return of the portfolio is highest for the level of volatility you are willing to assume. The inputs to this process are the expected returns, volatilities, and correlations of the assets available to you and a measure of how much risk you are willing to assume. The output is a portfolio allocation with the highest expected return for that level of risk. The mathematical process used to figure out the best allocation is known as *portfolio optimization*.

WHAT IS PORTFOLIO OPTIMIZATION?

If you were trying to figure out what particular combination of assets offered the highest expected return for a given level of volatility, you could just try a bunch of random portfolios and calculate the expected return for each one. If you did this enough times, you would find some portfolios have higher expected returns than others. Of course, the random portfolios would also vary dramatically in their risk levels. To find the best combination of assets to get the highest expected return for a given level of risk would take a ridiculous amount of time with this method, and furthermore, you would have a hard time deciding when you were done searching. Just because you found the best one so far does not mean that there might not be another asset mix out there that could do even better. So how do you solve this type of problem?

It turns out that with a few reasonable assumptions you can write an algorithm (called an *optimizer*) that will quickly identify the portfolio mix that yields the best expected return for a given level of volatility. Optimizing a portfolio is kind of like climbing a hill. The hill represents the expected return of the portfolio and the optimizer is simply finding the most direct path to the top of the hill. Instead of randomly stumbling around, an optimizer figures out which way is the fastest path to the top of the hill and walks in that direction.

Generally the goal of a portfolio optimization is expressed as maximizing an objective, like the expected return of the portfolio, while not violating one or more constraints. Constraints are just a fancy way of limiting the possible answers to issues that you care about. For instance, you might want to find the highest expected return portfolio with the same risk level as the S&P 500 index. In this case, the optimizer tries to find the highest expected return portfolio while limiting itself to mixes with the same risk as the S&P 500. More sophisticated optimizers like those used by Financial Engines are capable of solving problems with many types of constraints. For instance, you might want the highest expected return portfolio with the volatility of the S&P 500 index, no more than five holdings, and at least 20 percent allocated to international stocks. With a sophisticated portfolio optimizer, these types of problems are easily solved.

Using modern computing technology, portfolio optimization problems can be solved in just a few seconds, even when there are thousands of available investment options to choose from. However, this does not mean that good portfolios are easy to generate. Any optimization is only as good as the inputs used to specify the problem. Portfolio optimizers require estimates of the future volatility, returns, and correlations of the assets being considered. If these inputs are not accurate, then the resulting optimized portfolios will be inaccurate as well. If you have garbage inputs, even the most sophisticated optimization algorithm will generate garbage outputs. The art of effective portfolio optimization is in properly specifying the economic inputs of the problem. The actual optimization calculations are relatively easy.

From earlier discussions, we know that we can generate reasonably accurate estimates of the volatilities and correlations of different asset classes by analyzing historical returns. We also know that for someone with average risk tolerance, the market portfolio allocation is likely to represent an efficient portfolio, one with the highest expected return for that level of risk. The problem is that we cannot generate accurate estimates of expected returns from history directly since there is too much statistical uncertainty in the data for the length of time we have to analyze.

The idea with reverse optimization is to flip the traditional portfolio optimization problem on its head. When you optimize a portfolio, you start with expected returns, volatility, and correlations for each asset, along with a desired level of risk, and you get an efficient portfolio as an output. With reverse optimization, instead of starting with expected returns, volatilities, and correlations and solving for an optimal portfolio, we use an observed efficient portfolio (e.g., the market portfolio) to solve for the quantity that we do not know (expected returns). In this case, we use the estimated volatilities and correlations from history to solve for the set of expected returns that would result in the observed market portfolio. Since we believe the market portfolio is efficient, this should yield the set of expected returns that are consistent with observed market holdings of each asset class. In other words, the expected returns represent the market consensus estimates that result in the observed market portfolio.[2] If you feed these expected returns into a portfolio optimization (along with the volatility and correlation estimates) you should get the market portfolio as an output.

So what does the market portfolio say about the relative expected returns of different asset classes? Since the market portfolio changes over time, the expected returns of each asset class also adjust with market conditions. However, somewhat surprisingly, asset class expected returns tend to be relatively stable, typically varying by only a few tenths of a percent per

TABLE 4.4 Market Consensus Real Expected Returns Estimates from January 2007

Asset Class	Real Expected Returns
Cash	1.7%
Intermediate Government Bonds	2.6%
Long-Term Government Bonds	3.6%
Corporate Bonds	3.4%
Mortgage Bonds	3.3%
Foreign Bonds	3.5%
Large-Value U.S. Equities	7.0%
Large-Growth U.S. Equities	7.6%
Mid-Value U.S. Equities	6.9%
Mid-Growth U.S. Equities	8.3%
Small-Value U.S. Equities	7.4%
Small-Growth U.S. Equities	8.0%
Europe	7.1%
Pacific	6.4%
Emerging Equities	6.6%

Source: Financial Engines calculations.

year as the market valuations of different asset classes evolve. There are a number of very interesting relationships between the market consensus expected returns of different asset classes.

Table 4.4 shows the estimates of asset class expected returns based on information from the Financial Engines model as of January 2007. These estimates reflect market consensus real expected returns for each of the asset classes in Financial Engines' fifteen asset class factor model. These forward-looking estimates are expressed in real terms (adjusted for inflation), and are arithmetic averages (as opposed to annualized cumulative returns).

Your first reaction might be, "Wow, these numbers seem low." But keep in mind that these estimates are real returns, adjusted for inflation. Most of the return numbers you hear from your broker or advisor are quoted in nominal terms (not adjusted for inflation). Since what you care about is ultimately how much you can purchase with your wealth, it is important to focus on real returns instead of nominal returns. A 5 percent nominal expected return might sound okay, but if inflation turns out to be 3.5 percent, you are left with a real return of only 1.5 percent. These estimates help you understand what reasonable expected returns are for each asset class, after accounting for the impact of inflation. Also, many people have expectations for future returns that are wildly out of whack with reality. You'll note that there are no values above 10 percent. Don't fall into the trap of expecting the stock market to have average returns of 15 or 20 percent per year. Such returns are highly unlikely over long time periods.

While the specific numbers will vary with different time periods, it is instructive to examine some of the salient aspects of the market consensus expected returns:

Equity asset classes have higher expected returns than fixed-income asset classes. The consensus expected returns for the equity asset classes are uniformly higher than those of bonds. Economists call this gap the *risk premium*. The risk premium is the difference between the expected return from a risky asset and the expected return from holding a riskless asset (like a Treasury bill). The higher expected returns follow directly from the higher market risk associated with equities relative to bonds. Since the equity asset class returns are more volatile and are more sensitive to overall market outcomes, they provide higher expected returns than bonds. This does not mean that equities will always have higher returns than bonds in a given time period, but merely that in the future we should expect higher returns from equity than from bonds.

Longer-term bonds have higher expected returns than shorter-term bonds. The consensus expected returns for long-term bonds are higher than the expected returns for intermediate and short-term bonds. The explanation is that long-term bonds are more sensitive to changes in interest rates than shorter-term bonds. Because the payoffs from longer-term bonds are further out in the future, their value is more sensitive to changes in current interest rates. This creates a stronger correlation with overall market returns and commensurate higher expected returns.

Growth stocks have higher expected returns than value stocks. Consensus expected returns for growth stocks are higher than those for value stocks across different sizes of firms. This may seem surprising given the mountain of literature in recent years proclaiming the benefits of value investing, but it follows from straightforward economics. Growth stocks have higher correlations with the overall market, higher volatilities, and hence higher expected returns. This is not to say that you should prefer growth stocks over value stocks in your portfolio, as value stocks also come with lower volatility and lower correlations with the overall market, but if higher expected returns are your goal, a growth-oriented portfolio will provide higher exposure to market risk.[3]

Foreign stocks do not have higher expected returns than domestic stocks. From the standpoint of a U.S.-based investor, foreign equities do not have higher expected returns than domestic equities, despite their higher overall volatility (especially with the consideration of a home country bias). The reason is that the U.S. market is a bigger share of the overall global market, and hence is more highly correlated with the global market portfolio than the European, Pacific Rim, or emerging market economies. In effect, foreign equities do not need higher expected returns to become desirable holdings since they are good diversifiers for U.S. holdings. The expected returns for emerging markets equities clearly demonstrate this effect. Despite being the most volatile asset class historically, it has lower expected returns than any of the domestic equity asset classes. The reason is that emerging markets are less correlated with the global market than other equity asset classes, and hence have lower expected returns. However, their lower correlations with other equity assets make them a desirable part of a diversified portfolio.

Small capitalization stocks have similar expected returns to large capitalization stocks. In most time periods, small-capitalization stocks and mid-capitalization stocks will have slightly higher expected returns than large-capitalization stocks. However, the size effect is modest and the expected returns tend to be within a few tenths of a percent of one another.

Whether it is desirable to hold one or more of these asset classes in a portfolio depends not only on expected returns, but also the risk and correlations of each class. The market consensus expected returns will vary with market conditions and the relative valuation assigned to each asset class. They will also vary with the level of risk associated with each asset class (which changes over time in response to market conditions). Finally, the correlations between asset classes also change over time and can influence expected returns. All other things being equal, asset classes with lower correlations with the overall market will have lower expected returns.

MARKET PORTFOLIO SIMULATIONS

Now that we have described the composition of the market portfolio, and the expected return estimates implied by the market allocations of each asset class, let's take a look at the risk and return characteristics of the market portfolio in terms of wealth outcomes. As of January 2007, the market portfolio had an expected real rate of return of about 5.5 percent.[4] What does this imply about risk and return tradeoffs?

Using Financial Engines' simulation technology, we can generate thousands of potential scenarios for how such a portfolio mix will perform over different investment horizons. Table 4.5 shows the results of these simulations for an initial $10,000 investment. Note that the results are stated in terms of today's dollars (that is, the future portfolio values are adjusted for inflation).

As you can see in Table 4.5, the estimated median portfolio value increases with the investment horizon. Similarly, the upside value (represented by the 95th percentile of the wealth scenarios) also increases, but at a faster rate than the median. Remember, the upside value represents the portfolio outcome where 95 percent of the simulated values fall below. In contrast, the downside value (the 5th percentile) is relatively flat over the different horizons and actually increases at the longer horizons. It turns out that the portfolio median value is about double the initial investment at a horizon of 14 years. That is, about half the time you would expect to at least double your initial investment in the market portfolio over a 14-year period, adjusted for inflation.

One important note, which will be addressed in more detail in Chapter 5, is that the downside case (represented by the 5th percentile) is not the worst case scenario. If you visualize the distribution of portfolio

TABLE 4.5 Simulated Forecasts of the Adjusted Market Portfolio

	Value of $10,000 Initial Investment in the Adjusted Market Portfolio (in today's dollars)			
	At 1 Year	At 5 Years	At 10 Years	At 20 Years
Upside	$12,800	$19,200	$28,600	$57,700
Median	$10,600	$12,900	$16,500	$26,500
Downside	$8,850	$8,360	$8,700	$10,760

outcomes as a bell curve, the least likely cases are those in the tips of the bell curve.[5] The 5th percentile is the value such that only 5 percent of the portfolio outcomes are lower than that value. But there are portfolio outcomes that are even less probable. If you were to look at outcomes in the very tips of the bell curve, for instance the bottom 1 percent value, you will find that the portfolio values continue to drop with longer horizons. This is particularly true for portfolios with heavy allocations to equity. Thus while the downside values might not look too scary, there are possible outcomes that could result in much more significant losses, albeit with small probabilities.

There is no easy way to avoid these improbable, but potentially very negative outcomes with equity portfolios. The problem is that insurance against such outcomes is very expensive, since in severe market downturns nearly everyone (including the entity writing the insurance) will be experiencing bad times. The only way to avoid the possibility of such outcomes is to adopt a less aggressive investment mix with lower equity exposure (of course, this comes at the expense of lower expected returns). As I said before, there is, sadly, no such thing as a free lunch.

FINAL THOUGHTS

If we believe that the market portfolio accurately reflects the consensus expectations of all market participants, then the average investor should desire to hold an allocation that approximates the market portfolio allocation. This does not imply that all investors should want to hold the market proportions, since those with preferences for higher or lower levels of risk will choose to hold certain asset classes in higher or lower proportions. How one constructs a portfolio of assets to meet desired levels of risk will be addressed in Chapter 5. But the key lessons of the market portfolio are that unless your strategy varies with changes in the market portfolio, then you are implicitly making a market timing bet. Fixed rebalancing strategies often employed by advisors and fund companies are inherently contrarian strategies that imply bets against the market. While some institutional investors may be able to profit from such bets some of the time, individual investment strategies based on timing the market are likely to significantly underperform a more stable and long-term approach to diversification.

TAKE-AWAYS

- There is a lot of valuable information in the observed market portfolio—and you are well advised to use it. Avoid investment strategies that rebalance to fixed proportions—they are actually contrarian bets against the market. You should use strategies that adjust with the market portfolio to avoid market timing.
- The market portfolio is a good benchmark for the average investor, assuming a broad range of assets is available.
- Don't try to time the market (e.g., assume everyone else in the market is stupid). You are better off with a diversified strategy that you stick with over time.
- Higher expected return asset classes have more market risk. To get higher expected returns, you need to be willing to take more market risk.
- International asset classes do not have the highest expected return, but are good diversifiers and so should generally be part of your portfolio. Their relatively low correlations with the rest of your portfolio make them desirable holdings.
- When deciding on an asset allocation, start with the market portfolio allocation and tilt away from it toward higher or lower expected return mixes, depending on your time horizon and risk tolerance. Chapter 8 will provide more detail on this approach.

CHAPTER 5

Getting the Risk Right

First weigh the considerations, then take the risks.
—Helmuth von Moltke (1800–1891)

Selecting an appropriate risk level for your investments is one of the most important and daunting decisions in personal finance. While there is no single right answer, the appropriate level of investment risk will generally depend on your personal tolerance for risk, the length of your investment horizon, and the nature of your goal. Determining what risk level makes sense for you requires understanding the tradeoffs that exist between risk and expected return over different time horizons, and how these tradeoffs impact the chance of reaching your financial goals.

Some people are naturally bigger risk takers than others. Individual preferences for risk seem to be innately wired as a part of our brain chemistry, perhaps part of our genetic makeup. Of course, risk is everywhere in our lives, and our perception of that risk is often skewed. Many people worry about flying on an airliner, yet give no thought to a cab ride to the airport without wearing a seatbelt, which actually represents a far greater chance of injury or death. Many books have documented the wide range of preferences that people have for risk in their lives.[1] Such preferences govern our interest for risky sports like skiing or skydiving, how much insurance we choose to purchase, whether we always wear a seatbelt, and the types of careers we pursue, among many other life decisions. However, your love of extreme sports might not have much to do with your preferences for investment risk. You might be risk seeking in some parts of your life, but not in others. Age is also not a perfect proxy for risk preferences. There are conservative 20-year-old investors and swashbuckling 65-year-olds. When it comes to money, people are remarkably varied in their preferences for the tradeoff between investment risk and return. However, understanding your preferences for risk is a crucial part of the investing process.

Perhaps the most important decision you make in investing is selecting an appropriate level of risk. This one variable has a bigger impact on your range of investment outcomes than almost any other decision. Unfortunately, most of us are not endowed with a natural ability to quantify and evaluate the tradeoffs between risk and return. More often than not, decisions about risk are made in an ad hoc manner with little regard for the inherent tradeoffs that exist with any investment choice.

Investment risk is also a multidimensional concept—it means different things to different people. What does risk mean to you? Is it the chance of your investments dropping in value tomorrow? Is it the chance of failing to meet your financial goal? Is it the size of the potential shortfall if you fail to meet the goal? Or is it the amount by which your assets bounce up and down with the market? There are many ways to think about risk, and what is foremost in your mind might differ from what keeps your neighbor up at night. Fundamentally, risk comes from the fact that the future is uncertain. Depending on how the market performs, your investment outcomes will vary. Since there is no reliable way to predict the future, the choice of how much variation in future outcomes you are willing to accept is an important decision.

Selecting the right risk level for your investments is a little like picking the right color to paint your kitchen. There is no one right answer, but there are some obvious choices you want to avoid (fluorescent orange or hot pink come to mind). Within a wide range of personal taste, there is considerable discretion in what might be appropriate for you. So, too, it is with the tolerance for investment risk. The choice of paint for your kitchen will depend on objective factors (like the style of the house, number of windows, the angle with which the room faces the morning and afternoon sun, etc.) but also on your personal preferences. Perhaps you have a fondness for earth tones, while others may prefer the visual impact of saturated hues. As anyone who has ever remodeled a kitchen can attest, getting the right color can be challenging. Often it is not obvious what works (or does not work) until you walk into the freshly painted kitchen and experience it for the first time. Historically, a key problem with picking risk levels for investments has been an inability for investors to "try on" a choice before actually implementing it. However, times have changed.

A major breakthrough in personal investing has been the development of sophisticated simulation engines that enable investors to directly observe not just the expected value of an investment, but the full range of potential outcomes. Rather than answering arcane hypothetical questions in a risk questionnaire, investors can directly observe the upside and downside of any contemplated decision in actual dollars, and make an informed choice about the level of risk that feels right for them. This development by Financial Engines, and later other firms, places the tools routinely used by institutional investors into the hands of everyday investors for the first time. Through the *Personal Online Advisor* service, individual investors can now run sophisticated simulations of their investment portfolios to observe the tradeoffs between investment risk and the possible range of portfolio values in the future. In effect, these tools allow investors to interactively explore the tradeoffs between different investment decisions like savings, risk level, and length of investment horizon and see their impact on possible portfolio outcomes. This chapter illustrates the basic insights that come from the use of such outcomes-based investing tools.

HOW TO MEASURE RISK

The most commonly used measure of risk in financial economics is the standard deviation or volatility of returns—the extent to which returns vary around their average value. For financial instruments this is usually expressed as a percentage per year. For instance, the standard deviation of annual returns for the U.S. equity market is about 20 percent. The problem with measures like standard deviation is that they are abstract and have little meaning to people outside of financial or technical disciplines. Is a standard deviation of 20 percent per year high or low, good or bad?

One way of helping with this issue is to express portfolio volatilities in terms of the risk of the market portfolio. Since the market portfolio represents the risk of the average investor, a portfolio with the same risk as the market portfolio has a risk of 1.0 on this scale. If your portfolio had a risk of 0.5, we can say that it has 50 percent as much volatility as the average investor, while another portfolio with a risk level of 1.5 is taking 50 percent more risk than the average investor. This scaling makes it more intuitive to compare the risk levels of different portfolios, but it does not directly address the problem of how to make decisions about what level of risk is right for you.

It is also useful to point out that this measure of risk is a relative measure, since it is a proportion of the volatility of the market portfolio, which itself changes over time. A risk of 1.0 on this scale can mean a higher or lower standard deviation of returns, depending on the risk of the market portfolio at that point in time. If the market portfolio consists of a higher proportion of equities, the standard deviation risk of a 1.0 portfolio goes up. For instance, during the dot-com boom, the risk of the market portfolio increased significantly due to the higher valuations placed on equities versus bonds. When the value of the equity market went back down over 2001–2003, the volatility of the market portfolio also went back down. But a portfolio that has a risk of 1.0 always represents the risk of the average investor, and thus it is a useful benchmark regardless of the market portfolio allocation. Of course, this also suggests that overall preferences for risk for investors vary through time, depending on market circumstances. The question of how societal risk preferences might change over time is an active area of financial economics research.

In developing its online advisory services, Financial Engines did extensive research on how people think about financial risks and what measures of risk they found most intuitive. What we discovered was that the most easily understood measures focused on risk measured in dollars. Rather than evaluating standard deviations of returns, investors preferred to see their potential outcomes in dollars to understand the impact that investment risk might have on their ability to meet their goals. This meant calculating the full range of possible portfolio outcomes, and showing people the actual tradeoffs between risk and return measured in actual dollars. By evaluating the risk/return tradeoff in the context of their actual portfolio outcomes, it was much easier for people to make informed decisions.

It was also discovered that there were at least three distinctly different kinds of risk that most people cared about. The first type was long-term risk—how much money could be made or lost over their investment horizon. Financial Engines developed outputs that showed the median, upside, and downside scenarios for portfolio values. The downside showed how much money you might have if the market experienced poor performance (that is, 95 percent of the time you would expect to have at least that amount). The upside showed how much money you would have if the market experienced much better than normal outcomes (only 5 percent of the time would you have at least that amount). The median outcome represented a more typical result, showing the value that you would achieve or exceed 50 percent of the time.

The second type of risk was short term in nature. Specifically, how much money in dollars you might lose in the next 12 months if there was a significant (1 in 20 probability event) market downturn. As is demonstrated in the following sections, there is often a tradeoff between taking on higher levels of short-term risk and the median long-term portfolio outcome. Some investors are very concerned with the short-term loss number, while others tend to focus more on the long-term portfolio outcomes in making their decisions. Financial Engines found it helpful to show multiple sets of outputs

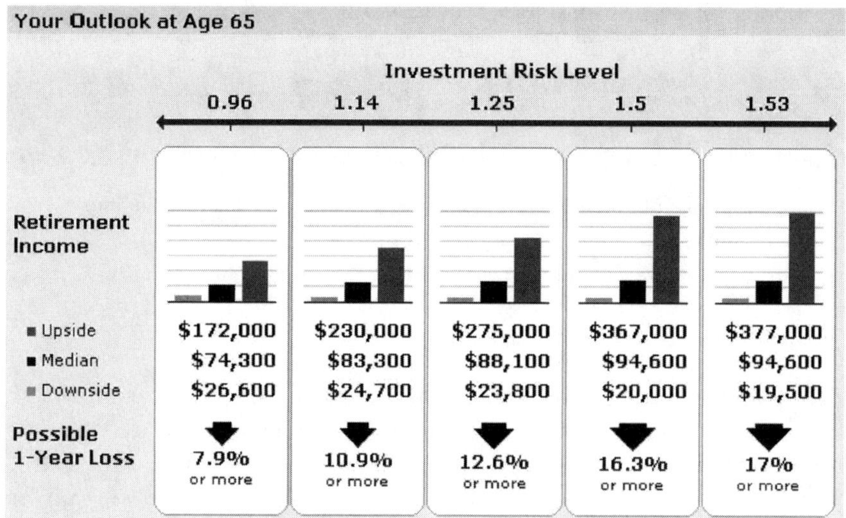

FIGURE 5.1 Illustration of Different Risk Levels and Simulated Portfolio Values

Source: Financial Engines.

for different portfolios so that investors could observe the tradeoffs between short- and long-term risk. Figure 5.1 shows an example of such a range of tradeoffs for a sample portfolio.

As you can see in this example, the median portfolio outcome rises with higher levels of risk, but the one-year loss measure also increases with higher levels of portfolio volatility. Of course there are many other ways of measuring investment risk, and institutional investors have a large toolbox of various risk measures at their disposal for different applications.

A third measure of risk that has been popularized by Financial Engines is the concept of the chance of reaching a particular financial goal. Using Monte Carlo simulation, it is possible to calculate what percentage of possible future scenarios result in outcomes that meet or exceed a desired goal. Risk is then expressed as the probability of failing to reach the goal. While usually not sufficient as the sole basis for decisions, this probability can be a very enlightening metric to consider. It makes plainly obvious when an investment strategy is at odds with a reasonable chance of success. To facilitate the quick interpretation of the probability of reaching a goal, Financial Engines developed a weather icon analogy to go with the percentage number. A gray and cloudy icon represents a poor chance of reaching the objective, while a bright and sunny icon shows that your chances are good.

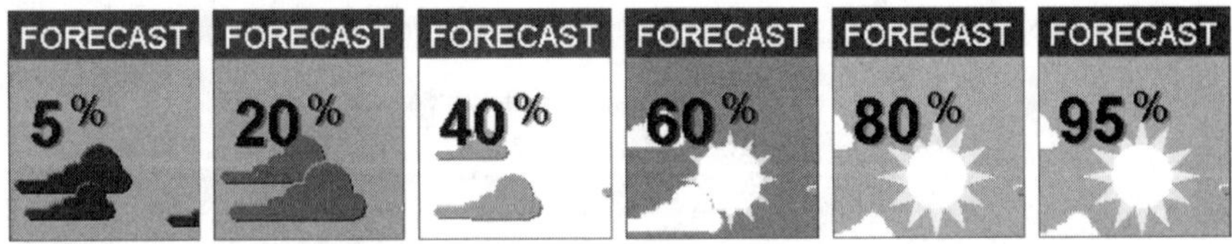

FIGURE 5.2 Range of Probabilities of Reaching a Goal Using Financial Engines' Forecast Icons

Source: Financial Engines.

The weather metaphor worked best among many others that were tested, in part because people have a natural understanding of the uncertainty associated with weather forecasts. If you read in the paper that there is a 60 percent chance of rain, you know this does not mean that it will rain for sure, but you likely want to bring along your umbrella for the walk to the train station.

Figure 5.2 illustrates a range of such icons across different levels of probability for reaching a goal.

ASSET MIX AND SHORT-TERM LOSS

The risk of an investment portfolio is determined by the types of assets held inside. In general, the larger the allocation to equities, the higher the overall volatility of the portfolio. However, the specific mix of asset classes held in the portfolio matters considerably in determining the overall level of risk. The volatility level of a portfolio determines a number of things, including how much money you might lose in a down market and the width of the future possible range of portfolio values over different time horizons. The higher the volatility of the portfolio, the more money you might lose in a bad market and the wider the spread of possible future outcomes.

When building good portfolios, you want to achieve the highest expected return for the level of volatility you select. That is, for a given level of volatility, you want to choose a mix of assets that provides the highest level of expected future returns. If you could find a higher level of expected return without taking on any additional volatility, then you would clearly want to take advantage of that opportunity. Similarly, if you could find a lower volatility portfolio offering the same level of expected returns, you would likely be interested.

TABLE 5.1 Portfolio Allocations by Risk Level

Portfolio Risk Level	0.2	0.4	0.6	0.8	1.0	1.2	1.4	1.5
Cash	100%	35%	25%	4%	0%	0%	0%	0%
Bonds	0%	55%	42%	50%	35%	19%	0%	0%
Large-Cap Stocks	0%	6%	17%	29%	33%	38%	43%	33%
International Stocks	0%	4%	14%	17%	20%	22%	29%	20%
Small- and Mid-Cap Stocks	0%	0%	2%	0%	12%	21%	28%	47%

Source: Financial Engines calculations as of May 2007.

As a first step, let us examine the relationship between portfolio volatility and the mix of asset classes in the portfolio. For the following examples, we will illustrate the characteristics of highly diversified and efficient portfolios across the risk spectrum. The underlying investments are assumed to be very low cost index funds that are representative of each asset class. The specific tradeoffs for a particular universe of mutual funds or stocks could be quite different, but this analysis will provide some basic intuition on how risk tradeoffs vary over various time horizons for broad-based asset classes.

Table 5.1 illustrates the asset allocations of efficient portfolios over different risk levels from the least risky mix to the mix with the highest expected growth rate.

Note that as you move up the risk spectrum different categories of assets move in and out of the efficient portfolio mix—first cash, then bonds, then various classes of equities. At the lowest risk levels, the portfolio allocations are dominated by cash and bonds. Representing the lowest risk portfolio is an allocation of 100 percent cash (for instance, a money market fund) with a risk score of 0.2, indicating that it has about 20 percent of the market portfolio's volatility. As you move up the risk spectrum, the portfolios become increasingly oriented toward equities, eventually crowding out any bonds or cash exposure. Even at relatively low levels of risk it is desirable to have some exposure to international equities. At a risk level of 1.0, the portfolio allocation mix is equivalent to that of an average risk-tolerance investor. At the upper end of the risk spectrum, the portfolios contain a mix of both domestic and international equity exposures and generally have exposures to stocks of multiple capitalization levels. The highest volatility efficient portfolio mix has a risk level of approximately 1.5. While it is possible to achieve efficient risk levels beyond 1.5 using diversified investments like mutual funds, the additional return received is generally not adequate to compensate you for the higher incremental volatility. For many typical

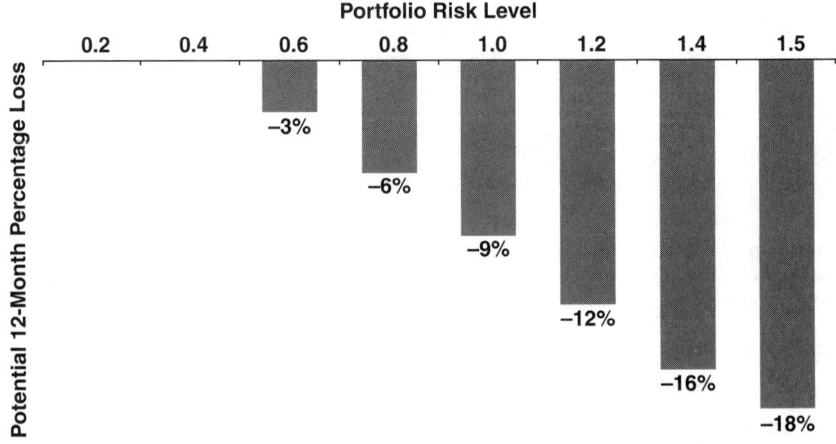

FIGURE 5.3 Potential 12 Month Loss by Portfolio Risk Level

Source: Financial Engines calculations as of May 2007.

investment universes, it is not desirable to strive for risk levels above about 1.5 on this scale.

Next, we examine how the short-term volatility of efficient portfolios varies with risk level. Figure 5.3 shows the percentage of your money amount of money that you could expect to lose over the next 12 months if there was particularly bad market performance (an event with a 1 in 20 probability of occurrence). That is, you could expect to see comparable losses over the next 12 months about one year in 20 if you held a portfolio of this risk level.

As you can see, the short-term potential loss is 0 percent for the least risky portfolios (not adjusting for inflation). This is not to say that such portfolios cannot suffer a loss in the next 12 months, but merely that the odds of such an occurrence are less than 1 in 20. As the risk levels increase, the short-term risk measure rises rapidly. Notice that the short-term risk of a portfolio with 1.2 risk is much more than double the short-term loss potential of a portfolio with 0.6 risk (a possible loss of 12 percent versus 3 percent).

Table 5.2 shows the short-term risk measure in relation to the total investment in equities.

For a portfolio with one-third equity exposure, you can expect to lose about 3 percent of the portfolio value in the next 12 months 1 time in 20. Doubling the equity exposure to two-thirds of the portfolio allocation increases the short-term loss amount by a factor of three, to about 9 percent. At the highest risk levels, a portfolio of 100 percent diversified equity

TABLE 5.2 Comparison of Total Equity Exposure and Short-term Loss Possibility

Portfolio Risk Level	0.2	0.4	0.6	0.8	1.0	1.2	1.4	1.5
Total Equity Exposure	0%	10%	33%	46%	65%	81%	100%	100%
Possible 12-Month Loss (1 in 20 chance)	0%	0%	–3%	–6%	–9%	–12%	–16%	–18%

Source: Financial Engines calculations as of May 2007.

exposure can expect to lose between 16 percent and 18 percent of its value over the next 12 months if markets perform poorly (depending on the types of equity held). Of course, each of these estimates is based on events with a 1 in 20 probability (or a 5 percent chance) of occurring.[2] To put this in perspective, this is a little less probable than the chance of flipping four heads in a row with a fair coin. There are clearly even less probable events that could cause losses greatly exceeding these numbers. In fact, for portfolios with higher equity exposure, the potential loss due to extreme market movements (see the section on Peso Problems) greatly exceeds the potential loss for portfolios that consist of mostly cash and bonds. The implication of this data is that the magnitude of potential losses that may be experienced over the next 12 months increases rapidly with the level of equity exposure in the portfolio.

RISK AND PORTFOLIO OUTCOMES

Now let's consider the relationship between long-term risk measures and portfolio risk levels over different investment horizons. For each of the following examples, we simulate the performance of a hypothetical portfolio (in today's dollars) at different levels of risk using the Financial Engines simulation engine. Specifically, Figure 5.4 shows the relationship between portfolio volatility and the downside, median, and upside portfolio values (in today's dollars) for a one-year horizon for an initial investment of $10,000. All forecast values are shown in today's dollars (the estimated values are adjusted for inflation) and for simplicity, we assume no taxes are due on the portfolio gains.

There are a number of interesting observations to make about this chart. First, the downside value (representing the amount that you would have after one year with a 95 percent probability) steadily decreases with

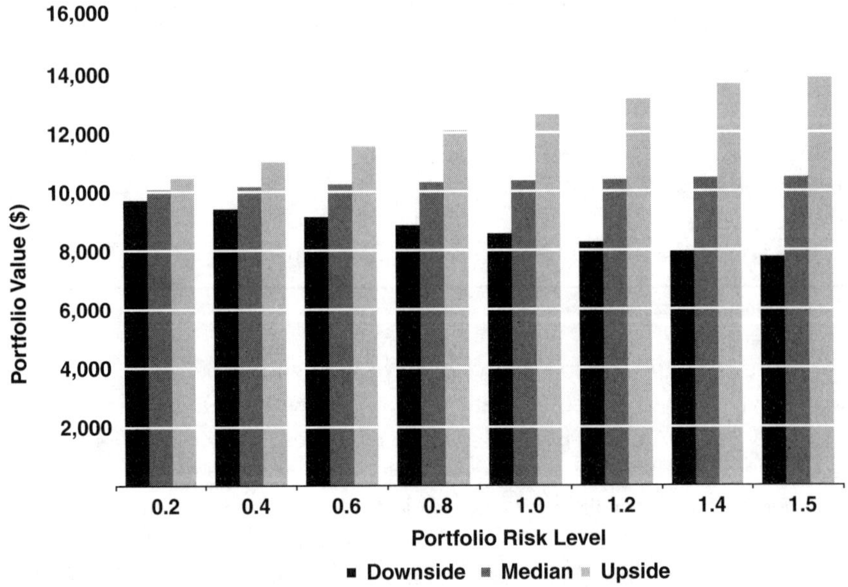

FIGURE 5.4 Portfolio Forecasts for $10,000 Initial Investment over a One-year Horizon at Different Risk Levels

Source: Financial Engines calculations as of May 2007.

higher levels of risk. At higher risk levels, the amount of money that you could lose with a 1 in 20 probability is about 20 percent in today's dollars.[3] The magnitude of the potential downside loss for the highest risk portfolio is over seven times that of the cash portfolio, measured in today's dollars.

Interestingly, the median portfolio value does not change much at all over a one-year horizon. Why? Because the higher expected return is partially offset by the higher volatility of the portfolio allocations. The higher volatility acts as a drag on the median portfolio value forecast, even though the expected returns of the investments are higher. For a one-year horizon, the median value for the highest risk portfolio is only 3 percent greater than that of the cash portfolio. *One can deduce from this relationship that there is little value from selecting higher risk investments when the horizon is very short (e.g., a year or less) unless you intend to bet on better-than-expected market performance.* Of course, if you are wrong about those market outcomes, you will end up with substantially less than you would have with the lower risk allocation.

The upside values (exceeded by only 5 percent of the portfolio outcomes) at one year, increase significantly with the higher risk allocations.

The upside value for the highest risk portfolio is 32 percent higher than that of the all-cash portfolio. You can also observe that the upside estimates begin to flatten out with the highest risk levels. For instance, moving from a risk of 1.4 to 1.5 (which increases the potential short-term loss), only increases the upside value by 1.5 percent at the one-year horizon—not much of a payoff for taking on additional volatility. The median value does not change much at all. For a short horizon (e.g., one year), the benefits of higher expected return investments are not that compelling for most investors. Most investors with short-term horizons prefer to keep their money invested conservatively in order to have more predictability in the final outcome. However, the story changes a bit at longer investment horizons.

Now we examine the relationships at a five-year horizon (see Figure 5.5). The downside values at five years still drop dramatically with the higher risk allocations. Actually, the differences in downside values are even more pronounced at five years than they are at the shorter one-year horizon. Over five years, the potential downside loss of the highest risk portfolio is more than nine times that of the all-cash portfolio.

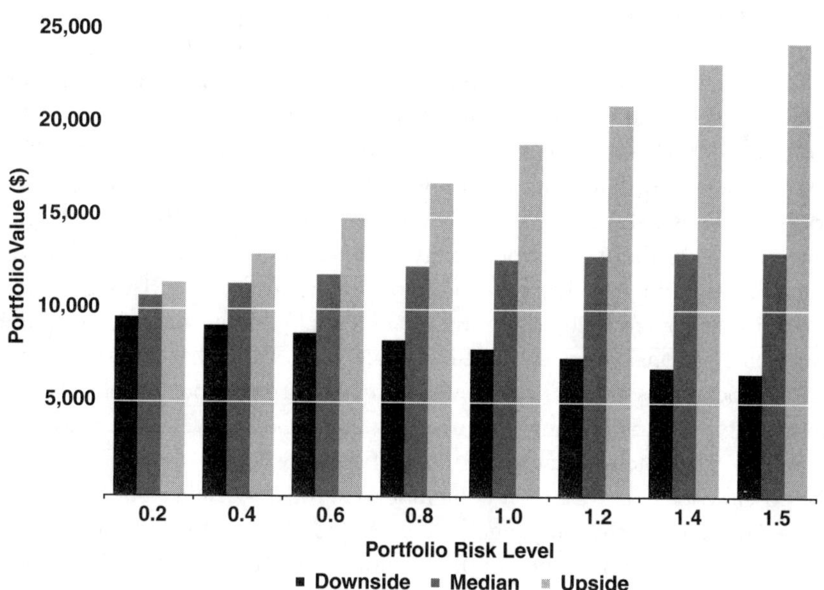

FIGURE 5.5 Portfolio Forecasts for $10,000 Initial Investment over a Five-year Horizon at Different Risk Levels

Source: Financial Engines calculations as of May 2007.

However, the median values also differ significantly across the risk spectrum. Remember, the median value is the middlemost value in the distribution. For a given range of outcomes, 50 percent of the outcomes will be below the median and 50 percent will fall above. In this case, the median value for the highest risk portfolio exceeds the cash portfolio median value by 22 percent. With the longer horizon, the median outcomes are more impacted by the higher expected returns of the equity allocations. Even with a risk level of 1.0 (the market portfolio), the median portfolio value exceeds the cash portfolio median outcome by about 18 percent.

The variation in upside values is even more pronounced at five years. The upside value for the highest risk portfolio is now a whopping 113 percent higher than that of the all-cash portfolio. If markets perform better than expected, you would be much better off with the higher equity allocations. An interesting calculation is to compare the differences in downside values versus the difference in upside values for the cash and highest risk portfolios. To get that opportunity for a potential 113 percent gain in the upside value, you must be willing to tolerate the possibility of losing about a third of your initial investment versus a potential loss of only 3 percent if you were to invest in cash. As you can see from the charts, as the horizon increases the distribution of possible portfolio values becomes increasingly skewed. The difference between the downside and median values is smaller than the difference between the upside and the median values. At a 20-year horizon, the chart is even more striking (see Figure 5.6).

Notice that the median values increase sharply as the portfolio risk level is increased, flattening out only at the highest increments of risk. Of course, the downside values steadily drop with higher levels of risk. With the longer horizon, there is the possibility of an extended string of bad market events that could significantly erode your initial investment. However, the downside values at a 20-year horizon are actually higher than those of the five-year horizon, particularly at the middle risk levels. This does not imply that the portfolios are less risky over a 20-year horizon, but simply that the probability of experiencing bad market outcomes is lower as the horizon increases. The catch is that while the probability is lower, the magnitude of the possible loss can be larger. Remember that the downside value is defined as the 5th percentile of the range outcomes (the value that you would expect to be below 5 percent of the time). The more extreme tails of the distribution (say, events with a 1 in 100 chance of occurrence) are more dramatic for the 20-year horizon than the five-year horizon. When you invest in a portfolio that contains lots of equity, you are running a greater chance of doing very poorly in very bad times than with a more conservative allocation, even if the odds are that you would beat the conservative portfolio most of the time.

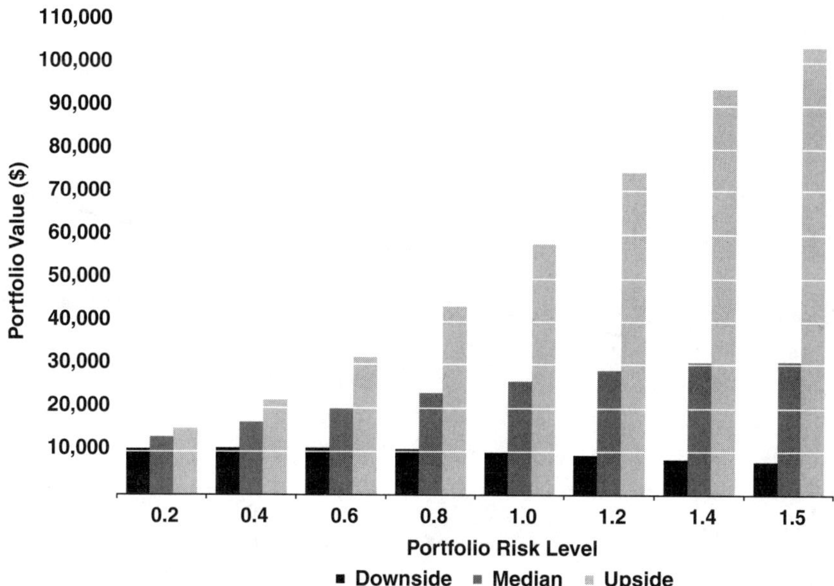

FIGURE 5.6 Portfolio Forecasts for $10,000 Initial Investment over a 20-year Horizon at Different Risk Levels

Source: Financial Engines calculations as of May 2007.

Over the 20-year horizon, the upside values are much higher than they are for the shorter periods. Over longer time periods, a few extraordinarily good returns can compound into impressive gains. Notice that the gap between the median forecast and the upside gets larger as the risk level increases and as the horizon gets longer. This implies that the average outcome is higher than the median outcome. Why? Because the small chance of really good outcomes drive up the average, but does not impact the median much since the probabilities are so small.

RISK AND TIME HORIZON

Another interesting way to look at the relationship between risk and investment horizon is to plot the outcomes of different levels of risk over different horizons. This shows how the outcomes change with lengthening investment horizons for different risk portfolios.

First, let's examine the outcomes for a conservative but diversified portfolio. Figure 5.7 shows the downside, median, and upside portfolio values

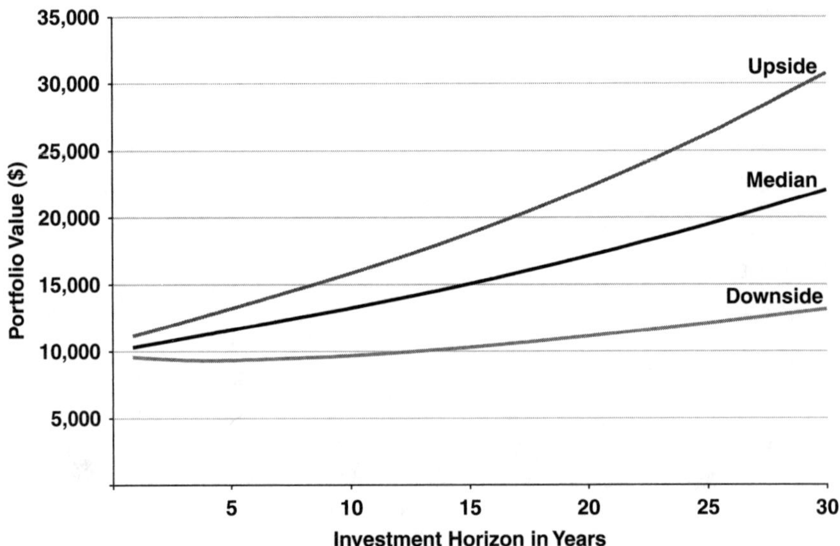

FIGURE 5.7 Portfolio Forecasts for $10,000 Initial Investment in 90 Percent Fixed Income and 10 Percent Equities (Risk 0.4) over Different Horizons

Source: Financial Engines calculations as of May 2007.

for a portfolio of risk 0.4 (corresponding to a mix of 90 percent fixed income and 10 percent equity) over horizons ranging from 1 year to 30 years.

What does this chart show us? Interestingly, the downside values are relatively flat over horizons from one year to 10 years, but the median values increase significantly the longer the horizon. Even for this conservative allocation, the range of potential outcomes (in today's dollars) is relatively wide, especially as the horizon increases. At 30 years out, you could expect to see portfolio values fall within the range of $13,000 to $31,000 about 90 percent of the time. That is not a trivial spread of potential outcomes. However, if you invest conservatively, you are highly likely to see a return on your investment (adjusted for inflation), particularly if your horizon is greater than 15 years or so.

Now compare Figure 5.7 to that of a portfolio with market risk (1.0). See Figure 5.8, corresponding to a portfolio mix of about 35 percent fixed income and 65 percent equities.

Note that the scale of the graph has changed significantly. For the riskier portfolio mix, the downside remains relatively flat up to horizons of about 20 years. Again the median forecast steadily climbs with longer

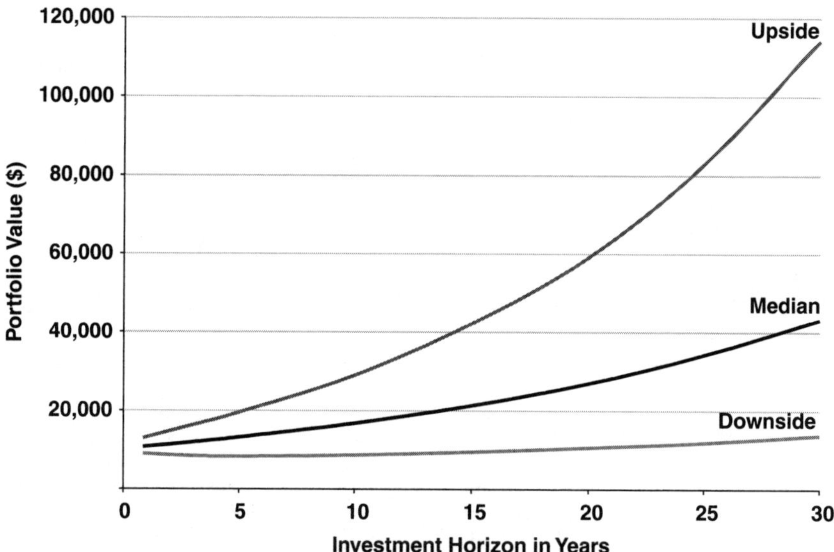

FIGURE 5.8 Portfolio Forecasts for $10,000 Initial Investment in 35 Percent Fixed Income and 65 Percent Equities (Risk 1.0) over Different Horizons

Source: Financial Engines calculations as of May 2007.

investment horizons. For a 30-year horizon, the median outcome of the risk 1.0 portfolio is actually 39 percent higher than the *upside* value for the more conservative 0.4 allocation. Surprisingly, the downside values are actually comparable, only 2 percent different. What this means is that you are quite likely (>95 percent of the time) to do better over the 30-year horizon with the higher risk portfolio allocation. However, in those rare circumstances where you do worse, you could do much worse than with the more conservative allocation (remember, there is no free lunch). What if we choose an even higher risk portfolio?

A portfolio with a risk of 1.4 corresponds to a diversified mix of 100 percent equity exposure (see Figure 5.9). The same general pattern applies to this case as in the previous lower risk portfolios. The downside case is relatively flat, while the median and upside increase substantially as the horizon lengthens. The downside for this mix (at the 5th percentile) is a bit lower than the 1.0 risk portfolio. Here the downside values are 80 percent to 85 percent of the downside values of the 1.0 risk portfolio across different horizons. But for horizons longer than 15 years, the median and upside values are significantly higher with the higher equity allocation. Of course, the

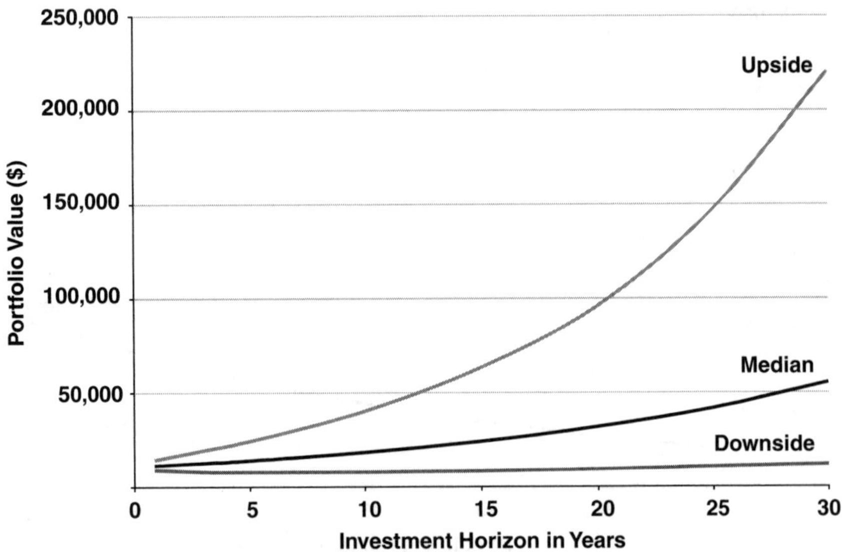

FIGURE 5.9 Portfolio Forecasts for $10,000 Initial Investment in 100 Percent Equities (Risk 1.4) over Different Horizons

Source: Financial Engines calculations as of May 2007.

upside values are dramatically higher with the additional volatility. If markets do much better than expected, a higher equity allocation clearly dominates.

To get a better idea of how the forecast values for each of these portfolios differ across the 1 to 30-year investment horizons, it is useful to plot the forecast percentiles for each mix on the same chart. Figure 5.10 shows the comparison of the downside (5th percentile) forecast values for the 0.4, 1.0, and 1.4 risk portfolios.

For shorter horizons, the downside values behave just as you would expect. The lowest values correspond to the highest risk portfolios. However, as the horizon lengthens beyond 25 years, the downside values for the 0.4 and 1.0 portfolios converge, with the 1.0 portfolio achieving a downside forecast slightly higher than that of the more conservative mix at the 30-year horizon. Remember that this is in contrast to the short-term risk measure, which uniformly gets worse with higher volatility portfolios. Also, while the 1.0 portfolio beats the 0.4 portfolio in downside values at long horizons, this does not imply that the 1.0 portfolio is lower risk. In fact, for more extreme events (for example, the 1st percentile value), the higher risk

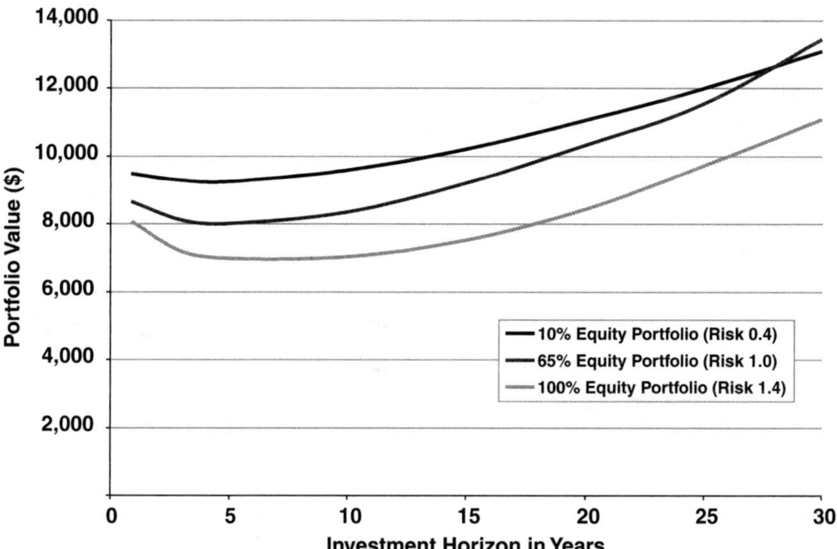

FIGURE 5.10 Comparison of Downside (5th Percentile) Portfolio Forecasts for $10,000 Initial Investment at Three Risk Levels over Different Investment Horizons

Source: Financial Engines calculations as of May 2007.

portfolio would do significantly worse than the more conservative one. But if you are focused on events that are likely to happen 95 percent of the time, the 1.0 portfolio appears better at the longest horizons.

Now let's look at the relationship between the median forecasts of the three portfolios at different horizons. See Figure 5.11.

Not surprisingly, the highest risk portfolio has the highest median forecast for all time horizons. Moreover, the longer the horizon, the greater the difference between the median forecast values of each portfolio. Again we see diminishing returns at the highest levels of risk. The median forecast for the 1.0 portfolio is not much below that of the highest risk allocation, except at the longest horizons.

Table 5.3 shows the percentage change relative to the initial portfolio value for each median outcome estimate. There are a couple of observations about this table that merit attention.

At very short horizons (less than three years), the differences in median outcomes for different risk levels are modest. At longer horizons, the differences in median outcomes are larger, showing the impact of higher risk

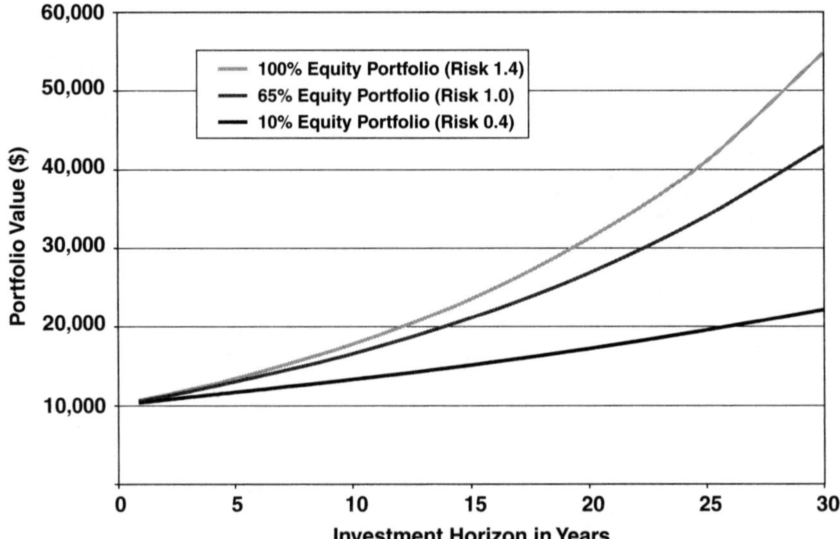

FIGURE 5.11 Comparison of Median (50th Percentile) Portfolio Forecasts for $10,000 Initial Investment at Three Risk Levels over Different Investment Horizons

Source: Financial Engines calculations as of May 2007.

TABLE 5.3 Percentage Change in Initial Portfolio Value for Median Outcomes

	Percentage Change in Initial Portfolio Value for Median Outcome by Horizon (years)							
Portfolios	1	3	5	10	15	20	25	30
10% Equity Portfolio (Risk 0.4)	2%	8%	15%	31%	49%	70%	93%	119%
65% Equity Portfolio (Risk 1.0)	4%	15%	28%	63%	109%	165%	237%	326%
100% Equity Portfolio (Risk 1.4)	5%	17%	32%	75%	132%	209%	306%	444%

Source: Financial Engines calculations as of May 2007.

TABLE 5.4 Percentage Change in Initial Portfolio Value for Downside Forecasts

	Percentage Change in Initial Portfolio Value for Downside Outcome by Horizon (years)							
Portfolios	1	3	5	10	15	20	25	30
10% Equity Portfolio (Risk 0.4)	−6%	−8%	−8%	−5%	2%	10%	19%	30%
65% Equity Portfolio (Risk 1.0)	−14%	−19%	−20%	−17%	−9%	3%	15%	34%
100% Equity Portfolio (Risk 1.4)	−20%	−28%	−31%	−30%	−25%	−16%	−3%	10%

Source: Financial Engines calculations as of May 2007.

levels. At all but the longest horizons, the median forecast of the market risk portfolio (1.0) is close to that of the more risky 100 percent equity portfolio (risk 1.4). This shows the diminishing returns aspect of taking on higher levels of volatility. A modest amount of additional volatility has a big impact, but the expected return gains from even higher levels of volatility begins to taper off.

Table 5.4 shows the corresponding percentage changes in initial values for the downside portfolio outcomes.

At the shorter horizons, differences in downside forecasts are significant among the varying risk levels. The 100 percent equity portfolio has nearly four times the volatility of the 10 percent equity portfolio at horizons of one to three years. At longer horizons, the differences in downside forecasts become less pronounced. At 30 years, the 10 percent equity portfolio downside outcome is only three times higher than the all-equity portfolio mix.

The bottom line here is that the benefits of higher risk portfolios only become significant when your investment horizon is long. At short horizons (less than five years) you get comparatively little benefit for taking on more volatility. There simply isn't much expected gain in the form of higher expected returns to compensate for the additional risk. However, at longer horizons the median outcomes of the portfolios diverge substantially. This means, on average, you are more likely to end up with higher levels of wealth with more equity exposure if your time horizon is long. Of course, the range of possible outcomes also increases in size with longer horizons.

FACTORS TO CONSIDER IN SELECTING A RISK LEVEL

The preceding section provides insights into the relationship between risk and investment horizon. Certainly, in making a choice about what level of risk to take, one should understand the nature of the tradeoffs between risk and investment horizon. There are, however, other factors to consider beyond risk/return tradeoffs in making a decision about the level of investment risk that is appropriate for you. To assist you with these decisions, here is a list of additional factors that you should consider in selecting the appropriate risk level for your investment portfolio.

- When will you actually need the money? Can the date be changed? A goal with a flexible horizon can be treated as a longer-term investment more so than one with a fixed deadline. If the market performs poorly, you can simply delay the goal. For instance, if you are saving for a vacation home and the market has a bad year, you can simply put off the purchase for another year or two.
- What is the consequence if you fail to achieve the goal? What if you fall a little short? Is this a minor problem, or a disaster? If you need the money to pay the rent (or some other critical need), then you cannot tolerate a shortfall in the portfolio outcomes. This will make you much less tolerant of downside uncertainty, and hence investment risk. But if you have more margin for error, you can afford to be more aggressive (for instance, saving for a child's college fund). If things don't go well, you might be able to alter the goal or how you plan to fund it.
- How comfortable are you with market fluctuations? Can you sleep at night with significant equity exposure? If you are anxiously watching the day-to-day gyrations in the market, then you are probably taking on too much risk for your comfort zone. Pick a level of risk that you are comfortable with and stick with it. Don't fall victim to the siren song of market timing—you will very likely be disappointed.
- If the investment portfolio performs poorly, how exposed are your other assets or income sources? Financial asset risk is just one measure of risk. If the market turns down and your investments are adversely impacted, how safe is your income? What about the value of your home? If events that could negatively impact your investments are highly correlated with your source of income or the value of your home, you should be less willing to take on high amounts of financial risk. Conversely, if your income is very secure (perhaps you work for the government), then you are more able to handle additional financial risk.

EXAMPLES OF INFORMED INVESTOR BEHAVIOR

A common question asked by investors contemplating what risk level is appropriate for them is "what do other people like me do?" Even if you have preferences that are likely to differ from your peers, it is still helpful to understand what other investors with similar goals are doing with respect to risk. An interesting question is how to define "people like me."

To answer this question and enhance the usability of its advisory services, Financial Engines engaged in research of what investment risk decisions people tend to make relative to their investment horizon. The company surveyed a large population of frequent users (several hundred thousand) of the Financial Engines *Personal Online Advisor* service. The goal was to determine what risk levels were selected by users of the service relative to their investment horizon. The research also examined the impact of variables other than investment horizon on risk choices (such as income, wealth, and gender), but found that investment horizon was by far the most important factor.

Since these users had a full range of simulation outputs available to them when selecting their desired risk level, it could be inferred that these revealed choices were based on a realistic assessment of the tradeoffs between risk and return. Note that the vast majority of the assets analyzed in the study were pegged for retirement, so it is important to qualify that these choices may not accurately reflect preferences for nonretirement goals (for instance, assets earmarked for college tuition). It is also true that someone with a one-year retirement horizon may not be planning to immediately begin drawing down his or her assets, and thus may have a longer implicit investment horizon. However, the results of this study provide a very interesting view into how people tend to weigh the benefits and disadvantages of different levels of risk depending on their investment horizon.

Of course, not everyone in the sample with the same horizon selected the same risk level for their investments. For each horizon studied, there was a distribution of risk levels reflecting personal risk tolerance and other factors beyond horizon that may have influenced the specific choice by each investor. Figure 5.12 shows the median selected risk levels by investment horizon, measured in years.

Qualitatively, there is a clear linkage between the median selected risk levels and investment horizon, with a preference for higher risk levels the longer the time to the goal. Investors with retirement horizons of one year had a median risk level of 0.87, which corresponds to a portfolio mix of approximately 50 percent fixed income and 50 percent equities. Those

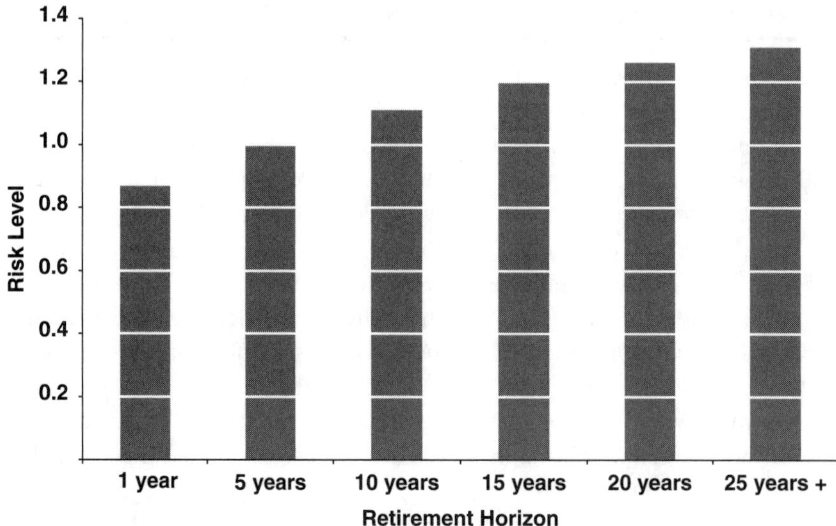

FIGURE 5.12 Median Portfolio Risk Levels by Retirement Horizon for a Large Population of Financial Engines Personal Online Advisor Users

Source: Financial Engines.

with retirement horizons of 10 years had a median portfolio risk of 1.1, which corresponds to a portfolio of 25 percent fixed income and 75 percent equities. Investors with horizons of more than 20 years had median risk levels corresponding to portfolios of at least 90 percent equity exposure.

The median risk levels for each retirement horizon are only part of the story. For each cohort of investors, there was a distribution of risk levels selected. For a given retirement horizon, different investors displayed varying preferences for investment risk. Figure 5.13 shows the spread between the 30th percentile and the 70th percentile for each investment horizon.

The range between the most risk averse and less risk averse investors was larger at the shorter horizons. That is, there is more variance in preferences for risk at the shorter horizons among this population. There are many reasons why this might be the case, including different times when the money may be accessed to generate income, the presence of other retirement assets, tolerance for volatility, other retirement income sources, and tolerance for uncertainty in the desired level of retirement income. At the higher risk levels, the variation in preferences is less dramatic. Fewer investors with long horizons choose to hold very conservative investment allocations.

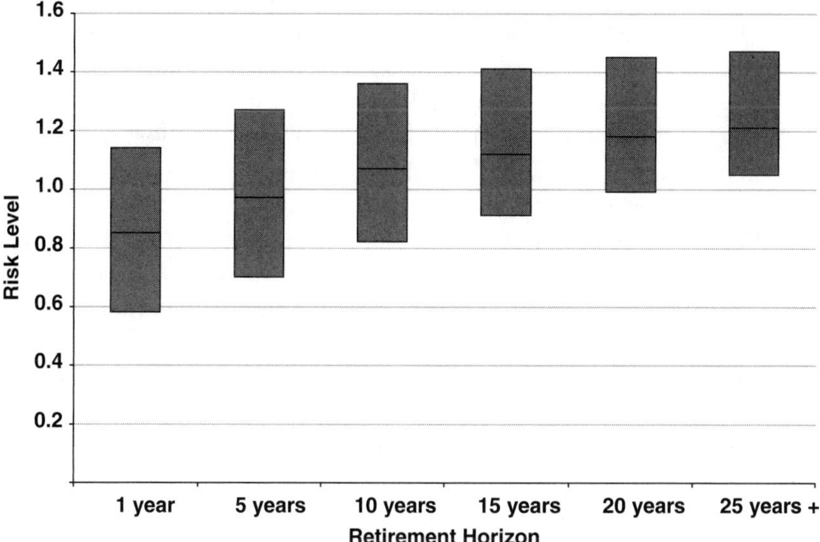

FIGURE 5.13 Range between 30th Percentile and 70th Percentile of Portfolio Risk Levels by Retirement Horizon for a Large Population of Financial Engines Personal Online Advisor Users

Source: Financial Engines.

The bottom line here is that there is a significant amount of variation in preferences across individuals when it comes to risk choices. For instance, the most risk-seeking investors with one-year horizons chose to hold more equity exposure than the most risk averse investors with 25-year horizons. These results underscore the notion that there is no single right answer for what level of risk is appropriate for a given person. It will always depend, to some extent, on the personal preferences of the individual. However, depending on your investment horizon, it is prudent to consider risk levels that result in more desirable outcomes the vast majority of the time.

TAKE-AWAYS

- Risk is a multifaceted concept that means different things to different people.
- The most important factors in selecting an appropriate risk level are time horizon and your tolerance for downside outcomes, both short and long term.

(Continued)

- There is a trade-off between long-term outcomes and short-term risk exposure, with higher long-term median outcomes coming at the expense of more short-term volatility.
- Don't fall into the trap of taking on more risk than you get compensated for. There are diminishing returns for taking on very high levels of investment risk.
- Very short horizons generally do not justify risky portfolios with substantial equity allocations. With short horizons, you don't get much benefit from the higher expected return relative to the cost of the greater volatility.
- However, even at retirement it will often make sense to have significant equity exposure. Just because you are retired does not mean you will need to immediately liquidate your portfolio.
- If your horizon is more than 10 years, consider having at least 60 percent of your assets devoted to diversified equities.
- How much risk is appropriate will depend on how much uncertainty you can tolerate in your goal. Goals that are more flexible in timing or amount (e.g., retirement) imply higher tolerance for risk, since you can make adjustments based on market outcomes.

CHAPTER 6

An Unnecessary Gamble

Take calculated risks. That is quite different from being rash.
—George S. Patton (1885–1945)

For much of modern history, personal investing revolved around the idea of buying and holding individual stocks. Consequently, many investors have embraced the idea that stock picking is the most effective way to generate wealth. The truth is, for the vast majority of individual investors, buying individual stocks to achieve investment goals is inefficient, risky, and costly. Stock picking represents an unnecessary gamble with higher risk and lower rates of expected growth than more diversified investment strategies. Moreover, few investors appreciate the impact of large individual stock holdings on portfolio risk. If you do choose to hold individual securities, make sure you mitigate the risk to your overall portfolio by keeping your holdings to a small fraction of your portfolio.

Okay, I admit it. Picking stocks can be fun. Even index investing advocates like Burton Malkiel admit to audiences that the temptation to pick stocks is difficult to avoid. It feels good to spot that hot company that nobody else noticed right before it takes off. You look smart and perhaps enjoy the envy of your friends and family. On the cocktail circuit, it is much more entertaining to discuss your latest prescient stock purchase or to debate the finer points of Jim Cramer's latest televised rant than it is to talk about how your 401(k) fund portfolio performed in line with market averages. Holding a diversified portfolio for the long term (if you are doing it right) is, well, boring, and it certainly doesn't make you look like a master of the universe. So yes, picking stocks can be an exciting hobby (at least for some people). But when it comes to the more serious objective of meeting financial goals like retirement, buying individual stocks is not a great strategy. In fact, it can easily be a disastrous one.

If you go back just a couple of decades, you would be hard pressed to find individual investors holding positions in anything *but* individual stocks and perhaps a few bonds. Indeed, the whole idea of "investing" meant buying stocks as opposed to putting your money in a savings account at the bank. Going back to the 1950s, about 90 percent of the shares of America's corporations were held by individual investors. Today about three quarters of the shares are held by professional investors like mutual funds, endowments, and pension funds. In the last few decades the concept of prudent investing has matured considerably to include investment products that are more suitable for personal investors than individual stocks. Products like mutual funds and exchange-traded funds (ETFs) provide easy and flexible diversification at low cost. However, many investors still believe that holding small numbers of stocks is the most effective way to generate wealth. Of course, they get a little push from brokerage firms and the financial media, who also profit from the stock-picking culture.

It may come as no surprise that the popularity of investing in individual stocks waxes and wanes with how the markets are doing. During the run-up to the dot-com bull market of the late 1990s, newspapers and magazines were filled with stories of dry cleaners and bartenders who had quit their jobs to pursue *day-trading* of stocks. Neighborhood book clubs transformed into investing clubs overnight, and kids dropped out of college convinced that they could make a fortune by spending a few hours a day in front of their computer trading NASDAQ stocks. It seemed as if every casual conversation turned to the subject of yet another technology miracle stock that was going through the roof. When the market eventually came back down in the early 2000s, the ranks of these newly converted stock traders thinned considerably. Many would-be day traders had to go back to their day jobs, often with quite a hit to their bank account. And almost everyone has a story, or has heard a story, of how they lost a ton of money on a stock pick that went south during this period.

There are at least three big problems with relying on individual stocks to build wealth. First, holding concentrated positions in a small number of individual securities exposes you to much greater risk than a more diversified portfolio built around aggregated products such as mutual funds or ETFs. Second, the rate at which such concentrated portfolios can be expected to grow is much lower than for comparable, but more diversified investment strategies. Third, unless you have several millions of dollars to invest, the costs of building an adequately diversified portfolio from individual securities can be quite high.

But what if you (or your broker) only pick good stocks? Surely there is a lot of money to be made? True, if you could identify stocks that will go up in value *after* you purchase them then you could make big profits. The press is filled with stories of people who have made fortunes speculating on stocks. "Buy low and sell high" sounds easy, but the devil is always in the details. As Will Rogers once said, *"Don't gamble; take all your savings and buy some good stock and hold it till it goes up, then sell it. If it don't go up, don't buy it."*

All kidding aside, for the reasons discussed in Chapter 2, consistently picking stocks that will *do well in the future* is extraordinarily difficult. The cards are really stacked against you. Billions of dollars are spent every year by brokerage firms, investment banks, hedge funds, mutual funds, and investment management companies on research to identify under- or overpriced stocks and other securities. If there are any easy opportunities out there, they have likely been well mined by professional investors. Sadly, picking stocks that outperform the market on a consistent basis has proven to be very difficult, even for the well-capitalized and sophisticated institutional investors. The notion that typical individual investors will be able to *consistently* identify such opportunities (using simple or complex methods) does not really stand up to even casual examination.

The good news is that you don't have to be a gifted stock picker to profit from the market. You don't even have to beat the market to be successful; you just have to make sure you get your fair share of the expected returns. The key is to ensure you are taking the right kind of risks, in particular those risks for which you earn expected returns. Financial economics teaches us that it makes sense for many investors to hold a significant portion of their assets in stocks—but the trick is to own a lot of them. Only then are you eliminating the unnecessary sources of risk from your investment portfolio.

My personal view is that most individual investors are better served by assuming that the market accurately prices stocks the vast majority of the time. I'm not saying the market always gets it right. The assumption that the market has already factored in all the relevant information into the price of the stock might not always be true, but it is quite likely to be true most of the time (and figuring out when it is not true is really hard). What this means is that when you purchase a stock, you should have no inherent expectations that it will perform better or worse than expected given its correlations with the overall market. This *does not* mean that stocks will have the same returns as the overall market, since stocks have much higher volatility and are affected by many things beyond the performance of the overall market. In fact, you can safely assume that a given stock will usually perform differently from the overall market. In any given time period, some stocks will do much better than the market, while others will substantially underperform. But on average, there will be no positive or negative bias to this performance. For every dollar invested in a stock that beats the market, there is another dollar invested in a stock that does worse. The winners and losers must add up to yield the overall market performance.

As we have seen in previous chapters, simply observing that some stocks greatly outperform the market during certain periods says almost nothing about whether it would have been possible to identify such opportunities prior to the run-up. Stock picking only works if you can identify the profitable opportunities *before* they transpire. Random noise and inherently unpredictable events play a significant role in the price movements of any individual stock and thus make picking good stocks a tricky exercise.

The goal of this chapter is not to be a buzz kill, but instead to illuminate some of the obvious and not so obvious perils of investing in individual securities. While picking stocks can be an exciting hobby, you should proceed with caution when it comes to your core investments. The vast majority of investors, even high net worth ones, are better off using more efficient investment vehicles to achieve their financial goals. If after considering my warnings, you still want to play around with stock picking, make sure that you treat it for what it is, a hobby, and make informed decisions that appropriately control your risk. If you are just looking for an adrenaline rush, perhaps you should look elsewhere, like an occasional trip to Vegas. You don't want to gamble with your financial future.

A DIFFERENT SORT OF BEAST

When I talk to many individual investors about stocks, particularly those with limited experience in the market, it is readily apparent that their perception of the risk-and-return characteristics of individual stocks is way off base. It is a natural tendency to think that the risk and return of a single stock must be comparable to that of a more diversified mutual fund. After all, a fund is simply composed of a collection of individual stocks. Why should the risk be that different?

The reality is that individual stocks are *much* more risky, and have different return characteristics, than more broadly diversified instruments like mutual funds. When you consider the very wide range of possible investment outcomes associated with a portfolio concentrated into one or a

TABLE 6.1 Comparison of Risk Levels for Popular Mutual Funds and Individual Stocks

Mutual Funds	Risk Level	Stocks	Risk Level
Vanguard 500 Index/Inv	1.5	Dell Inc	3.7
Washington Mutual Investors Fund/A	1.3	Merrill Lynch & Co.	3.1
T Rowe Price Mid Cap Growth Fund	1.6	Pfizer Inc	2.6
Vanguard Explorer	1.8	Tivo Inc.	5.5
Putnam International Equity Fd/A	1.5	Marriot International	2.4

Source: Financial Engines calculations as of January 2007.

few individual stocks, you realize that it is very different from investing in a diversified equity fund.

First of all, almost all individual stocks are much more risky than a broad-based portfolio like the S&P 500 index or a diversified equity mutual fund. The reason is that the performance of an individual stock is highly dependent on the fortunes of that particular company, whereas the performance of a fund is driven by the average performance of all the stocks in its portfolio. As an example let's compare the overall volatility estimates for some popular mutual funds with those of some popular individual stocks. Table 6.1 shows the relative total volatility of a group of mutual funds and individual stocks expressed as a proportion of market risk (remember that the market portfolio has a risk of 1.0 on this scale).

Many of the stocks on the right side of the table are actually constituents of the funds on the left. There are a few striking things about this table. First, the equity mutual funds are all concentrated around similar levels of risk, ranging from 1.3 to 1.8 times the volatility of the market portfolio. Despite the fact that they invest in different types of assets (large-cap stocks, small-cap stocks, international stocks), each mutual fund represents a diversified portfolio of many stocks, hence, limiting the risk. There are certainly mutual funds with higher and lower levels of risk (for instance, sector funds can be much more risky), but these funds are representative of the risks common to broadly diversified investments.

The individual stocks, on the other hand, have much higher and much more varied levels of risk. A more mature company in a less volatile industry like Marriot International has a risk level of 2.4, while a smaller technology company like Tivo, from a more volatile sector, has risk of 5.5 times that of the market portfolio. However, even the relatively sedate Marriot

International stock has 64 percent more volatility than that of the S&P 500 index fund. The more volatile Tivo stock has 267 percent more volatility than the S&P 500. As will become apparent, this large amount of additional volatility has profound implications for potential portfolio outcomes. Note that in the case of both funds and stocks, the specific risk levels of securities can change over time.

THE RISK OF INDIVIDUAL STOCKS

Where does all this extra risk come from? The risk of individual stocks comes from a variety of sources, but generally can be broken down into three major components: risk from the overall market, risk from industry-related factors, and risk from factors unique to the company itself. Each of these types of risk can impact the fortunes and thus the stock price of a given company. For instance, if the market as a whole drops, chances are that the stock price of most companies will fall as well. If the industry of a given stock is adversely impacted by a new regulatory mandate, it is likely that stocks in that industry may also suffer, or it may alter the competitive balance among firms in the market. Finally, if a company's new product fails to achieve success in the market, that failure might negatively impact the future value of the firm and cause its stock price to drop.

Remember from our prior discussions that the risk related to the overall market cannot be diversified away. No matter how many stocks you own, the fundamental risk correlated with the market will remain. When markets go up, your stocks will tend to go up, and vice versa. On the other hand, the industry- and company-specific risk factors can be diversified away by holding enough stocks from varied industries. In theory these types of risks can be virtually eliminated by holding a very broad cross-section of individual stocks. The specific events that impact one company generally will not impact another company. If you hold both stocks, the events that impact each company individually, tend to be averaged away.

Standard financial economic theory tells us that expected return is only earned for bearing market risk. Industry- and company-specific risks are easily diversified away and do not come with any additional expected return. Of course this means that the extra volatility from industry- and company-specific sources can sometimes work out in your favor (for it is precisely this extra volatility that allows individual stocks to dramatically outperform the market in some scenarios). But just because a stock *might* outperform the market does not mean that you get any expected benefit *on average*. As we demonstrated in Chapter 2, there is no inherent reason why expected return should be associated with risks that can easily be diversified away.

The bottom line is that if you want to earn the full benefit of the expected returns from stocks, you need to hold enough of them to diversify away the uncompensated industry and company risk. Otherwise, you are just taking on avoidable risk with no additional expected return.

With mutual funds, the vast majority of the risk (typically 95 percent or more for diversified funds) is related to the movements of underlying asset class exposures. Even for actively managed mutual funds, what happens with asset classes will have the greatest impact on the fund's returns. Another way of saying this is that if you want to guess the daily return on your large cap equity mutual fund, just take a look at the return on the S&P 500 index. Chances are the two returns will be quite similar on any given day.

Not so with individual stocks. In many cases, the majority of the risk comes from factors related to company-specific characteristics, not to the overall market. Different stocks have varying degrees of correlation with the overall market. Because of this correlation, stocks have expected returns that are dependent on the degree to which they move with the market. Stocks with lots of market correlation (like brokerage firms) tend to have higher expected returns than those with less correlation (like utility companies).

But the majority of the risk of an individual stock comes not from the market, but from factors that impact the industry and the fortunes of that one company. This may not be obvious when you look at the newspaper or your favorite stock web site each day. After all, when the Dow Jones index drops 300 points in a day, chances are your favorite stocks drop as well. But over the long run, most of the risk of an individual company's stock is not related to the market but to factors unique to that stock. For instance, a drug company's stock might fall precipitously when its latest drug fails to win approval from the Federal Drug Administration (FDA), even on a day where the market goes up.

Table 6.2 shows an interesting breakout of the components of risk from five popular individual stocks. The first column shows the proportion of the total risk (variance) of the stock that is related to movements in the market. This is the risk than cannot be diversified away by holding more stocks. The second column calculates the remaining risk that is related to industry- or company-specific factors (the two proportions sum to 100 percent by construction).

For Dell stock, about one-third of the total variance comes from its correlation with the market. The remaining two-thirds of the variance comes from factors related to its industry or from company-specific risks. In

TABLE 6.2 Proportion of Individual Stock Risk from Market Exposures

Stock	% of Risk from Market	% Company-Specific Risk	Total Risk
Dell Inc.	32.8%	67.2%	3.7
Merrill Lynch	41.8%	58.2%	3.1
Pfizer Inc.	44.5%	55.5%	2.6
Tivo Inc.	12.5%	87.5%	5.5
Marriot International	33.0%	67.0%	2.4

Source: Financial Engines calculations.

contrast, Merrill Lynch has a higher proportion of its risk due to market movements—not surprising for a financial services company whose fortunes are more closely tied to the stock market. But even for Merrill Lynch, the majority of the risk associated with the stock is due to factors that can be diversified away by holding a portfolio of many stocks. In the case of the most risky stock in our small sample, Tivo, the percentage of risk associated with the market is only 12.5 percent. The vast majority of the risk comes from company-specific factors. In each case, the proportion of the stock risk coming from the market is less than 50 percent.

What does this mean? *You can eliminate the majority of the risk associated with an individual stock by holding a broadly diversified portfolio of stocks.* When you hold many stocks, the company-specific risk factors are averaged away. A broadly diversified equity portfolio is not without risk, as the impact of market risk can be substantial, but the risk is far below what you experience with a single stock. The corollary is also true: if you choose to invest in a single stock, most of the risk you are taking is not related to the market. Accordingly, you take on much more risk than needed to earn the expected return associated with the stock. The magnitude of the company-specific portion of the volatility for stocks implies that it has a major impact on potential portfolio outcomes. Just how big might surprise you.

THE IMPLICATIONS OF INDIVIDUAL STOCK RISK

To give you an idea of the impact of the risk associated with individual stocks that is not due to the overall market, let's use the Financial Engines

TABLE 6.3 Simulated Forecasts of an S&P 500 Index Fund

	Value of $10,000 Initial Investment in the S&P 500 Index (in today's dollars)			
	At 1 Year	At 5 Years	At 10 Years	At 20 Years
Upside	$13,200	$23,600	$40,100	$100,000
Median	$10,400	$13,100	$17,400	$30,500
Downside	$8,170	$6,880	$6,890	$8,070

Source: Financial Engines calculations as of May 2007.

simulation engine to illustrate the range of portfolio outcomes with such strategies.

For a baseline reference, we will compare the results for several of the above stocks with an investment in a more diversified S&P 500 index fund. Table 6.3 shows the range of investment outcomes associated with a $10,000 investment in the S&P 500 index over different time horizons. To keep things simple we will assume no taxes and report everything in today's dollars (adjusted for inflation).

As noted before, the median portfolio values steadily increase as the horizon lengthens, culminating in a healthy forecast of $30,500 at 20 years. As we noted in Chapter 5, the downside values represented by the lower 5th percentile of portfolio outcomes drop until about 10–12 years out, when they begin to rise again. Of course the upside values, represented by the upper 5th percentile, rise at all horizons and become a larger multiple of the median value for longer holding periods.

Now let's take a look at a simulation for a portfolio consisting of a single individual stock. In the first example I show the results for a portfolio consisting entirely of Oracle common stock, which has a risk level of 3.9. Table 6.4 illustrates the portfolio outcomes.

As you can observe in Table 6.4, there are some big differences in the individual stock outcomes compared to those of the S&P 500 index fund. Even though Oracle is a component of the S&P 500 index itself (at the time of this writing), the simulated portfolio values are very different from the more diversified index results in Table 6.3.

The downside values are much lower, the upside values are much higher, and the median is strangely flat over the different horizons. To better understand how the higher volatility of an individual stock influences portfolio outcomes, look at the downside estimates for the various horizons

TABLE 6.4 Simulated Forecasts of an Investment in Oracle Inc. Common Stock

	Value of $10,000 Initial Investment in Oracle Inc. Common Stock (in today's dollars)			
	At 1 Year	At 5 Years	At 10 Years	At 20 Years
Upside	$18,500	$46,700	$94,200	$244,000
Median	$10,400	$10,200	$9,500	$7,800
Downside	$4,300	$1,300	$400	$100

Source: Financial Engines calculations as of May 2007.

in Table 6.4. One huge difference is that the downside value at a one-year horizon implies a potential loss of 57 percent of the initial investment if the stock performs poorly. Mutual funds (at least reasonably diversified ones) almost never see this kind of volatility, but these types of potential losses are common for individual stocks. In fact, unlike a mutual fund, it is quite possible for a single stock to lose *all* its value by going bankrupt. With a more diversified portfolio, the probability of bankruptcy outcomes quickly diminishes to an insignificant concern (unless you borrowed a lot of money to invest in the fund, a mistake that more than a few hedge fund managers have made over the years). Figure 6.1 shows a graph comparing the downside estimates for the Oracle and S&P 500 portfolios. The additional risk not only creates a higher probability of near term losses, but also the chance of bigger losses over longer time periods as well. In other words, things do not look any better in the long run.

Concentrating your portfolio into a single security increases your risk dramatically at all timescales. In fact, the longer you hold the stock, the worse the potential downside outcomes become. This has nothing to do with whether Oracle is a good company, it is simply a function of the higher volatility of the stock compared to a more diversified portfolio. Put almost any company with comparable risk characteristics in the chart, and it will look similar. This characteristic of the downside estimate is true of almost all stocks, and the higher the volatility of the stock, the more dramatic the effect. For many higher volatility stocks, the downside values can easily go to zero (bankruptcy) for horizons of more than a few years.

On the other hand, the upside values for the individual stock portfolio are also much higher, reflecting a significantly wider range of potential outcomes. If you get lucky and hit it big, a single stock can provide returns far beyond that of more diversified investments (this, of course, explains

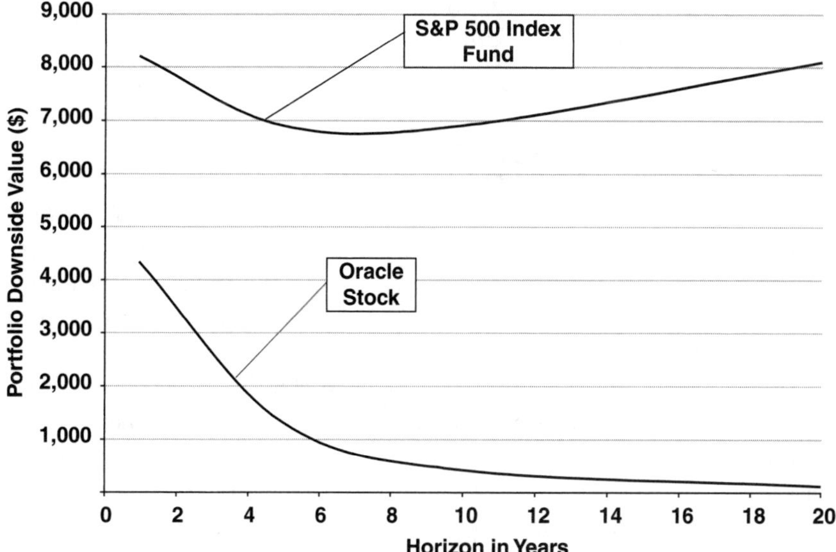

FIGURE 6.1 Comparison of Portfolio Downside Values for an Initial $10,000 Investment in Oracle Common Stock or an S&P 500 Index Mutual Fund

Source: Financial Engines calculations.

the allure of stock picking). But the probabilities of such extraordinarily positive outcomes are low. *A diversified portfolio has a much higher probability of ending up with more money, but a lower chance at that really big score.*

Perhaps most curiously, the median outcomes for the individual stock portfolio trend down as the horizons increase from one year to 20 years. The median estimate at 20 years is only $7,800 after adjusting for inflation. All that time to end up less than where you started? This is in stark contrast to the median outcome for the S&P 500, which steadily increases with longer investment horizons. What is going on here? Does Oracle stock have a negative expected return?

No, to the contrary. In fact, Oracle stock has an expected return that is about *40 percent higher than the S&P 500*. But that higher expected return comes with much higher volatility (more than two-and-a-half times as high as the S&P 500). It is this extra volatility that accounts for the big difference in median (and downside and upside) portfolio outcomes.

How can more risk imply lower median estimates than the S&P 500, even if the expected return of the individual stock is higher? The difference is that the individual stock portfolio has a much lower *expected growth rate* than the more diversified index fund.

EXPECTED GROWTH RATES

The concept of expected growth rates is an important one in personal investing. However, the difference between growth rates and expected returns is a nuance that trips up even experienced financial professionals. The distinction is based on the idea of compounding rates of return over multiple years.

When you are thinking about performance of an investment over a single year, then the annual expected return is a useful metric to measure the "typical" outcome from an investment portfolio. If you visualize the distribution of potential outcomes over a single year, which looks something like a bell curve, then the annual expected return will give you an idea of where the middle of that distribution lies. However, as you consider longer horizons of multiple years, the expected return becomes a less useful measure for making forecasts. You might think that you could estimate the typical outcome by just compounding the annual expected return for the number of years of your particular horizon. However, such a calculation would give you an unrealistic view of the expected outcomes of the portfolio. If you want to understand the typical outcome over longer periods, you want to calculate the expected growth rate of the portfolio.

Let's take a very simple example to make the point clear. Assume we have an asset, such as a publicly traded stock, that has only two possible and equally likely returns per year, an "up" state and a "down" state. In the up state the stock returns 5 percent, while in the down state it drops 5 percent in value. Over a single year, the expected return from the stock is just the average of the two possible returns, or 0 percent (5 percent + −5 percent = 0 percent). The median return (the return where half the returns are above and half the returns are below) is also 0 percent.

But consider what happens when we look at a two-year horizon, where the stock has an up return followed by a down return. The average of the two annual returns is still 0 percent, but the compounded rate of return over the two years is not zero. Say you invested $10,000 in the stock. After one year you would have $10,500: $10,000 × (1+0.05) = $10,500. But after year two, you would only have $9,975 in your account: $10,500 × (1−0.05) = $9,975. What happened? When your investment went up 5 percent it started from a base of $10,000. But when it fell 5 percent it

TABLE 6.5 Comparison of Average and Compounded Returns

Year 1	Year 2	Average Return	Cumulative Return
+5%	−5%	0%	−0.25%
+10%	−10%	0%	−1.00%
+25%	−25%	0%	−6.25%

started from the higher base of $10,500. The net loss was greater than the net gain since 5 percent of $10,500 is bigger than 5 percent of $10,000. You actually ended up *below* where you started. The more volatile the returns, the bigger the difference between the average return and the compounded rate of return. As Table 6.5 demonstrates, the expected return (the average) is always zero in our example, but the compounded return becomes more negative as the volatility of the returns increases. In addition to the 5 percent example, Table 6.5 shows the calculations for a stock where the up and down states are more volatile, with swings of plus or minus 10 percent and plus or minus 25 percent.

As you can see, the more volatile returns result in ever larger negative cumulative returns, even though the average returns over the two years are always zero.

What happens if the down state comes first and then the up state return is applied? You get exactly the same answer. If the drop comes first, it reduces the base on which the subsequent gain is calculated, leaving us again with less money than we started. No matter what the order of the returns, the impact of volatility over time lowers the cumulative rate of return. This property of cumulative rates of return applies in the more general case of multiple years and more realistic return possibilities. Since the cumulative rate of return is ultimately what you actually get from the investment, it is useful to focus on this measure when considering how a portfolio is likely to perform over multiyear periods. The annualized cumulative rate of return is typically called the *growth rate* of the portfolio. This leads to an interesting fact: *When returns are volatile, the cumulative growth rate will always be lower than the average return for a multiperiod horizon.*

It turns out that the expected growth rate is a close approximation to the annualized rate of return associated with the *median* portfolio outcome over a multiperiod horizon.[1] Remember that the median is the middle of the distribution of portfolio outcomes, the point where 50 percent of the outcomes are above and 50 percent are below. If you took the median portfolio outcome and calculated the annualized cumulative return consistent with that outcome, you would get approximately the expected growth rate of the asset. This in turn, implies something important about the distribution of portfolio outcomes for risky assets over multiyear periods. *The median portfolio outcome will always be lower than the average outcome.* Moreover, the higher the volatility of the asset, the bigger the difference between the average outcome and the median outcome.

This is a crucial point. When you hear advisors talking in terms of expected returns of investments, you might naturally assume that this return is representative of what you could expect. Our instinct is to assume that we should get the expected level of return about 50 percent of the time. But that is *not* what happens with risky assets over multiyear periods. For assets with high volatility like individual stocks or sector funds, the probability of achieving the expected outcome is *much less* than 50 percent. Alternatively, the median portfolio outcome will have a rate of return that is much less than the expected return of the asset. If you want to have an idea of what to expect for a risky asset, you should concentrate more on the *median* portfolio outcome, not the much less probable average outcome. Of course, you also need to recognize that you will often experience an outcome that is different from either the average or median result.

Let's look at some examples for some common types of investments. Table 6.6 shows the comparison of the expected returns (adjusted for inflation) of various types of assets and their corresponding expected growth rates.

As you can see, the expected growth rate of a very low volatility asset like a Money Market fund is the same as the expected return (or very close). For an asset with more volatility like the market portfolio, the drag of the additional volatility lowers the expected growth rate by about 0.7 percent

TABLE 6.6 Comparison of Expected Returns and Expected Growth Rates

Asset Type	Expected Real Return	Volatility (1.0 = Market)	Expected Growth Rate
Money Market Fund	1.6%	0.2	1.6%
Market Portfolio	5.6%	1.0	4.9%
S&P 500 Index Fund	7.2%	1.5	5.5%
Typical Large-Cap Stock	7.2%	3.0	0.3%

Source: Financial Engines calculations. Data as of January 2007. All expected returns are adjusted for inflation.

relative to the expected return. With an even higher volatility asset like an S&P 500 index fund, the expected growth rate is 1.7 percent lower than the expected return. Perhaps most striking are the results for a typical large-capitalization stock with three times the volatility of the market. Despite having an expected return that is about the same as the S&P 500 index fund, the expected growth rate is only 0.3 percent—an incredible 6.9 percent below that of the more diversified index fund! Of course the expected growth rates for a particular stock may be higher or lower than this example, but these estimates are broadly consistent with the expected growth rates for many commonly held stocks.

What causes this to happen? Over longer time periods, with the impact of compounding, the distribution of portfolio outcomes stretches out. One end of the distribution is bounded by zero (you can't lose more than you started with), but the other end is effectively unbounded. With high volatility assets like individual stocks there are small probabilities of *very* good outcomes (Bill Gates can provide personal testimony to this effect). The higher the volatility of the assets, the more stretched out the distribution becomes. Figure 6.2 shows an example of the shape of the distribution of portfolio outcomes for a typical equity mutual fund asset over 20 years compared with the distribution for a typical large-cap individual stock, assuming a $10,000 initial investment.

To make the graph easier to read, I have truncated the portfolio outcomes at $300,000, even though the individual stock investment has about a 2.5 percent chance of exceeding this amount. Notice how much more peaked the shape of the distribution is for the stock investment compared to the more diversified fund. Because the stock has such a long right hand tail of possible outcomes, the shape of the distribution becomes much more peaked around the initial investment value. For the stock, there is a 45 percent chance of ending up with $10,000 or less at the end of 20 years, compared with only an 18 percent chance of falling below the initial investment for the fund. Because the shapes of the distributions are so different, the median and means of the portfolio outcomes are also quite different. Table 6.7 shows the estimated mean and median outcomes for each simulation.

The stock portfolio actually has the higher mean (expected) outcome, but the fund portfolio has a much higher median outcome, almost twice that of the stock. What drives this result is that the stock portfolio mean is affected by the small probability of very good returns. However, the median outcome (which is associated with the portfolio growth rate) is not as sensitive to such events, since they are relatively few in number. When

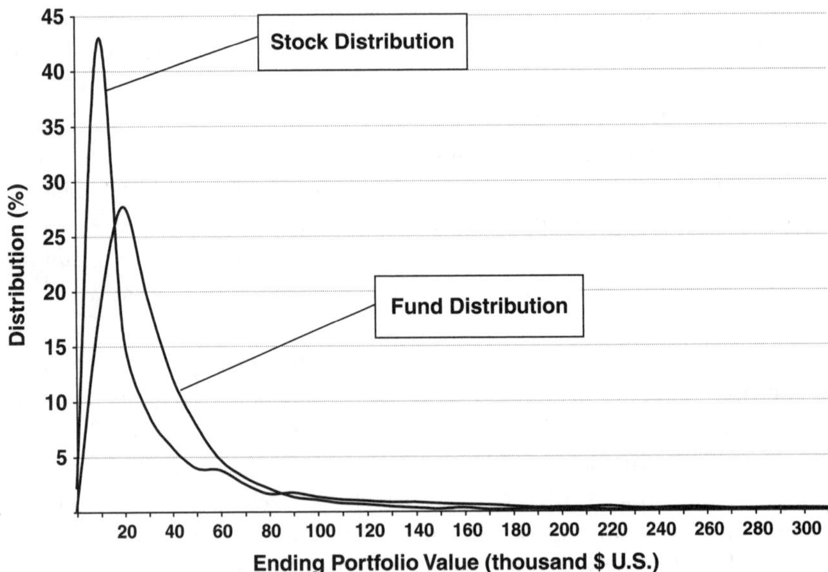

FIGURE 6.2 Comparison of Simulated Portfolio Outcomes for Hypothetical Stock and Mutual Fund over 20 Years

Source: Financial Engines calculations.

you calculate the median it does not matter how big the values are, only the number of outcomes above the value. The net effect is that there is a big gap between the mean outcome (associated with the expected return) and the median outcome (associated with the expected growth rate), particularly for the stock portfolio. In the case of the stock distribution, the median outcome is only 30 percent of the expected value, compared to 73 percent of the expected value for the mutual fund. This gap gets worse the higher

TABLE 6.7 Comparison of Median and Mean Portfolio Outcomes for Hypothetical Stock and Fund Simulations

	Median	Mean (Average)	Median as a Percent of the Mean
Stock Portfolio Outcomes	$12,600	$41,800	30%
Fund Portfolio Outcomes	$21,900	$29,800	73%

Source: Financial Engines calculations.

the volatility of the stock and the longer the investment horizon. Of course, these statistics will vary quite a bit depending on specific characteristics of the funds and stocks being evaluated. But the basic relationship—that the median outcome is a small fraction of the mean or expected outcome for most individual stocks—is quite robust.

One final point to keep in mind regarding portfolio growth rates is that small differences in growth rates over long time periods can create substantial differences in ending wealth. For instance, an increase of only 1.0 percent in the expected growth rate translates into approximately 28 percent more median wealth over a 25-year horizon for a reasonably diversified portfolio that includes equity (adjusted for inflation). Correspondingly small decreases in expected growth rates can have a large negative impact on portfolio outcomes, particularly over long horizons. Giving up small amounts of expected growth rates for longer horizons has a much larger impact on your accumulated wealth than you might imagine.

Certainly the possibility of catastrophic implosions in the value of an individual stock should give you pause before committing a large part of your portfolio to a single security. But even if you avoid a meltdown, the constant drag of the additional volatility implies a much lower growth rate over the long haul. Putting too much of your money in a single security is a poor gamble. Your odds of long-term success are much better with a more diversified portfolio.

Okay, a stock with 3.9 times the risk of the market has much more risky potential outcomes than a diversified fund. But what about a less volatile stock like Marriot International, with only 2.4 times the risk of the market portfolio? How different are the potential outcomes?

Table 6.8 shows the simulation outcomes for a portfolio consisting solely of Marriot International Inc. common stock. As before, we start with an initial investment of $10,000 and assume no taxes.

While the outcomes for the Marriot portfolio are certainly less volatile than those of Oracle, they more closely resemble the Oracle portfolio than they do the S&P 500 results. At one year, we see the potential to lose a substantial 35 percent of the initial balance if markets perform poorly. Like the results for Oracle, the long-term downside values fall with a lengthening horizon, though not quite as dramatically as the more volatile stock. With the lower volatility of Marriot International, the median outcomes do increase with longer horizons, though much more slowly than the diversified S&P 500 portfolio. In fact, at 20 years, the median outcome is still about half that of the more diversified portfolio. The upside outcomes are higher than the S&P 500, but not a lot. At 20 years the difference is only about 30 percent.

TABLE 6.8 Simulated Forecasts of an Investment in Marriot International Inc. Common Stock

	Value of $10,000 Initial Investment in Marriot International Inc. Common Stock (in today's dollars)			
	At 1 Year	At 5 Years	At 10 Years	At 20 Years
Upside	$15,600	$32,300	$55,900	$130,000
Median	$10,500	$11,500	$13,000	$15,800
Downside	$6,450	$3,590	$2,430	$1,490

Source: Financial Engines calculations as of May 2007.

As is evident from the results in Table 6.8, the basic characteristics of portfolios consisting of a single stock are similar across a wide range of stock volatilities. Individual stock portfolios are much more risky than fund or index portfolios, even when the stock is a relatively low-volatility security.

THE BIGGEST MISTAKE IN RETIREMENT INVESTING

One of the most common mistakes made in the retirement investing world, particularly among 401(k) participants, is over-concentration in an employer's stock. In an analysis of more than 100,000 401(k) participants from companies offering stock in their 401(k) plan, more than 54 percent of employees had stock concentration levels that were greater than 20 percent of their total account, an amount that is enough to significantly decrease their median forecasts. In fact, loading up on your employer stock is even worse than loading up on a random individual security. Why? Because chances are your job (and hence your future income) is likely to be highly correlated with how the company stock performs. If bad things happen to the industry or the stock of your employer, you are likely not only to lose your money on the investment, but possibly your job as well. As the unhappy former employees of Enron can attest, this double whammy effect can be devastating, particularly if you are nearing retirement. This implies that you should be even less likely to want to hold the stock of your employer than you would be to hold the stock of a random company. Unfortunately, surveys suggest that many employees do exactly the opposite, loading up on their employer stock in their retirement plan.

People often confuse a good company with a good stock. Your company may be the most amazing, creative, world-dominating, run-by-geniuses firm around, but that does not mean that the stock is undervalued. Chances are, all that good stuff about the company is already factored into its price by the market. To determine that something is undervalued, you have to have information about the future prospects of the firm that are not understood by the market. If it is public, you can bet that the markets have already digested the information. If the new information is private, you are prohibited by law from trading on it (this is called insider information). *Never make the mistake of assuming that a great company implies a great stock.*

Sometimes the impact of stock volatility can be counterintuitive. Consider an investor at the beginning of January in 1997. Let's say this investor consulted a magical genie and was offered a stock pick that would return an average of 37 percent per year for the next six years *guaranteed.* The genie states that there would be many bumps along the road, but the investment was guaranteed to have average annual returns of 37 percent. The investor does a quick calculation in his head and determines that if he invests $100,000 in the stock and gets an average annual return of 37 percent, then he stands to make about $560,000 over the next six years. Not a bad deal, right? Sure, there will be some volatility, but those guaranteed average annual returns look pretty good. The investor thanks the genie and promptly goes off to invest his $100,000 in the recommended stock.

Fast forward six years later to December 31, 2002. As promised by the genie, the stock pick has achieved annual returns of 37 percent over the six -year period. But the investor is astonished to see that his account balance is only $80,130. He actually lost 20 percent of his money! What the heck happened?

The stock in this example (JDS Uniphase Corp.) actually did have average annual returns of 37 percent over the period January 1, 1997, through December 31, 2002. But the growth rate (which takes into account the impact of the volatility) was an anemic -3.6 percent per year. The average return was pretty good, but the volatility of the stock's performance killed the growth rate. A graph helps explain what happened. As you can see in Figure 6.3, it was indeed a bumpy ride.

The stock had extraordinary performance in the period leading up to early 2000, but this was matched by equally poor performance in 2001 and 2002. The result was that average returns were strongly positive for the six year period, but the overall cumulative performance was poor. This is an extreme example, but clearly demonstrates the danger of focusing too much attention on average returns without considering the impact of

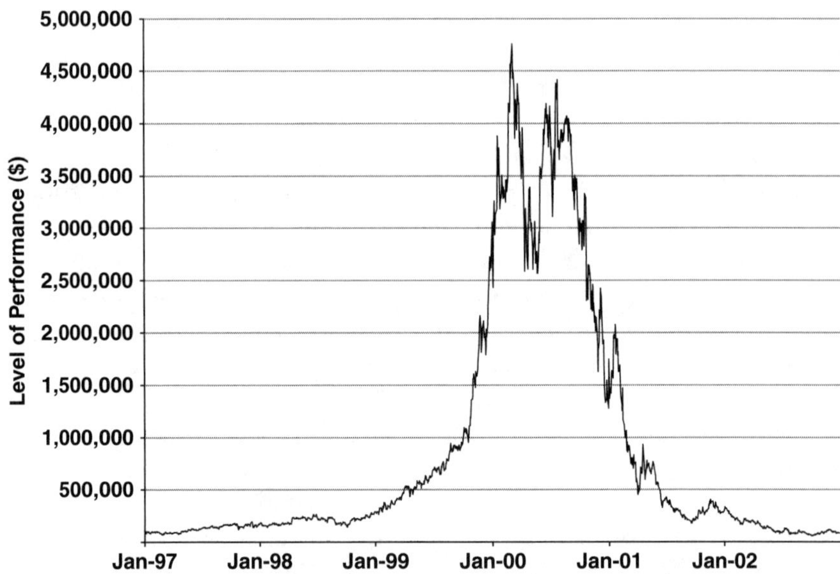

FIGURE 6.3 Performance of JDS Uniphase Corp. Common Stock from January 1, 1997, through December 31, 2002

Source: Data from Yahoo! Finance.

volatility. Remember that volatility matters a lot in accumulating wealth over time.

WHAT ABOUT MORE THAN ONE?

Clearly, putting all your money into a single stock is a risky proposition, no matter how strongly you believe in the company. But who puts everything into just one stock? Most (though not all) individual stock investors hold more than one security at a time. This raises the natural question of how many stocks you have to own before the portfolio becomes reasonably well diversified.

You can probably guess that the answer to this question is "it depends." Holding 10 stocks in equal proportions from varying industries and multiple countries is much less risky than a portfolio of 10 stocks, all from a single sector, with heavy concentration in just a few of them. To provide some intuition on this important question, let's examine portfolios of varying numbers of stocks and examine their risk characteristics and simulated portfolio

TABLE 6.9 Simulated Forecasts of an Equally Weighted Portfolio of Two Stocks

	Value of $10,000 Initial Investment in an Equally Weighted Portfolio of Oracle Inc. and Merrill Lynch & Co. Common Stock (in today's dollars)			
	At 1 Year	At 5 Years	At 10 Years	At 20 Years
Upside	$16,300	$36,500	$71,600	$216,000
Median	$10,500	$12,400	$15,100	$22,500
Downside	$5,900	$3,300	$2,200	$1,600

Source: Financial Engines calculations as of May 2007.

outcomes. To keep things simple, we will assume that all the portfolios are equally weighted across the constituent stocks. A portfolio with two stocks will be split 50/50, one with three stocks will have a third invested in each stock, and so on.

For the first example, consider a portfolio of two stocks from different industries: Oracle and Merrill Lynch. Table 6.9 illustrates the simulation results for a $10,000 initial investment ($5,000 in each in stock) over different horizons going out to 20 years. Again we assume no taxes and all values are adjusted for inflation (in today's dollars). Each year, the portfolio is assumed to be rebalanced to 50 percent in each stock.

There are a number of important differences between the outcomes for this portfolio and that of the Oracle-only portfolio. Adding together two stocks from different industries significantly reduces the risk of the portfolio, even though both constituent stocks are relatively volatile (at 3.9 and 3.1 times the market volatility, respectively). The downside values are still much lower than the diversified S&P 500 portfolio, but they are significantly higher than the single-stock Oracle-only portfolio. The median outcomes are also universally higher than the single stock portfolio, with a steady increase associated with longer horizons. However, the median outcomes still trail the S&P 500 with a 26 percent lower value at the 20-year horizon. Interestingly, the upside values are only modestly lower at the 20-year horizon compared to those of the single-stock portfolio. Clearly, holding more than one stock reduces the risk of the portfolio, resulting in significant improvements in both median and downside outcomes.

But if two is better, how about three?

Table 6.10 shows the outcomes associated with a portfolio of three stocks: Oracle, Merrill Lynch, and Pfizer.

TABLE 6.10 Simulated Forecasts of an Equally Weighted Portfolio of Three Stocks

	Value of $10,000 Initial Investment in an Equally Weighted Portfolio of Oracle Inc., Merrill Lynch & Co., and Pfizer Inc. Common Stock (in today's dollars)			
	At 1 Year	At 5 Years	At 10 Years	At 20 Years
Upside	$15,500	$33,200	$65,100	$198,000
Median	$10,600	$13,100	$17,100	$29,300
Downside	$6,500	$4,400	$3,600	$2,900

Source: Financial Engines calculations as of May 2007.

Adding a third stock from a different industry further reduces the risk of the portfolio. The downside values are still much lower than the diversified S&P 500 portfolio, but they are higher than the two-stock portfolio. At a 20-year horizon, the downside value for the three-stock portfolio is still 64 percent lower than the corresponding value for the S&P 500. However, the median outcomes steadily increase with longer horizons and now approximate the values for the more diversified S&P 500 portfolio. As for the upside values, they are only modestly lower than those of the two-stock portfolio.

If three are not enough—how about four stocks? Let's take a look. Consider an equally weighted portfolio (25 percent in each stock) of four stocks: Oracle, Merrill Lynch, Pfizer, and Marriot International. Table 6.11 shows the simulated portfolio outcomes over various horizons up to 20 years.

TABLE 6.11 Simulated Forecasts of an Equally Weighted Portfolio of Four Stocks

	Value of $10,000 Initial Investment in an Equally Weighted Portfolio of Oracle Inc., Merrill Lynch & Co., Pfizer Inc., and Marriot International Inc. Common Stock (in today's dollars)			
	At 1 Year	At 5 Years	At 10 Years	At 20 Years
Upside	$15,200	$30,500	$58,300	$171,000
Median	$10,800	$13,500	$17,800	$30,600
Downside	$7,090	$5,180	$4,460	$4,260

Source: Financial Engines calculations as of May 2007.

TABLE 6.12 Simulated Forecasts of an Equally Weighted Portfolio of Ten Stocks

	Value of $10,000 Initial Investment in an Equally Weighted Portfolio of Oracle, Merrill Lynch & Company, Pfizer, Marriot International, General Electric, Chevron, Citigroup, Target, Ford, and Dell Common Stocks (in today's dollars)			
	At 1 Year	At 5 Years	At 10 Years	At 20 Years
Upside	$14,800	$28,800	$52,800	$151,000
Median	$10,800	$13,800	$18,600	$34,200
Downside	$7,480	$5,870	$5,570	$6,140

Source: Financial Engines calculations as of May 2007.

With four stocks in the portfolio, the outcomes begin to look more like those of the diversified S&P 500 portfolio. The main differences are that the upside outcomes are higher, and the downside outcomes are still quite a bit lower. At 20 years, the downside outcome with four stocks at 20 years is still 47 percent lower than the S&P 500 portfolio. That is better than the 62 percent lower value for the portfolio of three stocks, but it still implies a significantly higher downside risk at longer horizons. The median outcomes look quite similar, implying that even modest diversification makes a big difference for median portfolio outcomes.

How about 10 stocks? Table 6.12 shows the simulated portfolio outcomes from a portfolio consisting of 10 large capitalization stocks: Oracle, Merrill Lynch & Company, Pfizer, Marriot International, General Electric, Chevron, Citigroup, Target, Ford, and Dell. Notice that these companies come from a mix of different industries.

With ten stocks, the outcomes continue to more closely resemble the results for the S&P 500 portfolio. But even with 10 stocks from different industries, the downside and upside values are still significantly more volatile than the diversified index. Individually, most of these stocks have expected returns that are somewhat higher than the S&P 500 due to leverage or exposures to higher expected return asset classes. This accounts for the slightly higher median forecast at 10 and 20 years. But the downside scenarios remain significantly below that of the broader index fund. At 20 years, the downside outcome is 24 percent less than that of the S&P 500 portfolio. What this demonstrates is that building a portfolio with a comparable range of outcomes as the S&P 500 requires a substantial number of stocks. Even

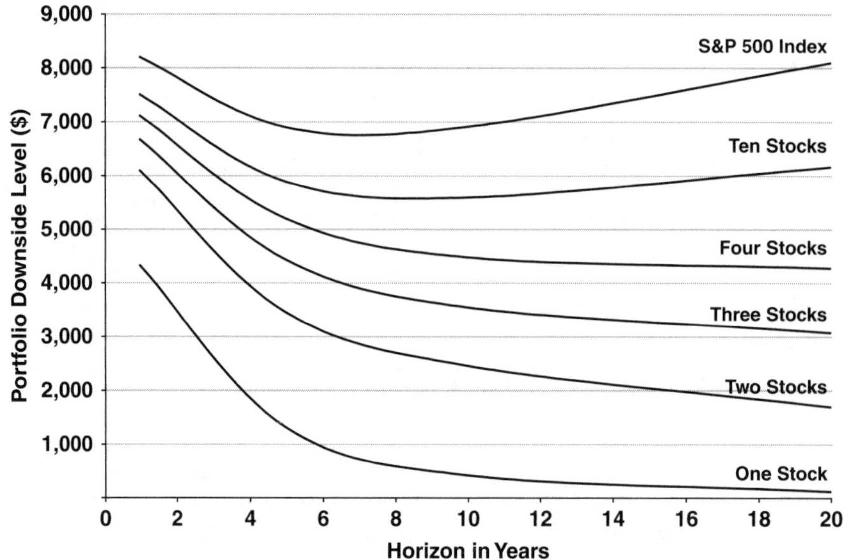

FIGURE 6.4 Comparison of Downside Outcomes for Portfolios of One, Two, Three, Four, and 10 Individual Stocks

Source: Financial Engines calculations as of May 2007.

a portfolio of 10 stocks from widely varying industries has a significantly wider range of outcomes than a broad-based index like the S&P 500.

To visually demonstrate how the downside risk changes with increasing numbers of stocks in the portfolio, consider the graph in Figure 6.4. This chart shows the downside outcomes (5th percentile) for a portfolio of $10,000 invested into different numbers of individual securities ranging from one to 10 stocks.

Figure 6.4 shows a classic case of what economists like to call diminishing returns. We see a big improvement moving from a single stock portfolio to one with two, three, and four stocks. But then the pace of improvement slows down. Getting to the same downside values as the S&P 500 requires a substantial number of individual stock holdings with varying industry exposures.

Before concluding this section, it is important to point out a few caveats to the previous results. First, the results will depend on the specific stocks used in the portfolios. If we were to repeat the above analysis with small-cap stocks we would see even higher levels of volatility and a wider range of outcomes. Also, our examples assumed that we were building portfolios out of stocks from varying industries. If we built a portfolio of stocks from a single sector, the additional diversification associated with higher numbers of stocks would be muted. Finally, our portfolios assumed that the stocks were equally weighted. If you concentrate your bets into higher allocations to a few stocks, the diversification of the portfolio will suffer.

DO YOU FEEL LUCKY?

When you concentrate your portfolio into one or a few individual stocks you are making a big bet. The bet is that your particular stock holdings will perform better than average—that you will end up somewhere in that Bill Gates side of the distribution of portfolio outcomes. If you don't believe that this will be the case, then you should invest in a more diversified portfolio, as this will at least provide returns in line with the market. Your chances on doing well with a diversified portfolio are much better, even if your chances of doing spectacularly well are a bit less. However, hope springs eternal, and many people go ahead and make the bet. An interesting question is how big of a bet is this? What are the odds that a given stock pick will beat a broad-based index of many stocks?

To shed some light on this question, Financial Engines analyzed the performance of stocks comprising three major indexes over the period 1995–2005: the S&P 500, S&P 400, and S&P 600. These three popular indexes represent the asset classes for large-capitalization, mid-capitalization, and small-capitalization U.S. stocks, respectively. In each case, we posed the question: What are the odds that a randomly selected single stock from these indexes would outperform the index itself over the 10-year period from 1995–2005?

For each index, we assumed hypothetical investors who randomly select a stock from the respective index. They invest all their money into this single stock and hold it for one month. At the end of the month, they replace the first stock with a second randomly selected stock from the same index. This stock is then held for a month and replaced with yet another stock. If the stock dies during the month (if it went bankrupt or was acquired) it is replaced with a new randomly selected stock and returns are chained together. This process is repeated for each month in the full 10-year period to generate a performance history for a portfolio invested in randomly selected individual stocks month by month. The performance of the single-stock strategy is then compared to the performance of the index itself over the same period. To reduce the noise in the calculations, the analysis above is

TABLE 6.13 Comparison of Single-Stock Strategy Performance to Index Performance: 1995–2005

	Median Single-Stock Cumulative Return	Index Cumulative Return	% of Returns Below the Index
S&P 500: Large-Cap Index	7.60%	11.40%	62.80%
S&P 400: Mid-Cap Index	7.40%	15.80%	74.10%
S&P 600: Small-Cap Index	3.40%	13.70%	74.60%

Source: Financial Engines calculations

repeated for 100,000 hypothetical investors in the single-stock strategy for each of the three indexes. For simplicity, we assume no taxes or transaction fees. The results of this experiment are detailed in Table 6.13.

As you can see, the median returns for the single-stock strategies are significantly lower than the returns for the three S&P indexes over the period 1995–2005. In each case, the median single-stock strategy underperformed the cumulative return of the index strategy by at least 3.8 percent per year. In the case of the small-cap S&P 600 index, the gap is over 10 percent per year! Since mid- and small-cap stocks tend to have higher volatility than large-cap stocks, the growth rates of single-stock strategies for the small- and mid-cap sectors are lower. Also, the percentage of single-stock strategies that underperform their corresponding index range from 63 percent for large-cap stocks to 75 percent for the small-cap strategies.

What this analysis suggests is that a strategy of selecting a single stock is likely to underperform a corresponding index over a multiyear period. This would be true if you held the stocks for longer than a single month as well. Additional diversification from holding a broad-based portfolio significantly increases the expected growth rate and the probability of beating a single-stock strategy.

HOW TO INVEST IN STOCKS SAFELY

Okay, so you have heard all my warnings about the dangers of over-concentration in individual stocks. But still you are not deterred. How much can you invest in a single stock and not pay too big a price in terms of risk?

It turns out that the company-specific volatility contributed to your portfolio from an individual stock position is proportional to the square of its allocation weight (the square is the weight multiplied by itself). For the nonmathematicians in the crowd this means that small allocations to a single stock are not much of a problem, but as the allocation weight increases it quickly becomes a big problem. For instance, if you allocate 10 percent of your portfolio to a single stock, then only 1 percent of the company-specific volatility of the stock is added to the risk of your total portfolio (since 10 percent × 10 percent = 1 percent). Even 1 percent of the company-specific risk of a stock can be meaningful, since individual stocks have much greater volatility than a more diversified portfolio, but with such a small weight the additional risk is not catastrophic.

If we double the exposure to 20 percent of the portfolio, the contribution of the individual stock volatility to the portfolio total increases to 4 percent (four times the volatility of the 10 percent allocation). On the other hand, if you invest 50 percent of your portfolio in a single stock, then the contribution to the total volatility of the portfolio increases to 25 percent—25 times the risk of the 10 percent allocation!

To give you an idea of how rapidly total portfolio volatility increases with higher individual stock allocations for a typical large-cap U.S. stock, look at the chart in Figure 6.5. The graph shows the total volatility of a

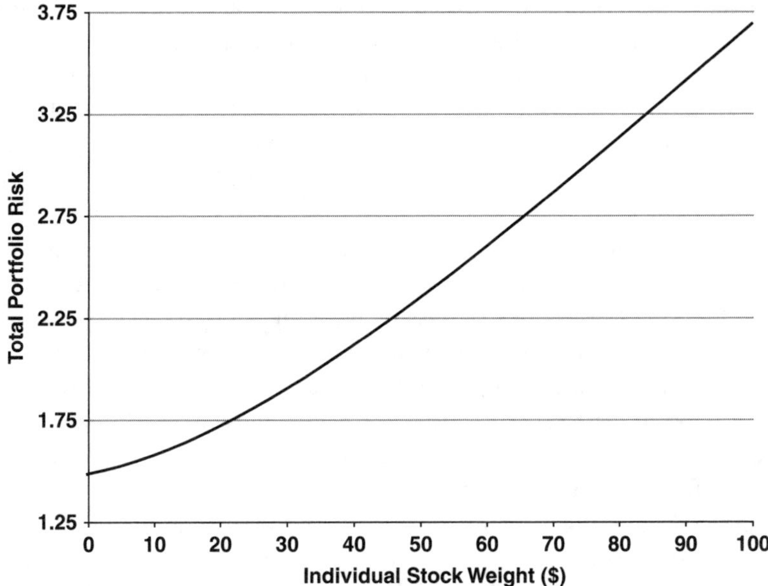

FIGURE 6.5 Total Portfolio Risk of a Mix of S&P 500 Index and Typical Large-Cap U.S. Stock

Source: Financial Engines calculations.

portfolio of the S&P 500 index and typical large cap stock as a function of the size of the individual stock allocation (measured in multiples of market portfolio risk).

As you can see in the chart, the risk of the portfolio rises steeply with the increasing proportions of the individual stock. In fact, the amount of money you could lose in the next 12 months (with a 1 in 20 probability) doubles when the stock proportion reaches only 45 percent of the total portfolio. In this example, we started with a relatively volatile portfolio of the S&P 500 index. If the starting portfolio had a lower volatility, the increase in risk with higher proportions of individual stock would look even more dramatic. The moral of this story is that the impact of individual stocks on total portfolio risk is modest for weights below about 20 percent, but the costs of stock concentration rise dramatically beyond that.

HIDDEN COSTS

A final consideration in trading individual stocks is the impact of transaction costs. When you trade individual securities, you are typically paying a brokerage commission fee to execute the trade. In addition, you are paying on average half of the difference between the posted *bid* and *ask* prices of the stock. The bid price represents the price you will get if you sell the stock, while the ask is the price that you can purchase the stock. The ask price will always be a little higher than the bid, with the difference between the two prices representing compensation for the entity that matches up the buyer and seller.

If you are trading the stocks in a taxable brokerage account, you must also take into consideration the costs associated with realized gains and losses. If you hold positions for less than a year, then the gains are subject to the standard income tax rates, which range up to 35 percent for federal taxes (as of 2007), and even more if you have to pay state income tax. If you hold positions for more than a year, you must generally pay capital gains taxes, which while less than income rates for most people, can still be a significant factor in realized returns.

The costs of trading a portfolio of even a modest number of individual stocks can be deceptively high. Consider an investor who holds a portfolio of 20 stocks and trades each of them on average three times per year (for instance, buying a stock, selling it, and replacing it with a different stock once per year). Some stock investors trade much more frequently than this, and others less so, but this is a plausible assumption for a moderately active investor. If we assume that the total portfolio value is $100,000, then the average position size is $5,000 per stock. Let's also assume that the average share price of the stocks in the portfolio is $20/share.

At most brokerage firms, you will pay a brokerage commission in order to execute a stock trade. We will assume that our hypothetical stock investor is trading at a discount brokerage firm and pays $14.95 in commissions per trade (in line with typical fees as of mid-2007). Based on these assumptions, our trader is going to pay about $900 per year in brokerage commissions. If we express these fees as a percentage of the total portfolio value (like a mutual fund expense ratio), this works out to an effective expense of 0.9 percent per year. Such fees are comparable to typical retail active mutual funds, and about four times higher than a typical index fund.

But that is not the only cost of trading. In addition to the brokerage commissions, our trader has to pay the difference between the current stock price and the ask price if they are buying, or the bid price if they are selling. On average, our trader has to pay about half the quoted spread between the bid and the ask price each time they transact. For stocks on the NYSE and NASDAQ exchanges, these half spreads average in the range of 0.25 percent to 0.75 percent of the share price, depending on the trading volume of the stocks (they can easily be much more than this for small-cap and thinly traded stocks). With the 0.75 percent assumption, the bid-ask spread costs add another $37.50 to the cost of each trade (assuming 250 shares per trade), more than double the cost of the brokerage commission itself. This works out to an additional $2,250 in costs per year.

Putting it all together, our moderately active trader is paying the equivalent of $3,250 in commissions and bid-ask spread costs per year, or 3.25 percent of the total portfolio value. As will be detailed in Chapter 7, this is a very significant annual cost that greatly reduces the expected returns with the stock-trading strategy. You can easily be giving up more than half the expected growth rate of the portfolio to the fees associated with even moderate levels of stock trading. To come out ahead, you will have to do much better than average on your stock picks.

Finally, if this portfolio were held in a taxable brokerage account, you would be subject to income tax rates (both federal and state) on any gains associated with the trades. Since the average holding period is less than a year, you would not qualify for long-term capital gains rates. This further erodes the after-tax expected growth rate of the trading strategy.

This analysis suggests that the costs of stock trading are an important consideration in estimating the potential gains from a portfolio of individual stocks. It is very difficult to demonstrate positive performance when coping with the drag of 3.25 percent in fees per year. In contrast, if you invested in a diversified fund product with costs of 0.25 percent per year, you would be paying only a small fraction of the fees associated with the stock portfolio. This is why you should strongly consider more cost-effective securities for your core investments. Of course, there are ways of reducing your trading costs by using specialized platforms and low-priced brokers. But the basic notion that trading individual securities is an inefficient investment strategy for most investors is difficult to dismiss.

DEALING WITH UNWANTED STOCK RISK

Despite your best efforts, there may be times when you are unable to avoid concentration in a particular stock. This can happen when your employer makes contributions to your retirement account in company stock but you are unable to diversify out of these positions due to vesting restrictions (though these types of restrictions are thankfully becoming less common).

In these circumstances, you may have to adjust the allocation of your other assets to compensate for the additional risk of the stock positions. On balance, this may make you less willing to take additional equity risk in your allocation. It may also make it desirable to adjust your exposure to asset classes that complement the exposures you have through your company stock. For instance, if your company stock has a high growth equity exposure, you might want to increase your exposure to value stocks or international equity in order to get the best diversification in your overall household portfolio. Chapter 8, which deals with the subject of smart diversification, will provide more details and examples of such allocation changes.

TAKE-AWAYS

- Investing in individual securities is an unnecessary gamble. You can do better, on average, by using more diversified instruments like mutual funds for your core investments.
- Individual stocks have much higher volatility than more diversified funds and their risk varies significantly across industries and different companies.

- The higher volatility of individual stocks implies much lower expected growth rates over multiyear horizons. For many individual stocks the expected growth rate is zero or even negative.
- The downside values for portfolios that consist of one or a few stocks are much lower than more diversified portfolios.
- When you invest in a diversified portfolio instead of a single stock, you give up a small probability of doing very well, but your overall chances of coming out ahead are greater.
- Most of the risk of individual stocks is not related to the stock market, but to factors specific to that company that can be easily minimized by holding many stocks across different industries.
- On average, the performance of a broad-based index will exceed the returns of a single-stock strategy about 60 percent to 75 percent of the time over a multiyear period.
- The costs associated with even moderate levels of stock trading can be a substantial drag on your expected returns, greatly exceeding the costs associated with mutual funds or exchange-traded funds. And it is even worse if you are trading in a taxable brokerage account.

CHAPTER 7

How Fees Eat Your Lunch

Spare no expense to save money on this one.
—Samuel Goldwyn (1882–1974)

The majority of individual investors profoundly underestimate the role that costs play in picking good investments. While institutional investors give careful consideration to investment expenses, most individual investors pay little heed to their impact. Inattention to the costs of investing can dramatically reduce the rate at which you build wealth. It is critical to understand how costs impact optimal portfolio construction and investment performance. The difference between the hypothetical performance of costless investments and the actuality of real-world costs can be startling.

Among the many things we purchase, investments are a curious species of product. As members of a consumer-oriented society, we are routinely conditioned to believe that if something costs more, it must be better. Often there is more than a nugget of truth to this view. After all, a Bentley offers certain improvements in comfort, materials, and craftsmanship (not to mention a better parking spot at the local country club) over the more prosaic choice of a Pontiac. High-quality clear diamonds cost much more than cloudy ones with obvious flaws. And houses on picturesque tree-lined streets cost more than those by the railroad tracks in the dodgy part of town. Across nearly all categories of products, you usually have to pay more for something of higher quality.[1] Should not the same be true for investment products?

The answer, curiously enough, is no.

IT'S BASIC ARITHMETIC

The value of an investment product like a mutual fund is its ability to generate returns and create wealth for you (often in combination with other investment products). The more wealth it can create per unit of risk, the better off and happier you will be (or at least richer).[2] All investment funds charge fees that detract from returns. Such fees represent compensation for the investment manager to manage the assets and provide services to shareholders. To shareholders, these fees are like a tax—they represent money that you don't get to keep and take away from net returns.

The financial services industry has come up with all kinds of ways to charge people for their services. Investment fees can be recurrent charges such as a mutual fund *expense ratio*, or one-time charges, as in the case of a *transaction fee* or a mutual fund *load charge*. In either case, the presence of these costs reduces the dollars you get to keep. Every dollar that goes into the pocket of an investment manager or broker is a dollar that does not end up in yours. There can be no debate about this reality. It is simple subtraction. All other things equal, a cheaper fund will have higher net returns than its more expensive peers. Of course, in reality, not everything else is equal, and so costs are one factor that must be weighed in consideration against other characteristics. They are, however, a particularly important one.

Some practitioners and investment managers argue that you don't need to be overly concerned with expenses as a good manager can earn far more than their incremental fee through excellent investment performance. While excess performance can easily overcome a fee difference in a given time period, the view that you can therefore ignore fees is just a bunch of hooey. Even the best investment managers have to work hard to overcome the impact of fees. And good performance by a manager does not take away the fact that *investment expenses always have a negative effect on portfolio returns*. A fund that charges a dollar of expenses lowers its expected net returns by *exactly* one dollar. There is no mystery here that requires fancy statistical analysis. It is simple subtraction.

As an example, consider two share classes of the same mutual fund with different levels of fees. Many mutual funds have multiple share classes of the same portfolio with varying expense ratios. These funds are typically marketed to different segments—for instance, one share class may be marketed to investment advisors and another class to corporate retirement plans. Usually the difference in fees is attributable to how the funds are distributed in different channels. Consider the Income Fund of America from the American Funds family, which comes in an R4 share class (symbol:

RIDEX) with an expense ratio of 0.64 percent per year, and an R5 share class (symbol: RIDFX) with an expense ratio of 0.34 percent per year. Both share classes of the Income Fund of America have exactly the same underlying holdings, same manager, and same portfolio characteristics. The only difference is that the R4 share class is 0.30 percent more expensive than the R5 share class. For the 12 months ending on October 31, 2007, the R4 share class of the fund returned a total of 13.13 percent for its shareholders. For the same period the less expensive R5 share class returned 13.47 percent. The difference in returns for the year was 0.34 percent, almost exactly matching the difference in expense ratios. As you can see, expenses have a very predictable effect on fund returns.

While fund expenses might seem small relative to the magnitude of investment returns in a given year, such fees are a big drag on your wealth accumulation over time. Furthermore, it is important to recognize that you always would have ended up with more money had the expenses been lower. Investment expenses represent the hurdle that a manager must overcome before he or she can even *start* to add value with management expertise. The lower the fees, the lower the hurdle, and hence the easier it is for a manager to add value for the investors in the fund.

It is interesting to contrast the attention paid to investment costs by institutional investors with that of most individual investors. Large pension funds with tens of billions to invest negotiate vigorously to reduce the investment expenses that they pay. The expense ratios of institutional funds (those not offered to the public) are often dramatically lower than those marketed to individual investors. Entire companies exist solely to help these institutions manage and reduce their investment expenses through better manager selection, more intelligent trading methods, and the use of low-cost electronic exchange networks. Finding ways to reduce the costs of investing directly adds to the net return enjoyed by the pension fund and thus makes it easier to meet future liabilities. Strangely, many individual investors don't seem to be getting the message, much to their detriment.

Fees for products like mutual funds vary widely. Among Financial Engines' retail mutual fund database, expense ratios vary from a low of only 0.03 percent to an astoundingly high 31 percent per year.[3] This incredible range of annual expenses charged to fund shareholders means that the most expensive funds are more than 1,000 times more costly than the least expensive options. Even automobiles don't show that kind of variation in price. A Bentley may be pricey, but it certainly does not cost 1,000 times more than a Pontiac. If we assume that you can get a Pontiac for $25,000, then a Bentley would need to command a price tag of about $25,000,000 to be comparable to the price variation seen in the mutual fund industry. Luckily, the very most expensive funds tend to have low asset balances, so at least most investors seem to recognize the folly of picking funds with expenses greater than 3 percent per year. According to Financial Engines' data, the total assets in funds with expense ratios above 3 percent per year was about $2.4 billion, or 0.02 percent of total mutual fund assets as of the beginning of 2007. But one still wonders what these "fee blind" investors are thinking (or not thinking).

What accounts for this incredible range of expenses? Actually, this is an interesting question generating some debate among economists. The range might be explainable if the highest expense funds have higher investment performance (gross of fees) than the lower expense funds. One could surmise that better managers are able to charge more for their investment expertise than less skilled managers. However, the evidence suggests that the higher expense funds actually have *worse* performance, even before expenses, than less costly funds. In an efficient market one would presume that the more costly, poor-performing funds should be driven out of business by the less costly and better-performing competition. The fact that this does not seem to be happening in the mutual fund market (at least not quickly) creates an interesting paradox for financial economists.[4]

As will be illustrated in upcoming sections, fund expenses are like termites. They can quietly eat away at the returns of your investments without you even realizing that there is a problem. Investment expenses grind away at your returns year by year, lowering the wealth that you accumulate over many years. Before you invest your hard-earned money in an investment product, make sure that you have checked out the soundness of its foundation. You want to have as little competition for those dollars of investment earnings as possible. An appropriate adage for investing might be "You get what you don't pay for."

BIG BUSINESS

If you follow the mold of about 99 percent of the adult population, you probably have no idea how much you pay in fees each year for your investment holdings. Most people can readily tell you their mortgage payment, how much they spend on a tank of gas, and how much they pay in medical bills, but they have absolutely no idea how much they are handing over to the various financial firms with whom they conduct business. This is not entirely by accident. Many financial firms are less than transparent about the magnitude of fees embedded in their offerings, and the standard of disclosure for such fees is an ongoing tug-of-war between the financial services industry and governmental regulators.

The aggregate numbers on the magnitude of investment fees are substantial. For example, look at the fees charged by mutual fund companies. According to the Investment Company Institute (an industry trade group for the mutual fund industry), mutual fund assets totaled $10.4 trillion at the end of 2006 (yes, that is *trillion* with a "t").[5] Equity mutual funds alone held $6.6 trillion in assets. The average fee for these equity funds was 1.07 percent per year on an asset-weighted basis. This implies that investors paid over $70.6 billion in management expenses and load fees for equity funds alone in 2006. In addition, there was over $1.5 trillion invested in bond mutual funds, generating an estimated $12.4 billion per year in fees. Money market funds accounted for another $2.4 trillion in assets and generated an estimated $9.6 billion in fees for the fund industry. Adding it all up you get to a grand total of $92 billion in annual mutual fund fees—a lot of money by anyone's standards. Putting these fees into perspective, $92 billion is equivalent to an average payment of about $300 per year for every man, woman, and child in the United States. And this estimate does not even include the many trillions of dollars managed by institutional investment managers outside of the mutual fund industry, nor the costs associated with brokerage commissions, transaction fees, custody fees, account fees, and other advisory fees. Needless to say, the investment management industry is a very big and lucrative business.

FOR EVERY WINNER THERE HAS TO BE A LOSER

Okay, so investment managers make lots money for their services. So do professional basketball players, architects, and doctors. They certainly deserve some compensation for their services. But do fund managers create value above and beyond the fees they charge?

On average, the answer for active fund managers is no. Why? Again, it is simple arithmetic.[6] The market as a whole is comprised of assets held by passive and active investment managers.[7] Active funds are those that attempt to beat the market averages by selecting securities that they expect to outperform. Passive funds simply invest in the market. The overall market return is just a weighted average of all the returns earned by passive and active investment managers. Before costs, the return on the average dollar invested in passive funds is equal to the average market return, since that is what they invest in. On a net-of-fees basis, the average passive manager underperforms the market average by an amount equal to the fees they charge.

But it must also be true that the weighted average return of a dollar invested in active funds (before fees) must equal the market return (since active + passive = the market). We also know that active management costs more than passive management due to the research and additional trading costs associated with active strategies. *Therefore, after costs, the average dollar invested in active funds will underperform the average dollar invested passively.* This statement depends only on basic math. It must hold for any time period and under any market conditions. This does not mean that a subgroup of active managers might not be able to outperform the market net of fees, but if they do, there must be a corresponding group of active managers that fail to beat the market for the math to add up. This is an example of a so-called *zero sum game* that economists often study. You can't have winners without corresponding losers. Unlike the kids in Lake Wobegon, not everybody can be above average in their performance. It may be possible for a minority of managers to do better than the market in a given time period, but the average dollar invested actively is guaranteed to underperform the market after accounting for fees. Of course, if you could identify the subgroup of active managers that will subsequently do better than the market, you could certainly beat the average. However, for reasons that we discuss in Chapter 9, this proves to be a challenging exercise.

To illustrate this relationship with some real data, I analyzed a database of 22,474 mutual funds (of all share classes) tracked by Financial Engines that were available to U.S. investors between January 1993 and May 2007. For each fund, an appropriate benchmark was estimated based on the investment style of the fund. For instance, money market funds were compared to the performance of cash returns, while equity funds might have a benchmark composed of exposures to one or more equity asset classes. For each fund, the performance of the portfolio returns was compared to the performance of the underlying asset class benchmark over the available life of the fund. Note that some of the funds went out of business prior to May 2007 and were liquidated or merged into other funds. The difference in performance between the fund and the underlying investment measures the manager's contribution to performance. A positive difference indicates that the fund beat an investment in a passive index fund with the same investment style, while a negative difference indicates that the manager underperformed a comparable index (you would have been better off with a similar-style index fund). Economists call this difference the *alpha* of a fund.

Alpha is just a shorthand measure of the value added or subtracted by the decisions of a fund manager. For instance, I might manage a fund investing in large-capitalization U.S. stocks, while my friend across town might manage a different fund with another portfolio of large-capitalization U.S. stocks. If my particular stock choices do well compared to the average performance of the large-capitalization U.S. stock asset class, then my alpha would be positive (I added some value with my choices). If my friend selected stocks that on average did worse than the large-capitalization U.S. stock asset class, then his alpha would be negative. In both cases we had the same investment style, but made different decisions on the specific securities to achieve that style. These decisions are where an active fund manager can add or subtract value relative to an index fund with the same investment style.

Using this definition, an index fund almost always has an alpha of zero (before adjusting for fees). Why? Because an index fund is designed to exactly track the performance of its underlying investment style. With an index fund there is no manager discretion to select securities different from those that compose the asset class itself. Index funds allow an investor to get the performance of the asset class, less the fees charged by the fund. The underlying investment style of a fund is often referred to as a *benchmark*. The benchmark represents the performance that a fund must achieve before the manager can be said to have added any value with his or her investment selections. Index fund performance closely tracks that of their benchmark, while an actively managed fund might outperform or fall short of the benchmark depending on the decisions of the manager.

So what do we see from the analysis of 22,472 mutual funds? The average mutual fund had a *negative* alpha of 1.15 percent. This means that the average mutual fund underperformed its investment-style benchmark by 1.15 percent per year.[8] That may sound like a modest number, but it implies that on average, you are giving up about 22 percent of the total expected return of the underlying asset classes to the combination of fees and manager performance.[9] Moreover, only 26 percent of the funds in the sample had positive alphas. This implies that only about one quarter of mutual funds were able to demonstrate performance that exceeded what you could achieve with a low-cost index fund. The proportion of active funds with positive historical alphas will vary from time period to time period, but over the last couple of decades, 60 percent–80 percent of active mutual funds have underperformed their underlying investment style.

IT STILL ADDS UP TO DOLLARS

Financial service firms have many ways of charging fees to their customers. You should at least be aware of the basic types of fees that you are likely to be charged, either by the fund company or by your investment advisor or broker. This is definitely one of those areas where ignorance is *not* bliss. Some fees vary with the amount of money invested in the product, while others (like brokerage commissions) are often fixed in magnitude.

Explicit Fees

The following section provides a brief discussion of the explicit types of investment fees that investors pay for funds and individual stocks.

Expense ratios: A fund expense ratio is the fee charged by the fund operating company for operational expenses and investment management fees. It is typically expressed as a percentage of the net assets (e.g., 1.0 percent or 100 basis points) of the fund and is updated annually. This fee is deducted from your investment returns as a shareholder of the fund on a daily basis. Some funds tie their expense ratios to the total assets of the fund or to investment performance, and so their expenses may change over time. All mutual funds have expense ratios, as do the nonretail institutional funds often found in large 401(k) plans.

12b-1 fees: These fees are fees charged by the mutual fund company to cover marketing, promotion, and distribution expenses. They are expressed as a percentage of net assets and are included as part of the overall expense ratio for the fund. 12b-1 fees are set at an annual level of 1.0 percent or less. Even so-called "no load" mutual funds can have 12b-1 fees embedded in their expense ratios, but not all mutual funds charge such fees. Often a portion of 12b-1 fees go to compensate brokers who distribute the funds to investors.

Loads: A load fee is a sales charge or commission that is added to the price of a fund when it is purchased or sold. There are *front-end loads,* which are added to the purchase price of a fund, and *back-end loads,* which apply to the price of the fund when it is sold. Usually, back-end load charges decay over time so that if you hold the fund for more than six to eight years you can avoid paying the load when you sell the fund. For mutual funds, front-end loaded funds are typically known as Class A shares, while Class B and Class C shares may involve back-end load charges. Front-end and back-end load fees are generally not charged to participants in defined contribution plans such as a 401(k) plan.

Redemption fees: These fees are a relatively recent phenomenon for most mutual funds. Redemption fees may apply if you choose to hold a fund for a short period of time. For instance, some funds charge a fee of 1.0 percent of the amount sold if the fund is held for less than 60 days. Unlike load charges, redemption fees are fairly common in defined contribution plans. Also, redemption fees are paid back into the fund, as opposed to going to the investment manager. Such fees exist to discourage investors from rapid trading in and out of the fund, which can raise the transaction costs for other investors in the fund. In many situations it makes sense to avoid incurring redemption fees, unless the benefits of getting out of a poor position are significant.

Transaction fees: Transaction fees apply when you purchase or sell certain funds in a brokerage account or brokerage window. Generally transaction costs are expressed in dollars and for fund trades are not tied to the size of the transaction. For instance, a brokerage firm might charge a transaction fee of $25–$50 for the purchase or sale of certain mutual funds. For stocks, the transaction fees are known as *brokerage commissions* and can vary widely in magnitude, depending on the nature of the account. Usually brokerage commissions for stocks are structured as a flat fee for trades up to a certain size, with a variable fee on shares above that amount. It is worth noting that for these types of fixed fees, the impact on your account is sensitive to the size of the transaction. For large transactions a $25 fee may not be meaningful, but if you have small transactions, especially if they are recurring, the fees can add up. For example, if you purchase $500 worth of a mutual fund that charges a $25 transaction fee, you are paying the equivalent of a 5.0 percent transaction fee ($25/$500 = 5 percent), which is a very steep hit to your expected returns.

Investment advisory fees: If your money is being managed by a registered investment advisor or financial planner, you may be paying an asset-based investment advisory fee on top of the fees for your investment funds. This fee is intended to cover the expense of allocating your assets, providing investment advice, and monitoring your portfolio over time. Such fees can vary widely depending on the level of services and the amount of assets under management. Typically, investment advisory annual fees range from 0.50 percent to more than 2.00 percent of assets under management.

Implicit Fees

In addition to the previously discussed explicit fees, there are also hidden or implicit fees that reduce the performance of mutual funds. These fees are almost never disclosed in advertising materials or a prospectus, but they can have a significant effect on your net returns.

Brokerage commissions: When a fund manager trades securities in the fund portfolio, he or she is required to pay brokerage commissions to the firm that processes the trades. These commissions are paid out of the assets of the funds, and hence detract from the net returns to investors. The more the fund manager trades, the higher the level of commissions. Generally mutual fund managers pay far less than individual investors for executing trades, but the costs can still be significant, particularly with active managers who trade frequently or those who invest in less mature markets with higher trading costs (such as developing countries).

Bid-ask spreads: When a fund manager makes a trade, in addition to brokerage commissions, she or he must pay the difference between the market price and the price at which she or he can buy the security (the ask) or the price that she or he can sell the security (the bid). The ask price exceeds the bid price and the difference between the two is known as the *bid-ask* spread. This spread between what it costs to buy a stock and what you can sell it for is part of the cost of executing a stock trade. Generally these costs are higher for stocks that have lower trading volumes and a smaller number of shareholders. This tends to be true for small-capitalization and some international stocks. For larger-company stocks with very deep trading volume, the spread between the bid and ask tends to be lower. Similar to brokerage commissions, the more frequent the trading by the fund, the higher the costs associated with paying the spread between the bid and ask prices in the market. Like brokerage commissions, these costs lower net returns to investors. It is particularly important to pay attention to bid/ask spreads when trading in securities with very low share prices, as the gap between the bid and the ask can be a significant percentage of the stock price itself. Not surprisingly, active mutual funds tend to incur much higher commissions and bid-ask spread costs than index funds due to their higher rate of trading.

What is interesting about these implicit costs is that they are widely estimated as being comparable in size to the explicit costs associated with expense ratios and loads.[10] One study estimates that the average cost to fund shareholders from brokerage commissions and trading spreads is 0.78 percent, and that the costs for specific funds can vary widely. This implies that many mutual funds have total costs in the range of 2.00 percent when these implicit costs are added to the explicit fees charged by the fund company (and even more for funds with load charges). As we will see, such fees have big implications for the ability of funds to generate wealth for you.

A WIDE, WIDE WORLD

As mentioned earlier, the range of expenses charged by different types of retail mutual funds is quite large. When shopping for funds, it can sometimes be difficult to know whether an expense ratio is low, high, or just typical for the type of fund you are evaluating. To assist with this effort, I have analyzed the expense ratios of common types of retail mutual funds to show the distribution of expenses you may encounter in the marketplace. This sample includes only those classes of funds that are typically marketed to individuals whose minimum initial purchase amount is $10,000 or less.

Table 7.1 shows the range of expense ratios for different types of retail mutual funds as of the middle of 2007.

As you can see, there is a wide range of fees charged by different types of funds. Less expensive share classes can be found if you are able to invest a larger amount of money. Often fund companies will offer institutional class shares with lower expense ratios for entities that are willing to invest $100,000 or more. Also, it should be noted that the lower-expense funds tend to have a larger share of the market than the higher-expense fee funds. This implies that investors are paying some attention to the costs of investing in mutual funds and that lower-cost funds are capturing more investor dollars than higher-priced funds.

TABLE 7.1 Expense Ratios for Different Types of Retail Mutual Funds

Percentile	Money Market Funds	Bond Funds	Equity Funds
5th	0.29%	0.50%	0.56%
25th	0.56%	0.76%	1.16%
Median	0.71%	1.00%	1.52%
75th	0.97%	1.53%	2.02%
95th	1.49%	1.80%	2.50%

Source: Financial Engines analysis.

As for patterns, the median money market fund is less expensive than the median bond fund and the median bond fund costs less than the median equity fund. Where should you draw the line when purchasing a fund? You almost always want to avoid funds with expense ratios in the upper quartile of their peer group. For instance, it will almost never be worthwhile to pay more than 2.00 percent in fund expenses for an equity mutual fund. *As a general rule of thumb, you should focus your attention only on those funds in the lowest quartile of expenses for their fund category.* This means expense ratios of less than 0.56 percent for money market funds, less than 0.76 percent for bond funds, and less than 1.16 percent for equity funds. However, a good argument can be made for even lower thresholds, particularly with equity funds. There are a large number of reasonably priced, high-performing equity funds with expense ratios below 0.80 percent per year. These days, when there are so many funds and managers to choose from, there is little incentive to put up with unreasonable fund expenses.

One final point on fund fees. In many 401(k) retirement plans, particularly for larger employers, investors will have access to institutional fund managers who often charge far lower fees than comparable retail mutual funds. Often, institutional fund managers charge fees that are only 10 percent to 50 percent of those charged by mutual funds. Clearly, these investments can be a very good deal for participants in the plan. Moreover, the presence of such funds can make it profitable to keep your money in the plan after you leave the company, even if you might have greater fund choice in a retail IRA rollout account. Don't let the brand names of retail mutual funds distract you from taking advantage of a great deal with less well-known, but very cost-effective institutional fund products.

HOW FEES EAT YOUR LUNCH

Let's make all this discussion of fees a bit more concrete. First, consider two funds that have the same underlying assets, but two very different levels of fees (as of May 2007), the Fidelity Spartan 500 Index Fund (FSMKX) with an expense ratio of 0.10 percent per year, and the Morgan Stanley S&P 500 Index Fund (SPIBX) with an expense ratio of 1.38 percent per year.

Both funds are passively managed funds designed to track the performance of the S&P 500 index. As such, they hold virtually identical portfolios, representing an asset-weighted index of large-capitalization U.S. stocks. Essentially the only major difference between the two funds is the level of expenses that they charge to their investors. The Fidelity Spartan 500 fund

TABLE 7.2 Comparison of S&P 500 Index Funds with Different Fee Levels

	Value of $10,000 Initial Investment in Two S&P 500 Index Funds			
	Morgan Stanley S&P 500 Index Fund SPIBX	Fidelity Spartan 500 Fund FSMKX	Difference in Wealth Accumulation Over 30 Years	Percentage Difference
	1.38% Expense Ratio	0.10% Expense Ratio		
Upside	$163,000	$210,000	$47,000	29%
Median	$37,100	$53,400	$16,300	44%
Downside	$7,050	$10,400	$13,350	48%

Sources: Financial Engines calculations and mutual fund annual reports.

(symbol: FSMKX) is one of the least expensive large-cap index funds available to typical retail investors (the minimum investment is $10,000 at the time of this writing). The Morgan Stanley S&P 500 fund (symbol: SPIBX) is one of the more expensive index funds on the market, with an annual expense ratio of 1.38 percent per year. So how big of a difference is this 1.28 percent per year difference in fees? Let's look at an example forecast of $10,000 in each fund over 30 years. To keep it simple we assume that there are no taxes or transaction fees on either fund. Table 7.2 shows what the portfolio outcomes look like over a 30-year holding period.

The median portfolio value estimates at 30 years differ by a whopping 44 percent! Remember that these two funds have virtually identical risk and identical holdings. The only significant difference is that the Morgan Stanley fund has an annual expense ratio that is 1.28 percent higher than the Spartan fund. While 1.28 percent might seem like a small amount, over 30 years that difference in fees creates a big disparity in ending wealth. The result of the higher expense ratio is that you will pay $16,300 more in fees over 30 years in the median outcome—a lot of money. Note that the percentage difference in return given up to fees is even larger when the fund performance is poor. That is, you give up more of your return to fees precisely when your overall returns are the lowest. In the upside case, which represents very strong market performance, you end up paying a whopping $47,000 in additional fees over the 30 years. Think about what you could do with an extra $47,000 in your pocket.

Clearly, an informed investor will prefer the fund with higher ending outcomes across the board. This is one of the rare situations in financial economics where there really is a dominant choice. If you can get exactly the same portfolio for less money, you should. You may recall in an earlier chapter that I said there was no free lunch in investing. Actually, that is only mostly true. When it comes to expenses, there is no downside to lowering investment fees. If the only difference between two investment products is the level of the fees, then the lower fee product will have a higher expected return (net of fees) without any additional risk. The impact of selecting the lower expense ratio fund is a substantial increase in the expected return of the portfolio, and hence a big increase in predicted wealth.

Of course this example is a stark one. Different S&P 500 index funds are easily compared since they hold the same stocks and track the same index. But what about other types of mutual funds? How much do differences in expenses account for variations in expected returns?

To answer this question, let's examine the characteristics of some popular and widely held mutual funds. First, we'll look at some popular equity funds that primarily invest in large-capitalization U.S. stocks (generally companies with market values above about $5 billion). To understand how expenses affect returns, we can compare the expected returns of a fund against the expected returns of the underlying assets themselves. In a perfect world, one could achieve the expected returns of the underlying assets by investing in a no-cost index fund. Of course, we don't live in a perfect world, and we usually have to pay expenses to invest in a fund. The difference between the expected return of a costless portfolio with the same investment style and the return of the actual fund reflects the impact of the explicit and implicit costs of the funds. It allows us to calculate how much of the potential return of the underlying assets is eaten up by fund expenses. For the purposes of this calculation, we will assume that the managers of the funds are not adding or subtracting any performance beyond the returns of the investment style, which is true on average but may not be true for every fund.

Our sample is drawn from the database of retail mutual funds tracked by Financial Engines. The five mutual funds in Table 7.3 represent five of the largest funds with at least 75 percent exposure to large-capitalization U.S. stocks as of May 2007. Some of these funds have load charges, which we assume are not paid by investors in this hypothetical example (this would be true if these funds were held in a 401(k) account).

As you can see in Table 7.3, there is a considerable range in the amount of expected return lost to fund fees. The fees on these funds range from a low of 0.18 percent for the Vanguard Index fund to a high of 0.87 percent for the Davis Venture fund. In other words, the highest expense fund has

TABLE 7.3 Comparison of Expected Return Lost to Fees for Five Large-Capitalization U.S. Stock Mutual Funds

Fund	Expected Return Lost to Fees
Vanguard 500 Index/Inv	2.7%
Washington Mutual Investors Fund/A	9.6%
Fidelity Blue Chip Growth	9.9%
Fidelity Equity Income	10.9%
Davis New York Venture/A	12.6%

Source: Financial Engines calculations, based on data as of May 2007.

nearly five times the fees of the lowest expense fund. At the low end, the Vanguard 500 Index fund, with its low expense ratio and low turnover, loses only 2.7 percent of its estimated expected return to fees, while the Davis New York Venture fund loses 12.6 percent of its estimated expected return to fees. This, of course, means that the Davis New York Venture fund has to post considerably better performance than the Vanguard fund before it can add to the net returns of fund shareholders. It is like running a race with a ball and chain attached to your ankle. You may think you are a faster runner, but the extra weight will surely slow you down. No matter how naturally fast you are, the extra drag of higher fees reduces your overall speed.

Now let's look at some results for some popular small- and mid-cap funds. Again, as shown in Table 7.4, the range of expected return lost to fund expenses varies considerably. The fees on these funds vary from a low of 0.22 percent for the Vanguard Mid Cap Index fund to a high of 1.19 percent for the Calamos Growth Fund (not including the front-end load). Again, this is a big range of fees. The most expensive fund has 5.4 times the expenses of the least costly fund. In general, the expense ratios for

TABLE 7.4 Comparison of Expected Return Lost to Fees for Five Small- and Mid-Cap U.S. Stock Mutual Funds

Fund	Expected Return Lost to Fees
Vanguard Mid Cap Index/Inv	3.6%
Vanguard Explorer	9.4%
T Rowe Price Mid Cap Growth Fund	11.5%
Fidelity Mid Cap Stock	11.6%
Calamos Growth/A	16.3%

Source: Financial Engines calculations, based on data as of May 2007.

TABLE 7.5 Comparison of Expected Return Lost to Fees for Five Bond Mutual Funds

Fund	Expected Return Lost to Fees
Vanguard Intermediate Term Treasury/Inv	10.0%
Maxim Bond Index	16.7%
TCW Total Return Bond Fund/N	23.7%
UBS PACE Funds: Strategic Fixed Income/P	30.4%
Northern US Government Fund	37.9%

Source: Financial Engines calculations, based on data as of May 2007.

small- and mid-cap funds tend to be a bit higher than those of large-capitalization equity funds. The Vanguard fund gives up only 3.6 percent of its expected return to expenses, while the Calamos gives up a whopping 16.3 percent of its expected returns to the combination of fund expenses and the implicit costs of trading by the fund manager.

When you get to bond funds the situation is even more striking. Because bond funds have lower expected returns due to the lower returns of fixed-income assets versus equities, fees have an even greater impact. Let's examine results for five popular fixed-income funds with at least 90 percent exposure to bonds (Table 7.5).

In general, bond funds tend to have lower expense ratios than equity funds, though that is not always the case. The least expensive bond fund in our group, the Vanguard Intermediate Term Treasury fund, has an expense ratio of 0.26 percent, while the most expensive fund (UBS PACE Funds: Strategic Fixed Income) has fund fees of 0.93 percent per year. Again we see a substantial difference between the fees of the low-cost funds and those of the higher-priced alternatives. What is striking about Table 7.5 however, are the fractions of expected returns lost to the fund fees. Even in the case of the relatively inexpensive Vanguard fund, about 10 percent of the fund's expected returns are lost to fees. However, for the two most expensive funds (the UBS PACE and Northern U.S. Government funds), fees devour an astonishing 30 percent and 38 percent of total expected returns, respectively. That is, as an investor in these funds, you are giving up about one third of your total expected return from these assets in the form of fees. Clearly, the bottom line here is that you should be very cost conscious when selecting bond mutual funds. Paying a little too much has a big impact on your net expected returns.

Finally, let's examine the impact of fees on the expected returns of money market funds. It is a not-so-well-kept secret in the financial services

TABLE 7.6 Comparison of Expected Return Lost to Fees for Five Money Market/Cash Mutual Funds

Fund	Expected Return Lost to Fees
Vanguard Prime Money Market	17.4%
Fidelity Cash Reserves	27.0%
Western Asset Money Market/A	30.6%
Centennial Money Market Trust	40.1%
Schwab Money Market Fund/Sweep	44.3%

Source: Financial Engines calculations, based on data as of May 2007.

business that money market funds are a major source of profits for fund companies and brokerage firms. Often one of these funds is the default fund for "sweep accounts," where your money goes when you sell assets and do not specify a specific destination for the proceeds. As a result, these sweep account funds tend to accumulate considerable assets. Firms have realized that customers tend not to pay much attention to the fees associated with these funds, since they are not specifically selecting the fund. Table 7.6 shows the analysis for five large money market funds.

Money market funds suffer from the same problem as bond mutual funds—since they invest in lower expected return assets, net expected returns are very sensitive to fund expenses. In fact, money market funds invest in the lowest expected return assets, like U.S. Treasury bills, high-quality commercial paper, and certificates of deposit. In general, money market funds tend to have somewhat lower average expense ratios than other bond funds, but the range of expenses is still quite wide. In our list of five popular cash and money market funds, the expenses range from a low of 0.29 percent (Vanguard Prime Money Market) to a high of 0.74 percent (Schwab Money Market Fund/Sweep). Even the relatively low-expense Vanguard fund is forfeiting over 17 percent of its total expected return to fees. In the case of the more expensive Schwab Money Market Fund, an investor is giving up more than 44 percent of the total expected return to fund fees! In fact, only one of our five funds gives up *less* than 25 percent of its total expected return to fund fees. Keep in mind that the variation in the historical returns of these funds due to differences in their underlying assets is very small. Money market funds tend to invest in basically the same types of short-term fixed-income assets, and hence get the same kinds of returns (gross of fees). Many investors and some advisors will select a money market fund based on its historical net returns. Sometimes funds that invest in slightly lower-credit quality instruments will post slightly higher returns. But the real predictor of future performance is actually the fees of the fund. When picking a place for your short-term cash, it pays to be *very* cost conscious. The cheapest money market fund will almost always be the best choice (assuming the credit quality of the underlying assets is high).[11]

So, how do you make sense of all this analysis on fund fees? Table 7.7 provides a handy reference to estimate the impact of fund fees in terms of the total expected return for common types of mutual funds. For each category of mutual fund, I have estimated the percentage of total expected return that is given up for every 0.10 percent increase in fund fees. As you can see, the impact is more modest for high expected return funds like small- and mid-cap funds, and quite large for low expected-return funds like money market funds. The exact amount of expected return lost to fees will vary a bit from fund to fund, but Table 7.7 provides useful estimates when comparing funds and their relative expense ratios.

For money market funds, an incremental 0.10 percent (10 basis points) in additional fees implies that you give up 6 percent of the total expected return of the fund's underlying assets. If the money market fund costs 0.25 percent more than an alternative fund, you are giving up the equivalent of 15 percent of the total expected return. For a large-cap equity fund, 0.50 percent in additional expenses implies a reduction of 7.2 percent in the total expected return of the fund. The bottom line here is that it pays to be cost efficient in your investing choices, particularly for funds that invest in lower expected-return asset classes like bonds and cash.

TABLE 7.7 Percentage of Total Expected Return Lost to Fees

	Percentage of Total Expected Return Lost		
Fund Type	**+0.10%** Incremental Fee	**+0.25%** Incremental Fee	**+0.50%** Incremental Fee
Money Market/Cash	6.0%	15.0%	30.0%
Bonds	3.3%	8.3%	16.7%
Large-Cap Stocks	1.4%	3.6%	7.2%
Small/Mid-Cap Stocks	1.3%	3.2%	6.4%
International Stocks	1.5%	3.6%	7.3%

Source: Financial Engines calculations.

IT'S A HEAVY LOAD TO BEAR

The previous analysis examined the impact of mutual fund expenses, both implicit and explicit, on net expected returns. To keep the analysis simple, I excluded the consideration of load fees (both front- and back-end loads). In the 401(k) world, you generally will not encounter load fees. However, in the retail brokerage world many mutual funds have load charges of up to 5 percent and even higher.

Class A shares of mutual funds typically carry a front-end load charge. The load fee is paid up front and thus is deducted from your initial investment in the fund. The load fees are generally intended to compensate the broker or advisor for the costs of selling the fund or for providing investment advice. For instance, the Van Kampen Growth & Income Fund (ACGIX) carries a front-end load charge of 5.75 percent in addition to its ongoing expense ratio of 0.79 percent (as of May 2007).

When you purchase a load fund, you are giving up a significant portion of your investment right up front. When you invest $10,000 in a fund with a 5.75 percent front-end load, it is like taking a match and burning $575 of your money. That $575 is gone forever. Obviously this has a significantly negative impact on your wealth accumulation over time. However, unlike an expense ratio, the average cost per year depends on how long you hold the fund in your portfolio. If you hold the fund only for one year, you are effectively paying fund expenses of 5.75 percent plus the fund's normal expense ratio. This is a terrible investment decision under almost any circumstances. In effect, you are forfeiting nearly all of the expected return of an equity fund if the holding period is only a single year. The same would be true for bond funds, though the front-end loads tend to be a bit smaller than in the case of equity funds.

Of course, if you hold the fund for 20 years the situation is a bit different. In effect, you are amortizing or spreading out the impact of the initial load charge over a longer period of time. As a simple rule of thumb, you can take the load charge and divide it by the number of years you expect to own the fund to arrive at the annual net expense. For instance, if you purchase a fund with a front-end load charge of 5.75 percent and hold the fund for 10 years, you are effectively paying additional fees of 0.575 percent per year plus the expense ratio. Even over 10 years, this is not a trivial amount. Holding the fund for 20 years would cut this impact in half. But no matter how long you plan to hold the fund, the load charge up front negatively impacts your wealth accumulation forever. Once that money is deducted from your account, it is gone forever and is unable to accumulated future returns.

Some funds charge back-end loads that are charged to your account if you sell the fund in the first several years of ownership. The same type of analysis applies to this situation as well. Often this class of funds has higher expense ratios as well. Unless you are highly confident that you will hold the fund for a long enough period (typically more than five or six years), the additional costs of the load charge in addition to the expense ratio can be burdensome. Load charges have a very large impact of future net returns.

What does this mean? Well, unless you plan to hold a load fund for a long time (at least 10 years), or you believe you are receiving advisory services from your broker or advisor that are worth the payment of the load fee, you should avoid funds with front-end or back-end loads. Purchasing loaded funds and holding them for only a few years virtually guarantees poor performance on a net returns basis. Even if you plan on holding the fund for a lengthy period of time, you can usually find no-load alternatives with equal or lower total expenses and comparable performance.

FEES AND THE BIGGER PICTURE

Earlier I demonstrated how fees can chew up a large percentage of the possible expected returns offered by different kinds of mutual funds. To help make the analysis more concrete, let's examine some longer-term forecasts of funds with similar investment styles, but varying levels of fees. With these simulations, you can directly observe how fees impact potential wealth accumulation.

Let's look at a few examples from a group of no-load funds that invest primarily in U.S. Equities.[12] Table 7.8 shows three funds with varying levels of fees that meet these criteria as of May 2007.

TABLE 7.8 U.S. Equity Mutual Funds with Varying Fees

Fund Name	Symbol	Expense Ratio
Elite Growth and Income Fund	ELGIX	1.39%
Dreyfus Fund	DREVX	0.74%
SSgA S&P 500 Index Fund	SVSPX	0.18%

Sources: Financial Engines and fund annual reports as of May 2007.

These funds have similar investment styles, though they vary in their investment selection strategies. Two of the funds, the Elite Growth and Income fund and the Dreyfus fund, are actively managed, while the third (the SSgA S&P 500 index fund) is passively managed. Both the Elite and the Dreyfus funds are in the standard range of expenses for actively managed equity mutual funds, with the Elite fund on the higher side of that range, and the Dreyfus fund on the lower end of the spectrum.

To illustrate the differences, I have run 10-year simulations of a $10,000 initial investment in each fund. We assume no taxes are paid on the proceeds, and all the forecast values are presented in today's dollars (adjusted for inflation).

As you can see from Figure 7.1, there is a clear relationship between the forecast values and the expense ratios of each of the funds. The most expensive fund has the lowest forecast values, while the least expensive fund has the highest. In fact, the median forecast value for the SSgA fund is 21 percent higher than the Elite fund and 9 percent higher than the Dreyfus

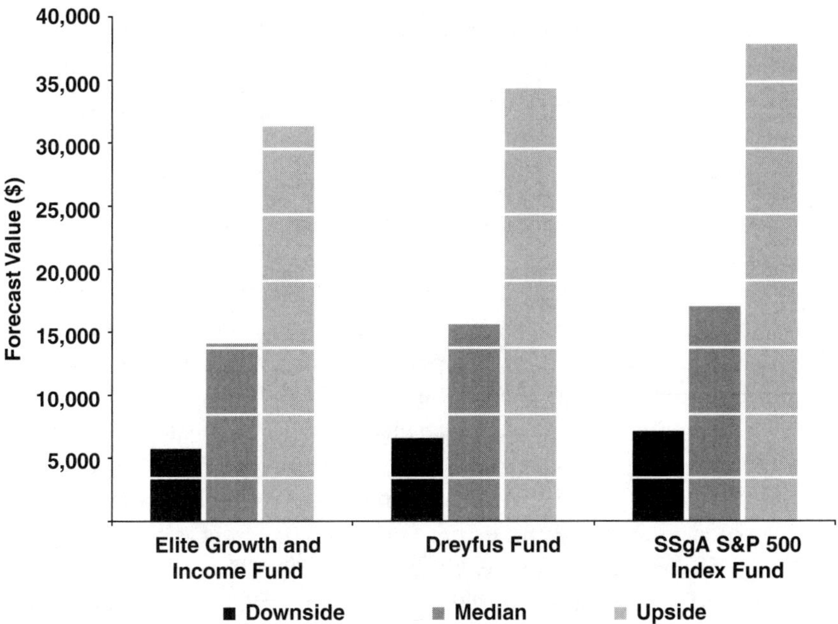

FIGURE 7.1 Simulation Results for Three Large-Cap Equity Funds over 10-year Horizon

Source: Financial Engines calculations as of May 2007.

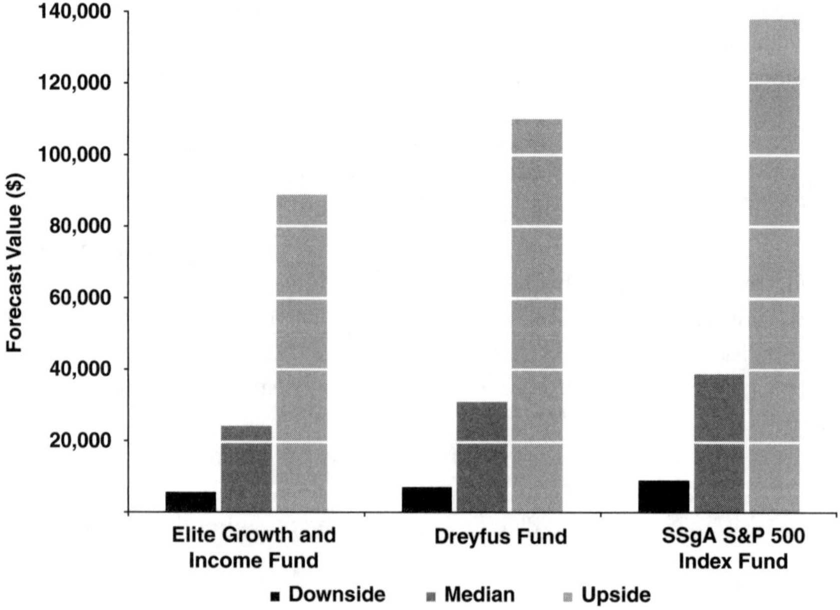

FIGURE 7.2 Simulation Results for Three Large-Cap Equity Funds over a 25-year Horizon

Source: Financial Engines calculations as of May 2007.

fund over a 10-year horizon. These are significant differences in wealth accumulation.

Over a longer horizon, the differences become even more striking. Figure 7.2 shows the chart for a 25-year investment horizon. With the impact of compounding over a longer time period, the differences in ending wealth outcomes for the three funds are far greater.

The lowest expense fund has a median outcome that is 60 percent higher than the higher-expense Elite Growth & Income Fund ($38,800 versus $24,200). Think about that for a moment. The difference between paying an expense ratio of 0.18 percent versus 1.39 percent is approximately 60 percent in higher median wealth measured over 25 years. Most people would regard an outcome with 60 percent higher wealth as *much* better. In fact, there are very few opportunities in the investing world where you can get 60 percent higher expected wealth without taking on significantly higher risk. Paying less in expenses is easy and requires no skill, yet the benefits are tremendous over long time horizons.

Now expense ratios alone do not account for all the differences in the observed forecasts (implicit costs due to portfolio turnover and manager performance had a modest impact as well), but it is clear that higher expenses mean lower wealth accumulation potential. Expenses have a highly predictive and substantial impact on future expected returns for mutual funds.

PRACTICAL CONSIDERATIONS

When selecting funds and managing your assets, it pays to devote substantial attention to the costs of investing. Unlike many types of products, the fees associated with investment funds directly detract from the net value you receive. This does not imply that the cheapest investment fund will always be the best choice (as we will see in Chapter 9, there is more to selecting good funds than fees alone). But it does mean that paying incremental investment fees without comparable value being provided in return is something to be avoided. Make sure the fees are reasonable and that you fully understand how the fees you pay add up. If you decide to purchase a fund with a higher expense ratio or a load charge, be sure you understand the value that you are receiving for the additional fees.

Here are a few pitfalls to avoid when considering investment fees:

- Avoid equity funds with high levels of turnover (more than 150 percent per year). To check, consult the web for statistics on the fund's rate of turnover. High fund turnover dramatically increases the implicit costs embedded in mutual funds, particularly for equity funds and international funds. You won't find these costs explicitly stated in a prospectus (at least not yet), but they still have a big impact on future expected returns. Bond fund turnover is less of a concern as the costs of trading are usually much lower.
- Beware of sweep accounts in brokerage accounts (the fund that your money defaults to when you don't specify a destination). Don't allow large amounts of your money to sit around in high-expense sweep money market or cash accounts. These accounts are often highly profitable for brokerage firms. You can often do better by explicitly moving your money into less expensive options when you sell positions.
- Try to avoid purchases of transaction fee funds, unless your transaction is of significant size. For small transactions, these fees can be a crushing burden to your returns. As a rule of thumb, your transaction costs should

be less than 1 percent of your total purchase for any transaction. For instance, if it costs $25 to purchase a fund, make sure you are buying at least $2,500 of the fund at one time. This, of course, means that you almost always want to avoid transaction fee funds when setting up a periodic investing plan.

- Avoid front-end or back-end load funds unless your horizon is lengthy and you don't plan to sell the position for at least 10 years. Even if held for five years, a fund with an up-front load fee of 5 percent is substantially more expensive than a comparable no-load fund choice. The only exception to this rule would be if the advisory services you expect to receive from your advisor or broker outweigh the additional fees. However, if you are paying your advisor with commissions based on load charges, be aware that they may have conflicts of interest both in terms of the funds they recommend and how often they will recommend a change in your portfolio holdings.

Unlike institutional investors, most individuals don't pay much attention to the costs of investing. *Yet, investment expenses have the biggest impact on your ability to accumulate wealth.* Don't fall into the trap of seeing your rightful share of investment earnings end up in the pockets of others. It is hard enough to stay afloat on the roiling seas of investment markets without the added weight of high expenses. Do yourself a favor and pack light for the voyage.

TAKE-AWAYS

- Investing without consideration of the costs and their impact on your returns is extremely unwise.
- Given the alternatives available today, you should generally avoid equity funds with expense ratios above 1.00 percent. For bond funds, avoid expense ratios above 0.75 percent. If the fund is passively managed, you should not be paying more than 0.40 percent per year in fund expenses.
- You should never pay more than 0.50 percent per year for a money market fund if you can avoid it.
- Avoid equity funds with high turnover (more than 150 percent per year). The high turnover increases the total costs of the fund. Turnover ratios are readily available from several online sources, including Yahoo! Finance and Google Finance.

- Don't purchase funds with front-end or back-end investment loads if you can avoid them, particularly if you don't plan to hold the fund for at least 10 years. You are generally better off selecting comparable no load funds, or paying an advisor an explicit flat or asset-based investment advisory fee for advice or management. This allows you to avoid conflicts of interest that can compromise the quality of advice that you receive.
- Take advantage of institutionally priced products if you can get them through your employer retirement plan. Many large companies offer very attractively priced funds in their defined contribution plans. Institutional fund expenses are typically only 10 percent–50 percent of comparable retail mutual fund expenses. If you can invest in such funds, they often represent an excellent value.

CHAPTER 8

Smart Diversification

A man sits as many risks as he runs.
—Henry David Thoreau (1817–1862) *Walden*

Diversification is an extremely important part of good investing practice. However, the concept is also often misunderstood and misapplied. Being diversified means taking only those risks that come with expected rewards. Building a well-diversified portfolio is critical to a successful long-term investment strategy. Getting it right requires understanding the benefits of diversification as well as how factors like costs, other household assets, and the types of investments available to you influence portfolio decisions. There is more to good diversification than simply matching an asset class pie chart. In this chapter, we explore the keys to an effective approach to portfolio diversification.

When it comes to the investment literature, the concept of diversification is generally lumped in with the flag, apple pie, Tiger Woods, and dear old Mom as "things that are undeniably good." Indeed, proper diversification is an important characteristic for any well-designed investment strategy. Why is diversification so important? *Because a properly diversified portfolio means you are only taking risks for which you are likely to be rewarded.* To the economist, diversification means getting rid of unnecessary risk. If you are not properly diversified, you could be getting more return for your level of risk, or correspondingly, you could lower your risk without reducing your expected return. Put another way, when you are improperly diversified, you are making bets that have no expected benefit—you are just assuming more risk. It is like getting your paycheck from your boss, but then deciding to flip coins on the side for plus or minus 10 percent of your pay. You may get lucky if the outcome works out in your favor, but on average, you are as likely to lose as you are to win. There is no expected value to the additional risk. Unless you are an inveterate gambler, you would probably prefer to just get the paycheck and avoid the unnecessary coin flipping.

However, taken to an extreme, striving for complete portfolio diversification can actually hurt investment performance. When you seek investment advice from a professional advisor, asset class diversification is usually the starting point for the conversation. Sometimes it seems like asset class diversification is the only topic worth discussing. Among many advisors, it has become almost religious dogma that asset class diversification is the most important factor in investment decision-making. Certainly, appropriate asset class diversification is important. But it is not the only thing that matters. Investment costs, the quality of investment options, and restrictions on the types of investments you hold can have a big impact on the most appropriate strategy for diversification. More troubling, asset class diversification is a commonly used rationalization to sell investors funds and investment products that are unneeded or inappropriate.

THE GOALS OF DIVERSIFICATION

The basic goals of any diversification strategy are to take the minimum amount of risk required to get a desired expected return and to only take risks that provide additional expected return. You cannot eliminate investment risk with a diversified strategy, but you can mitigate the impact of bad outcomes by spreading out your exposures to more than one type of asset. The idea is that if something bad happens in the market that impacts one part of your portfolio, your other investments in different asset classes may be spared the same fate. Appropriately allocated, a well-diversified portfolio will have risk exposures that partially offset one another. Since it is unlikely that unrelated risks would all break the same way, a diversified portfolio gains added protection by spreading its bets across assets with lower correlations. The risk that is left over is the fundamental market risk, which cannot be diversified away no matter how many funds, bonds, or stocks you own. Diversified portfolios are less susceptible to damage from a single part of the market blowing up.

An important attribute of diversification is the necessity of thinking about it at the highest level—the household portfolio. Too often, investors make the mistake of evaluating the diversification of their assets at the account level. For instance, you might think your 401(k) is appropriately diversified, but fail to consider the impact of the significant cash position in your savings account, or the holdings of company stock from your *Employee*

Stock Purchase Plan. Viewed in the aggregate, it is quite possible that your portfolio could be seriously out of whack. Diversification is a holistic concept; it only makes sense when viewed in terms of your entire portfolio. That is not to say that there is anything wrong with diversifying individual accounts on a stand-alone basis, but the real test of whether a portfolio is adequately diversified depends on the characteristics of the household mix, not an individual account.

THE BIG PICTURE

To get started, we will examine the difference between diversification at the account level and at the household level and how fund quality can play a role in asset allocation decisions. In Chapter 5, I presented target asset class allocations to maximize the expected return for each level of risk in a world where you could invest directly in the asset classes themselves (or equivalently in low-cost index funds that mimic asset classes). These optimal mixes were based on market consensus expectations for expected returns based on data as of January 2007. Table 8.1 illustrates the composition of these efficient portfolios across the risk spectrum. Remember that a portfolio of risk 1.0 on this scale has the same volatility as the overall market portfolio.

Of course, as the market portfolio shifts over time, these efficient allocations will adjust with changes in the market proportions of different asset classes. But these changes tend to occur gradually over time, so Table 8.1 illustrates reasonable portfolios in a world where you have a very wide choice of options available to you.[1] Note that these proportions would be desirable for an overall household portfolio and would not necessarily be appropriate for individual accounts. An example makes this point more clear.

TABLE 8.1 Efficient Asset Mixes for Different Levels of Risk

Portfolio Risk Level	0.2	0.4	0.6	0.8	1.0	1.2	1.4	1.5
Cash	100%	35%	25%	4%	0%	0%	0%	0%
Bonds	0%	55%	42%	50%	35%	19%	0%	0%
Large-Cap Stocks	0%	6%	17%	29%	33%	38%	43%	33%
International Stocks	0%	4%	14%	17%	20%	22%	29%	20%
Small- and Mid-Cap Stocks	0%	0%	2%	0%	12%	21%	28%	47%

Source: Financial Engines
Calculations based on January 2007 data.

Consider a working couple, Bill and Hillary (names have been changed to protect the innocent), each of whom has a 401(k) plan through their respective employers. Bill is working for a small consulting company with a small 401(k) plan comprised of relatively costly mutual fund choices. Hillary, on the other hand, works for a large company with an excellent 401(k) plan consisting of institutionally priced funds covering a range of asset classes. Both have $200,000 invested in their accounts and both agree that they would like to aim for a target risk of 1.0, or the risk equivalent to the overall market portfolio given their planned retirement date in about 10 years.

The catch is that Bill's plan has a decent large-capitalization U.S. equity option, but only mediocre cash, bond, small-capitalization equity, and international equity funds to choose from. His bond options are high priced and poor performers. His international option has similar poor performance and high fees. On the other hand, Hillary has excellent fund options across the board to choose from, with good performance and very low fees relative to Bill's 401(k) plan.

To examine the impact on optimal allocations for Bill and Hillary, we will use the Financial Engines *Personal Online Advisor* service to generate recommendations. This analysis reflects both the asset allocation and the fund-specific characteristics of each account. First, let's consider what the optimal allocations should look like if we considered each account separately, taking into consideration the respective quality of the fund options available to Bill and Hillary. At a target risk level of 1.0, Bill's desired allocation is shown in Table 8.2.

Bill should invest some money in bonds but a bit less than he might if better fixed-income options were available. Since the bond options in his plan are less desirable, Bill is better off putting more money in the

TABLE 8.2 Recommended Allocation for Bill's 401(k) Account in Isolation

Asset Class	Allocation at Risk 1.0
Cash	8%
Bonds	27%
Large-Cap Stocks	48%
International Stocks	15%
Small- and Mid-Cap Stocks	2%

Source: Financial Engines calculations.

cash and equity options in the plan to achieve the desired level of risk. Relative to the ideal allocations in Table 8.1, he is also underweighted in international equities and small-cap equities and overweighted in large-cap domestic equity. Because the quality of the options providing exposure to international and small-cap equity are poor in his plan, it makes sense these asset classes would be less desirable to Bill. It does not mean he should ignore the value of asset class diversification, but the high costs of these asset classes alters the optimal fund mix to achieve the highest expected return at a 1.0 risk level. The portfolio optimizer takes into consideration the quality of the options in determining the appropriate allocation of the funds in Bill's plan (more on this later).

When it comes to adjusting a target allocation based on the quality and cost of the available funds, it is worth noting that *relative differences* are what matter. For instance, if your 401(k) plan charges an administrative wrap fee of 0.25 percent on all assets to pay for recordkeeping services, this fee would have no impact on the target allocation. Why? Because the fee impacts all the options in the plan in the same way. Only when there are relative differences between the options does it make sense to adjust the target asset allocation. Of course, most of the time, there are significant relative differences between the fund options available in an account.

As for Hillary, her plan is pretty strong across all the asset classes. Table 8.3 demonstrates an optimal allocation for her plan if it were considered in isolation.

As you can see, Hillary's optimal allocations look a lot more like the example in Table 8.1, where it is possible to invest directly in the underlying asset classes. She does not have any cash exposure, and her bond, domestic equity, and international equity allocations look similar to the ideal case. The reason for this is that she is able to achieve high-quality exposures to each

TABLE 8.3 Recommended Allocation for Hillary's 401(k) Account in Isolation

Asset Class	Allocation at Risk 1.0
Cash	0%
Bonds	36%
Large-Cap Stocks	36%
International Stocks	19%
Small- and Mid-Cap Stocks	9%

Source: Financial Engines calculations.

of the asset classes through her plan at low cost (unlike her less fortunate husband). This means that there is little reason to alter her target allocation based on the relative quality of the options. She is able to maximize her expected return without compromising asset class diversification.

Now let's look at how the allocations are impacted by considering the two accounts together. What happens when we consider the two accounts not in isolation but as a total household portfolio? If we consider the two accounts as part of the same household, then the portfolio optimizer can consider the possibility of holding some types of assets in one account, and different allocations in the other. This provides an important additional degree of flexibility. Even if one account has no good options in a particular asset class, the optimization can still achieve a diversified household portfolio by placing certain asset exposures in one account and different assets in the other account.

If we assume that Bill and Hillary optimize their household portfolio across both accounts, we get the following allocations, as shown in Table 8.4.

The joint allocation of the total household portfolio in the right hand column looks pretty similar to the target allocation for risk 1.0, assuming you could invest directly in the asset classes. The only significant difference is the somewhat higher cash exposure. But look at the allocations for Bill and Hillary's accounts individually. Since Bill has poor international and small-cap options in his plan, the optimization gets those exposures almost entirely from Hillary's account. Doing this while hitting the overall target risk level of 1.0 requires moving more of the desired bond exposure over to Bill's account. Here the value of getting the high-quality international and small-cap exposure in Hillary's account outweighs the penalty of using some of Bill's mediocre bond funds. The 10 percent cash exposure shows the impact of the poor bond funds, since it becomes advantageous to increase

TABLE 8.4 Recommended Joint Allocation for Hillary's and Bill's 401(k) Accounts

Asset Class	Bill's Allocation	Hillary's Allocation	Joint Household Allocation at 1.0 Risk
Cash	20%	0%	10%
Bonds	44%	6%	25%
Large-Cap Stocks	36%	36%	36%
International Stocks	0%	41%	20%
Small- and Mid-Cap Stocks	0%	17%	9%

Source: Financial Engines calculations.

exposures to cash and equity rather than bonds to get the same level of risk. What is striking about the two portfolios is that they have substantially different risk levels. Hillary's account has a risk of about 1.3, while Bill's is much more conservative at about 0.8 times market risk. If you blindly were applying the standard 1.0 risk allocation to both accounts, the overall efficiency of the household portfolio would suffer. By taking into account the relative quality of the options across the two accounts, you can construct a better portfolio.

WHY HIERARCHY IS BAD FOR PORTFOLIOS

I'm going to let you in on a dirty little secret in the financial services industry. The standard process for ensuring asset class diversification often results in building a portfolio of less than desirable funds. How? Because it creates the impression that you need to fill in every one of those pie chart slices with the "best" fund of that asset class, and often these funds come with high fees or load charges that actually harm the overall quality of your portfolio. Many of these abuses occur not because of bad intentions, but simply because the advisor or broker is following a flawed process.

When you visit an advisor or a broker, chances are you will be asked to complete a risk tolerance questionnaire of some sort. Based on your answers to these questions, you will be assigned a recommended model portfolio—a generic target asset allocation. No matter what your other assets are, or what options you have to choose from, if you answer the questions in the same way, you will typically get the same model asset class portfolio. The process then shifts to identifying investments to achieve this target asset allocation.

When this approach is followed, the portfolio construction process is being divided into two distinct and separate steps—asset allocation followed by investment selection. Among economists, this process is known as *hierarchical asset allocation* because there is a rigid hierarchy of steps—first asset allocation, and then fund selection. There are a few problems with this approach. First, the target asset allocation ignores the actual funds you can choose from. Instead, it is based on the assumption that you can invest directly in the underlying asset classes, or equivalently in zero-cost index funds. However, you almost never get to invest in zero-cost index funds, but instead in a range of mutual funds with varying fees, different degrees of active management, and diverse levels of performance. In fact, these available investments usually have markedly different risk-and-return characteristics than a zero-cost index fund. If the risk-and-return characteristics of the assets available to you are different, then the target asset allocation needs to be adjusted to account for these differences.

Second, the hierarchical method assumes that funds can be categorized into single asset classes. This is rarely the case. In fact, most funds have a mix of underlying asset class exposures. A large-cap growth fund might have significant exposure to mid-cap stocks or even value stocks. A global fund might have a mix of domestic and international exposures. And certainly a balanced fund or lifecycle fund will have a mix of asset class exposures. But the hierarchical model does not know what to do with these multi-asset class funds. They don't fit neatly into any of the pie slices and thus they create a problem. Usually such products are simply excluded from the choice set or they are categorized according to their largest asset class exposure. Of course, this means you may end up with a very different asset allocation than intended when finished with filling in the slices of the pie.

Third, the hierarchical method treats the asset allocation decision as *infinitely* more important than the investment selection decision. That is, no matter what the quality or costs of the investment options available to you, with the hierarchical model, achieving the target asset allocation is paramount. You could have the worst bond funds in the world to choose from, but your target asset allocation would still say to hold bonds if that is consistent with your risk preferences. This is inherently suboptimal. With the hierarchical approach, the selection of investments is conditional on a potentially bad target allocation decision made under unrealistic assumptions. The result is often a less than optimal portfolio.

Finally, the whole process of hierarchical asset allocation is tilted toward selecting narrowly focused (single asset class), actively managed, and often expensive funds. Why? Because the selection process typically focuses on selecting the best fund option for each slice in the asset allocation pie. Usually "best" is defined as the fund with the best historical performance in its asset class. For any given asset class in any given time period, the best historically performing fund is almost always an actively managed and often relatively expensive fund. Low-cost index funds will almost never be at the top of the performance list because they are designed to match the return of their asset class, not beat it. In any given time period, some active funds will do well and some will do poorly, but there will almost always be some active funds that do well and end up at the top of the performance list. If your advisor ranks on past performance, these will be the funds you select regardless of whether there is any reason to believe that such performance will be repeated in the future (usually it won't). Actively managed funds, particularly those that are narrowly focused on a specific asset class and have lots of fund-specific risk, tend to be higher priced than other funds. With the hierarchical asset allocation process you often end up with a portfolio of many actively managed and high-fee funds to achieve your target asset allocation. In fact, you might have been much better off with a selection of more broad-based index funds to achieve a diversified portfolio. But the hierarchical process does not facilitate such decisions.

Why do so many investors and financial professionals use the hierarchical approach? Well for one, it's pretty simple to explain. You pick an asset allocation target and then you pick some funds. But another reason has to do with the power of conventional wisdom.

In 1986 Gary Brinson, Randolph Hood, and Gilbert Beebower wrote a very influential paper in the *Financial Analysts Journal*. This study evaluated the performance of 82 pension plans in the late 1980s to see what factors accounted for the variation in returns among the different funds. The study determined that 94 percent of the *variance* in returns could be explained by the underlying asset allocation strategy of the plans. Variance is a measure of how much a value moves around its average value. In this case, the returns of the pension funds tended to move in the same direction of the underlying asset allocation the vast majority of the time. This seems like a very powerful finding. However, the significance of this study is frequently misunderstood. While asset class exposures explain a large percentage of the variation in fund returns (at least for broadly diversified pension funds), they do not explain a similarly high percentage of the *level of returns* for many assets. When you invest in an asset, it is important to consider both the level of returns (the mean) as well as the variation (volatility). Most funds held by individual investors have risk-and-return characteristics that are very different from the performance of asset classes. An example makes this point evident.

Consider an S&P 500 index fund that charges 10 basis points (0.10 percent) in management expenses. An investor in this fund could expect to receive the performance of the U.S. large-cap equity asset class, less the cost of owning the fund. Now consider an otherwise identical fund with a 150 basis point expense ratio (1.50 percent). In both cases, the asset class exposures of the fund (large-cap equity) explain approximately 100 percent of the variation in returns. *Yet, the two funds have very different expected returns due to the difference in expenses*. Over a 25-year horizon, the cheaper fund would be expected to yield a median portfolio value about 40 percent higher than the more expensive fund, adjusted for inflation and net of fees. Obviously, differences of this magnitude in median outcomes are highly relevant to financial planning decisions. Despite the fact that the asset allocation fully described the variation in returns for both funds, it failed to differentiate the enormous gap in performance due to expenses. This is a crucial flaw in the conventional wisdom that asset allocation explains 90 percent of the performance of a portfolio. It does not. For diversified portfolios, asset allocation might explain 90 percent or more of the *variance* in returns, but it says nothing about the level of performance. As an investor, you care about the level of performance a great deal.

The key issue here is that stocks and mutual funds held by individual investors have several characteristics that cause their performance to differ, sometimes dramatically, from their underlying asset class exposures. In addition to expenses and transaction costs, actively managed mutual funds often have additional risk due to changes in investment style or sector concentration (e.g., technology stocks). Individual stocks have dramatically higher risk than their asset class category due to company- and industry-specific risk factors. And finally, taxes can have a significant impact on the number of dollars a strategy may yield in the future for a given investor. An asset allocation strategy that is blind to these differences is very likely to give you the wrong answer. *The next time your broker or advisor makes the claim that investing is 90 percent about asset allocation, challenge this thinking.* Asset class diversification is important, but so is appropriate investment selection, especially when it comes to considering the impact of fees, manager performance, and taxes.

So how does this approach sometimes lead to bad advice? Often, a target asset class allocation will be broken down into narrowly defined investment categories. For instance, there might be a target for large-cap value, large-cap growth, mid-cap, small-cap, and so on. For each asset class category, there is a corresponding slice of the allocation pie that needs to be filled in. This makes it easy for the broker or advisor to focus on filling in the slices of the pie, rather than on evaluating the cost and quality of the fund options. If you slice up the investment world into smaller categories, it becomes more convenient to justify the need for a separate fund to achieve each asset class exposure. When asset class diversification is defined as the supreme objective, you can rationalize constructing the portfolio with narrowly defined and perhaps more expensive funds in order to meet the target allocation. Certainly many advisors understand these issues and make sure that their clients are building their portfolios with high-quality funds. But it is easy to convince a naïve investor that he or she needs an overpriced small-cap value fund with good past performance to complete their target allocation, regardless of whether the fund would actually improve the overall expected return and risk of the portfolio. The argument boils down to "if investing is 90 percent asset allocation" then "fund selection and expenses aren't that important." This is wrong. Appropriate fund selection matters a great deal in portfolio construction. As we will see in the next section, there are significant limits to the value of asset class diversification.

THE VALUE OF ASSET CLASS DIVERSIFICATION

Asset class diversification is a very desirable goal in portfolio construction. Having exposure to multiple asset classes decreases the risk of a single market sector doing damage to your portfolio. It also allows you to achieve the highest level of expected return for a given level of risk. An efficient portfolio (the highest return for that level of risk) will generally have exposures to multiple asset classes, unless you are at the extremes of the risk spectrum. But like everything in life, asset class diversification has its limits. Using the techniques of modern portfolio theory, it is possible to calculate and quantify the benefits of asset class diversification. The results of this analysis may surprise you.

To shed some light on this subject, consider an experiment where an investor has the ability to invest in any of the 15 asset classes used in the Financial Engines advice model.[2] These 15 asset classes represent the majority of investments held by individual investors. One way of calculating the value of asset class diversification is to ask the question: what if our investor could invest in all the asset classes except one? For instance, suppose the investor had the ability to invest in any of the 15 asset classes except for small-cap value stocks. What is the penalty associated with the inability to get small-cap value exposure in a portfolio?

First, a little background. The expected value of asset class diversification can be measured in terms of annual expected return. If you think about the range of efficient portfolios with the highest expected return for each level of risk, removing the ability to invest in one or more asset classes reduces the expected return of the set of efficient portfolios. In other words, the expected return that was attainable with all the asset classes may no longer be reachable when one or more of them are removed from consideration. The amount that the frontier drops can be measured in terms of expected return. One can then compare the cost in expected return with other types of costs—for instance, mutual fund expense ratios. If an asset class is missing, then a sophisticated portfolio optimizer will substitute other combinations of asset class exposures in order to get as close to the unconstrained portfolio expected return as possible for that level of risk. It is important to note that these estimates reflect the *expected* value of asset class diversification. In any given time period, the actual realized value of having exposure to that asset class could be higher or lower than the expected value. Of course, there is no way to know beforehand which way the market will move.

Obviously, the cost of losing access to a particular asset class depends on the target risk level of the desired portfolio. If you are very risk averse and are interested in a portfolio of cash and bonds, then there is very little cost to eliminating small-cap growth equity as an option since you would not want to hold it anyway. Similarly, the inability to invest in short-term bonds represents no penalty for an investor who desires a portfolio with 100 percent equity exposure.

So what is the value of asset class diversification? Table 8.5 provides some estimates of the maximum loss in expected return for excluding various asset classes based on the Financial Engines asset class model.

For each asset class, Table 8.5 shows the corresponding maximum loss in expected return across different levels of risk. Note that these values are rounded to two decimal places. To read the table, pick an asset class and

TABLE 8.5 Estimation of the Value of Asset Class Diversification

Asset Class	Maximum Loss in Expected Return
Cash	0.24%
Intermediate Bonds	0.02%
Long-Term Bonds	0.00%
Corporate Bonds	0.01%
Mortgage Bonds	0.02%
Non-U.S. Bonds	0.01%
Large-Value Equity	0.06%
Large-Growth Equity	0.05%
Mid-Value Equity	0.05%
Mid-Growth Equity	0.05%
Small-Value Equity	0.01%
Small-Growth Equity	0.01%
European Equity	0.04%
Pacific Rim Equity	0.02%
Emerging Markets Equity	0.02%

Source: Financial Engines calculations.

look at the number in the right hand column. For instance, if you had to give up the ability to invest in mid-cap growth stocks, but could invest in anything else, you would be foregoing a maximum of about 0.05 percent or 5 basis points of expected return, depending on your target risk level. Across the spectrum of 15 asset classes, the annual costs of giving up the ability to invest in a given asset class ranges from less than 0.01 percent to 0.24 percent (1 to 24 basis points).

If this does not sound like much of a penalty, you are right. The reality is that you can do almost as well by combining other available asset classes (like mid-cap value and small-cap growth) to compensate for the missing mid-cap growth. The low magnitudes of these estimates are surprising, even to experienced advisors. A standard assumption is that asset class diversification has a large impact on estimated portfolio expected returns. However, as you can see, the expected return impact of giving up a single asset class is considerably less dramatic than you might expect.

The most important asset class, at least for low risk levels, is actually cash (or very short-term fixed income). If you don't have access to the cash asset class, you cannot even achieve the lowest portfolio risk levels. At slightly higher risk levels you pay a penalty of up to about 0.24 percent of your expected return. The next most valuable asset class in the table is large-cap value equity at 0.06 percent. The other asset classes have even less incremental value to the overall portfolio's expected return.

What is going on here? The short answer is that asset classes generally have relatively high correlations with one another. For instance, mid-cap growth stocks are highly correlated with large-cap growth and small-cap growth stocks. When mid-cap growth stocks go up, chances are that large-cap and small-cap growth stocks increase as well. Intermediate-term government bonds and mortgage bonds are also very highly correlated, as are corporate and intermediate-term government bonds. The correlations are not perfect, but they are good enough so that if one asset class is missing, an optimizer can mostly compensate by leveraging the other available asset classes. You pay a bit of a penalty for not being able to invest in a specific asset class, but in general the cost is relatively low on a forward-looking basis. The results in Table 8.5 evaluated relatively narrowly defined asset classes. What if we bundle up the results into somewhat larger categories?

Table 8.6 illustrates the results for somewhat more broadly defined asset classes.

TABLE 8.6 Estimation of the Value of Asset Class Diversification with Broad Asset Classes

Asset Class	Maximum Loss in Expected Return
Cash	0.24%
Bonds	0.23%
Large-Cap Equity	0.06%
Mid-Cap Equity	0.05%
Small-Cap Equity	0.01%
International Equity	0.10%

Source: Financial Engines calculations.

Even when we aggregate the narrow asset classes from Table 8.5 into broader definitions, we still see that removing an asset class from consideration has a relatively modest impact on portfolio efficiency. If you lacked the ability to invest in any kind of bonds of greater than one-year maturity, you would be giving up a maximum of only 0.23 percent of expected return, depending on your risk level. As we saw in Chapter 7, fund expense ratios can easily vary by multiples of 0.23 percent and thus dominate the expected return benefits of additional asset class diversification. On the equity side of the ledger, the costs of skipping specific asset classes are even more modest. As long as you have the ability to invest in some type of equity, the benefits of having access to multiple classes of equity based on market capitalization is limited. For instance, the cost of not being able to invest in small-cap U.S. equity as an asset class will only cost you about 0.01 percent of your expected return. Not being able to invest in international equity costs the U.S.-based investor only about 0.10 percent in expected return.

Interestingly, value and growth stocks are somewhat less correlated, and so the cost of not being able to invest in growth or value equities is a bit more than missing a category based on company size. However, in all cases, the expected cost of missing a specific asset class in a portfolio is fairly modest.

While these specific estimates for the value of asset class diversification are based on the assumptions implicit in the Financial Engines factor model, you will get very similar results for a wide range of other possible model assumptions. Unless you assume that different equity asset classes have very low correlations (which is contradicted by the available empirical and historical evidence), the benefits of spreading your investments across multiple equity asset classes can generally be measured in a handful of expected basis points.

To be fair, there may be other reasons why you would prefer to hold a broadly diversified asset class portfolio other than maximizing expected return for a given level of volatility. For instance, you might take the point of view that there are certain economic conditions that might cause big dislocations in the performance of asset classes that normally have high correlations. If there were the possibility of such events, then erring on the side of more asset class diversification would make sense. This argument probably has more credence for diversifying across domestic and international equity asset classes. It is at least plausible that there might be conditions under which the performance of domestic and foreign stock markets may significantly diverge in times of economic stress, though this is increasingly unlikely with continuing global integration of financial markets.

DIVERSIFICATION AIN'T WHAT IT USED TO BE

All of this is to say that the benefits of asset class diversification depend on how correlated the underlying asset classes are. In a world where you are investing in assets that don't move together very often, the benefit of diversification can be considerable. But if all the investment choices available to you always tend to move together, say with the global market portfolio, the benefit of diversifying across multiple investments is going to be muted. This may sound like a bad thing for investors, but it really suggests that the need for diversification is less pronounced than it used to be. Decades ago, it was possible to find markets where the correlations with the overall global market were relatively low (e.g., developing countries). While there are still stock markets with relatively low correlations with the overall global market, they are increasingly hard to come by. The culprit is globalization of trade and the integration of financial markets. As the economies of various countries become increasingly integrated with the world market, the opportunities for diversification, at least across the equities of different countries, become less prevalent. The headlines today are filled with stories of how events in one market have an impact in markets across the globe. For instance, the sub-prime mortgage crisis in the United States in 2007 had ramifications for financial service firms and monetary policy around the globe. It is becoming increasingly difficult to find asset classes or different countries with low correlations with the overall global market. When assets are more highly correlated, then you don't need as many of them to create a diversified portfolio. And in the future, we should expect the assets of different countries to become even more highly correlated.

This does not mean that the overall risk of investing is increasing, but merely that investment opportunities are becoming increasingly dependent on the fortunes of the overall global market and less related to the idiosyncratic factors of a particular sector or region. So while the opportunity for asset class diversification is diminishing for investors, there is also less need for it. In fact, some economists argue that increasing global integration is reducing the risk of the overall market, pushing asset values higher (and expected returns lower). Remember: you cannot diversify away the risk of the global market and it is this risk that generates expected returns. It is likely in the future that the fortunes of the global market will have an increasingly big impact on your personal portfolio outcomes.

DIVERSIFICATION AND INVESTMENT CHOICES

Now that we have covered the basic concepts, let's examine some portfolio examples to understand how the quality and costs of your investment choices should impact your desired asset allocation.

Consider a 401(k) investor; we'll call her Nancy, who has an account with a $100,000 balance. We'll assume that Nancy is interested in a portfolio with moderate risk, aiming for a target of 1.10 times the risk of the market portfolio. To keep things simple, we'll assume that Nancy can invest in a group of low-cost passive bond and domestic equity funds from Fidelity. The goal of this example is to demonstrate how the availability of international fund options of varying quality and costs has an impact on the desired portfolio allocation.

First, consider the case that best approximates a world where Nancy can invest directly in the underlying asset classes. We will use this lineup to develop a baseline allocation for comparison purposes. In the baseline case, the fund options in Nancy's plan are a spectrum of passive Fidelity funds, including a very low-cost international index fund, the Spartan International

TABLE 8.7 Recommended Fund Allocation for Nancy's 401(k) Account

Fund	Efficient Allocation at Risk 1.10
Fidelity Government MM Fund	0%
Fidelity Spartan Intermediate Treasury Bond Index	0%
Fidelity Spartan Long-Term Treasury Bond Index	29%
Fidelity Spartan International Index	24%
Fidelity Spartan 500 Index	33%
Fidelity Spartan Extended Market Index	14%

Source: Financial Engines calculations.

Index fund (symbol: FSIIX). This lineup approximates what you might see if you worked for a larger employer with institutionally priced fund options. The other funds in the lineup include a money market fund, intermediate and long-term government bond funds, an S&P 500 index fund, and an extended market index fund providing small- and mid-cap domestic equity exposures. With this lineup, Nancy can get low-cost exposures to each of the desired asset classes. Because the available asset class exposures are based on low-cost options, this lineup provides a clear test of the desirability of different asset classes when an investment vehicle has characteristics that are different from the asset class itself.

Table 8.7 shows the lineup of funds in Nancy's account and the target allocation to achieve an efficient portfolio at a risk level of 1.10.

As you can see in Table 8.7, the optimal allocation for the risk 1.10 portfolio includes exposures to bonds, domestic equities, and a sizable commitment to international equities. Given the ability to invest in all asset classes with high-quality, low-cost options, Nancy would be prudent to select a highly diversified portfolio that combines multiple asset class exposures. Table 8.8 shows the corresponding asset allocation of the risk 1.10 portfolio allocation.

The underlying asset exposures of this fund lineup predictably match the declared objectives of each fund. So in the case where Nancy can choose from the full spectrum of asset classes with high quality and reasonably priced options, we see a target allocation that is balanced among bonds, domestic equity, and international equity.

But what if the choices were not so clear cut? What if the only international option in Nancy's account was a bit more expensive and had poorer historical performance?

TABLE 8.8 Recommended Asset Allocation for Nancy's 401(k) Account

Asset Class	Portfolio Allocation at Risk 1.1
Cash	0%
Bonds	29%
Large-Cap Equity	33%
International Equity	24%
Small/Mid-Cap Equity	14%

Source: Financial Engines calculations.

For instance, at the time of this writing, the Schwab International Index Fund (symbol: SWISX) from the Schwab Funds family has an expense ratio of 0.50 percent per year (compared to 0.10 percent for the Fidelity Spartan International Index fund), and has somewhat negative historical performance relative to its investment style. However, based on the Financial Engines peer ranking, this fund would still be expected to outperform approximately 97 percent of its peers with similar investment styles on a forward-looking basis. What does the optimal allocation look like with the Schwab International Index Fund substituted for the low cost Fidelity Spartan International Index Fund as the plan's international equity choice? Table 8.9 shows the results of the modified fund lineup for Nancy's 401(k) plan.

Here we see a modest difference in the overall allocation, with the international fund getting a 20 percent allocation at the target risk level of 1.10. Despite the higher cost of the international fund, it still makes

TABLE 8.9 Recommended Fund Allocation for Nancy's modified 401(k) Account

Fund	Efficient Allocation at Risk 1.10
Fidelity Government MM Fund	0%
Fidelity Spartan Intermediate Treasury Bond Index	0%
Fidelity Spartan Long-Term Treasury Bond Index	30%
Schwab International Index Fund	20%
Fidelity Spartan 500 Index	35%
Fidelity Spartan Extended Market Index	15%

Source: Financial Engines calculations.

TABLE 8.10 Recommended Fund Allocation for Nancy's modified 401(k) Account

Fund	Efficient Allocation at Risk 1.1
Fidelity Government MM Fund	0%
Fidelity Spartan Intermediate Treasury Bond Index	0%
Fidelity Spartan Long-Term Treasury Bond Index	35%
SSgA International Stock Selection Fund	6%
Fidelity Spartan 500 Index	35%
Fidelity Spartan Extended Market Index	24%

Source: Financial Engines calculations.

sense to hold a portfolio of the assets in international equity. However, the optimal target allocation to international equities is lower due to the impact of the higher fund fees and lower predicted performance. On balance, the lower predicted performance of the Schwab fund reduces the desirability of holding international equities from 24 percent to 20 percent at the target risk level of 1.10.

But what if the fund was replaced by an even more expensive international fund choice?

Table 8.10 shows the optimization results for a portfolio where the international option is exchanged for the SSgA International Stock Selection Fund (symbol: SSAIX), an actively managed international equity fund with an expense ratio of 1.00 percent.

Here the allocations look quite different from the baseline case. The allocation to international equities is much lower, at about 6 percent of the total portfolio. Instead of holding international equities, the optimization places more money into the S&P 500 index, small-, and mid-cap domestic equities to achieve the highest return for the target level of risk. Why does the optimization retain 6 percent and not zero? Because there are diminishing benefits to getting exposures to asset classes as the proportion increases. The first little bit of international exposure is more valuable than the last little bit. So even though the international exposure is expensive relative to the domestic equity choices, it still pays to have a little bit of international allocation.

Even though the SSgA International Stock Selection Fund is a pretty good fund, expected to outperform about 85 percent of its peer group, it is still substantially more expensive than the domestic equity options in the plan (which average about 0.10 percent per year). The Financial Engines peer group ranking takes into account the expense ratio, turnover and trading costs, manager performance, and the level of active risk in the fund. With an expense ratio of 1.00 percent per year, it costs about 0.90 percent more to get international exposure in this lineup than it does to get domestic equity exposure. As we saw in the previous section, the benefits of international diversification are largely overwhelmed by the *additional cost of getting international exposure relative to the other options in the plan*. This last point is key. If the domestic equity options in Nancy's plan were more costly, then the differential gap between the costs of domestic and international exposure would be lower and hence we would see a greater international allocation.

Finally, what if the differential cost of obtaining international asset class exposure was even higher?

For instance, as of May 2007 the Hartford International Capital Appreciation Fund (symbol: HNCAX) from the Hartford Funds family has an expense ratio of 1.60 percent per year and has underperformed its style benchmark by about 2.5 percent per year in recent years. Based on the Financial Engines peer ranking, this fund would be expected to outperform only 31 percent of its style peers on a forward-looking basis. What does the fund allocation look like with the Hartford International Capital Appreciation Fund substituted for the Fidelity Spartan International Index Fund?

Table 8.11 shows the results of the modified fund lineup for Nancy's 401(k) plan.

Where did the international exposure go? With this substitution, we have finally reached the point where the cost and performance differential

TABLE 8.11 Recommended Fund Allocation for Nancy's Modified 401(k) Account

Fund	Efficient Allocation at Risk 1.10
Fidelity Government MM Fund	0%
Fidelity Spartan Intermediate Treasury Bond Index	11%
Fidelity Spartan Long-Term Treasury Bond Index	25%
Hartford International Capital Appreciation Fund	0%
Fidelity Spartan 500 Index	35%
Fidelity Spartan Extended Market Index	29%

Source: Financial Engines calculations.

between the available domestic equity funds and that of the international option overwhelms the benefits of international asset class diversification. While this is an example constructed to demonstrate the point (an account with institutionally priced domestic index funds combined with a relatively high-priced active international equity fund is not the norm), there comes a point where the benefits of international asset class diversification no longer makes sense. In this case, Nancy could do better by taking a mix of domestic and bond exposure to get a higher expected return portfolio for this level of risk. How much better?

Let's assume that Nancy is 45 years old and plans to retire at age 65. We will further assume that she is saving $10,000 per year into her plan and that her company is matching the first $4,000 for a total contribution of $14,000. Using the Financial Engines simulation model, we can forecast the range of potential values of her 401(k) balance in 20 years.

Table 8.12 shows the results of the portfolio simulation at the optimal fund allocations assuming that Nancy ignores the Hartford International Capital Appreciation Fund in favor of a diversified portfolio consisting of the low-cost bond and domestic equity options (using the allocations from Table 8.11).

TABLE 8.12 Recommended Allocations and Portfolio Value Forecasts for Nancy's 401(k) Account with No International Fund Allocation

Fund Lineup	Optimal Allocation at Risk 1.10	Portfolio Value (in today's dollars)	
Fidelity Government MM Fund	0%	Upside	$2,220,000
Fidelity Spartan Intermediate Treasury Bond Index	11%	Median	$1,060,000
Fidelity Spartan Long-Term Treasury Bond Index	25%	Downside	$464,000
Hartford International Capital Appreciation Fund	0%		
Fidelity Spartan 500 Index	35%		
Fidelity Spartan Extended Market Index	29%		

Source: Financial Engines calculations.

As you can see, even without the international exposure, Nancy is likely to accumulate a substantial nest egg, with a median portfolio value of $1,060,000 adjusted for inflation. However, she is paying a cost for not having a better international fund, as she could have done even better with access to the Fidelity Spartan International Fund. In this case she is making allowances for the lower quality of her only international option and doing the best that she can.

What if Nancy blindly applied the standard target allocation and put 24 percent of her money in the more expensive and poorer performing Hartford International Capital Appreciation Fund anyway? If we assume that she applies the same target asset allocation as shown in Table 8.7 to this plan (like she would do if she were following the standard hierarchical asset allocation strategy), we get the results shown in Table 8.13.

Note that the risk of this portfolio is actually slightly higher (at 1.12 times the volatility of the market portfolio) than the one shown in Table 8.12 due to the higher risk of the Hartford fund relative to the index fund in Table 8.7. As you can see, Nancy would pay a substantial price for blindly following a target asset allocation without considering the impact of the quality of the fund options in her plan. In this case, the cost of following the original target asset allocation ranges from $31,000 to $80,000 in lower portfolio values depending on market performance (these values are adjusted for inflation). For the median portfolio value, Nancy can expect to see $60,000

TABLE 8.13 Recommended Allocations and Portfolio Value Forecasts for Nancy's 401(k) Account with Allocation to a More Expensive International Fund

Fund Lineup	Optimal Allocation at Risk 1.12	Portfolio Value (in today's dollars)	
Fidelity Government MM Fund	0%	Upside	$2,140,000
Fidelity Spartan Intermediate Treasury Bond Index	0%	Median	$1,000,000
Fidelity Spartan Long-Term Treasury Bond Index	29%	Downside	$433,000
Hartford International Capital Appreciation Fund	24%		
Fidelity Spartan 500 Index	33%		
Fidelity Spartan Extended Market Index	14%		

Source: Financial Engines calculations.

less in retirement savings in 20 years if she makes the mistake of ignoring the impact of fund characteristics in diversifying her 401(k) account.

This analysis for the value of international diversification can be applied to the benefits of other types of asset class diversification as well. For instance, it will sometimes make sense to give up small-cap diversification if the costs of achieving small-cap exposure are high enough relative to the other equity options in the plan. Typically, if the gap in expenses between funds representing various equity asset classes is greater than about 0.8 percent, then it will make sense to reduce or possibly eliminate the more expensive asset class from your allocation. In general, you need to pay close attention to the cost and quality of the fund options available to you before determining the optimal asset allocation.

THE BIG PICTURE: PART II

Another common mistake in building a diversified portfolio is to ignore the impact of other household assets on your investment choices. When deciding what to do with a particular account, you need to take into consideration other financial assets you hold and their correlation with the investments that you are managing. For instance, if your brokerage account is invested aggressively in a small number of growth stocks, you might want to pursue a more conservative strategy with your 401(k) account to compensate for the additional risk. You may also want to invest in securities with more of a value or international exposure within your 401(k) in order to balance the heavy domestic growth equity exposure.

Let's review a couple of examples to demonstrate the point, one illustrating the impact of holding low-risk assets outside of an account, and another showing the impact of holding high-risk assets in addition to the primary account.

The Impact of Low-Risk Household Assets

Helen is a long-time employee at a large telecommunications company. Having been with the company for 20 years, Helen has diligently saved her way to an accumulated 401(k) balance of $250,000. Helen is still 15 years away from retiring and has decided that she is comfortable with a risk level of 1.1 times the market portfolio (corresponding to roughly a mix of 75 percent equity and 25 percent bonds). In addition to her 401(k) balance, Helen has accumulated a balance of $110,000 in her company's

TABLE 8.14 Asset Allocation for Helen's 401(k) Account

Asset Class	Portfolio Allocation at Risk 1.10
Cash	9%
Bonds	14%
Large-Cap Equity	40%
International Equity	26%
Small/Mid-Cap Equity	11%

Source: Financial Engines calculations.

Cash Balance plan. Cash Balance plans are relatively common among larger employers as an alternative to traditional Defined Benefit plans. The idea behind a Cash Balance plan is that contributions are made by the employer into an employee account that earns a fixed or variable level of interest each year, often tied to Treasury bond yields. The amount of money contributed by the employer is usually dependent on the compensation of the employee. As far as investment exposures go, the presence of a Cash Balance account increases the exposure to fixed-income asset classes. Because the value of the plan is sensitive to interest rates changes (like a bond), a Cash Balance account increases your exposure to cash and bond asset classes.

Helen looks at the asset allocation of her 401(k) portfolio shown in Table 8.14 and thinks that she has her portfolio allocation about right.

Helen's 401(k) asset allocation shown in Table 8.14 indeed has a risk level of about 1.10 times the market when evaluated in isolation. She has about 23 percent of her account in cash and bonds, with the remaining balance spread across different equity asset classes. But does she really have an appropriate mix when we take into account her Cash Balance plan?

The answer is—not really. When we consider the impact of her Cash Balance plan, Nancy's portfolio allocation looks quite different. Table 8.15 shows the impact on her asset allocation, considering the Cash Balance plan and the 401(k) plan jointly.

Actually Helen's total portfolio is quite a bit more conservative than she suspects. Taking into consideration the impact of her Cash Balance account, her overall allocation to cash and bonds is 46 percent, with only 54 percent in equities. Relative to the volatility of the market portfolio, this portfolio has a risk level of 0.88. If Helen wants the investment outcomes associated

TABLE 8.15 Asset Allocation for Helen's 401(k) Account with Her Cash Balance Plan Included

Asset Class	Portfolio Allocation at Risk 0.88
Cash	6%
Bonds	40%
Large-Cap Equity	28%
International Equity	18%
Small/Mid-Cap Equity	8%

Source: Financial Engines calculations.

with a portfolio of risk 1.10, she needs to adjust the allocation of her 401(k) plan to be more aggressive. Attaining a diversified portfolio at the desired risk level of 1.10 requires that Helen increase the equity allocation of her 401(k) account significantly. Table 8.16 shows the required asset allocation for her 401(k) plan in order to a balance out the additional fixed-income exposure of her Cash Balance plan.

Helen's 401(k) portfolio is now almost entirely allocated to equities, with a risk level of 1.45. With this allocation, the overall asset allocation of Helen's assets (including the Cash Balance plan) meets her desired risk level of 1.10. This particular example shows that it may be necessary to modify your investment strategy to seek higher risk if you have low-risk assets that you cannot change. In other cases, the impact of outside assets may not dramatically influence the choice of risk level, but it may alter the desirable asset class exposures in your investment portfolio. Of course, there can also

TABLE 8.16 Revised Asset Allocation for Helen's 401(k) Account

Asset Class	Portfolio Allocation at Risk 1.45
Cash	0%
Bonds	0%
Large-Cap Equity	72%
International Equity	12%
Small/Mid-Cap Equity	16%

Source: Financial Engines calculations.

be cases where the presence of higher-risk outside assets can cause you to seek a lower-risk investment strategy, as in the next example.

The Impact of Higher-Risk Household Assets

Stan is a senior exec at a large biotechnology company (Genentech) and has been aggressively saving in his 401(k) plan for years, accumulating a total of $300,000. Stan figures he will retire in about 15 years and is willing to tolerate a reasonable level of volatility. He decides that his desired risk level is about 1.25 times the market portfolio volatility (which corresponds to about a 90 percent allocation in equities for his plan). Based on his great performance, Stan was recently awarded a substantial number of restricted shares in the common stock of his employer, worth approximately $80,000 at the current stock price. The problem is that Stan is not able to sell these shares for several years. Stan is worried about the additional risk of these shares and thinks he should be doing something different with his 401(k) allocation in order to take into account his restricted stock position. It turns out that Stan's intuition is correct.

First, consider the situation where Stan does not have any restricted stock shares and is just investing the $300,000 in his 401(k) account from among the options available to him in the plan. Table 8.17 shows the

TABLE 8.17 Recommended Allocations for Stan's 401(k)

Fund Lineup	Portfolio Allocation at Risk 1.25
Fidelity Money Market Fund	0%
Fidelity Short-Term Bond Fund	0%
Fidelity Government Income Fund	0%
PIMCO Total Return Fund	0%
T. Rowe Price Capital Appreciation Fund	0%
American Funds Capital World Growth and Income Fund	35%
Fidelity Low-Priced Stock Fund	23%
Dodge and Cox International Stock Fund	14%
T. Rowe Price Blue Chip Growth Fund	0%
Vanguard S&P 500 Index Fund	28%
Fidelity Small Cap Stock Fund	0%
Vanguard Explorer	0%

Source: Financial Engines calculations

TABLE 8.18 Recommended Asset Allocation for Stan's 401(k) Account

Asset Class	Portfolio Asset Allocation at Risk 1.25
Cash	1%
Bonds	9%
Large-Cap Equity	37%
International Equity	33%
Small/Mid-Cap Equity	20%

Source: Financial Engines calculations.

recommended 401(k) fund allocation for Stan, assuming no outside assets at a risk level of 1.25.

This portfolio is mostly invested in equities (about 92 percent), and has a short-term loss potential of 11.9 percent over the next year if markets perform poorly (a 1 in 20 chance of this loss or more). There is a mix of passive and active funds in the portfolio reflecting a spectrum of various asset classes. Table 8.18 shows the corresponding asset allocation of his portfolio.

The recommended asset allocation for Stan includes a mix of domestic and international equities, with significant exposure to both large-cap and small- and mid-cap stocks.

With the addition of the $80,000 in shares of Genentech stock (symbol: DNA), the risk of Stan's portfolio increases substantially, increasing to 1.52 times the volatility of the market portfolio. His short-term risk also increases significantly, with a possibility of losing 16 percent or more of his portfolio in the next year if markets perform poorly. To get back to the desired level of risk for his overall account, Stan needs to make some adjustments.

Table 8.19 shows the recommended allocation for Stan's account, taking into consideration his desired risk level (1.25) and the impact of his restricted position in Genentech stock.

The recommended allocation in Table 8.19 has significantly less volatility, reflecting the need to balance the additional risk coming from the Genentech stock holdings. What changes do we see? First of all, the portfolio has significantly more cash and bonds than Stan's initial portfolio. The higher fixed-income exposure is necessary in order for the overall portfolio to achieve a risk level of 1.25. Since the risk of the company stock is large (over three times the volatility of the market portfolio), Stan needs to become more

TABLE 8.19 Recommended Allocations for Stan's 401(k) with $80,000 in Restricted Company Stock

Fund Lineup	Portfolio Allocation at Risk 1.25
Fidelity Money Market Fund	0%
Fidelity Short-Term Bond Fund	0%
Fidelity Government Income Fund	25%
PIMCO Total Return Fund	15%
T. Rowe Price Capital Appreciation Fund	0%
American Funds Capital World Growth and Income Fund	35%
Fidelity Low-Priced Stock Fund	0%
Dodge and Cox International Stock Fund	12%
T. Rowe Price Blue Chip Growth Fund	0%
Vanguard S&P 500 Index Fund	13%
Fidelity Small Cap Stock Fund	0%
Vanguard Explorer	0%

Source: Financial Engines calculations.

conservative in his 401(k) investments to compensate for the additional risk. In addition, the presence of the company stock position tends to crowd out much of the small- and mid-cap domestic equity exposure in the original mix. In the original portfolio, small- and mid-cap exposure accounted for 20 percent of the total equity exposure, while in Table 8.19, that percentage drops to only 3 percent of total equity exposure. Why? Because Genentech stock and other companies in its industry tend to be correlated with the movements of mid- and small-cap equities. Given that type of exposure, it makes sense for Stan to underweight his small- and mid-cap exposure in his 401(k) plan. Similarly, it makes sense for Stan to increase the international equity exposure of his 401(k) assets as a proportion of his total equity exposure. In the original portfolio in Table 8.17, international equity comprised 37 percent of the total equity exposure, while in Table 8.19 international equity accounts for 53 percent of the total equity exposure. Again, the idea is to find exposures that complement the assets held outside of the 401(k) account. In Stan's case, this means lower risk, less mid- and small-cap exposure, and a stronger tilt toward international equity.

In this example we see two separate impacts of the restricted company stock holdings. First, Stan needs to lower the risk of his 401(k) assets in order to maintain the desired risk level for his overall portfolio. Second, Stan needs to adjust the asset class exposures of his 401(k) plan to account for the exposures of the Genentech stock position. Depending on the characteristics of the particular stock, the optimal asset class exposures in the 401(k) plan will vary. Of course, these recommended allocations are based on the fact that Stan cannot sell his restricted stock positions. Once his restricted shares can be sold, Stan should revisit his 401(k) allocations to ensure that he is appropriately diversifying his company stock exposure.

The difficulty is that coming up with the right fund and asset allocation often requires some analysis. Unless the circumstances are very simple, it will not always be intuitively obvious how to adjust your portfolio to meet your overall risk target and to achieve the optimal asset class exposures. Of course, having access to appropriate tools can help. With the purchase of this book, you have the ability to evaluate an appropriate allocation for your personal investments by using the Financial Engines *Personal Online Advisor* service.[3] By specifying the available investment choice set as well as identifying any outside assets that might affect the risk of your household portfolio, you can receive personalized recommendations on the appropriate fund and asset allocation to meet your objectives. Often the results can be illuminating.

THE SEARCH FOR BETTER DIVERSIFICATION

A final topic in the area of diversification is the popularity of so-called "alternative" asset classes for use in building individual portfolios. Depending on who you listen to, alternative asset classes may consist of the following types of assets (among others):

- Real estate
- Real estate investment trusts (REITs)
- Commodities (including precious metals)
- Hedge funds
- Treasury Inflation Protected Securities (TIPS)

The appeal of alternative assets is based on their relatively low correlations with the overall market portfolio. In recent years, mutual fund companies and other investment firms have been offering various types of funds and investment products based on alternative asset classes to their customers, especially among higher net worth individuals. While such assets may sometimes have low correlations with the stocks and bonds that comprise the core of most individual portfolios, there are good reasons to be cautious in evaluating the benefits of holding significant portions of your portfolio in such assets (with the possible exception of TIPS). As a rule, such alternative investments tend to have higher expenses than more traditional assets. The issue is that you have to consider more than just the correlation of alternative asset classes with your portfolio. Expected returns (particularly on a net-of-fees basis) are also critically important in determining whether it makes sense to hold them as part of your total portfolio. After all, you can easily add uncorrelated risk to your portfolio by flipping coins for $1,000 with your friend. Such an investment strategy would be uncorrelated with your stocks and bonds, but of course, there is no expected value from such an exercise; it only increases the volatility of your portfolio outcomes. More risk with insufficient expected reward is not a good idea.

Real Estate

With the rise in residential real estate values over the last decade, more and more investment managers and advisors have been marketing the benefits of real estate as a part of a well-diversified portfolio. Indeed, real estate of all types comprises a significant fraction of overall global wealth. For many U.S. investors, home equity is the single largest financial asset they own. Many individual investors have made considerable sums of money by investing in houses, apartments, and condominiums. In fact, in the United States, there is a large industry devoted to teaching people the ins and outs of real estate investing. But what role should real estate play in a well-diversified investment portfolio?

Many investment managers and advisors claim that real estate should be thought of as a separate asset class with desirable characteristics, particularly as a hedge against future inflation. The argument is that when inflation spikes up, the prices of real estate are likely to follow suit. Among financial economists, the perspective on whether real estate should be treated as a separate asset class (like bonds and stocks) is somewhat mixed, although most agree that real estate is an important component of global wealth that is differentiated from other types of assets. Unlike most other financial assets, real estate has some special characteristics that change its risk and return properties.

First, real estate tends to be relatively difficult and costly to buy or sell. Economists call such assets *illiquid* since they are difficult to exchange into cash on short notice, unlike, say, a publicly traded stock. Second, you can't easily sell real estate without owning the property first. This makes hedging the risk of a real estate downturn difficult, unlike stocks and bonds, where short selling—i.e., selling something before you actually own it, is common. For instance, if you wanted to protect yourself against a downturn in the value of your stock portfolio, there are many financial strategies that you can use to eliminate the market risk (of course, at a cost). With real estate, it is much more difficult to find assets whose values are inversely related to specific properties. Finally, the primary economic value of real estate in the long run is the value of the land. Buildings are typically a wasting asset, in that their value declines over time with age and use. It is generally accepted that land values should increase with global economic growth, but the volatility of such values may be high and may vary considerably across geographic locations.

There is evidence that real estate returns do behave differently than stocks and bonds. But the performance of real estate varies widely by type and geographical location. An individual holding direct real estate is subject to significant geographical and sector risk unless the investment is through a highly diversified real estate fund. However, even if real estate offers some incremental diversification potential, how much should you own?

Most individuals already have substantial holdings in real estate in their portfolio (in the form of their household residence). In fact, in some parts of the country, the value of home equity is by far the biggest financial asset that most people have. In addition, when you hold a broad-based portfolio of stocks (like the S&P 500) you also hold an interest in a substantial portion of the institutional quality commercial real estate in the United States. More than half of all commercial real estate in the United States is owned by large, publicly traded corporations. When you buy their stock, you also get an ownership stake in the value of their assets, which include real estate. Given the prominent role that real estate already plays in most investment portfolios and the likely presence of a large personal investment in residential real estate, a strong case can be made that most people are typically *overconcentrated* in real estate. This is particularly true if your real estate holdings are concentrated in a single geographical region.

The bottom line is that you likely should not be investing a large portion of your financial assets in direct real estate, particularly if you already own a home. If you do choose to hold real estate, make sure that you pay attention to fees and that you invest in a broadly diversified real estate portfolio. Concentrating your wealth in a single sector, location, or type of property (say, Southern California apartment buildings) can be very risky if the market turns against you, especially if you borrow heavily to purchase the properties. In a downturn, you may find that you are unable to sell your properties at a reasonable price, which can result in an inability to pay off the loans. Real estate prices, like other financial assets, can be very volatile in difficult market conditions. However, there are securities that make it somewhat easier to achieve diversification with real estate, which is the topic of our next section.

Real Estate Investment Trusts (REITs)

A related alternative investment type is the *Real Estate Investment Trust*, or *REIT*. These funds invest in and manage real estate properties and are required to distribute their income from such properties (including the gains from sales) to their shareholders. As such, REITs tend to pay high-dividend yields, making them poor choices for a taxable account (since income tax rates are higher than capital gains taxes for most investors). Different REITs specialize in various kinds of real estate, including office buildings, industrial buildings, shopping mails, and apartments. There are a number of mutual funds that invest strictly in REITs in the United States. In general, REIT funds tend to be correlated with the small-cap value sector of the market and bonds combined with a lot of fund-specific volatility, depending on how diversified the fund is. The bond exposure of such funds depends on the degree of leverage that they employ (how much they borrow to purchase the property in their portfolio). Real estate investment trust returns can be quite volatile over time, with interest rates shocks and credit market changes sometimes creating sharp dislocations in the value of the underlying real estate assets, particularly if the portfolio of properties is limited to a particular sector or region. Often the assets are relatively illiquid and difficult to sell in times of economic stress.

It is true that REITs have performance characteristics that cause them to behave differently from most stocks, which may make them look like attractive diversifiers. Even if you account for the overall market exposure, REITs will typically have leftover risk that is common to other REITs. But remember that when you own a portfolio of stocks, you also get significant real estate exposure from the assets of the corporations. Given the relatively short history of such funds, it is not clear that REITs provide a meaningful improvement in the diversification of individual portfolios. And even if they do, the magnitude of such holdings to get the benefit should be fairly small. For most people it will not make sense to put more than about 10 percent of your assets in REITs, even if the costs are low. Like mutual funds, the expenses of REIT funds can vary dramatically, so you need to be careful of the fees.

Remember, even if you do not invest in real estate or REITs directly, your portfolio still has significant exposure to real estate. Moreover, the incremental value of REIT exposure in a portfolio is relatively small. If you own a home already, you probably have enough real estate in your household portfolio.

Commodities

Commodity investments are based on the value of various goods, including oil, natural gas, steel, aluminum, corn, soybeans, ethanol, and many other types of raw materials. Commodities have received considerable press in recent years, with the prices of oil and various other raw materials rising significantly. Interestingly, there was a similar surge of enthusiasm around commodity investments in the 1970s with rising oil prices and inflation in the United States. It is relatively easy to invest in commodities by using *futures contracts*, financial instruments that provide a contractual obligation to buy or sell a specific quantity of a certain commodity in the future. By putting up an amount of cash as margin, one can gain exposure to a large amount of various commodities. More recently, a few investment firms have begun to offer commodity exposure in the form of exchange-traded funds (ETFs), which make commodity investing even more straightforward.

Many advisors and money managers have noted that some of these commodity investments appear to have low correlation with the stock market. Certainly this is true of some types of commodities, including agricultural goods, energy products, and certain industrial materials. If you use recent historical data to estimate returns and correlations, you might come to the conclusion that commodities are a useful class of investments in a diversified portfolio. But low correlations with the market are not enough to make them desirable elements of your portfolio. A desirable investment needs to have positive expected returns that are commensurate with the risk when held in a diversified portfolio. Unfortunately, there is no strong consensus among financial economists that commodity assets should even have a positive expected return in the long run, much less one warranting a significant investment of an individual's portfolio.

Unlike financial assets whose returns are based on the growth of the overall economy, commodity prices tend to rise and fall with economic demand, new technologies, and even geopolitical events. While their prices certainly fluctuate, it is not obvious that there should be a positive or negative trend in the long run. Remember from our discussion on the use of historical data in Chapter 4 that relying on short time periods to estimate expected returns is very susceptible to error.

Many economists suggest that over the long run, commodities have a zero expected return with positive volatility. Merely adding an investment to your portfolio with low correlation does you no good unless it also has expected return. Without a positive expected return, it is just adding noise. There are good reasons to be very skeptical of claims based on historical rates of return, no matter how dramatic. Past returns have virtually no bearing on the future returns of commodities and the funds that invest in them. Finally, the costs of commodity funds, exchange-traded funds (ETFs), and managed pools can be high relative to more conventional investments, further limiting their appeal. After deducting costs, you can make a strong argument that many commodity investments actually have negative expected returns.

Hedge Funds

Hedge funds are investments with the ability to invest in a wide variety of strategies, including the use of leverage (borrowing), currency speculation, and the use of complex options and derivatives. Unlike mutual funds, hedge funds can invest in almost anything they desire, including using borrowing to greatly magnify their investment exposures. Traditionally, hedge funds were marketed only to sophisticated wealthy investors and large institutional investors like pension funds. In the last decade, there has been an explosion in the number of hedge funds available. Increasingly, these products are being packaged for sale to less-wealthy individual investors, often in the form of fund-of-funds (a fund that invests in multiple underlying hedge funds).

The investment strategies of hedge funds run the gamut from relatively low-risk strategies to highly speculative and risky bets on all kinds of economic variables. Hedge funds have marketing appeal for their ability to post high levels of return when their strategies pay off. Of course, there is always a downside, as sometimes hedge funds fail spectacularly. In 1998 a famous hedge fund called Long Term Capital Management (symbol: LTCM), lost billions in a just a few weeks, triggering such concerns in the financial markets that the Federal Reserve Bank was forced to intervene and restore order. Hedge funds are also often marketed as having VIP status given their history as vehicles for wealthy investors.

It is tough to generalize about hedge funds as a class, since individual funds vary so widely in their investment strategies. They certainly don't meet the standard for an asset class. Despite that, there are two big issues that should give you pause before investing your hard-earned money into a hedge fund. The first issue is costs. Hedge funds often charge investment management fees of 2 percent–5 percent or more, plus a percentage of the profits if the fund performs well (ranging from 20 percent to 50 percent). To make matters worst, most individual investors only get access to such funds through vehicles called *fund-of-funds*. These funds simply invest in the portfolios of multiple hedge fund managers, in exchange for an additional management fee on top of the underlying fees from the hedge funds themselves. By piling high fees on top of high fees, you can easily find yourself holding an asset with a zero or even negative expected return. Such products might be a great idea for the hedge fund manager, but chances are they are not such a good deal for you.

Hedge funds are also particularly susceptible to the "Peso Problem" risks described in Chapter 2. While hedge fund strategies vary widely, they often involve complex positions that amount to selling insurance against very bad downside market events. Sometimes these bets involve purchasing positions that can be very difficult to sell in poor market conditions. Essentially, they place bets that markets will continue to perform in normal ranges. This works great most of the time. But when uncommon downside market scenarios happen (like the currency/debt crises of 1998 or the subprime mortgage crisis of 2007), these strategies can blow up, sometimes spectacularly. In 2006, a hedge fund by the name of Amaranth Advisors lost over $6 billion in just *one week* after ill-timed bets on natural gas futures. Investing in hedge funds is kind of like walking through a minefield. As long as you avoid the mines, everything can look good. But one false step and kablooey!

Admittedly, the vast majority of hedge funds do not self-destruct, but the potential for outsized losses based on complicated strategies involving lots of borrowing and illiquid securities is significant. There is no big secret here; strategies that involve the prospect of outsized gains also come with the possibility of big-time losses if things do not go as planned. Most individual investors would be better served with a more conventional portfolio mix, even if that sounds a lot more pedestrian and less sexy than a hedge fund.

Treasury Inflation-Protected Securities (TIPS)

A final alternative investment that is receiving much attention recently is Treasury Inflation-Protected Securities (or TIPS, as they are more commonly known). Treasury Inflation-Protected Securities are treasury securities where the value of the principal is indexed to the *Consumer Pricing Index* (CPI), a measure of inflation in the United States. They are different from normal Treasury bonds in that they protect investors from the impact of future inflation. Because they protect investors from erosion in principal due to inflation, they pay interest rates that are lower than traditional Treasury securities of the same maturity. The lower interest rate reflects the market's consensus expectations about future inflation. In recent years, there have been a number of mutual funds and exchange-traded funds set up to invest in a spectrum of individual TIPS bonds with varying maturities.

Unlike some of the other alternative asset classes, TIPS do offer something unique—the ability to explicitly protect your portfolio against inflation. Assuming that the cost of the exposure is reasonable (relative to the other choices available to you), it may make sense to have a modest allocation to TIPS for those of you who are more risk averse, particularly if you are concerned about future inflation. In fact, TIPS are lower risk (in real terms) than comparable maturity Treasury bonds due to the fact that they have inflation protection built in.

One small problem with TIPS is that the supply of such bonds is somewhat limited. The TIPS market is not nearly as deep as the market for traditional Treasury bonds, and so not all maturities are available to investors. Still, TIPS offer a unique hedge against inflation that can be a useful part of a diversified portfolio (assuming you don't have to pay too much for it).

TAKE-AWAYS

- Diversification is important, but it is not a panacea. A diversified portfolio may still have considerable risk, depending on the amount of exposure to the overall market.
- Evaluate diversification at the household portfolio level, not at the individual account level.
- If you are forced to hold assets with high or low risk outside of your primary portfolio, make sure that you consider their impact on your optimal allocation.
- Diversification has significant but finite economic value. The cost of not being able to invest in a single asset class is typically less than 0.50 percent on a forward-looking basis.
- The most important dimension of diversification is being able to spread your assets across stocks and bonds.
- The next most important type of diversification is the mix between domestic and international equity.
- Don't overpay for diversification. If it costs you incrementally more than about 1.0 percent to get exposure to a given asset class, you will usually be better off skipping over that investment in your allocation.

- Don't make the mistake of overpaying to fill every little slice of an asset allocation pie chart. Focus on the most important areas of diversification first (stock/bonds, domestic/international), then worry about the nuances of lesser asset class exposures. Often you can do better by purchasing funds with broader asset class exposures like a total stock market index fund.
- Keep investments in alternative investments like real estate, commodities, and hedge funds to a small part of your portfolio if you choose to hold them, and be very wary of high fees, particularly any fund with an expense ratio above 1.25 percent.

CHAPTER 9

Picking the Good Ones

Prediction is very difficult, especially about the future.
—Niels Bohr (1885–1962)

Selecting good funds means finding investments with desirable future risk and return characteristics, based on the best information available today. Many investors and advisors spend far too much time obsessing about which funds performed best in the past. Figuring out the best performing fund from last year is easy, but it only counts if you actually held the fund last year. Good fund selection means paying attention to predictive factors that impact future risk and returns. Even with the best techniques you won't be able to perfectly predict fund performance, but there are a number of factors that can improve your investment selection. This chapter introduces the most important factors in making good fund choices for your investment portfolio, and shows you how to avoid big mistakes.

Since you are now eight chapters into this book, I feel the liberty to spring a little pop quiz on you. Figure 9.1 illustrates the historical performance of six different actively managed mutual funds (Funds A–F) over the last 10 years. Each of the funds has the same investment style and volatility characteristics. Your task is to identify which of the funds is the best choice for your investment portfolio going forward. Look carefully. Which one would you prefer to own?

Okay, so I cheated a little bit in creating these performance charts. Each of these six fund histories was hypothetical, created on a computer to have certain desired properties. Each fund was invested in the same type of assets with the same risk characteristics. The only differences between them were in the amount by which the funds would be expected to outperform their underlying investment style due to manager skill. The variation in historical performance observed in the graphs in Figure 9.1 is due to the performance of different securities held by each fund, even though they were investing with the same general investment style.

So which one is the best fund on a forward-looking basis?

The answer is Fund D. Surprised? Like most people you were probably seduced by the funds with the highest past performance. In fact, Fund D has far and away the best *expected* performance of the group. By construction, Funds A, B, C, E, and F have exactly the same expected returns and *no manager skill at all*. Economists and investment professionals call the component of performance due to the manager's skill the *manager alpha* of the fund. In this example, all the funds (except for D) had expected manager alphas of zero. That is, on average, the managers of these funds are not expected to add any value beyond the expected returns of their investment style. Fund D, on the other hand, was constructed to have a skillful manager who is expected to add 1.5 percent per year in additional return, which is a very sizable amount for a mutual fund. However, due to the randomness of market returns, the stocks selected by this manager happened to not be the best performers over this particular 10-year period. Over the long run, Fund D is expected to outperform the other funds by an average of 1.5 percent per year. But that does not mean that it will always outperform its peers over any given time period. It just means that Fund D is more likely to do better than its peers in the future.

What is the point of this example? Investors are naturally attracted to funds with impressive past performance. In fact, many studies have shown a strong link between past performance and the inflows of new money into mutual funds. The problem is that the random variation in returns due purely to chance mostly obscures the relatively small differences in expected manager alphas of mutual funds. Searching for mutual funds with good expected manager alphas is like listening for a cricket chirping in a room full of people at a boisterous happy hour—there is a lot of noise drowning out the sound you are straining to hear.

Over the long run, a fund with a higher expected manager alpha (net of fees) is likely to outperform peers with similar investment styles. But just because a fund has a higher expected manager alpha, does not *guarantee* better performance. Even the best fund managers have a good bit of volatility in their performance—nobody wins all the time. Even over multiyear periods, funds with substantially worse expected returns can nonetheless outperform their more attractive peers. Conversely, really good funds can underperform poor funds for lengthy periods of time. This makes selecting good funds quite difficult. *But on average, funds with higher expected manager alphas (adjusted for fees) will tend to outperform funds with less*

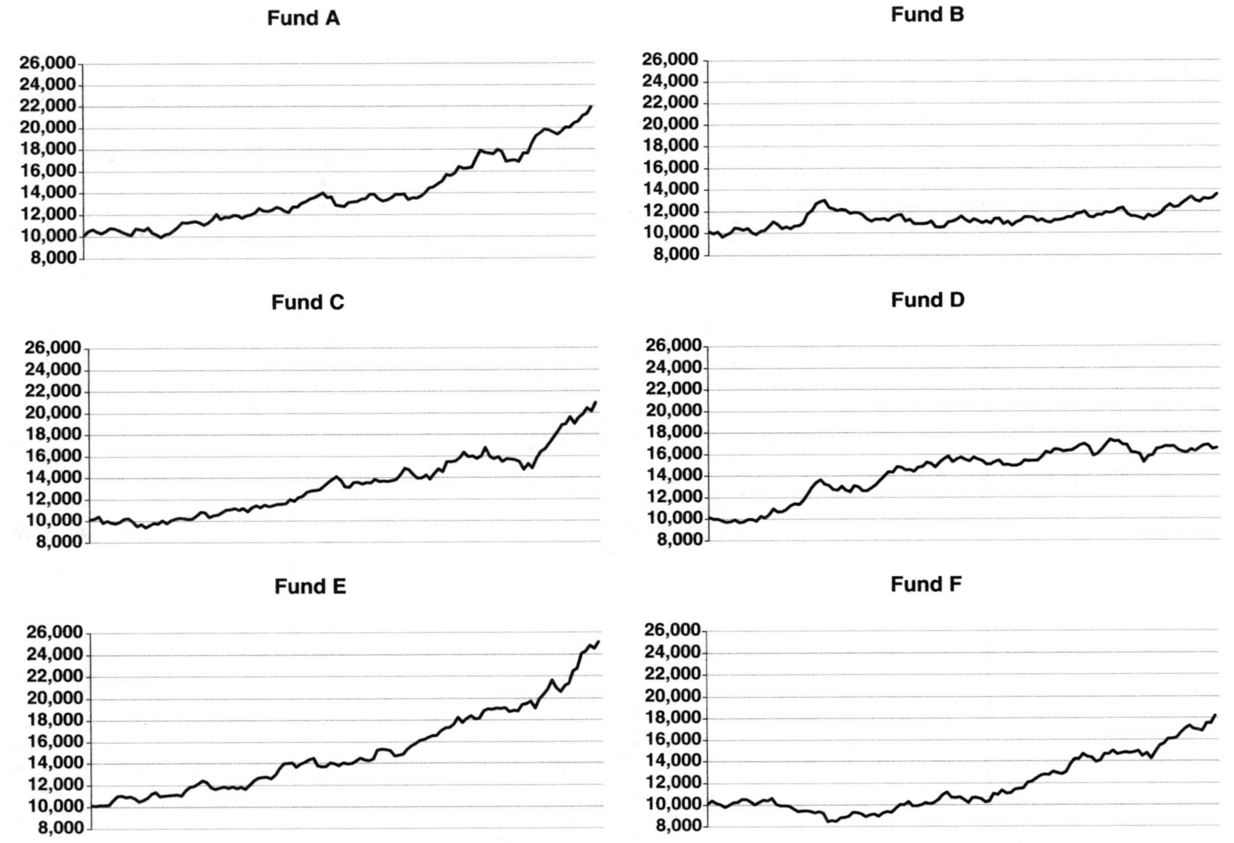

FIGURE 9.1 10-year Performance Histories of Six Example Equity Mutual Funds with a $10,000 Initial Investment

Source: Financial Engines.

desirable characteristics but similar investment styles. However, just because a fund manager is expected to outperform does not mean that he or she is guaranteed to do so.

So how *do* you pick good investment funds? While the process is not trivial, there are techniques that can be applied to separate out the good, the bad, and the ugly among investment alternatives.

THE STUFF THAT MATTERS

Selecting high-quality investments is an exercise in tradeoffs and calculated risk taking. The goal is to end up with a portfolio of investments that *in combination* have desirable risk and return characteristics. The value of a fund is not its performance in isolation, but how it contributes to the risk and expected return of your portfolio as a whole. Since the risk and return of an investment depends on many factors, the intelligent investor must carefully weigh competing objectives to arrive at a good decision.

While there are many types of investments that individuals may choose to own, most investors should have the majority of their assets invested in pooled investment vehicles such as mutual funds, institutional funds, or exchange-traded funds. I will limit my discussion of investment selection to these three classes of investments. As has been noted in previous chapters, these types of investments are the prudent and most cost-effective choices for most investors. I'll leave the tips on stock picking to those authors of a more speculative nature.

Mutual funds are retail investments vehicles managed by registered investment management companies. These funds are registered for sale to the public and are regulated by the Securities and Exchange Commission (SEC). Unlike other types of funds, mutual funds have certain restrictions on their investment strategies, including tight limits on the amount of borrowing or leverage that can be used by the managers. They must also abide by strict regulations on keeping track of the market value of portfolio assets. Open-ended mutual funds are priced daily at the close of the market and must allow shareholders to redeem their shares at any time. A mutual fund trade executed in a given day will be transacted at the closing *net asset value* of the fund (the value of all the stock positions in the fund at the close of the market) on that day. Many mutual funds are listed on the NASDAQ exchange and their daily closing prices can be easily found online or in a daily newspaper. Mutual funds may be passively or actively managed.

A passive mutual fund is designed to mimic the performance of a certain segment of the market by tracking an index, while active funds attempt to outperform the market through a combination of market timing and investment selection. Active mutual funds account for about 90 percent of the total assets invested in mutual funds in the United States as of mid-2007.

Institutional funds are like mutual funds, but are not registered for sale to the investing public directly. Typically most individuals will have access to institutional funds only through their employer retirement plan, particularly if they work for a larger employer. Institutional funds form the bulk of investments in traditional Defined Benefit pension funds. Institutional funds often have management fees that are considerably lower than those of retail mutual funds. Like mutual funds, institutional funds may be actively or passively managed. From the viewpoint of an investor, there is little difference between investing in institutional funds or mutual funds, other than the fact that institutional funds tend to have lower fees and are not listed on stock exchanges (and thus you will not find them listed in the newspaper).

Exchange-traded funds (ETFs) are the new kid on the block for individual investors and are rapidly growing in assets, although the total holdings are still a small fraction of the total represented by aggregate mutual fund assets. From the investor's point of view, an exchange-traded fund is much like a traditional mutual fund except that it trades continuously during the day like a stock. An exchange-traded fund is really a basket of stocks that is divided into shares. Exchange-traded funds are listed on various stock exchanges, and like stocks, you can borrow on margin to increase the size of your position. They also can be sold short like a stock, allowing you to take negative (short) positions in the market if you think a part of the market is going to drop in value. For instance, if you feel that the S&P 500 is likely to drop in value, you could speculate on this prediction by selling short an exchange-traded fund that tracks the S&P 500 index. If the S&P 500 drops in value, you could later cover the short position at a lower cost than your initial sale, pocketing the difference as profit.

One important difference with exchange-traded funds is that you pay brokerage commissions to trade them, much like individual stocks. This implies that you need to be extra careful about the transactions costs associated with small, regular purchases of exchange-traded funds, as the fees can quickly mount. If you are participating in a program of regular savings, you should probably use no-transaction-fee mutual funds for the investments. As of 2007, there were several hundred exchange-traded funds available on U.S. exchanges, with more than $500 billion in assets, reflecting a wide variety of investment styles and industry sectors. Currently, the majority of exchange-traded funds are designed to track a declared index, hence they are passively managed. In many respects, most exchange-traded funds act a lot like index mutual funds in terms of their risk-and-return characteristics, though some of them are more narrowly specialized in specific sectors than many funds. There are also exchange-traded funds that invest in bonds, commodities, and other assets besides equities. Because of their flexibility and relatively low costs, exchange-traded funds have become quite popular with both institutional and individual investors in recent years.

There are many considerations in selecting good investment funds for your portfolio. Among the factors that a savvy investor will want to consider are:

- Your tolerance for risk
- Investment style of the fund
- Fund expenses
- Implicit costs due to trading by the fund
- Manager performance (if actively managed)
- Fund-specific risk
- Length of investment track record
- Tax efficiency (income and capital gains distributions)

Each of these factors can impact the relative desirability of a fund for your portfolio. Most of these factors impact the expected returns or risk of an investment fund. However, none can be considered in isolation. One must weigh the relative impact of different fund attributes in order to answer the question of whether a particular fund is right *for your portfolio*.

Unfortunately the exercise is further complicated by the fact that many of these attributes, notably investment style, turnover, manager performance, and fees may change over time. Any specific fund recommendations are subject to being out of date in the future as circumstances change. This suggests a couple of important pointers regarding fund selection:

1. Ensure that you are relying on reasonably up-to-date information when selecting investments.
2. Periodically review your investment choices (or perhaps have someone do it for you) to ensure that your choices and allocations remain consistent with your objectives and remain appropriate, given changing fund characteristics and market conditions over time.

In the following sections, I will show how the preceding factors interact to influence expected fund performance. To make the discussion more concrete, I will use snapshots of example retail mutual funds to illustrate the points. However, note that this fund information is only up to date through mid-2007. You should not rely on the specific statistics in this book to make investment selections without first ensuring that the information is still timely and accurate. Conveniently, with the purchase of this book, you have access to the Financial Engines *Personal Online Advisor* service to provide updated information on an ongoing basis.

IT'S ABOUT THE FUTURE

While it may sound patently obvious, the most important thing you can do in selecting investment funds is to focus on the future, not what has happened in the past. Most of the fund ratings you see and read about in the press are simply reflections of how a fund has performed in the past. As I will illustrate, this type of information can be useful, but only to the degree that it helps you understand what the *expected* risk and returns of the fund are likely to be in the future.

As an investor, you don't get credit for good past performance unless you happened to have owned the fund before the good returns happened. *Good funds are not defined by how well they have performed in the past, but how well they are likely to perform in the future.* This sounds like an obvious observation, but I am consistently surprised by how many investors, even sophisticated ones, are led astray by defining a good fund as one with good past performance. As we will see, there are other factors that have a big influence on expected *future* performance, including how much emphasis (if any) you should place on the historical track record of the fund manager.

Making good fund choices requires knowledge of which factors are most important and how they interrelate to create an overall future performance estimate.

RISK TOLERANCE AND FUND CHOICE

The first question in the investment selection process is how much risk you want in your investment portfolio. If you have a very short-term goal, say paying your tax bill next quarter, or you are looking to build a very low-risk portfolio, you should probably not be spending a lot of time evaluating small-cap growth mutual funds. Even the best small-cap growth fund is not likely to be an appropriate match for your horizon and risk preferences (at least for a large part of your portfolio). Similarly, if your tolerance for risk is high or your time horizon is long, you likely don't want to waste time evaluating money market funds. They are simply not going to be a major element of your investment decision.

As we saw in the previous chapter, picking an appropriate risk level is not the same thing as selecting a target asset allocation, since the style and quality of your fund choices matter. The goal with portfolio allocation is to pick the best mix of investments from your available choice set to get the highest expected return for the level of risk that you are willing to bear. The choice of risk level will largely determine the general mix of equity and fixed-income assets that are appropriate for your portfolio, but the specific funds will depend on a number of factors, including costs and manager performance. The starting point to the process is your desired risk level. Asset allocation is actually a consequence of the best investment selections to reach your target risk level. The investment selection process implicitly determines your asset class allocation. However, there are some general properties of asset allocation that are relatively consistent across different investment choice sets. Even if you have investment options of varying costs and quality, you will still generally want to hold certain kinds of assets to achieve specific levels of portfolio risk.

Chapter 5 provided a detailed look at selecting portfolio risk levels that are consistent with your investment objectives. The specific choice of risk level will depend on your investment horizon, your comfort level with investment risk, and the nature of your goal. However, there are some general consequences of different portfolio risk levels. If you are seeking a portfolio that is less risky than the overall market portfolio, such as a risk level of 0.8 (representing 80 percent of the volatility of the market portfolio), then you will want to hold a majority of your portfolio in fixed income (bonds and cash). Similarly, if you are looking for a portfolio that is close to the risk of the overall market, say in the range of 0.8–1.2 times market risk, then your investment choices will consist of a mix of fixed income and equity funds. Finally, if you are looking for a portfolio risk level of more than 1.2, you can safely assume that your choices will consist primarily of equity funds.

INVESTMENT STYLE

The investment style of a fund—what kinds of exposures it has to different asset classes—is a very important factor in estimating its future risk and return. No matter how good a bond fund manager may be, a bond fund will still behave mostly like bonds. Funds inherit the properties of the asset classes that they invest in. This is precisely why asset allocation explains more than 90 percent of the variation in returns for most mutual funds. Bond funds mostly act like bonds and equity funds mostly act like equities, irrespective of how well they are picking securities within their asset classes. Some funds, such as balanced and lifecycle funds, invest in a mix of fixed income and equities with varying proportions. Depending on the relative proportions, they may act more like bonds or stocks. But the fundamental fact remains that the underlying investments in a fund largely govern the risk and correlations of the fund and in most cases the majority of the expected return as well.

An important consideration in evaluating factors that influence a fund's expected performance is the necessity of comparing against a relevant peer group. Most of the predictive factors in fund performance are dependent on the investment style of a fund. For instance, to determine if a money market fund is expensive, you want to compare its expenses against other money market funds, or perhaps short-term bond funds providing similar levels of risk and return. The expense ratio of a very different type of asset, say a small-cap growth fund, is not really relevant to your determination of whether a money market fund is high priced.

This idea extends to other factors as well. In looking at the consistency of a manager's performance track record, you want to consider the typical level of risk taken by other managers with similar investment styles. For instance, money market funds tend to have much more consistent manager performance than small-cap equity funds. That is, the performance of small-cap equity managers varies much more widely than that of money market fund managers. Consequently, you would not want to compare the consistency of the track record of a money market fund manager against the track record of an equity manager. Otherwise you would have an apples-to-oranges comparison that would shed little light on either fund's properties.

One way of addressing these issues is to rank various characteristics of funds based on a peer group with similar investment styles. In other words, you want to evaluate money market funds against the characteristics of other money market funds, equity funds against other equity managers, and so on. The closer the investments style of the funds, the more relevant the comparison. A key motivation for this approach is that you are comparing investments against the group of likely alternatives. For instance, if you don't choose a particular money market fund, the alternative investments are likely to be other money market funds.

Since Financial Engines does not put funds into rigid asset class categories, we use techniques to create a weighted peer group of funds based on how close the investment style is to the fund in question. For each fund, we determine a peer group of funds with similar investment styles weighted by how closely they match the style of the fund. Funds with more similar styles are weighted more strongly in the peer group than funds with more disparate investment styles. The result is a custom peer group for each fund in the Financial Engines database. With this peer group, we can rank funds on various measures, including expenses, fund-specific risk, performance, and turnover to determine how they rate relative to similar style funds. For instance, we can determine that a fund's expenses are in the lowest 10 percent of peers with similar investment styles.

Why does investment style matter so much? Because each fund inherits the expected return and risk of its underlying assets. Depending on the fees, turnover, and manager performance, a given fund can deviate from the performance of its investment style, but the underlying investment exposures still play a prominent role in explaining the fund performance. As we saw in the previous chapter, a well-diversified portfolio will generally consist of a number of different asset class exposures. Of course the quality of the available fund options will have an impact on the optimal asset class exposures of the portfolio in addition to the target risk level.

Table 9.1 shows the largest and most prominent investment styles in optimized portfolios of increasing risk, assuming that you have a wide variety of reasonably priced fund alternatives.

The list of asset class exposures in Table 9.1 is not exhaustive, as long-term U.S. government bonds, Pacific Rim equities, mid-cap value U.S. equities and other types of assets have a place in diversified portfolios as well, but the magnitudes of the optimal allocations for these classes tend to be smaller than for those assets listed in the table.

Starting at the low end of the risk spectrum in Table 9.1, a diversified portfolio will consist of predominantly cash and short- to intermediate-term bonds (or perhaps municipal bonds if you are investing in a taxable account). For risk levels of 0.6 and 0.8, the portfolios grow to include exposures to mortgage and corporate bonds as well as large-cap U.S. equities (usually including both value and growth equities). Moving further up the risk spectrum at 1.0 and 1.2, the optimal portfolios now consist of mostly equity exposure, with U.S. large-cap value, U.S. large-cap growth, and European equities forming the largest exposures. As we move to the highest risk portfolios at 1.4 to 1.5 times market risk, the mix shifts to 100 percent equity and an increasing weigh on growth equities.

TABLE 9.1 Primary Investment Styles in Diversified Portfolios by Risk Level

Portfolio Risk Level (1.0 = Market Risk)	Approximate Fixed Income/ Equity Mix	Largest Portfolio Investment Styles
0.2	100 / 0	Cash
0.4	90 / 10	Cash Intermediate-Term Bonds Municipal Bonds (for taxable accounts)
0.6	67 / 33	Cash Intermediate-Term Bonds Municipal Bonds (for taxable accounts) Large-Cap Value U.S. Equities
0.8	55 / 45	Intermediate-Term Bonds Mortgage Bonds Corporate Bonds Municipal Bonds (for taxable accounts) Large-Cap Value U.S. Equities
1.0	35 / 65	Intermediate-Term Bonds Mortgage Bonds Municipal Bonds (for taxable accounts) Large-Cap Value U.S. Equities Large-Cap Growth U.S. Equities European Equities
1.2	20 / 80	Mortgage Bonds Municipal Bonds (for taxable accounts) Large-Cap Value U.S. Equities Large-Cap Growth U.S. Equities European Equities
1.4	0 / 100	Large-Cap Value U.S. Equities Large-Cap Growth U.S. Equities Mid-Cap Growth U.S. Equities European Equities
1.5	0 / 100	Large-Cap Value U.S. Equities Large-Cap Growth U.S. Equities Mid-Cap Growth U.S. Equities Small-Cap Growth U.S. Equities European Equities

Source: Financial Engines.

Of course, the actual quality of the funds available to you will have an impact on the specific asset class exposures that make sense in your portfolio, but the Table 9.1 provides some rough intuition on the kinds of asset class exposures that might be appropriate for different levels of risk. One final thing to keep in mind is that there are many funds (such as total stock market index funds) that offer exposures to multiple asset classes in varying proportions within a single fund. They, too, can be excellent building blocks of a well-diversified portfolio, even though they may not fit into a particular asset class category. Because they cover multiple asset classes, such funds are often excluded from the traditional hierarchical asset allocation exercise, even though they may be superior to a portfolio of more narrowly specialized funds.

FUND EXPENSES

Of all the factors that go into predicting future fund performance, fund expenses are among the most informative and easiest to model. As I discussed in Chapter 7, fund expenses have a highly predictable impact on fund performance. All other things held equal, higher fees mean lower net of fees performance for fund shareholders. On average, the impact of an additional 1.0 percent in higher fees is 1.0 percent lower expected returns to the fund shareholder.

After investment style, fund fees are the single most important factor in predicting future fund performance. Unlike manager performance, which is subject to noise due to random variation, fund fees are highly predictive. Their impact on future fund returns is inescapable. That is not to say that funds with higher fees cannot sometimes outperform lower fee counterparts when their investment strategies do well, but the higher-fee fund would have done *even better* had the fees been lower. Every dollar kept by your investment manager or broker is a dollar that you do not get to keep yourself.

To make the impact of fees more concrete, consider a selection of mid-cap U.S. equity funds with varying degrees of fund expenses taken from the Financial Engines database. Each of these funds has at least 80 percent exposure to the U.S. mid-cap asset classes. However, they differ significantly in fund expenses. Table 9.2 shows the expense ratio of the funds and the median portfolio forecast for a $10,000 investment in the fund over 10 years using the Financial Engines simulation engine.

Table 9.2 clearly illustrates the strong relationship between fees and projected fund performance. Consistently, the higher-fee funds have lower

TABLE 9.2 Portfolio Forecasts for Selected Mid-Cap Equity Funds ($10,000 Investment over 10 Years)

Fund Name	Symbol	Annual Expense Ratio	Median Portfolio Forecast
Vanguard Mid Cap Index/Inv	VIMSX	0.22%	$17,647
Dreyfus Index Funds: Midcap Index Fund	PESPX	0.50%	$16,978
Hartford HLS MidCap Value/IA	HMVIX	0.78%	$16,811
PIF Partners MidCap Growth/Instl	PPIMX	1.00%	$14,864
Harbor Funds Mid Cap Growth Fund/Ret	HRMGX	1.18%	$14,931
AIM Technology/Inv	FTCHX	1.57%	$13,056
Firsthand Funds: Technology Leaders Fund	TLFQX	1.95%	$11,870
Van Kampen Technology/B	VTFBX	3.03%	$10,181

Sources: Financial Engines calculations and mutual fund annual reports as of May 2007.

expected forecast values than the lower-cost funds. However, the relationship is not exact, as there are other fund characteristics that have an impact on the forecast as well. Notably, the funds differ in their level of turnover, fund-specific risk, and historical manager performance. To truly understand the future performance of a fund, you must consider these other factors in addition to the expense ratio.

PREDICTING MUTUAL FUND PERFORMANCE

Once you have an idea of the portfolio risk level and types of asset class exposures you are looking for, the question remains: How do you select from among the thousands of funds with similar investment styles? After all, at the time of this writing, there are over 17,000 mutual funds to choose from in the United States—a bewildering array of choices and management styles.

There are two primary dimensions to consider in predicting any fund's performance: expected risk and expected return. The expected risk of a fund (usually measured by its volatility) is largely driven by its underlying investment style. Generally, a money market fund will have low risk, a bond fund moderate risk, and an equity fund higher risk. Most of the risk of the fund is derived from the types of investments in its portfolio. However, if the fund is actively managed, there will be an additional amount of fund-specific risk related to the management style of the fund. This is because the manager of the fund takes on some additional risk by deviating from the market proportions in the underlying asset class. For instance, a small-cap growth manager might concentrate her or his holdings in particular industries that she or he believes are undervalued rather than hold a broad-based portfolio of small-cap growth stocks. For some funds, this active management risk component is very small (for index funds, it is nonexistent). For others, it can be quite large and can make the fund significantly more risky than an index fund with the same investment style. A fund that changes its investment style over time can also increase fund-specific risk. When you hold such a fund, your estimate of the future investment style of the fund is uncertain. It may have more or less of certain asset class exposures in the future than it has now. This increases the risk of holding the fund since you don't know what its future investment style is going to be.

Funds also differ in their expected returns. Just as a fund inherits volatility from its underlying assets, a fund also receives expected return from the investments in its portfolio. But depending on the characteristics of the fund, its expected return can vary from that of the underlying asset classes in the following ways:

1. Expenses and trading costs will lower the expected return of a fund relative to its underlying assets.
2. Expected manager performance (alpha) can be positive or negative, which may have an influence on future expected returns.
3. Finally, the tax efficiency of a fund (or lack thereof) can determine its after-tax expected return for investors holding the fund in a taxable brokerage account.

It may come as a surprise, but the vast majority of mutual funds actually have *negative* expected performance relative to their underlying investment style. That is, most mutual funds are expected to underperform their underlying asset class exposures on a going forward basis, primarily due to the impact of expenses and the costs of trading. Most mutual funds charge management and administrative expenses and incur trading costs that detract from the net return going to shareholders. In addition, many active mutual fund managers underperform their investment style benchmark (negative manager alphas), which can also contribute to negative expected performance in the future. This does not mean that such funds have negative overall expected returns, but just that they can be expected to lag the returns from their investment style. Remember from our earlier discussion that on average, actively managed funds must have negative performance due to the impact of fees. Some managers may do better than average, but this implies that other managers must be doing worse than average.

With any fund selection methodology, it is important to recognize that there are serious limits to the ability to predict the future. After all, if it were that easy, then we would all be filthy rich. At best, we can find factors that will explain future performance *on average*, but for a given fund over a given time period there are many unpredictable events that can influence overall returns. Even the best fund selection methodology will only be right some of the time. This does not mean, however, that you should throw up your hands in despair. Following a rigorous selection process for your investment funds will make a difference in your performance over time. You won't always pick funds with the highest future performance, but you will avoid mistakes and have a better chance of reaching your goals in the long run.

Manager performance, properly measured, is somewhat predictive of future returns, but the effect is relatively weak and is subject to lots of statistical noise. Accordingly, we have to apply a hefty discount to the observed historical performance in order to correctly predict future performance. Since past performance is subject to random variation in returns, you cannot project that past performance will repeat in the same way. Given this fact, it is important to properly weigh the impact of historical performance in developing reasonable forecasts for future returns, which requires understanding not just the magnitude of the historical manager alpha, but also how consistent the performance was and for how long a period it was demonstrated by the manager.

All other things held the same; the performance of a manager with a longer and more consistent track record will be more predictive of future performance than one with a sporadic and shorter history. Managers with long track records of consistent outperformance are somewhat more likely to continue to outperform their investment style in the future. The same is true for managers who underperform their investment style; managers with consistently poor performance are somewhat more likely to underperform in the future relative to their investment style. But the impact of past manager performance is far from perfectly predictive. At best, the past performance of a fund is only partially indicative of the performance we might expect in the future. This has big implications for how you want to select funds. Factors like expenses are highly predictive, while manager performance is only somewhat predictive. If you can get additional performance for sure (say with lower fees), that is worth more than equal expected performance with a lot of uncertainty (by, say, betting on a good manager).

RATING FUNDS

The following examples look at the expected performance characteristics of several different types of mutual funds to illustrate how various factors combine to impact future risk and expected returns. This same process can be applied to institutional funds found in your employer retirement plan, though the required data can be more difficult to obtain. The following analysis is predicated on the methodology used by Financial Engines to evaluate and rate investment funds. It represents the efforts of more than a decade of financial research into the factors that influence mutual fund performance.

All analysis in this section is based on information as of May 2007. As such, you should treat these evaluations as snapshots in time. As time goes by the manager performance and other characteristics of funds are likely to change, potentially rendering these evaluations unreliable. The objective of working through these examples is to provide some insight into how various fund characteristics combine to generate an expectation of future investment performance. When using these techniques to select funds for your own investment portfolio, it is important to rely on up-to-date information (like that in the Financial Engines *Personal Online Advisor* service).

For this discussion, I have limited the examples to funds with at least $25 million in assets under management and at least 36 months of trading history. I have also limited the selections to those that have minimum initial investment amounts of $10,000 or lower, and excluded all funds with front- or back-end load charges. This last constraint is to simplify the comparisons to funds with similar fee structures. In short, these criteria ensure that we are looking at no-load funds that are available to typical individual investors, are likely to be around for awhile, and have track records of reasonable length. In some cases, the mutual funds may be closed to new investors at this time. The discussion of these specific funds should not be viewed as providing investment advice to any individual investor.

Bond Funds

The first type of investment we will examine are bond mutual funds. First, we decompose the expected performance of some popular bond and short-term fixed-income mutual funds. Our first example is the Bond Fund of America/R2 (symbol: RBFBX) from the American Funds family of mutual funds. This particular fund is a no-load version of a popular front-end load

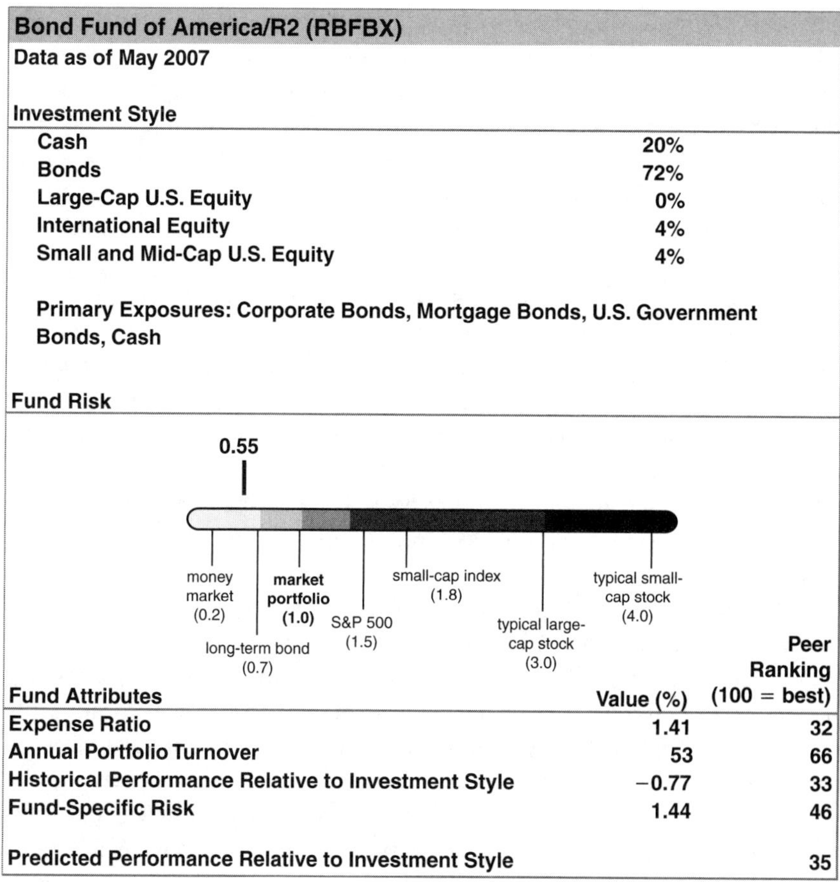

Bond Fund of America/R2 (RBFBX)
Data as of May 2007

Investment Style

Cash	20%
Bonds	72%
Large-Cap U.S. Equity	0%
International Equity	4%
Small and Mid-Cap U.S. Equity	4%

Primary Exposures: Corporate Bonds, Mortgage Bonds, U.S. Government Bonds, Cash

Fund Risk

Fund Attributes	Value (%)	Peer Ranking (100 = best)
Expense Ratio	1.41	32
Annual Portfolio Turnover	53	66
Historical Performance Relative to Investment Style	−0.77	33
Fund-Specific Risk	1.44	46
Predicted Performance Relative to Investment Style		35

FIGURE 9.2 Characteristics of the Bond Fund of America/R2 (RBFBX)

Sources: Financial Engines and mutual fund annual report.

fund with the same name. In this case the share class is known as R2 shares, created to make the fund more accessible to retirement plan investors in 401(k) plans where load charges are not permitted. The Bond Fund of America invests primarily in corporate, mortgage, and intermediate term government bonds. It also has smaller exposures to foreign bonds, cash, and equities. Figure 9.2 shows some important characteristics of the Bond Fund of America.

The investment style of the fund shows that 92 percent of its performance is related to the returns of bonds and cash. Note that cash is defined as fixed income exposure with less maturities of one year or less. But the fund also has modest exposures to small, mid-cap, and international equity. Why? This particular fund contains a small amount of equities in addition to fixed-income investments. However, certain bonds can actually have equity-like characteristics even if they hold no stocks if there is significant risk that the bonds could default. The higher the default risk of the bond, the more equity-like a bond will behave. In this case the performance of the Bond Fund of America is partially related to the movements in small, mid-cap, and international equities.

Compared to other bond funds with similar investment styles, this particular fund has a relatively high expense ratio at 1.41 percent. Ranked against its peers, less than a third of similar bond funds have expense ratios that are higher than the Bond Fund of America/R2. As we saw in Chapter 7, an expense ratio of this magnitude eats up a sizable portion of the expected returns of a bond fund (net of inflation). In this example, the expense ratio alone consumes 42 percent of the expected return (net of inflation) from the underlying bond assets in the fund—a pretty steep price to pay as a shareholder.

The fund has reported annual portfolio turnover of 53 percent, implying that the manager traded 53 percent of the portfolio positions in the previous year. Relative to similar bond funds, this is not an unusual level of trading activity. About two thirds of similar bond funds have annual turnover of 53 percent or higher. When a fund invests in short-to-intermediate bonds, some trading is required to replace positions that mature with new bonds. Since the cost of trading bonds is much lower than equities, portfolio turnover is a less important factor in explaining expected returns for bond funds than it is for equity funds. In this case, the implied costs of the portfolio trading only reduce the expected returns of the funds by a few basis points per year.

The impact of expenses and trading costs on expected fund performance is highly predictable. As a starting point, a good measure of a fund's predicted performance is to take the expected returns of the underlying assets and subtract the fund expenses. This baseline calculation is a critical part of any estimate of future fund performance. *Failing to adjust for the impact of fund expenses in predicting future performance is indefensible.* However, the more interesting part of predicting future fund performance is to consider the influence of manager performance. How does the manager add or subtract future expected return with a particular management approach?

Figure 9.2 also shows the historical performance of the fund relative to its average investment style. This measure quantifies the average annual performance of the fund relative to its underlying investment style on a net-of-fees basis. Often this number is referred to as the historical *manager alpha*. If the fund beat the performance of its investment style, the manager alpha is positive, and if it fell short of the performance of the underlying asset classes, the number is negative. In this particular manager alpha calculation, the complete return history of the fund is used to calculate the manager alpha, with more recent returns weighted heavier than those in the more distant past.[1]

According to this measure, the Bond Fund of America has underperformed its investment style by about 0.77 percent per year in recent years after accounting for fees. This implies that you would have done better with a passive investment with the same investment style over this time period, assuming you paid less than 0.77 percent in expenses for a comparable index fund.

If the performance net of fees was negative, did this manager add any value? Interestingly, we would expect that the fund would underperform its investment style by about 1.41 percent per year (the value of the expense ratio) due to the negative drag of expenses on expected returns. In this case, the fund manager was actually able to earn back some of those fees by demonstrating good performance. Before fees, the manager of this fund actually beat the investment style benchmark by about 0.64 percent per year. However, after deducting expenses, the net performance was a negative 0.77 percent per year relative to its investment style. The question is, how much weight should be placed on the possibility that the manager will be able sustain such performance in the future? To answer this question, we need to evaluate how consistent the performance track record was over time.

The fund-specific risk metric measures how consistent the manager's performance was relative to its investment style. The smaller the number, the more consistent the fund manager's performance over time. In this case, the volatility due to manager performance for Bond Fund of America's manager was about 1.4 percent per year. As bond managers go, this turns out to be a pretty typical number. About 46 percent of similar bond funds had fund-specific risk of this amount or higher. The management style of this fund was about as consistent as the median bond fund with a similar investment style.

Since the manager of the Bond Fund of America was adding value (before deducting fees), the predicted performance of the fund relative to its investment style is actually a bit better than the baseline estimate that only accounts for fees. Given the length of the track record (about 60 months) and the consistency of the results (typical for its investment style), we should place a positive weight on the expectation that the manager will continue to add value in the future (before fees) through its investment strategy. However, the weighting of past performance in predicting future performance should still be relatively small. Because there is variation in the historical track record and that this performance was demonstrated for a limited period of time, there is considerable uncertainty in the prediction of future manager performance. Because of this uncertainty, you need to reduce the weight that you place on the probability that the historical track will repeat itself. Of course, the actual performance of the fund in the future could be higher or lower than your prediction, but the correct statistical assessment of the observed performance is a small positive weight on history. The precise weighting of history can be determined by analyzing thousands of funds over long time periods to determine the statistical relevance of past manager performance in predicting future performance, given fund characteristics.

Putting all the factors together, the Bond Fund of America/R2 fund is expected to outperform about 35 percent of its peers with similar investment styles. A peer ranking of 35 percent implies that about two-thirds of similar investment style funds would be predicted to outperform the Bond Fund of America/R2 class in the future. The most important factors influencing this performance assessment are the relatively high expense ratio, partially offset by the good observed performance of the manager. In the end, the high expense ratio proves to be too tall a barrier to overcome, even for a manager with good investment performance over about five years of returns. As we noted earlier, bond funds are particularly sensitive to having their expected returns decimated by high fund expenses. As a shareholder, you don't get to enjoy the benefits of the good manager performance, because the fund's expense ratio more than covers the value added by the investment manager.

Now let's examine another bond fund with somewhat different characteristics. Our next example is the Fidelity Intermediate Government Income fund (FSTGX). The summary statistics for the fund are shown in Figure 9.3.

The investment style of the Fidelity Intermediate Government Income fund shows that 100 percent of its performance is related to returns of bonds and cash. The overall risk level of the fund is 0.41 times the volatility of the market portfolio, reflecting the fact that most of the assets are relatively short-term bonds guaranteed by the U.S. government with comparatively little risk.

In contrast to the previous example, this particular fund has a relatively low expense ratio at 0.45 percent compared to other comparable funds. Ranked against its peers, 93 percent of similar bond funds have expense ratios that are higher than the Fidelity fund. As a consequence, a relatively

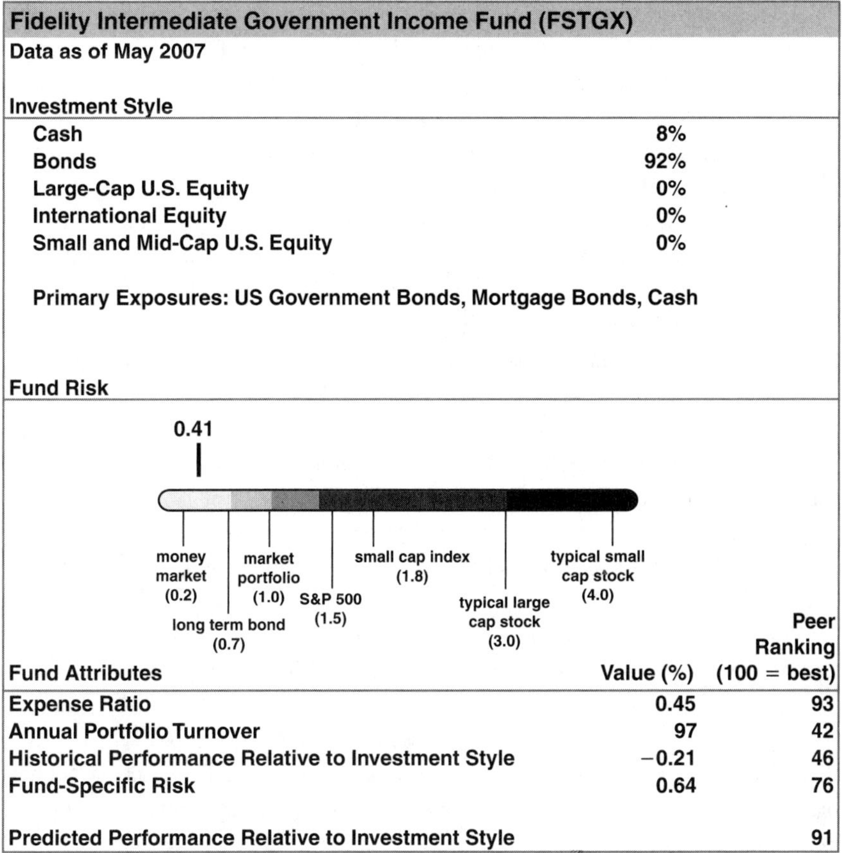

Fidelity Intermediate Government Income Fund (FSTGX)

Data as of May 2007

Investment Style	
Cash	8%
Bonds	92%
Large-Cap U.S. Equity	0%
International Equity	0%
Small and Mid-Cap U.S. Equity	0%

Primary Exposures: US Government Bonds, Mortgage Bonds, Cash

Fund Risk

Fund Attributes	Value (%)	Peer Ranking (100 = best)
Expense Ratio	0.45	93
Annual Portfolio Turnover	97	42
Historical Performance Relative to Investment Style	−0.21	46
Fund-Specific Risk	0.64	76
Predicted Performance Relative to Investment Style		91

FIGURE 9.3 Characteristics of the Fidelity Intermediate Government Income Fund (FSTGX)

Sources: Financial Engines and mutual fund annual report.

modest 18 percent of the total expected return (net of inflation) from the underlying assets is consumed by fund expenses. This makes the fund one of the more cost-effective funds in its peer group, despite being actively managed.

The Fidelity Intermediate Government Income fund reported annual portfolio turnover of 97 percent in the previous year, reflecting a relatively active management strategy and the necessity of more frequent reinvestment of shorter-maturity bonds. Compared to similar bond funds, about 42 percent of its peers with similar investment styles had higher turnover rates. But since the costs of such bond portfolio turnover are quite low, it has a negligible impact on the predicted returns of the fund.

Looking at manager performance, the Fidelity Intermediate Government Income fund underperformed its investment style by about 0.21 percent per year after accounting for fees. Again, as a baseline, we would expect that the fund should underperform its investment style by at least 0.45 percent (its expense ratio) due to the negative drag of expenses on expected returns, so this performance shows that the manager is adding some value through security selection. Before fees, the manager of this fund beat the fund's investment style benchmark by about 0.24 percent per year. Moreover, the Fidelity Intermediate Government Income manager's performance was achieved with only 0.64 percent per year in additional volatility. Compared to similar bond funds, this is in the lower quartile of volatility, implying a high degree of management consistency over time. About 76 percent of similar bond funds had fund-specific risk of this amount or higher. When evaluating the manager performance of this fund, the high consistency of the results makes it more plausible that such performance may be exhibited in the future.

Since the manager of Fidelity Intermediate Government Income was adding value (before deducting fees), the predicted performance of the fund relative to its investment style is higher than the baseline estimate. Given the long length of the track record (about 228 months), and the highly consistent nature of the manager's results, this fund has a higher probability of the manager continuing to add value (before fees) through its investment strategy. But again, the value added by the manager is relatively modest in magnitude compared to the overall expected returns of the fund.

Putting all the factors together, the Fidelity Intermediate Government Income fund is expected to outperform about 91 percent of its peers with similar investment styles. The primary factors influencing this assessment are the comparatively low expense ratio and the steady positive manager performance of the fund. These two factors imply a high likelihood that the Fidelity Intermediate Government Income fund will continue to outperform its peer group on a going-forward basis.

Large-Cap Funds

Now let's evaluate some funds that primarily invest in the equities of large-capitalization U.S. companies. Our first example is the Wilshire Large Company Growth Fund (symbol: DTLGX). As its name would indicate, this fund invests primarily in the stocks of large U.S. companies with high sales

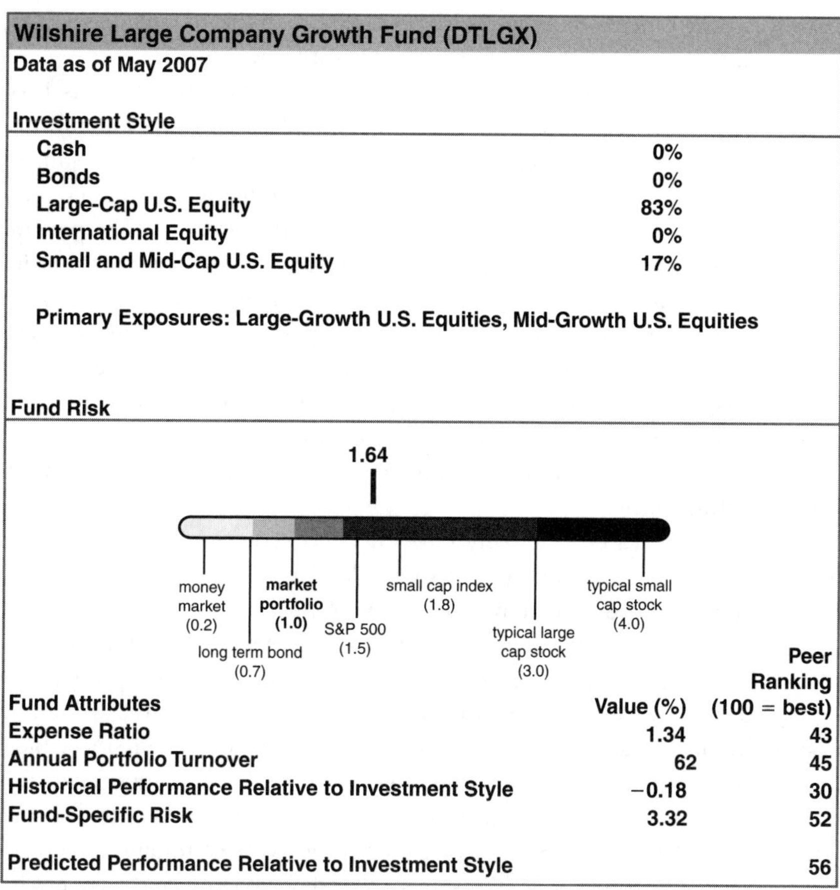

Wilshire Large Company Growth Fund (DTLGX)

Data as of May 2007

Investment Style

Cash	**0%**
Bonds	**0%**
Large-Cap U.S. Equity	**83%**
International Equity	**0%**
Small and Mid-Cap U.S. Equity	**17%**

Primary Exposures: Large-Growth U.S. Equities, Mid-Growth U.S. Equities

Fund Risk

Fund Attributes	**Value (%)**	**Peer Ranking (100 = best)**
Expense Ratio	**1.34**	**43**
Annual Portfolio Turnover	**62**	**45**
Historical Performance Relative to Investment Style	**−0.18**	**30**
Fund-Specific Risk	**3.32**	**52**
Predicted Performance Relative to Investment Style		**56**

FIGURE 9.4 Characteristics of the Wilshire Large Company Growth Fund (DTLGX)

Sources: Financial Engines and mutual fund annual report.

and earnings growth. Figure 9.4 shows the relevant summary statistics for this fund.

The investment style of the Wilshire Large Company Growth Fund shows that about 83 percent of its performance is related to the returns of large-cap growth stocks, and 17 percent to small- and mid-cap growth stocks in the United States. Unlike the previously analyzed bond funds, the risk of this equity fund is relatively high, at 1.64 times the volatility of the market portfolio. Given the fact that the fund concentrates in growth-oriented securities, it has volatility that is somewhat higher than the more balanced S&P 500, which includes both growth and value large-cap stocks.

Growth stocks tend to move more dramatically with the movements in the overall market and hence tend to be more volatile over time.

The expense ratio of the Wilshire Large Company Growth Fund is 1.34 percent per year, which places it near the middle of the pack for funds with similar investment styles. Ranked against peers, 43 percent of similar large-cap growth funds have expense ratios that are higher. In general, equity funds have higher expected returns than bond funds, so the impact of expenses as a *proportion* of total expected returns is less onerous, but in absolute terms, a loss of 1.34 percent per year to fees is still a meaningful loss. For this fund, 22 percent of the total expected return from the underlying equity assets is consumed by fund expenses. This may be a more modest proportion of total expected return because of the higher expected return assets in the fund, but it still has a big impact on expected portfolio outcomes. Never underestimate the impact of fund expenses on your future wealth accumulation.

The Wilshire Large Company Growth Fund reported annual portfolio turnover of 62 percent. Compared to similar large-cap equity funds, this is pretty typical. Approximately 45 percent of peers have annual turnover higher than this amount. However, unlike the previous bond fund examples, turnover is a bigger factor in estimating future expected returns for equity funds. The reasons are that it costs more to trade stocks than it does to trade bonds. Due to the impact of brokerage commissions, bid-ask spreads, and market impact costs, we estimate that this fund gives up more than 0.15 percent per year in expected return in addition to the impact of the fund's expense ratio. In general, the costs of trading large-cap U.S. equities are lower than the costs of trading smaller and less liquid stocks.

Now let's take a look at the fund manager's historical investment track record. The Wilshire Large Company Growth Fund underperformed its investment style by only 0.18 percent per year after deducting fees. This is quite good performance since we would expect that the fund should underperform its investment style by at least 1.34 percent, based on fund expenses. Before fees, the manager of this fund actually beat its investment style benchmark by about 1.2 percent per year. This is quite good manager performance for funds of this investment style.

Moreover, the Wilshire Large Company Growth Fund manager accomplished this feat by taking on only an average amount of additional risk for its investment style. About 48 percent of similar large-cap equity funds had fund-specific risk above that of the Wilshire fund. Given the magnitude of the manager outperformance, we would expect that the fund-specific risk would tend to be higher than average, but this manager has done a nice job of adding value without taking on a lot of additional volatility.

Since the manager of Wilshire Large Company Growth Fund was adding value (before deducting fees), the predicted performance of the fund relative to its investment style is higher than the baseline estimate. This fund also has a relatively long track record, spanning more than 14 years, so there is ample history to evaluate the performance and consistency of the fund manager.

Putting all the factors together, the Wilshire Large Company Growth Fund is expected to outperform about 56 percent of its peers with similar investment styles. Despite the very good performance before fees, the relatively high expense ratio of the fund brings the projected performance back down to close to the median fund in its category. This is an example where good manager performance is the victim of the relentless drag of fund expenses. Even good managers find it difficult to overcome the impact of higher fund fees. Had the expenses been lower, this fund would have been an even more attractive holding for large-cap equity exposure.

Now consider another large-cap equity fund, the American Century Income & Growth Fund (symbol: BIGRX). This fund invests primarily in a combination of U.S. large-cap value and growth stocks. Figure 9.5 shows the relevant summary statistics for this fund.

Most of the investment performance of the fund is related to large-cap U.S. equities (86 percent). The fund also has small exposures to mid-cap U.S. equity and a smaller percentage in international equities. Because of the higher-value equity exposure, the American Century Income & Growth Fund has lower volatility than the more growth-oriented Wilshire fund, with a risk rating of 1.46 times the market portfolio. This is roughly comparable to the volatility of the S&P 500 index.

The expense ratio of the American Century Income & Growth Fund is a relatively low 0.67 percent per year, which places it in the lowest 12 percent of funds with similar investment styles. Because of the lower fees, this fund only gives up a modest 9 percent of the expected return from the underlying equity assets to fund expenses. The lower expense ratio makes it much easier for this fund manager to provide value to shareholders.

In terms of turnover, the American Century Income & Growth Fund trades relatively frequently compared to its peers, with an annual turnover of 63 percent. Approximately 41 percent of peers have higher annual turnover. However, the fund is certainly not an extreme example of high turnover among its peers. It's level of trading activity is only slightly above the median fund with a similar investment style.

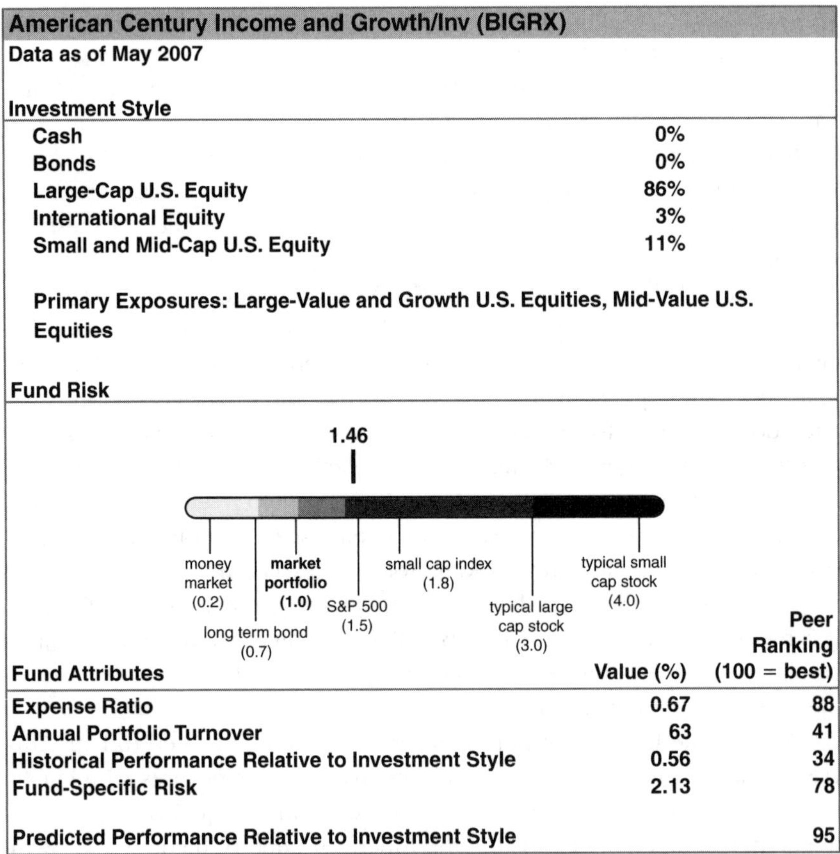

American Century Income and Growth/Inv (BIGRX)

Data as of May 2007

Investment Style	
Cash	**0%**
Bonds	**0%**
Large-Cap U.S. Equity	**86%**
International Equity	**3%**
Small and Mid-Cap U.S. Equity	**11%**

Primary Exposures: Large-Value and Growth U.S. Equities, Mid-Value U.S. Equities

Fund Risk

Fund Attributes	**Value (%)**	**Peer Ranking (100 = best)**
Expense Ratio	**0.67**	**88**
Annual Portfolio Turnover	**63**	**41**
Historical Performance Relative to Investment Style	**0.56**	**34**
Fund-Specific Risk	**2.13**	**78**
Predicted Performance Relative to Investment Style		**95**

FIGURE 9.5 Characteristics of the American Century Income & Growth Fund/Inv (BIGRX)

Sources: Financial Engines and mutual fund annual report.

Looking at manager performance, the American Century Income & Growth Fund *outperformed* its investment style by 0.56 percent per year after deducting fees. This is quite impressive performance, since we would expect that the fund should underperform its investment style by about 0.67 percent per year due to fund expenses. Before fees, the manager of this fund beat its investment style benchmark by a substantial 1.23 percent per year. Even more impressively, the manager accomplished this feat while taking only comparatively little active management risk compared to its peer group, ranking in the lowest 22 percent of similar funds. The fact that the performance was so consistent increases our confidence that the manager will be able to achieve similar performance in the future. If the manager performance had been less consistent, it would force us to further discount the observed historical performance since there would be greater uncertainty about whether it could be maintained. In this case, the long track record and steady performance gives us greater confidence in the future good performance of the manager.

Unlike the previous example with the Wilshire fund, the good manager performance of the American Century Income & Growth Fund is not consumed by the fund expenses and the costs of turnover. In fact, this fund has a significantly higher predicted performance than the baseline estimate. Given its characteristics and performance, the American Century Income & Growth Fund is expected to outperform about 95 percent of its peers with similar investment styles. By keeping the fees to a reasonable level and demonstrating highly consistent good manager performance, this fund is expected to outperform the vast majority of its peer group. This is an example of where an active fund manager is able to provide additional value to shareholders by keeping fees to modest levels, and demonstrating a long track record of consistent outperformance.

Small- and Mid-Cap Funds

Now let's examine some small- and mid-cap equity funds. Such funds tend to be more volatile than their large-cap counterparts. Partially this is due to the fact that smaller companies tend to be more volatile than larger ones. But also, small- and mid-cap fund managers tend to pursue more active investment strategies that increase the fund-specific risk of their funds. What would constitute a highly active strategy for a large-cap fund is only the middle of the road in the world of small- and mid-cap managers. In fact, the average small- and mid-cap fund has more than twice the fund-specific risk of the average large-cap equity fund. This implies that small- and mid-cap funds have a lot more variation in their manager performance than do large-cap funds. A wider spectrum of performance means more opportunities for both very good and very bad manager performance. Remember that the higher the volatility in manager performance, the higher the risk of the fund. With a very active manager, you increase your odds of seeing performance that differs significantly from the underlying investment style. Let's examine a couple of example funds to see how various factors play a role in predicting future performance.

The Dreyfus Founders Funds: Discovery Fund/F (symbol: FDISX) invests primarily in the stocks of small- and mid-sized U.S. companies with

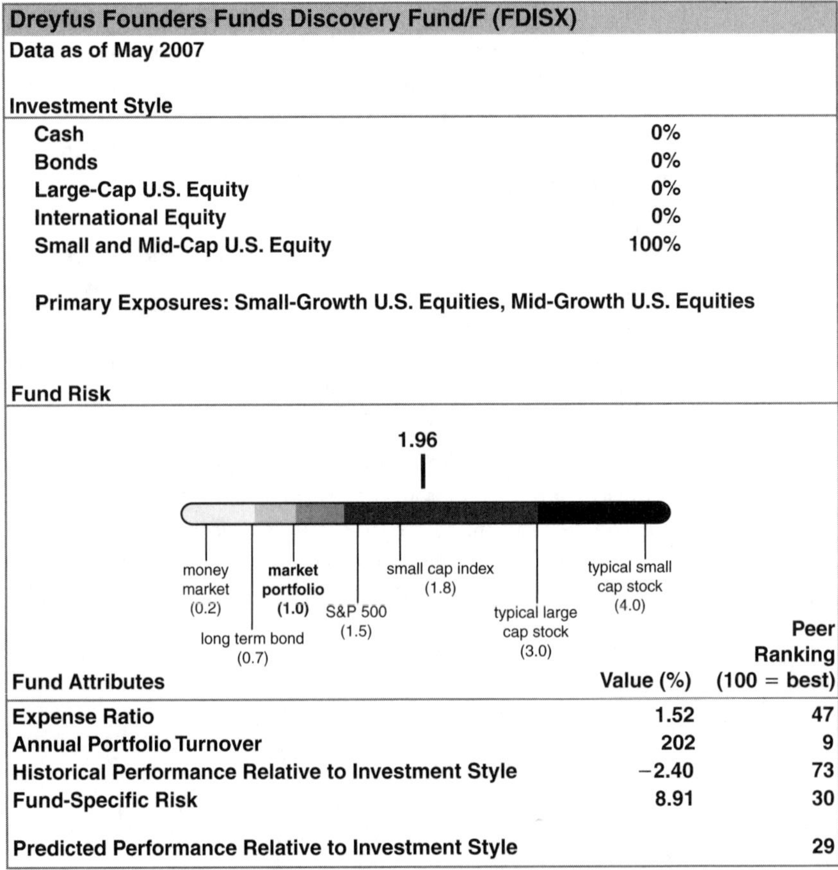

Dreyfus Founders Funds Discovery Fund/F (FDISX)

Data as of May 2007

Investment Style

Cash	0%
Bonds	0%
Large-Cap U.S. Equity	0%
International Equity	0%
Small and Mid-Cap U.S. Equity	100%

Primary Exposures: Small-Growth U.S. Equities, Mid-Growth U.S. Equities

Fund Risk

Fund Attributes	Value (%)	Peer Ranking (100 = best)
Expense Ratio	1.52	47
Annual Portfolio Turnover	202	9
Historical Performance Relative to Investment Style	−2.40	73
Fund-Specific Risk	8.91	30
Predicted Performance Relative to Investment Style		29

FIGURE 9.6 Characteristics of the Dreyfus Founders Funds: Discovery Fund/F (FDISX)

Sources: Financial Engines and mutual fund annual report.

high sales and earnings growth. Figure 9.6 shows the relevant summary statistics for this fund.

The investment style of the Dreyfus Discovery Fund shows that 100 percent of its performance is related to small- and mid-cap U.S. equity returns. Because of the higher volatility associated with small- and mid-sized companies, the risk rating of this fund is about twice the volatility of the overall market portfolio at 1.96. This kind of volatility is not that uncommon for funds that specialize in small- and mid-cap equities, but is significantly above the volatility for equity funds that invest in larger companies.

The expense ratio of the Dreyfus Discovery Fund is 1.52 percent per year, which is typical for active mutual funds with similar investment styles. Ranked against peers, 47 percent of similar funds have expense ratios that are higher. The Dreyfus fund gives up about 19 percent of the total expected return from the underlying equity assets to fund expenses, a considerable, but not overwhelming fraction. Partially this is due to the higher expected returns of the underlying small- and mid-cap growth assets.

As of May 2007, the fund reported turnover of 202 percent per year. This is a very high turnover rate for an equity mutual fund. Even among other small- and mid-cap equity funds, only 9 percent of peers have portfolio turnover higher than this amount. Due to the impact of brokerage commissions and bid-ask spreads, we estimate that this fund gives up at least an additional 0.60 percent in expected return beyond the impact of the fund-expense ratio.[2] When a manager engages in this level of trading activity, the additional costs become a significant drag on expected performance. The trading activity could turn out to be valuable if the trades result in better fund performance, but the costs associated with the trading raise the bar that the manager has to overcome before they can add value for shareholders. Such turnover can also make the fund much less tax efficient due to the more frequent realization of short-term capital gains when the manager sells positions in the portfolio. In Chapter 11 we will examine in more detail the impact of taxes on wealth accumulation.

Given the high level of portfolio turnover for the Dreyfus fund, we would expect this to be a very actively managed fund with significant additional risk beyond its underlying asset allocation. Indeed, the fund-specific risk is fairly high for this style of investment. Holders of this fund can expect an additional 9 percent per year of added volatility above and beyond the risk associated with the underlying mid- and small-cap assets. The Dreyfus Discovery Fund is thus substantially more risky than a comparable small- or mid-cap index fund. Again, the impact of this active management risk is much greater uncertainty about the future returns and performance of the fund. Unlike an index fund, the returns of the Dreyfus fund have the potential to vary significantly based on the performance of the specific securities in the fund portfolio. But how did the manager of this fund perform relative to its investment style?

As of May 2007, the Dreyfus Discovery Fund had underperformed its investment style by 2.40 percent per year after deducting fees, according to Financial Engines' analysis. Given the expense ratio of the fund, we would expect that the fund should underperform its investment style by at least 1.52 percent per year. The fact that this fund did worse indicates that, even before fees, the manager of this fund underperformed its investment style benchmark by about 0.9 percent per year. The bets it made on specific securities held in the portfolio did not perform particularly well. Some of this underperformance is due to the implicit fees paid by the manager for the high level of portfolio trading, but some of it is simply poor performance of the securities selected by the manager.

However, given the high volatility associated with the investment strategy, there is considerable uncertainty as to whether this historical performance is likely to repeat in the future. Basically, given the volatility of the manager's strategy, there is little information about future expected returns in the observed manager track record because it is so volatile. If it were positive, we would not have much confidence that it would continue. But the same goes for negative performance. Given the uncertainty, we have to attribute a large portion of the historical performance, positive or negative, to simply random luck. So even though the observed performance was negative in this case, there is little reason to expect that it will behave the same way in the future. Going forward, the performance could be better or worse than historically observed, but it is likely to be different. What this means is that you should not place a very big weight on the historical track record of this fund. Only managers with long track records of *consistent* positive or negative performance should receive a significant weight on history. So even though the observed performance of this fund was less than impressive, we have to admit the possibility that the negative manager alpha was simply due to bad luck, rather than the investment acumen of the manager.

Putting all these factors together, the Dreyfus Discovery Fund is expected to underperform about 71 percent of its peers with similar investment styles. The primary factors influencing this assessment are the relatively high expense ratio, very high portfolio turnover and fund-specific risk, and the negative performance of the fund relative to its investment style. Basically, this fund offers relatively expensive exposure to small- and mid-cap equities with a significant amount of additional volatility. You might get lucky in the future with such a fund, but it does not look like a good bet, given the alternative funds out there with the same investment style.

But what about a small- and mid-cap fund that is expected to do well versus its peers? The T Rowe Price Small-Cap Stock Fund (symbol: OTCFX) also invests primarily in the stocks of small-cap value and growth equities.[3] Figure 9.7 shows the summary statistics for the fund. At the time of this analysis (May 2007), it also behaved as if it held a small portion of its assets in cash.

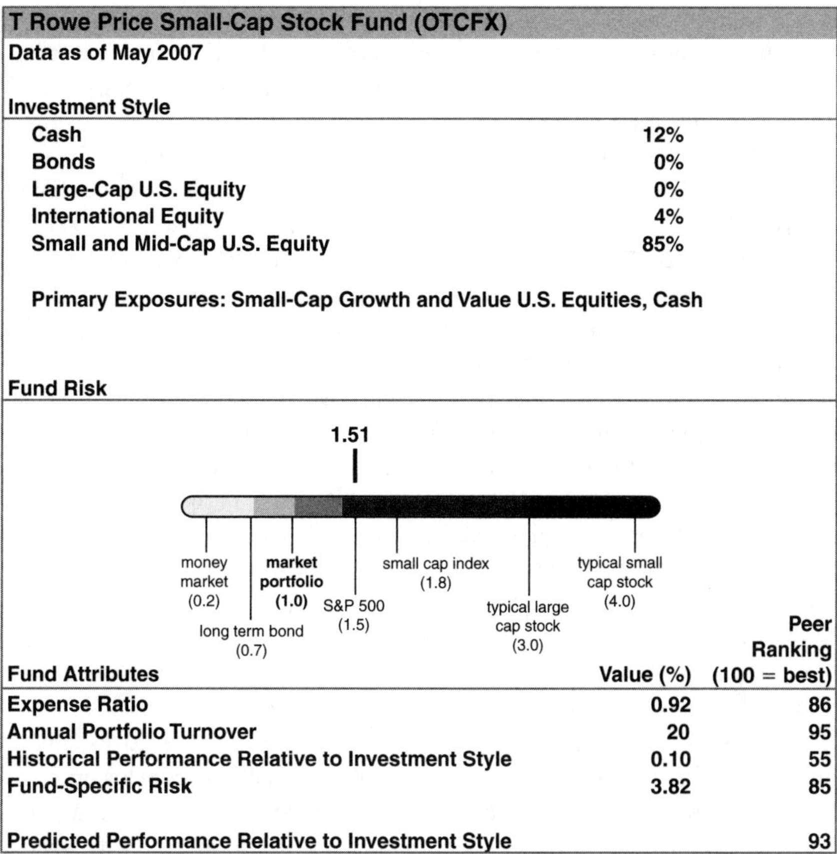

T Rowe Price Small-Cap Stock Fund (OTCFX)

Data as of May 2007

Investment Style

Cash	**12%**
Bonds	**0%**
Large-Cap U.S. Equity	**0%**
International Equity	**4%**
Small and Mid-Cap U.S. Equity	**85%**

Primary Exposures: Small-Cap Growth and Value U.S. Equities, Cash

Fund Risk

Fund Attributes	**Value (%)**	**Peer Ranking (100 = best)**
Expense Ratio	**0.92**	**86**
Annual Portfolio Turnover	**20**	**95**
Historical Performance Relative to Investment Style	**0.10**	**55**
Fund-Specific Risk	**3.82**	**85**
Predicted Performance Relative to Investment Style		**93**

FIGURE 9.7 Characteristics of the T. Rowe Price Small-Cap Stock Fund (OTCFX)

Sources: Financial Engines and mutual fund annual report.

The investment style of the T. Rowe Price Small-Cap Stock Fund shows that about 85 percent of its performance is related to the returns of small-capitalization U.S. companies. With the higher volatility associated with small-cap stocks, the risk of this fund is about 1.5 times the volatility of the market portfolio. While still reasonably volatile, it is quite a bit less risky than the more actively managed Dreyfus fund in the previous example. Lower fund-specific risk accounts for some of the reduced fund volatility, even though it shares a broadly similar investment style with the Dreyfus fund.

The expense ratio of the T. Rowe Price Small-Cap Stock Fund is 0.92 percent per year, which is on the lower end of active mutual funds with similar investment styles, but still markedly higher than most passively managed index funds and institutional small-cap funds. In the Financial Engines database, over 86 percent of similar small-cap funds have expense ratios that are higher than the T. Rowe Price Small-Cap Fund. Not surprisingly, the T. Rowe Price fund gives up only 14 percent of the total expected return of its underlying equity assets to fund expenses, a pretty low number compared to many of its peers.

As of May 2007, the fund reported turnover of only 20 percent per year. Again, unlike many of its actively managed peers, this is a pretty low number for an active small- and mid-cap fund. In fact, fully 95 percent of similar funds report higher turnover than that of the T. Rowe Price Small-Cap fund, and most of those with lower portfolio turnover values were index funds. Because of the relatively low turnover rate, the fund is also considerably more tax efficient than many of its actively managed peers.

Unlike the Dreyfus fund, the T. Rowe Price Small-Cap fund adds only a moderate amount of additional risk based on its investment strategy. A holder of this fund takes on an additional 3.8 percent per year of additional volatility beyond the risk of the underlying asset classes. Compared to its peers, only 15 percent of similar funds had lower fund-specific risk, and most of those were index funds. Thus the manager performance of this fund was quite consistent over time, compared to its peers.

So how did the manager of this fund perform relative to its investment style? As of May 2007, the T. Rowe Price Small-Cap Stock Fund had outperformed its investment style by 0.10 percent per year after deducting fees. Before fees, the manager of this fund outperformed its investment style benchmark by a healthy 1.0 percent per year. Moreover, the fund accomplished this feat without taking on much in the way of additional risk. Because the consistency of the performance was high, it is more plausible that the observed track record is more likely to be repeated in the future. This does not mean that you should simply project the historical performance going forward, but it does imply that the manager deserves some future credit for beating the investment style benchmark in a consistent way.

Putting all the factors together, the T. Rowe Price Small-Cap Stock Fund is expected to do better than 93 percent of its peers with similar investment styles. The primary factors influencing this assessment are the modest expense ratio, low turnover and fund-specific risk, and the strong positive performance of the fund relative to its investment style. Overall, this fund compares very favorably to its peers with similar investment styles.

International Funds

Finally, let's examine a couple of international funds to demonstrate how different combinations of fund characteristics influence projected performance. International funds are often more volatile than many domestic funds, as they may invest in less-developed markets and in companies that are more dependent on specific regions or sectors. However, international funds are desirable parts of a diversified portfolio due to the lower correlations of their assets with domestic stocks and bonds. Of course, some funds are better than others at delivering good performance and asset class diversification.

Our first example is the UBS PACE Funds: International Emerging Market Equity Fund (symbol: PCEMX), which invests primarily in the stocks of emerging market international equities. Figure 9.8 shows the relevant summary statistics for this fund.

The investment style of the UBS International Emerging Market Equity Fund shows that 93 percent of its performance is related to the performance of international emerging markets, with some small exposures to domestic equity. The overall risk of the fund is a relatively high 1.8 times that of the market portfolio. Emerging markets funds like this one invest in the stocks of companies from developing markets. Typically, the stock markets of developing countries like Chile, Malaysia, China, and India are more prone to global economic shocks, currency crises, and political instability. Accordingly, emerging market funds tend to be fairly volatile compared to domestic equity funds and those that invest in the more developed countries of Europe and Asia. However, emerging markets have very good diversification potential, especially for U.S.-based investors, and thus are desirable investments as part of a balanced portfolio. The higher risk of the fund does not translate into higher volatility of your overall portfolio since the movements of the emerging market funds tend to be less correlated with domestic equity.

The expense ratio of the UBS International Emerging Market Equity Fund is 1.98 percent per year (as of May 2007), which is definitely on the high end for retail mutual funds with similar investment styles. Ranked against peers in the Financial Engines database, only 25 percent of comparable emerging market funds have higher expense ratios. In general, emerging markets funds tend to have higher expenses than other asset classes, reflecting the higher costs of research and trading in developing markets. Because of these high fees, the UBS fund gives up about 30 percent of the total expected return from the underlying assets to fund expenses.

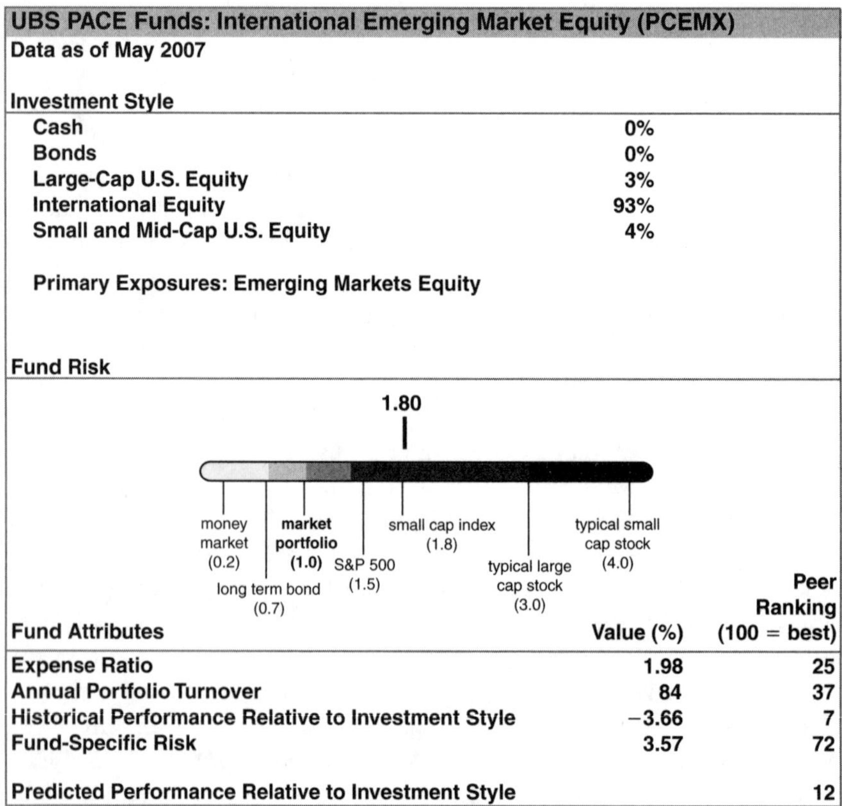

UBS PACE Funds: International Emerging Market Equity (PCEMX)

Data as of May 2007

Investment Style

Cash	0%
Bonds	0%
Large-Cap U.S. Equity	3%
International Equity	93%
Small and Mid-Cap U.S. Equity	4%

Primary Exposures: Emerging Markets Equity

Fund Risk

Fund Attributes	Value (%)	Peer Ranking (100 = best)
Expense Ratio	1.98	25
Annual Portfolio Turnover	84	37
Historical Performance Relative to Investment Style	−3.66	7
Fund-Specific Risk	3.57	72
Predicted Performance Relative to Investment Style		12

FIGURE 9.8 Characteristics of the UBS PACE Funds: International Emerging Market Equity Fund (PCEMX)

Sources: Financial Engines and mutual fund annual report.

Obviously this expense ratio has a marked impact on the expected returns of the fund.

As of May 2007, the fund reported turnover of 84 percent per year. This is a moderately high turnover rate for an actively managed emerging markets mutual fund. In this case, the UBS fund's turnover places it in the highest 37 percent of turnover for its peer group.

Despite the relatively high turnover, the fund only adds a modest amount of additional volatility for an actively managed fund, at about 3.6 percent per year. Relative to the fund's peer group, this is a pretty low number, reflecting relatively consistent management performance. More than 72 percent of comparable funds have higher levels of fund-specific risk than the UBS fund. The relatively low fund-specific risk means that the historical performance of the fund's manager is more relevant for predicting future performance.

Unfortunately, as of May 2007, the UBS International Emerging Market Equity Fund had underperformed its investment style (emerging markets) by about 3.7 percent per year net of fees. This is rather poor manager performance. Given the expense ratio and high turnover of the fund, we would expect the fund to underperform its investment style by about 1.8 percent per year. In this case, the fund actually underperformed its investment style by an average of –1.7 percent per year *before* fees were subtracted. With the high expense ratio of the fund, the net returns to shareholders were substantially worse than what would have been achievable with a more reasonably priced emerging markets index fund.

So what is the bottom line? The UBS International Emerging Market Equity Fund has a relatively high expense ratio, high turnover, and poor historical performance. Because its fund-specific risk is modest, the historical performance is a more meaningful indicator of future fund performance. Unfortunately, the weight of history is bad news for this fund, as the historical performance relative to its underlying investment style is negative. This fund is thus somewhat more likely to underperform its peers in the future, based on the research underlying fund performance. All together, the UBS International Emerging Market Equity Fund is expected to underperform about 88 percent of its peer group.

Our final example is the Dodge & Cox International Stock Fund (DODFX), a popular diversified international equity fund. Figure 9.9 shows the relevant summary statistics for this fund.

The investment style of the Dodge & Cox International Stock Fund shows that 84 percent of its performance is related to international equities, with some smaller exposures to large- and small-cap U.S. equity. The overall risk of the fund is about 1.4 times that of the market portfolio, considerably less risky than the more-specialized UBS emerging markets fund. The Dodge & Cox fund invests in a diversified portfolio of developed countries in Europe and Asia, as well as in less-developed emerging markets.

The expense ratio of the Dodge & Cox International Stock Fund is a low 0.66 percent per year (as of May 2007), which is pretty reasonable for an active international equity mutual fund, though still higher than most international index funds. Ranked against peers in the Financial Engines database, only 3 percent of comparable international funds have

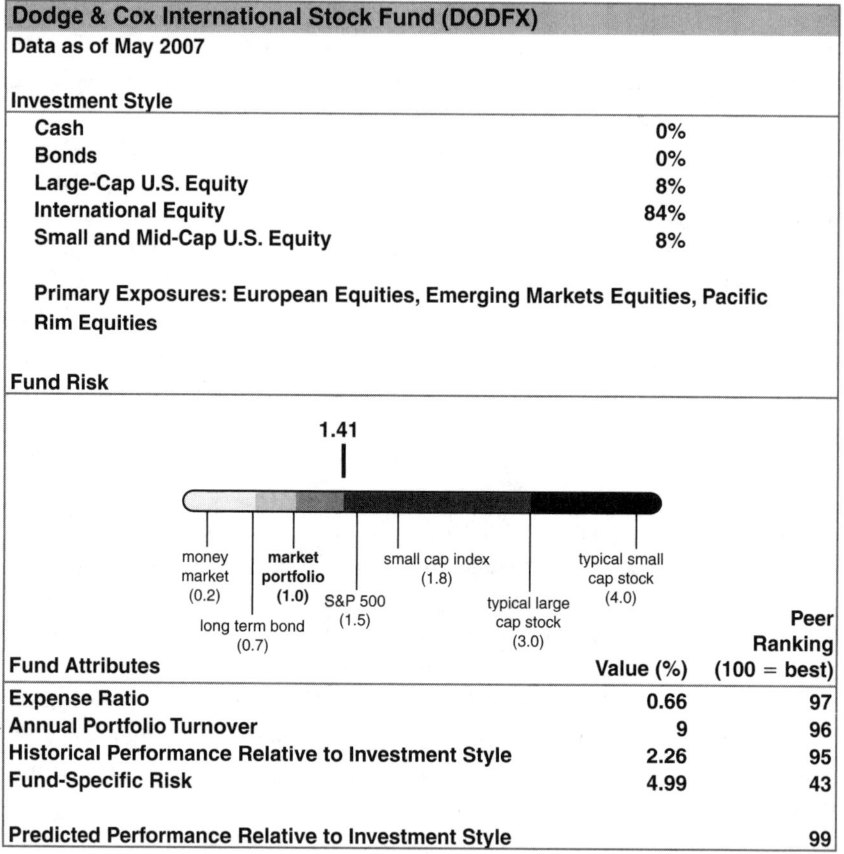

Dodge & Cox International Stock Fund (DODFX)
Data as of May 2007

Investment Style	
Cash	0%
Bonds	0%
Large-Cap U.S. Equity	8%
International Equity	84%
Small and Mid-Cap U.S. Equity	8%

Primary Exposures: European Equities, Emerging Markets Equities, Pacific Rim Equities

Fund Risk

Fund Attributes	Value (%)	Peer Ranking (100 = best)
Expense Ratio	0.66	97
Annual Portfolio Turnover	9	96
Historical Performance Relative to Investment Style	2.26	95
Fund-Specific Risk	4.99	43
Predicted Performance Relative to Investment Style		99

FIGURE 9.9 Characteristics of the Dodge & Cox International Stock Fund (DODFX)
Sources: Financial Engines and mutual fund annual report.

lower expense ratios, and most of those are index funds. Accordingly, the Dodge & Cox fund loses only 10 percent of the expected returns of the underlying assets to fund expenses.

As of May 2007, the fund reported turnover of 9 percent per year. This is a very low turnover rate for an active international equity mutual fund, comparable to that of an index fund. The low turnover means that the fund is paying less in the form of brokerage commissions and bid-ask spreads than its more active peers, and thus shareholders are keeping more of the expected returns of the underlying assets. Only 4 percent of international equity funds have turnover below that of the Dodge & Cox International Stock Fund.

The Dodge & Cox International Stock Fund has fund-specific risk that is pretty typical for an active international equity fund at about 5 percent per year in additional volatility. About 43 percent of comparable funds have higher fund-specific risk, so this fund is in the middle of the pack when it comes to fund-specific risk. The manager of the fund is clearly placing some bets that differ from a diversified index fund with a comparable investment style.

As of May 2007, the Dodge & Cox International Stock Fund had outperformed its investment style by about 2.3 percent per year net of fees, which represents strong positive performance. Given the expense ratio and turnover of the fund, we would expect that the fund should underperform its investment style by about 0.7 percent per year if the manager was adding no value. The Dodge & Cox International Stock Fund actually outperformed its investment style by an average of 2.9 percent per year before subtracting fees, which is evidence of very good manager performance.

Putting it all together, the Dodge & Cox International Stock Fund has a low expense ratio, low turnover, and very good historical manager performance. Because its fund-specific risk is moderate, the historical performance of the Dodge & Cox fund is meaningful in predicting future performance, but the weighting on history should still be modest since there is considerable uncertainty about future performance. Based on this analysis, the Dodge & Cox International Stock Fund is expected to outperform about 99 percent of its peer group, placing it among the best international equity mutual funds in terms of predicted performance relative to its investment style.

PUTTING THE PIECES TOGETHER

As we have seen, the difficulty with good fund selection is that the problem depends on many considerations, some of which are in tension with one another. It is difficult to come up with general rules of thumb that work well in all situations.

As illustrated in the previous examples, there are several fund characteristics that have a big influence on expected fund performance. Prominent among these factors is cost. It is clear from the research on fund performance that expenses are the single most predictable influence on future fund returns. Making sure that you are keeping expenses to reasonable levels is the most important criterion in selecting good funds, whether you choose to use index funds or active funds.

In the advisor community, debates rage on as to whether active or passive funds are the best choice for individual investors. There is little doubt that the average index fund outperforms the average active fund. In fact, a passive index fund will outperform the majority of comparable active funds in most time periods. But some active funds will do better than index funds. The only reason to select active management is the confidence that, after deducting fees, the manager you select will be able to add sufficient value in the future to beat the performance of the underlying investment style. Determining just which managers will accomplish such a feat turns out to be a challenging task, making confident predictions all the more difficult.

A central problem is that active fund management is what economists call a *zero sum game*. For an active manager to beat the market, he or she would have to trade with someone who underperforms the market. Not all active managers can be winners. *For every winner there has to be a corresponding loser.* Furthermore, active management costs more than running an index fund so, after deducting costs, the performance of the average active manager will be lower than the overall market, and therefore lower than the average index fund. But this does not mean that active management is a hopeless exercise.

As demonstrated in the preceding examples, there are managers who add considerable value above and beyond their fees over lengthy periods of time. But the central challenge is identifying these good managers before the fact. The best we can hope for is to make educated judgments about which managers are *more likely* to do well in the future relative to their investment style. Since the future is uncertain, it does not makes sense to simply extrapolate from history to predict the future. The impact of historical manager performance should be discounted to account for the fact that the past is unlikely to repeat itself exactly, whether the manager performance was positive or negative.

In the context of the Financial Engines fund methodology, both passive and active funds are subjected to the same analysis. The question analyzed is: does this fund offer desirable future risk-and-return characteristics after accounting for investment style, turnover, fees, and historical performance relative to an appropriate benchmark? The result of this analysis is that there are actively managed funds with reasonable fees and long track records of good performance that are competitive with low-cost index funds. So, in one sense, the methodology is agnostic when it comes to the active/passive debate. However, the significant majority of actively managed funds are not competitive with low-priced index funds. The higher expenses of such active funds are too large a hurdle for most managers to overcome. Beware of the tendency to rank funds based on past performance. Simply ranking on past performance within categories, which many advisors, web sites, and advisory services do, misses the most important factor in future fund returns, namely the impact of fees and costs. The predictable result is poor advice.

WHAT IT TAKES TO RANK AMONG THE BEST

So what does it take to rank within the top 10 percent of mutual funds in terms of expected performance? There is a wide spectrum of different fund characteristics that lead to good expected performance, but here are a few statistics of interest based on the Financial Engines mutual fund database as of May 2007.[4]

- The most expensive mutual fund ranked by Financial Engines in the top 10 percent of its peers for expected performance had an expense ratio of 1.36 percent, and only 4.5 percent of the top-ranked funds had expense ratios above 1.0 percent.
- The average expense ratio of this group is 0.44 percent, and the median fund had an expense ratio of only 0.36 percent per year.
- Historical manager performance relative to the underlying investment style ranges from an impressive high of +30 percent to a low of –5 percent per year. Interestingly, only 46 percent of the top-ranked funds had positive manager performance on a net of fees basis.
- For top-ranked *bond* funds, the highest expense ratio was 0.75 percent and the average was 0.28 percent.
- For top-ranked *large-cap* equity funds, the highest expense ratio was 0.77 percent and the average was 0.36 percent.
- For top-ranked *small- and mid-cap* funds, the highest expense ratio was 1.35 percent and the average was 0.66 percent.
- For top-ranked *international equity* funds, the highest expense ratio was 1.32 percent and the average was 0.71 percent.

Investments that meet these criteria will include both index funds and actively managed mutual funds. As of May 2007, the list of funds that are expected to outperform 90 percent or more of their peers contained more than 1,300 mutual funds from a large number of fund families. You can identify these funds by consulting the Investment Scorecards in the *Personal Online Advisor*. Many of these funds were index funds, but a large number were actively managed. Clearly you won't go wrong with picking low-priced index funds to provide the bulk of your investment portfolio needs. It is possible to find good active managers as well, but this requires careful consideration of costs, fund-specific risk, turnover, performance relative to investment style, and a willingness to monitor your portfolio closely over time. If you do want to pursue actively managed funds in the hopes of outperforming the market, be realistic about the level of effort required and also recognize that despite your efforts you may still fall short of what you could have achieved through an index fund strategy. For instance, the choice between an active fund with an expense ratio of 1.0 percent and a manager expected to add 0.60 percent of expected return per year, on average, and an index fund with an expense ratio of 0.40 percent is easy. You would always want to choose the sure thing in the index fund since the average net performance is the same. With the active fund you are making a bet that the manager will earn back the fees, but this is not a sure thing. Of course that manager might turn in performance that beats the expectation of 0.60 percent, but then again maybe he or she won't. On average, you would get the same net performance, but the risk is lower with the index strategy.

If you are not willing to put the effort into fund selection and monitoring, or are not willing to compensate a qualified advisor to do it for you, then the easy and safe approach is to use passively managed funds to build the bulk of your diversified portfolio. You are virtually guaranteed to outperform more than two-thirds of the actively managed funds with low-cost index funds. You won't beat the market, but you will get your fair share of the market returns. With good performing, reasonably priced active funds you might occasionally do better, but you might not. Remember that even the best active managers may underperform their investment style a significant portion of the time.

TAKE-AWAYS

- Fund expenses, including expense ratios and costs due to portfolio turnover, are important predictors of future investment performance.
- Generally you should avoid bond funds with expense ratios above 0.75 percent, large-cap funds with expense ratios above 0.75 percent, and small/mid-cap and international funds with expense ratios above 1.0 percent.

- Past performance is generally a weak predictor of future returns and is only relevant when the investment style and consistency of the manager's performance is taken into consideration.
- It is best to evaluate funds on how they behave, not what they label themselves. Some funds have very different investment styles than what their names might suggest.
- Compare the performance of funds against peers with similar investment styles. Bond funds should be evaluated against similar bond funds, and equity funds should be evaluated against similar equity funds.
- A manager with good historical performance is not guaranteed to repeat such results. As such, you should significantly discount history when predicting future investment performance.
- Low-cost index funds will beat the performance of most active mutual funds in most time periods. Finding high-quality active managers is difficult and time consuming. Unless you are willing to invest the effort, you should consider index funds as the most appropriate holdings for your core assets.
- Institutional funds like those sometimes found in the 401(k) plans of large companies are often much lower cost than mutual funds. Take advantage of these options if they are available to you.

CHAPTER 10

Funding the Future

If you would be wealthy, think of saving as well as getting.
—Benjamin Franklin (1706–1790)

Saving money to achieve financial goals is a tug of war between current wants and future needs. Investing requires some personal discipline, as funds put aside for the future cannot be spent today. One key lesson in funding financial goals is that time matters a great deal. The earlier you start saving, the easier it is to accumulate wealth. But when investing to achieve future goals, you must also take into account the impact of investment risk. There is a tradeoff between the level of confidence in reaching a goal and how much current income you are willing to commit to the effort. For a given investment horizon, higher confidence usually implies saving more. A successful plan requires being realistic about the amount of savings and the time required to achieve a high probability of success. Beyond the mantra of "start saving early," there are some surprising relationships between portfolio risk, time horizon, savings rates, and the chance of reaching financial goals.

Ultimately, investing boils down to a tradeoff between today and the future. You can increase the wealth of your future self by saving and investing a larger portion of your current income. Of course, this means the current you has to live on a bit less. At the risk of being repetitive, there really is no free lunch when it comes to investing. If you want to be certain that you will reach a future financial goal, and you aren't willing to wait longer, then you will have to save more. Supporting a \$300-a-month frappuccino habit now probably means feeling the pinch later in life (or at least being able to pinch an inch). The key to smart investing is making appropriate tradeoffs between your current financial needs and those you will face in the future. This sounds easy, but requires a bit of discipline. After all, by saving an extra \$300 per month, you can easily accumulate wealth of \$150,000 or more in today's dollars over a 25-year period.

Unfortunately, most of us are prone to focus more on immediate gratification than the needs of the future and grayer versions of ourselves. Saving for financial goals like retirement or our kids' college education is one of those activities where it is very easy to procrastinate. You immediately feel what you give up now, but can only speculate about the future benefit. When it comes to tough choices, giving up $100 this month seems to count more than having extra income in 30 years, even if giving up $100 per month today means a good chance of having $500 per month in additional retirement income for life.

I am going to spare you the long lecture on why it is so important to get started early with a savings program and focus instead on the more practical concerns of how to save to achieve goals with a high probability of success. Virtually every personal investing book ever written devotes many pages to the value of compounded returns and the importance of regular savings. These are very important concepts to embrace and understand, but there is more to the story than "get started early."

A central problem facing many investors is just *how* to invest their savings in order to have the best chance of reaching a goal. For instance, how much do I need to save in order to have a good chance of having adequate retirement income? Because both future market returns and inflation are uncertain, the answer to this question is not so obvious. The fact that future returns are uncertain means there is variability in investment outcomes. With any given investment and savings strategy, there will be scenarios where the goal is reached and others where you may fall short. How do you make the best decisions to maximize your chances of success? Finding the answers to these questions requires understanding the relationship between the key variables of time, risk, and savings.

At a high level, developing a savings plan is a bit like playing a game of financial Whac-A-Mole. You can save less, but you will need to invest for a longer period of time. Or you can take less risk, but you need to save more. You can invest for a shorter period of time, but only if you save more. Each decision is linked with the others and there is no way to improve one objective without giving up something elsewhere.

THE BENEFITS OF BEING FLEXIBLE

During the meandering path of our lifetimes, there are many types of financial goals that we strive to reach. Some goals are short term in nature, such as having enough money to pay the taxes to Uncle Sam next quarter or paying for that trip to Hawaii next spring, while others might span decades of time, such as investing for the retirement of you and your spouse or partner. Clearly the size of a goal matters, but there are other characteristics that have an impact on your investment plans as well. The objective with saving and investing is to accumulate sufficient assets over a period of time so that you can adequately fund a goal. When setting up an investment plan, there are a few considerations about goals that are important to evaluate:

- **Time horizon**: One of the most important factors is how long you have to accumulate assets. The longer the time period, the less you have to save. Also, if the goal is far in the future (e.g., retirement), then you have more flexibility in the appropriate investment strategy. If the goal is short term in nature, your investment choices will typically be more limited.
- **Flexibility in time**: Some financial goals have a rigid time horizon. For instance, your child may plan to go to college in four years, the summer after completing high school. In this situation, it is not easy to delay the need for the first year's tuition and room and board (although you could take out a loan to defer the full cost). For other goals, like retirement, the specific horizon may be inherently more flexible. As an example, you might choose to delay retirement by a year or two if markets perform particularly poorly. The point here is that goals with variable time horizons create additional flexibility for an appropriate investment strategy. If things don't go as planned, you might be able to delay the goal to ultimately reach success.
- **Flexibility in size**: For some financial goals, the amount of money needed is known in advance and is fixed. For instance, maybe you need to make a property tax payment next April of $15,000. In this case, the tax assessor is not going to take $13,000 if markets happen to perform poorly. You need to come up with exactly $15,000 next April. For other types of goals, the amount needed might be squishier. Perhaps you are saving money for the purchase of a vacation cabin in 5 years. You might like to have $100,000 to purchase the cabin of your dreams, but maybe you would be willing to settle for an $80,000 one a little farther away from the lake if markets don't perform as well as expected. For goals with less rigid funding requirements, you can accept more investment risk than for goals with very specific requirements. If markets don't perform very well, then you have the option to reduce

your expectations a bit. In many ways, this idea is similar to the flexible time horizon mentioned above.

- **Lump sum versus recurring**: Another consideration is whether the money to fund the goal is needed all at once (lump sum), or whether it will be paid out over time. For instance, you typically don't need to come up with the full cost of a 4-year college education all on the first day of classes. The payments will be generally spread out over a 4-year period. In effect, goals with recurring payments have a longer time horizon than lump sum goals, depending on the length of the period over which the payments occur. Of course, retirement goals are a special class of recurring payments, since the length of time that you (and perhaps your spouse) will need retirement income depends on your lifespan. Since we don't know when we are going to die, this creates the need for a string of income payments with an uncertain end date.

In the examples that follow, I will demonstrate how to construct savings strategies that will help you to reach different kinds of financial goals. But keep in mind the idea that flexibility—either in terms of timing or the size of the goal itself—is an important consideration when selecting an appropriate savings and investment strategy.

TAXABLE AND TAX-DEFERRED SAVINGS

Today, there are a variety of different types of investment accounts that can be used to save for future financial goals. For retirement savings, the most prevalent account types are defined-contribution plans such as 401(k)s and traditional *Individual Retirement Accounts* (IRAs). What makes these accounts valuable is that in most cases, the accounts can be funded with pretax dollars and accumulate assets without having to pay any taxes until the funds are distributed from the accounts, typically after retirement. For IRA accounts, there are strict limits on the amount of income you can earn to qualify for the ability to make pretax contributions and the total amount of the contributions is limited (up to $6,000 per year in 2008 across all IRA accounts). For employer retirement plans like the 401(k), the contribution limits are generally higher. In 2008, the pretax contribution limit for 401(k) plans was set at $15,500 per year ($20,500 if you are over 50. Of course, in addition to the 401(k) and IRA, there are many other types of retirement savings account types, including 403(b), 457, SEP-IRA, and SIMPLE IRAs, among others.

By funding an account with pretax dollars, you are lowering the taxes that you have to pay now. Paying fewer taxes now is a good thing. Every dollar you put into a traditional 401(k) is a dollar deducted from your taxable income, which lowers what you have to pay in state and federal taxes. This property of deferring taxes into the future is one of the fundamental benefits of being able to contribute to a defined contribution plan like a 401(k). In addition, your investments accumulate returns without having to pay capital gains taxes on the appreciation or income taxes on the income distributions (interest and dividends) until you begin taking money out of the accounts. This means that your investments will grow faster over time. Because of this benefit, it usually makes good sense to take advantage of the opportunity to invest in tax-deferred accounts when planning for long-term goals like retirement. This is doubly true when your employer matches your contributions into a 401(k) plan. An employer match is essentially "free money" and you would be foolish not to save enough to maximize your employer matching contributions. But even for contributions above those that maximize the employer match, tax-deferred accounts like the 401(k) provide a significant benefit for long-term wealth accumulation.

In the last 15 years, new types of IRAs and 401(k) plans have been introduced by Congress called *Roth* accounts. Unlike a traditional IRA or 401(k) plan, the Roth versions of these accounts only accept after-tax contributions, meaning there is no immediate tax benefit, but the assets in the account accumulate tax-free just like a normal 401(k) or IRA. Furthermore, unlike the traditional versions of the accounts, you will not owe any taxes on the accumulations when you begin distributions. Instead of paying taxes on the back end, you are paying the taxes up front with a Roth account. Roth 401(k) plans are currently offered by only a small number of employers at the time of this writing, but are expected to become more widely available in the years ahead.

There is quite a bit of confusion in the marketplace regarding whether you should put money in a regular IRA or 401(k) versus the Roth versions of the accounts. In many situations, there is little difference between the two account types in terms of money that you will accumulate over time.[1] Essentially, the primary issue in determining whether to choose one account type over the other comes down to what you think about your future tax rates relative to your current tax rates. If your current tax rates are the same as your future tax rates when you retire, and you are not fully maxing out your pretax contributions limit, then there is no real difference between the traditional 401(k) plan and the Roth version (or for the IRA). Whether you pay the taxes on the back end with the traditional accounts, or pay them up front with the Roth versions, you get the *identical* answer if the tax rates pre- and post-retirement are the same.

If you believe that your future tax rates will be *lower* than your current tax rates (which is quite plausible for many people in their peak earning years), then the traditional 401(k) will be a better choice, since it provides an immediate tax benefit by accepting pretax contributions. But if you believe that your future tax rates will be *higher* than your current rates, then the Roth account will be a better choice, since it allows you to avoid the payment of future taxes at the higher rate. Remember, that in both cases, the assets in the account accumulate capital gains and dividends without having to pay taxes along the way.

There is one caveat to this description, which is that if you are currently maxing out your pretax contribution limit for your 401(k) plan (set at $15,500 per year in 2008), and you have the desire and ability to save even more, then the Roth 401(k) may provide additional benefits. Why? Because a dollar held in a Roth account is worth more than a dollar held in a traditional 401(k) account, since you have already paid the taxes on it. In a traditional account, you still have to pay taxes on the money in the account when it is distributed. In the Roth account, you have already paid the taxes when you put the money in. In effect, a Roth 401(k) account allows you to put more wealth into it than a traditional account (after adjusting for taxes). If you have the money to save more now and desire to do so, a Roth 401(k) plan or Roth IRA allows you to effectively get more money into the account, even though the contribution limits are the same. However, if you are not able to max out your pretax savings in a traditional 401(k) account, this effect has less impact on your account type preferences. For most people, you will not be making much of an error with either the traditional or the Roth versions of the accounts. *It is far more important to take full advantage of one of the retirement account options than to get hung up on which one is best for you.* Don't let the choice between Roth and traditional 401(k) paralyze you from regularly saving into your employer retirement plan.

So what if you have exhausted your pretax and Roth savings opportunities? Then you should consider taxable savings through a brokerage account. With appropriate investment selection, you can achieve very respectable asset growth rates in a taxable account, despite having to pay income and capital gains taxes on the earnings. The key is to select investments that are highly *tax efficient*. That is, pick investments that will not generate large annual taxable distributions that detract from your after-tax portfolio growth rate. As we will see in Chapter 11, there is a wide range of tax efficiency among investments typically held in taxable accounts. Luckily, there are a number of very tax-efficient alternatives that the intelligent investor can use to generate good results.

HOW MUCH DO YOU NEED?

For goals like a vacation home or college tuition, it is usually not too difficult to figure out how much money you will need to be successful. Though sometimes, for goals like a college education, it can be challenging to determine how much inflation is likely to occur over your investment horizon. For retirement planning, however, the question of how much income you might need can be a complex issue. The principal problem is that you don't know up front how long you will need to fund your retirement income. While it is relatively easy to calculate our expected lifespan, we don't know whether we are going to fall short of the average or perhaps live much longer than expected. In the arena of retirement planning, dropping dead early does not pose much of a financial issue, but living too long can be a real pain in the pocketbook. Running out of money before you are ready to say goodbye to this world is not a great idea.

In the mid-1990s, I once evaluated a popular retirement planning software product that gave you a red or green light depending on whether you were on track to retire successfully. Since your estimated lifespan was used to determine the length of time for which retirement income would be needed, the software asked several questions about your health. Among them was whether you smoked regularly. Often, by answering yes, you could change your projection from red to green! Don't have enough to retire comfortably—try smoking! Obviously I don't recommend chain smoking as a prudent way to reduce your retirement income needs, despite its likely effectiveness. Figuring out how to deal with uncertain longevity is a key issue in retirement planning and few people can accurately predict their own lifespan.

There are many strategies used by investors to estimate the amount of retirement income that they will need, and how much money is required to generate such income. The topic is sufficiently complex that I will not attempt to cover it in a comprehensive way here. But I can provide some simple guidelines that make picking a reasonable retirement goal an easier task. One way to think about your needs in retirement is to consider what kind of retirement salary would allow you to maintain your pre-retirement standard of living. If you are living comfortably on $100,000 per year now (pretax), then how much money will you need to maintain your comfortable lifestyle after you retire? For most people, the answer is a number *less* than the income in the year prior to retirement (in today's dollars). That is, for most folks, the amount of income you will need in retirement is often less than what is needed while you are working. For instance, when you are retired, you no longer have to save for retirement. In addition, you may have paid off your home mortgage by then. Perhaps you are able to downsize your house now that the kids are off to college. Often, transportation costs go down without the daily commute into the office. True, some costs may go up in retirement. For instance, you may want to go on more frequent vacations, taking advantage of your free time. Also, medical costs might increase in your retirement years, depending on your quality of health and access to retiree medical benefits.

In determining your retirement income goal, you need to consider all the major puts and takes together to determine your income needs. This can be a rather personalized calculation depending on your financial, marital, tax, and health circumstances. However, the general consensus among advisors and economists who study such things is that most people will need approximately 60 percent to 80 percent of their pre-retirement income in order to maintain their standard of living. Of course, your mileage may vary. For some people, the number could actually be significantly higher than their pre-retirement income, while others may get along for much less. One factor that can strongly influence this calculation is whether you have access to retirement health care and adequate insurance coverage for catastrophic or long-term care needs. As an example, if you are comfortably living on $100,000 per year in pretax income, and plan to retire in a year, then you are likely to need between $60,000 and $80,000 in pretax income for as long as you live in order to maintain your standard of living.[2] But keep in mind that individual circumstances may vary widely.

The Financial Engines *Personal Online Advisor* service actually suggests setting up two different retirement income goals, a *desired* income goal for how much you would like to strive for, and a *minimum income* goal you would be willing to live on if necessary. The default values for these income goals are set at 70 percent and 50 percent of your pre-retirement income, respectively. The basic idea is that you want to have a reasonable shot at reaching your desired goal, and be quite certain that you will have enough to support your minimum retirement income goal. You can, of course, adjust both of these goals to better reflect your circumstances and preferences if desired.

One important consideration is that your income (and thus your standard of living) will tend to increase over time, even adjusted for inflation.

This is particularly true if you are younger or in the early stages of your career. This means that you need to take into consideration that your income in the year prior to retirement will likely be higher than your current income due to the impact of future raises and adjustments. You might assume that you would be comfortable in retirement living on 70 percent of your *current* income, but you may be disappointed when you actually get there. What seemed like a comfortable standard of living at age 40 might not look so great when you reach age 55. It is easy to lose track of the gradual increase in how much money you spend to support your lifestyle. Things that were once luxuries have a curious habit of turning into necessities. It is always a good idea to periodically review your retirement goals in response to changes in income or financial circumstances.

In the *Personal Online Advisor* service, this adjustment is calculated for you based on an assumption that your income will increase by 1.5 percent per year, adjusted for inflation. This assumption is consistent with the estimates used by many pension funds, but it might not always be appropriate for your situation. If you believe that your future income growth will be higher or lower, then you should update the default assumption accordingly. The key point is that you want to compute your retirement income needs relative to the standard of living that you will enjoy immediately prior to retirement, not relative to your current income.

FROM WEALTH TO INCOME

Once you have figured out your desired retirement salary, the next step is to determine how much money you need to accumulate to afford such an income. What makes this challenging is that you don't know how long you are going to live. Economists call this uncertainty *longevity risk*, and it is one of the more challenging issues in personal financial planning. If you could accurately predict your lifespan, future inflation, and future investment returns, then it would be a trivial calculation to determine what retirement income could be supported from a given portfolio value. But each of these quantities is uncertain, so the problem of figuring out how big your nest egg needs to be is a bit more complicated. Of course, how much money you will have in the future is also uncertain, since it depends on future market returns which are impossible to predict with any certainty. A comprehensive treatment of how to maximize retirement income from accumulated financial assets is well beyond the scope of this chapter and could easily fill another book. But there are some techniques that can provide some useful insights.

One way to simplify the conversion of accumulated wealth into an estimate for retirement income is to consider the amount of income that could be "locked in" for as long as you live. For instance, you could go to an insurance company and ask how much income, adjusted for inflation, will they guarantee for you as long as you live in return for the value of the assets in your retirement portfolio. The insurance company would then implement a strategy that provides guaranteed payments for as long as you might live. Such a guarantee of retirement income is called an *annuity*. If you wanted to, you could fully annuitize your portfolio and convert its value into a stream of income payments that will last as long as you live. This strategy gets rid of longevity risk, investment risk, and even inflation risk if the annuity is adjusted for inflation. It does not matter how long you live, or what happens in the market, you will continue to receive constant payments in retirement. However, when you die, there would be no assets available for your heirs. The insurance company gets rid of the longevity risk by pooling your assets with those of lots of other people. The insurance company cannot predict who will live a long time and who will die early, but with a large enough pool of people they can accurately predict the distribution of payments they will need to make on average. In effect, those who outlive their life expectancy are subsidized by those who pass away earlier than expected. The insurance company only has to worry about the average life expectancy of the annuity applicants to correctly price the annuity. Of course, the annuity is only valuable to the investor if the insurance company is around to pay the benefits when they are due. Accordingly, you are well advised to purchase such products only from those companies with the highest credit ratings and stability.

While most investors typically don't end up converting all their assets into annuities at retirement, the resulting income estimate from such a calculation does provide a reasonable estimate of how much income your portfolio value could support. As such, the inflation-adjusted annuity value of your portfolio is a good proxy for how much income you can afford to lock in over your lifetime if you wanted to. Financial Engines uses this inflation-adjusted annuity value to convert portfolio values into income estimates. It is not meant to be an exact estimate, as you may choose to follow a different retirement income strategy other than fully annuitizing your wealth, but it does provide a credible idea of the standard of living you could afford in retirement.[3] One thing to keep in mind is that this income estimate assumes that *all* of your retirement wealth is used to generate income. This means none of the money is bequeathed to your heirs. Obviously, if you

TABLE 10.1 Inflation-Adjusted Income Estimates Based on a Portfolio Value of $1,000,000

	Constant Inflation-Adjusted Income Estimates	
Retirement Age	Male	Female
60	$56,369	$52,451
61	$57,914	$53,693
62	$59,554	$55,009
63	$61,298	$56,402
64	$63,144	$57,876
65	$65,105	$59,436
66	$67,189	$61,089
67	$69,396	$62,844
68	$71,748	$64,714
69	$74,282	$66,720
70	$77,007	$68,885

Sources: Financial Engines calculations and 1994 Group Annuity Mortality (GAM) table.

plan to leave money to family or charity, then it will reduce the retirement income that you will be able to afford through annuitization.

Table 10.1 provides some sample estimates of the inflation-adjusted annuity value of a $1,000,000 retirement portfolio assuming that you retire at different ages, calculated for the estimated lifespans of both males and females.

Table 10.1 assumes for each retirement age that you fully annuitize the portfolio at the beginning of retirement. For instance, a male retiring at age 64 with $1,000,000 would be able to generate retirement income of approximately $63,000 per year for life. One thing that immediately strikes you about this table is that women seem to be getting a raw deal. Why are income values for women significantly lower than the values for men? Fortunately, there is a straightforward explanation. The reason for the lower income estimates for women is simply that they live longer than men. Because male lifespans are shorter on average, it costs less to guarantee future income to a man than it does for a woman. Whether you actually choose to annuitize your portfolio, or simply manage the investments and generate income yourself, you need to account for the higher average lifespan of women when developing a retirement plan. The other striking thing about

TABLE 10.2 Required Portfolio Values at Retirement to Achieve $100,000 in Inflation-Adjusted Income for Life

	Portfolio Values Required to Fund $100,000 in Inflation-Adjusted Income for Life	
Retirement Age	Male	Female
60	$1,774,000	$1,907,000
61	$1,727,000	$1,862,000
62	$1,679,000	$1,818,000
63	$1,631,000	$1,773,000
64	$1,584,000	$1,728,000
65	$1,536,000	$1,682,000
66	$1,488,000	$1,637,000
67	$1,441,000	$1,591,000
68	$1,394,000	$1,545,000
69	$1,346,000	$1,499,000
70	$1,299,000	$1,452,000

Source: Financial Engines calculations.

the table is how the income-equivalent values increase rapidly as you select later retirement ages. Again, the reason is expected lifespan. If you delay retirement by a year, there is one less year in expectation that you will need to fund your retirement income. Delaying retirement can be a very effective strategy for those who are late to the savings game.

With a reasonable retirement income strategy, you can assume that your retirement assets will yield inflation-adjusted income of approximately 5.6 percent to 7.7 percent of assets per year for men, and 5.2 percent to 6.9 percent per year for women, depending on your age at retirement and other circumstances. If you do not choose to use annuities in your retirement strategy (and thereby miss the benefit of pooling longevity risk), you may need to reduce your income expectations a bit.[4]

Table 10.2 shows the approximate portfolio values (in pretax terms) required in the year of retirement for single male or female investors to achieve $100,000 in inflation-adjusted income for life.

From Table 10.2 we see that it costs about 15 percent more to retire at age 60 than it does to retire at age 65 for a man, while a woman would need about 13 percent more to retire 5 years earlier. Again, the difference is a bit smaller for women as they are expected to live longer. Unfortunately for us guys, giving up a year of retirement saves more money because there are expected to be fewer retirement years to worry about. Of course, you can use the estimates in Table 10.2 to estimate the required retirement savings for any desired retirement salary. For instance, if you wanted to know approximately how much money is needed to afford a pretax retirement income of $75,000 per year at age 62 for a woman, you would multiply the value in the table by 75 percent ($1,818,000 × 0.75 = $1,363,500).

Now that you have some ballpark estimates of what you might need, the next step is to determine how much you will need to save and for how long in order to accumulate these kinds of retirement assets.

THE MYTH OF ABSOLUTES

Many advisors and retirement calculators still rely on savings models that assume a fixed rate of return for your investment portfolio. With such deterministic assumptions, it becomes a relatively simple calculation to determine whether a goal is reached or not. Either you have enough money or you don't. The problem is that these analyses rely on two flawed assumptions—that future market returns are constant through time and that they are known in advance. Sure, if we could talk to a magic genie who could tell us how our investments would perform, it would be easier to figure out how much to save, but that is not the world we live in (unless you happen to be hitting the Pinot Noir a little too heavy). Any savings plan must take into account the reality that market returns vary over time in unpredictable ways. Of course, this means that portfolio outcomes are also uncertain and therefore there is no black and white answer to the question "will I have enough?" You won't know for sure whether you are going to reach a certain level of wealth in the future. The best you can do is estimate *how likely* you are to get there. Portfolio simulation, like that provided in the Financial Engines *Personal Online Advisor* service, can be a big help in answering these types of questions.

An interesting consequence of thinking about investment performance in a probabilistic way is that the main objective is to have *high confidence* that you will be successful in reaching a goal. It is very expensive to guarantee that you will have a certain amount of money in the future, but if you can tolerate some uncertainty, you can likely fund your future goal with significantly less savings. How confident do you need to be? The answer varies depending on the type of goal and the consequences for falling short. If you are paying your taxes next year, you want to be very confident that you will have sufficient assets to meet the liability. This implies a very conservative investment strategy that does not expose you to the possibility of coming up short. But if you are saving for retirement, there may be some wiggle room in the amount that you will need. A minor shortfall might be less of a problem, easily accommodated by being a bit more frugal or perhaps delaying your retirement date or taking a part-time job.

As you will see in the examples that follow, there is a tradeoff between the amount that you are willing to save and how confident you can be about achieving a goal. The more you save, the more confident you are about having enough to meet the goal. Let's take a look at a simple example to illustrate the point.

Meet Frank, a long-time engineer at an oil company who is saving to purchase a vacation home in Idaho in about 10 years. Frank is lucky enough to have built up a significant defined-benefit pension at his company over the last 24 years, and so he has some extra income to spend on making his future retirement that much nicer. As an avid outdoorsman, Frank is looking to spend some serious time in the mountains once he retires from his job. Frank figures a cabin in the area of Idaho he likes will cost him about $300,000 in today's dollars. So far, Frank has amassed about $150,000 toward his goal. He has invested his savings in a diversified portfolio of low-cost index funds through a mutual fund brokerage window. Given his time horizon, Frank figures he should be investing in a portfolio that includes both stocks and bonds, so he has selected a portfolio with risk 1.0 (remember, risk 1.0 equals the same volatility as the market portfolio). In his particular case, the portfolio consists of about 37 percent bonds and 63 percent stocks. To purchase his dream home, Frank has been putting aside an extra $1,000 per month into his vacation home account. First, let's see how this investment strategy is doing in terms of getting Frank to his eventual goal of $300,000 (adjusted for inflation and after taxes) in 10 years.

Figure 10.1 shows the forecast results from the Financial Engines *Personal Online Advisor* service for Frank's vacation cabin account assuming he continues to save $1,000 per month (after tax) and invests it in his brokerage account in a low-cost index fund portfolio with risk 1.0. The portfolio outcomes are shown in today's dollars (adjusted for inflation) and take into account the estimated taxes that Frank will have to pay on the dividends and capital gains from his portfolio.

According to the simulation, Frank has a 75 percent chance of reaching his target goal of $300,000 in 10 years if he maintains his $1,000-per-month savings rate and keeps his portfolio risk level at 1.0. Note that the median outcome for his investment plan is a healthy $358,000, well in excess of his target goal. To be pretty sure of hitting his goal, he needs to aim for a median portfolio value that is significantly higher than his actual goal, in this case about $58,000 higher. If markets perform poorly over the next 10 years, then Frank could be looking at an account value of only $225,000. Obviously this might require Frank to revisit his goals if things were to turn out this way. On the other hand, if markets perform much better than expected, the upside value of $530,000 would allow Frank to buy a nicer place, or perhaps augment that vacation home with a fancy new fishing boat. Alternatively, he could go ahead and buy his dream vacation home a year or two earlier than he was previously planning.

As you can see in Figure 10.1, the range of portfolio outcomes over the 10-year horizon is relatively large. The upside case is more than twice as big as the downside scenario. This means that Frank needs to plan for a significant amount of uncertainty if he wants to maintain a portfolio risk of

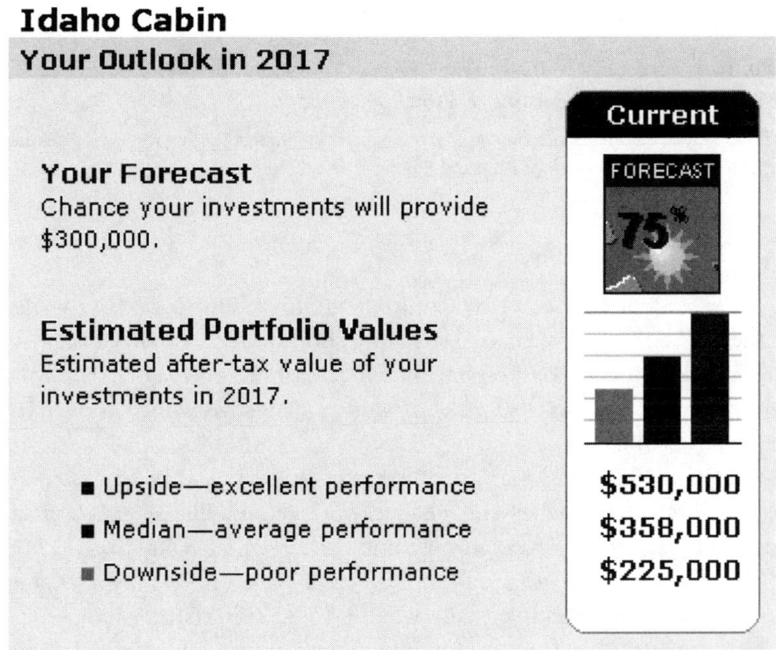

FIGURE 10.1 Forecast Results for Frank's Idaho Cabin Account with Savings of $1,000 per Month and a Balance of $150,000 in 2007

Source: Financial Engines. Copyright © 2007 Financial Engines. All rights reserved. Note: Weather forecast icons are a trademark of Financial Engines.

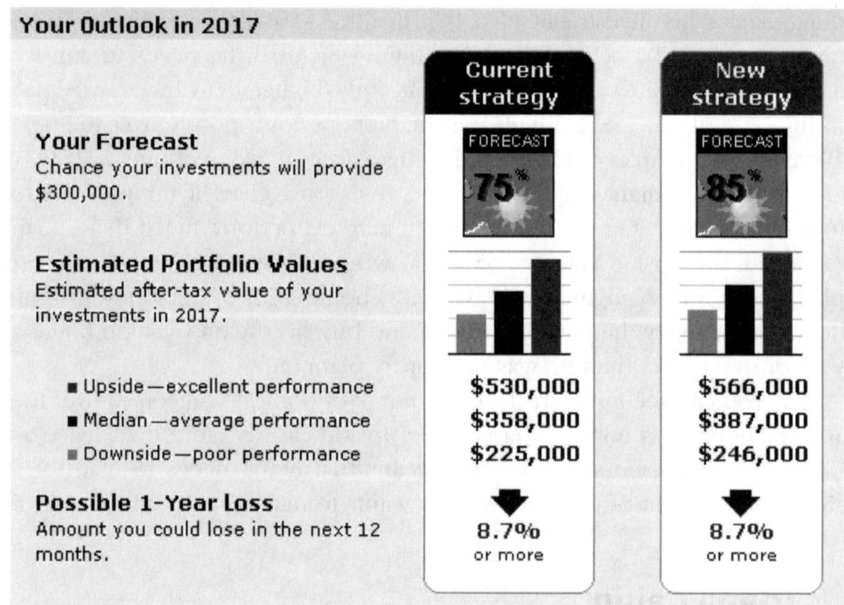

FIGURE 10.2 Forecast Results for Frank's Idaho Cabin Account with Savings of $1,250 per Month and a Balance of $150,000 in 2007

Source: Financial Engines. Weather forecast icons are a trademark of Financial Engines.

1.0. A 75 percent chance of reaching his goal is pretty good, but it means that there is a 25 percent chance of falling short of the $300,000 target. What if Frank wanted to be 85 percent confident of hitting his goal? Figure 10.2 shows the result of increasing his monthly savings from $1,000 per month to $1,250 per month.

The extra $250 per month of savings does a few things to Frank's forecast. First, it increases the chance of reaching his $300,000 goal to 85 percent. Second, his median outcome rises from $358,000 to $387,000. It also significantly improves his downside case, which now shows a value of $246,000. But what if Frank *really* wanted to be sure that he had $300,000 for the cabin 10 years from now while maintaining a portfolio risk level of 1.0? How much would he need to save to create such a plan?

To get to a 95 percent chance of success, Frank would need to increase his monthly savings to about $1,700 per month. Figure 10.3 shows the result of the forecast if Frank increases his savings to $1,700 per month.

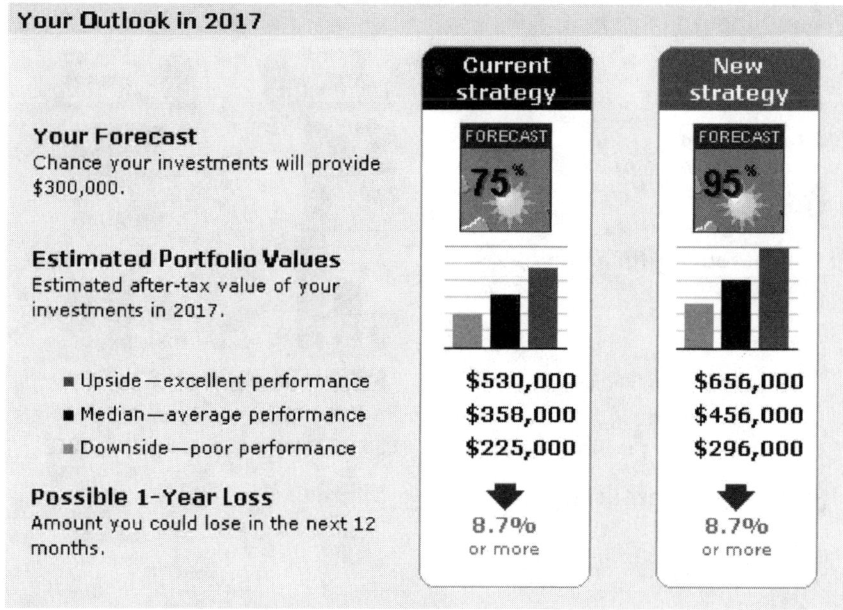

FIGURE 10.3 Forecast Results for Frank's Idaho Cabin Account with Savings of $1,700 per Month and a Balance of $150,000 in 2007

Source: Financial Engines. Weather forecast icons are a trademark of Financial Engines.

Notice that it requires a much higher savings rate (about 70 percent higher) to go from a 75 percent chance of reaching the goal to a 95 percent chance of reaching the goal. This demonstrates a fundamental point. *If you need to be really confident of hitting a future goal, then you will need to save significantly more*. Confidence costs money. You might ask, well couldn't Frank increase the confidence level of reaching his goal by investing in a less risky portfolio. Certainly, he can reduce the range of portfolio outcomes by selecting a less risky portfolio mix. But this does not necessarily reduce the amount of savings required to get to achieve a particular goal. Why? Because when you select a lower risk portfolio, you also lower the expected returns of your investments. Stocks have higher volatility than bonds, but they also have higher expected returns. Depending on the length of the time horizon and the shape of the distribution of outcomes, this can actually reduce the chances of reaching a goal. For instance, if Frank were to invest in a portfolio of risk 0.5 (50 percent of the volatility of the market portfolio) with his current savings of $1,000 per month, he would *decrease* his chance

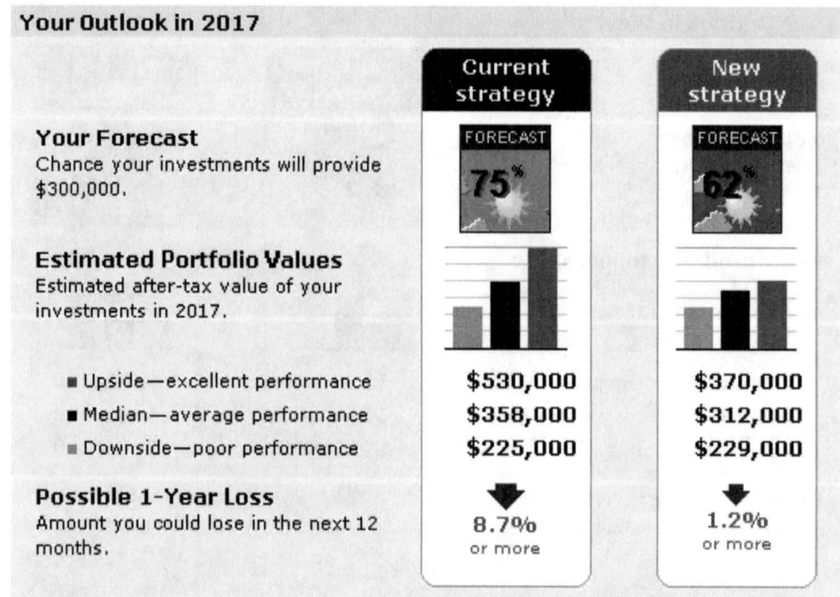

FIGURE 10.4 Forecast Results for Frank's Idaho Cabin Account with Savings of $1,000 per Month, Comparing Portfolios of Risk 1.0 and Risk 0.5, Based on a Balance of $150,000 in 2007

Source: Financial Engines. Weather forecast icons are a trademark of Financial Engines.

of reaching his goal to only 62 percent. Figure 10.4 compares his original forecast to one with a portfolio mix of risk 0.5.

As you can see in Figure 10.4, the lower risk portfolio mix reduces the range of possible outcomes significantly. The difference between the upside and the downside scenarios is about $140,000, compared with a difference of about $300,000 for the risk 1.0 portfolio. But notice that the median outcome for the lower-risk portfolio is actually $46,000 *lower* than the higher-risk portfolio. This shows the impact of the lower expected return assets in the less risky portfolio mix. In this case, it also reduces the chance of reaching Frank's $300,000 goal to 62 percent from the previous 75 percent. But what if Frank wanted to be 95 percent sure of reaching the goal? Is the lower-risk portfolio a better way to be more confident?

In this case, the answer is a qualified yes. To achieve a 95 percent chance of reaching his goal, Frank would need to save about $1,650 per month. With the higher risk 1.0 portfolio, his required savings was

$1,700 per month. Using the lower risk portfolio, Frank can reduce his required savings by $600 per year or about $6,000 over the 10-year savings period. So with a lower-risk portfolio mix, Frank can slightly reduce his required savings to be 95 percent sure of hitting his goal. Of course, if he is willing to accept a little more risk of falling short of his $300,000 target, he can reduce his required savings substantially.

In our experience at Financial Engines, many investors seem to be comfortable with forecasts in the range of 75 percent to 85 percent probabilities of hitting their goals. This seems to indicate a sweet spot between being reasonably confident about your chances for success versus having to significantly increase savings to protect against possible shortfalls. From this simple example, we again see the reality of "no free lunch" when it comes to investing. To achieve a certain goal in the future with high confidence, you need to be willing to save enough to make sure that most portfolio scenarios end up above your target. High confidence generally requires a more conservative investment strategy and higher savings.

RISK, TIME, AND SAVINGS

Now let's examine some of the relationships between savings, portfolio risk level, and time horizon in a more systematic way using the Financial Engines simulation engine. In the following examples, I will assume that the investment goal is to accumulate $100,000 in today's dollars.

To keep things simple, I will ignore the impact of taxes on accumulated returns and treat everything in pretax dollars. This means that I am assuming that you are not paying taxes on the savings, nor on the earnings from the investments. If you were saving into a 401(k) account with pretax dollars, then the following results can be used to determine the savings required to get to $100,000 in pretax terms. Of course, you would then need to pay the taxes on the $100,000, which would reduce the amount you have to spend, depending on your personal tax rates. In contrast, the examples with Frank in the previous section assumed after-tax savings and taxable account accumulations, which required the annual payment of taxes on capital gains and dividend distributions along the way. What does this mean? The following examples are estimates of what it takes to get to $100,000 in pretax dollars with a tax-deferred account like a 401(k) or 403(b). If you are using taxable accounts to save, you will need to put aside more money to compensate for the impact of taxes to fund the account with the same number of dollars. The amount of the additional money will depend on your tax rate.

Also, in the following examples all the savings and portfolio values are adjusted for inflation (in today's dollars). This makes it easier to compare future amounts in terms of today's purchasing power. Of course, this means you will need to increase the dollars you save each year to keep up with inflation. The idea behind these examples is to help you develop some basic intuition about how portfolio risk, time horizon, and savings interact to determine the confidence with which you can hit a particular financial goal. The general results are quite robust across typical situations encountered by investors, but be careful of drawing conclusions about the specific savings rates without first modeling the actual investment portfolio you are using in the *Personal Online Advisor* service.

Time Is Your Friend

First let's look at how your time horizon impacts savings decisions. Consider the following question: How much would you need to save on an annual basis in order to reach a goal with 75 percent confidence? Consider the case of an investor trying to accumulate $100,000 (adjusted for inflation) with a diversified portfolio invested at a risk level of 1.0. Figure 10.5 shows how the required annual savings decreases as your time horizon gets longer.

Notice that the required savings rate drops rapidly as the number of years in your investment horizon goes up. For instance, if you are saving for five years, you would need to save $19,200 annually to reach your goal with 75 percent confidence. But if you had 10 years to save, you would only need to save $8,800 per year to reach the same goal. Doubling the length of time you save decreases the required annual savings by more than half. In fact, you only need to save 46 percent as much for 10 years as you do for 5 years. This means the total investment to reach the goal is lower for the 10-year horizon ($88,000 versus $96,000 for the 5-year horizon). As you can see, time is your friend when it comes to accumulating wealth. The longer you have, the easier it is to reach the goal. Over 20 years, you would only need to save about $3,600 per year to have a 75 percent chance of reaching $100,000, which is much less than one-fourth the annual savings required over the five-year horizon.

Interestingly, if you only had one year to reach your goal and you invested in a portfolio of risk 1.0, you would actually need to start with *more* than $100,000 in order to be 75 percent sure of ending up with $100,000. In fact, you would need to save about $103,100 in order to be 75 percent sure you would have at least $100,000 after a year. Why? Because when you invest in a portfolio of risk 1.0, which has an allocation of approximately

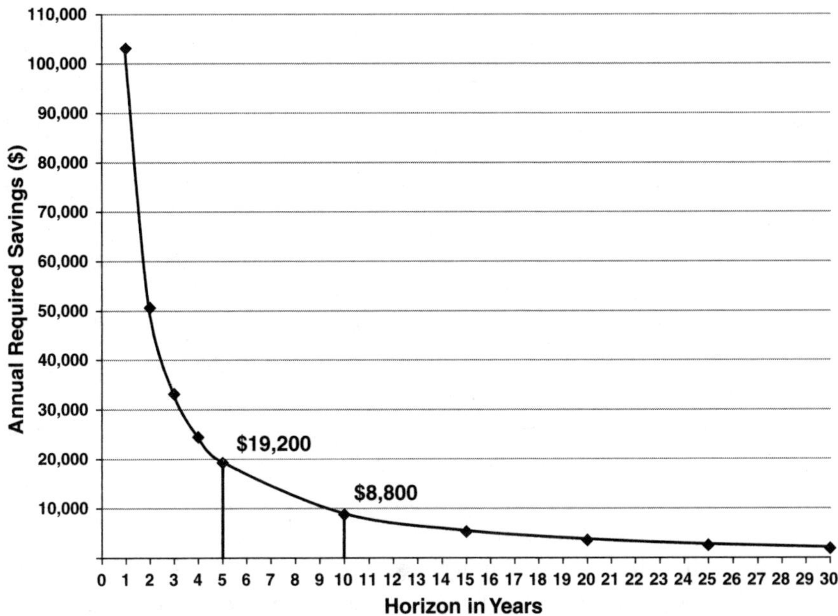

FIGURE 10.5 Required Annual Savings to Achieve $100,000 with 75 percent Confidence with a Risk 1.0 Portfolio

Source: Financial Engines calculations.

65 percent equities, there is a significant chance that you could actually lose money if markets performed poorly over the year. This implies something important about short-term goals—*it generally does not make much sense to invest aggressively with a short-term horizon if you require a high level of confidence*. In this case, you would be better off with a low-risk portfolio in order to be 75 percent confident of having $100,000 after a year. If you really need exactly $100,000 in a year, then you should consider putting the money into short-term treasury bills or some other very safe investment like a certificate of deposit (CD). Of course, if you are willing to deal with more uncertainty in the outcome, then it may make sense to consider a riskier portfolio. For instance, if you only needed to be 50 percent confident of having $100,000 in a year, then you would only need to invest about $95,400 in a risk 1.0 portfolio to achieve the goal.

This brings us to an interesting question: What kind of portfolio is best for reaching a goal with 75 percent confidence over different time horizons? Should you invest conservatively, or select a mix with more equity exposure? The answer, it turns out, depends on your time horizon. For shorter horizons it will be cheaper to invest in a more conservative portfolio, but for longer horizons you can reach a goal with 75 percent confidence by investing in a diversified portfolio with more equity and a higher volatility. Table 10.3 shows the required annual savings needed to achieve $100,000 with 75 percent confidence based on five different risk portfolios and various time horizons.

For instance, if your time horizon is 5 years, and you invest in a portfolio with 1.25 risk, you will need to save about $19,470 per year to have a 75 percent probability of reaching $100,000 (pretax). The highlighted entries in the table show the *minimum savings* required to achieve the goal with 75 percent confidence for each time horizon. As you can see from Table 10.3, it is cheapest to invest in the conservative 0.20 portfolio if your horizon is one year and you need to be at least 75 percent sure of reaching your goal. Even so, the amount of savings required is the same as the goal ($100,000). This is because of the potential impact of future inflation. Investments in cash (which is consistent with a 0.20 portfolio risk) are expected to basically just keep up with inflation. For a 1-year horizon, the higher risk portfolios imply higher levels of savings in order to maintain a 75 percent confidence.

However, you can see that by the four-year horizon, the investment strategy that yields the lowest required savings changes. Now the 0.75 risk portfolio (which corresponds to about 40 percent equity) has the lowest level of required savings. What causes this shift? The 0.75 risk portfolio has higher expected returns than the lower-volatility portfolios and over longer time periods this improves the chance of ending up above the goal. As you further increase the investment horizon, you see that the portfolio that yields the lowest required savings to hit $100,000 with 75 percent confidence becomes increasingly higher risk. With a 25-year horizon, you minimize your required savings by selecting a portfolio with risk 1.25, which corresponds to an asset mix with about 90 percent equity. Now keep in mind that the probability of reaching a goal may not be the only objective you care about. It might also matter how much you fall short in those bad market scenarios. For instance, you might want to partially base your decision about portfolio risk on the downside outcomes as well as the chance of hitting your desired goal. The *Personal Online Advisor* provides you with information on the range of possible outcomes as well as the chance of success to help you make an informed decision.

If you want to calculate the savings required for a goal other than $100,000, you can simply multiply or divide the corresponding table entry

TABLE 10.3 Required Annual Savings to Achieve $100,000 with 75 Percent Confidence (in today's dollars)

	Investment Horizon (Years)									
	1	**2**	**3**	**4**	**5**	**10**	**15**	**20**	**25**	**30**
Risk 0.20	$100,000	$49,710	$32,920	$24,530	$19,500	$9,440	$6,090	$4,420	$3,420	$2,750
Risk 0.50	$100,940	$49,820	$32,790	$24,290	$19,180	$8,980	$5,590	$3,910	$2,910	$2,250
Risk 0.75	$101,890	$50,110	$32,880	$24,280	$19,110	$8,780	$5,360	$3,660	$2,660	$2,010
Risk 1.00	$103,080	$50,640	$33,200	$24,480	$19,240	$8,760	$5,280	$3,550	$2,540	$1,880
Risk 1.25	$104,500	$51,280	$33,610	$24,780	$19,470	$8,820	$5,270	$3,520	$2,480	$1,820
Risk 1.50	$106,020	$52,030	$34,130	$25,180	$19,780	$8,960	$5,350	$3,560	$2,500	$1,820

Source: Financial Engines calculations.

by your goal as a proportion of $100,000. For instance, if you want to know the annual savings required to reach $250,000 over 10 years with a 1.0 risk portfolio, you simply multiply the table value by 2.5, which yields a required savings of 2.5 × $8,760 = $21,900 per year.

Confidence Costs Money

The previous section demonstrated how the required savings to hit a goal decreased with longer investment horizons. It also showed that the portfolio risk level that minimized the required savings also varied with the investment horizon. If your investment horizon is short and you want to be pretty sure you will hit your goal, then you will prefer to invest in a more conservative portfolio mix. Similarly, if your horizon is long and you are willing to accept a lower level of confidence that you will achieve the goal, it will generally make sense to invest in a more aggressive portfolio to lower your required savings.

But what is the relationship between the level of confidence and the total cost of reaching a goal? Not surprisingly, it turns out that higher levels of confidence cost more money. Table 10.4 shows the required annual pretax savings to achieve $100,000 in today's dollars (pretax) for different levels of confidence and investment horizons of 5, 10, 20, and 30 years.

For each table entry, I have calculated the required annual savings to achieve the $100,000 goal with different levels of confidence for each horizon. Note that the portfolios used to create the forecasts vary in risk. In each

TABLE 10.4 Required Annual Savings to Achieve $100,000 with Different Levels of Confidence (in today's dollars)

Confidence of Reaching Goal	Investment Horizon (Years) 5	10	20	30
50%	$16,560	$7,040	$2,510	$1,160
60%	$17,690	$7,700	$2,860	$1,380
70%	$18,710	$8,430	$3,290	$1,650
75%	$19,110	$8,760	$3,520	$1,820
80%	$19,500	$9,070	$3,770	$1,990
90%	$20,080	$9,800	$4,370	$2,480
95%	$20,490	$10,120	$4,810	$2,890

Source: Financial Engines calculations.

case, I have selected the portfolio risk that minimizes the required savings rate. For lower levels of confidence and longer horizons, the portfolio risk is higher, while shorter horizons and higher confidence levels imply lower portfolio risk levels.

As you can see in Table 10.4, the required annual savings increases sharply with higher levels of confidence. For the five-year horizon, it costs 24 percent more to be 95 percent sure of reaching the goal than it does to be only 50 percent confident. However, this gap gets much larger for longer time horizons. At 30 years, it costs a whopping two-and-a-half times more to be 95 percent sure than it does to be only 50 percent certain of reaching the goal! The reason is that more time creates a wider range of possible portfolio outcomes, like the branches of a tree spreading out. But this wider range of outcomes includes some bad ones, and the only way to make up for poor market performance without changing the time period is to compensate with more savings. Hence it costs more to be highly confident of reaching the goal, particularly for longer investment horizons.

To make the point visually, Figure 10.6 shows the total amount of savings required to reach the $100,000 goal for different levels of confidence and varying horizons. The total savings is just the annual savings required multiplied by the time horizon. For instance, it costs a total of $83,400 to be 70 percent confident of reaching the $100,000 goal over 10 years ($8,340 × 10 = $83,400). Remember that all savings rates shown are adjusted for inflation and expressed in terms of today's dollars.

Figure 10.6 clearly illustrates two basic facts: it costs less to fund a goal the longer the investment horizon and it costs more to fund a goal with higher levels of confidence. At all levels of confidence, you can achieve the goal with less money if you start saving earlier. But the cost of being more confident in reaching the goal increases sharply as you approach the 95 percent level of confidence. In fact, the cost of being 95 percent sure of having $100,000 in today's dollars in five years is actually *more* than $100,000. Why? Because you have to guard against the effects of future unanticipated inflation. If you invest conservatively, there is no guarantee that your investments will keep up with inflation over multiyear horizons (unless you are using an inflation-protected security like TIPS).

Now let's look a little more closely at how portfolio risk levels vary depending on the investment horizon and desired level of confidence. The estimates in Table 10.3 applied to the case where you wanted to be 75 percent sure of hitting your goal. What do the minimum savings strategies look like when you need to be 95 percent sure of hitting your goal? Table 10.5 shows the result of this simulation analysis.

TABLE 10.5 Required Annual Savings to Achieve $100,000 with 95 Percent Confidence (in today's dollars)

	Investment Horizon (Years)									
	1	2	3	4	5	10	15	20	25	30
Risk 0.20	$102,190	$51,290	$34,210	$25,650	$20,490	$10,120	$6,620	$4,860	$3,800	$3,080
Risk 0.50	$106,590	$53,460	$35,690	$26,740	$21,350	$10,420	$6,700	$4,810	$3,670	$2,900
Risk 0.75	$110,720	$55,550	$37,110	$27,850	$22,250	$10,840	$6,920	$4,930	$3,710	$2,890
Risk 1.00	$115,120	$57,780	$38,650	$29,020	$23,210	$11,320	$7,220	$5,120	$3,820	$2,950
Risk 1.25	$120,160	$60,330	$40,430	$30,440	$24,380	$11,980	$7,650	$5,430	$4,060	$3,130
Risk 1.50	$126,000	$63,380	$42,640	$32,130	$25,840	$12,840	$8,280	$5,900	$4,430	$3,430

Source: Financial Engines calculations.

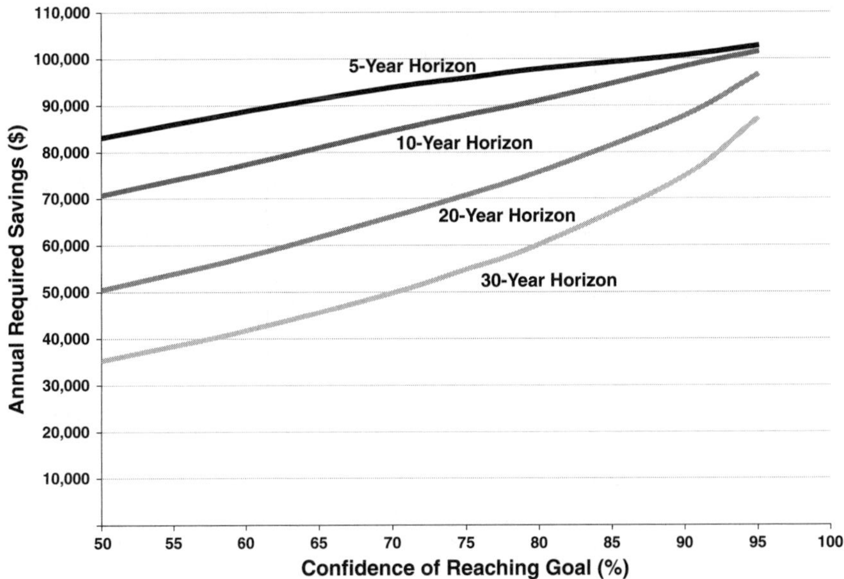

FIGURE 10.6 Total Required Savings to Achieve $100,000 Goal (Adjusted for Inflation) with Different Levels of Confidence over 5, 10, 20, and 30 Years

Source: Financial Engines calculations.

As you can see, to be 95 percent confident of hitting the goal requires a more conservative investment strategy to minimize the required savings. With horizons of 15 years or less, you are better off investing in the most conservative 0.20 risk portfolio to minimize your required savings. However, for horizons of 20 years or more, you can slightly reduce your required savings by investing in portfolios of up to risk 0.75.

In addition, notice that the required savings amounts are significantly higher than those in the table for the 75 percent level of confidence. This is particularly true for the longer investment horizons. For the 30-year horizon, it requires 60 percent more savings to be 95 percent sure of reaching the goal than it does to be only 75 percent confident hitting the mark. As the investment horizon gets longer, the range of possible portfolio outcomes gets wider. This means that you have to guard against downside investment performance possibilities by saving more, on average.

What if you are willing to settle for only a 50 percent chance of hitting the goal? In this case, the median estimate of the simulation would equal your investment goal. Table 10.6 shows the required savings rates needed to have a 50 percent chance of hitting $100,000 over different time horizons.

TABLE 10.6 Required Annual Savings to Achieve $100,000 with 50 Percent Confidence (in today's dollars)

	Investment Horizon (Years)									
	1	2	3	4	5	10	15	20	25	30
Risk 0.20	$98,560	$48,790	$32,240	$23,980	$19,030	$9,140	$5,860	$4,230	$3,250	$2,600
Risk 0.50	$97,090	$47,610	$31,180	$22,980	$18,070	$8,300	$5,080	$3,500	$2,560	$1,950
Risk 0.75	$96,130	$46,850	$30,510	$22,360	$17,480	$7,790	$4,630	$3,090	$2,190	$1,610
Risk 1.00	$95,430	$46,360	$30,070	$21,950	$17,090	$7,460	$4,340	$2,820	$1,950	$1,400
Risk 1.25	$94,860	$45,950	$29,710	$21,620	$16,790	$7,220	$4,120	$2,630	$1,780	$1,250
Risk 1.50	$94,330	$45,610	$29,440	$21,380	$16,560	$7,040	$3,970	$2,510	$1,680	$1,160

Source: Financial Engines calculations.

Now the highest risk 1.50 portfolio with 100 percent equity exposure minimizes the required savings to hit the $100,000 goal with a 50 percent level of confidence. Why? Because the 1.50 risk portfolio has the highest expected growth rate of all the different allocations. The portfolio with the highest expected growth rate will also have the highest median outcome, and hence the best chance of reaching a goal with a 50 percent probability. The bottom line here is that if you are willing to accept a 50 percent chance of falling short of the goal, then it will usually make sense to seek the investment strategy with the highest expected growth rate, regardless of the time horizon. However, recognize that this strategy will also have the widest range of potential outcomes. If you miss your goal, you might miss by a lot. Most of the time it *will matter* how big the shortfall is if things don't turn out the way you plan. If the downside possibilities are not palatable, then you should seek a lower risk strategy and plan to save more.

By dropping the confidence level to 50 percent, you are able to substantially reduce the required savings rate to achieve the $100,000. For instance, for a 20-year horizon, it would cost you about $4,810 per year to achieve 95 percent confidence, but only $2,510 per year to reach the goal with 50 percent confidence—about half as much. The bottom line here is that confidence costs money. The only way to be more confident of reaching a financial goal is to invest more conservatively and save more. There is no getting around this fundamental fact in investing.

WHAT IT TAKES TO GET THERE

Obviously putting together a comprehensive retirement savings plan requires a bit of analysis. One important consideration is what sources of income, like Social Security or pension benefits, you may be able to rely on in addition to your financial assets. The *Personal Online Advisor* service can be very helpful in figuring out the answers for your own personal situation. However, to help you develop some intuition, let's summarize the basic ideas about funding future goals:

- **Time is your friend**: The more time you have, the easier it is to achieve a financial goal with high confidence.
- **Confidence costs money**: Achieving a goal with very high confidence is much more expensive than allowing for the possibility of falling short if markets perform poorly.

- **Risk is a two-edged sword**: Higher-risk portfolios yield higher expected returns and growth rates. But this higher expected performance comes at the cost of a wider range of possible outcomes.

Let's say you are planning for retirement at age 65 and want to be able to maintain a retirement income of $50,000 per year (pretax) for as long as you live, in addition to any Social Security income you will receive. You also want to be 75 percent confident that you will be able to achieve your desired retirement income by age 65. Your primary savings vehicle is your 401(k) plan with a good selection of low-cost funds, and an employer match of $0.50 on the dollar for the first 6 percent of contributions. Finally, we will assume that you have zero assets to start, which as we will see is either no big deal, or a significant problem, depending on when you start saving for retirement.

What kind of savings is required to reach your goal if you start at age 30, 35, 40, 45, 50, or 55? Since the answers depend on whether you are male or female, we will calculate the required savings for both genders. Table 10.7 shows the required savings rates and the appropriate portfolio risk to achieve the goal of $50,000 per year in retirement income with 75 percent confidence.

The results clearly demonstrate the "time is your friend" element of savings. If you start at age 30, the required savings to achieve a 75% chance of having $50,000 in retirement income at age 65 is a relatively modest $9,750. But if you wait to start just five years later, the required savings jumps to $13,500. Start saving at age 40 and you need to save a considerable $18,750 a year to reach the goal. And if you have the misfortune to start saving at age 50, the required savings jumps to a steep $39,500 per year, including $24,000 of after-tax savings.

TABLE 10.7 Required Annual Savings to Have 75 Percent Chance of $50,000 in Retirement Income at Age 65 (Male)

Savings Start Age	Pretax Savings	After-Tax Savings	Total Required Annual Savings
30	$9,750	$0	$9,750
35	$13,500	$0	$13,500
40	$15,500	$3,250	$18,750
45	$15,500	$11,000	$26,500
50	$15,500	$24,000	$39,500

Source: Financial Engines calculations.

TABLE 10.8 Required Annual Savings to Have 75 Percent Chance of $50,000 in Retirement Income at Age 65 (Female)

Savings Start Age	Pretax Savings	After-Tax Savings	Total Required Annual Savings
30	$10,250	$0	$10,250
35	$14,250	$0	$14,250
40	$15,500	$4,250	$19,750
45	$15,500	$12,750	$28,250
50	$15,500	$27,000	$42,500

Source: Financial Engines calculations

Table 10.8 shows the corresponding estimates for a female investor. Due to the longer expected lifespan and longer retirement, the required savings numbers are somewhat higher. In general, it will cost a woman between 5 percent and 8 percent more in terms of required savings to achieve the same retirement income as a man of the same age.

Note that for people starting at age 40 or older, the required savings implies maximizing your allowable pretax contributions and saving the surplus into a taxable account. Just because you have maxed out the contributions to your 401(k) does not mean that you cannot benefit from saving more in your brokerage account. As we will see in Chapter 11, the key to accumulating assets in a taxable account is investing tax efficiently.

There is a caveat associated with this analysis, which is that it assumes a constant savings rate over time. In reality, most people will alter their retirement savings rates multiple times over their lifetime, depending on their financial circumstances and needs. On average, people tend to save less when they are younger and then ramp up their retirement contributions as they age. But as we all know, many life events such as purchasing a home, losing a job, paying for college, having kids, or an unanticipated illness can result in a reduction or suspension of savings for a period of time. Often your ability to save money will go up significantly over time as you pay off your house, get the kids through college, and deal with other major financial responsibilities. In general, the idea of ramping up savings over time is perfectly rational behavior, since most people have lower incomes when they are young than during their peak earning years. Of course, following this savings pattern means you really do have to ramp up your savings as you approach retirement. And don't underestimate the value of putting some money away early. Contributing even modestly to a retirement plan early in your career can pay big dividends.

Finally, when evaluating a savings plan, it is important to periodically revisit the plan and its assumptions as your circumstances change. Maintaining a robust retirement plan is not a "set and forget" exercise. You should update your projections at least once a year to determine whether you remain on track. Once you have set up your goals and investments in the *Personal Online Advisor* program, you can easily update your forecast as your circumstances change.

TAKE-AWAYS

- Time is your friend when funding future goals. Get started early if you can and it will reduce the required savings to get there.
- Confidence costs money. Since future investment returns are uncertain, there is no guarantee that you will reach your target goal. If you want to be very confident of reaching a goal, you will need to save more of your current income and invest more conservatively.
- Higher-risk portfolios have higher expected returns, but a much wider range of possible outcomes. Make sure you can live with the portfolio outcomes if markets perform worse than expected.
- Be realistic about funding goals; there is no free lunch when it comes to investment risk and savings. Make sure your savings plan is reasonable given your time horizon and portfolio risk level by running it through a realistic investment simulation like that found in the Financial Engines *Personal Online Advisor* service.
- Adjust your risk level to be consistent with your horizon. For longer investment horizons, it will usually make more sense to invest in portfolios with higher allocations to equities to maximize your chances of reaching a goal.
- All other things held equal, it will cost a woman more to fund her retirement than a man of the same age due to her longer expected lifespan.
- Set up savings plans so you don't have to think about them much—leverage your own inertia by making regular automatic contributions to your retirement accounts. Out of sight, out of mind is a great goal with long-term savings. And make sure you maximize the free money available from your employer match.

CHAPTER 11

Investing and Uncle Sam

Taxation with *representation ain't so hot either.*

—Gerald Barzan

Unlike institutional investors such as pension funds and university endowments, we individual investors usually have to pay taxes on our investment gains and income. Besides taking some of the fun out of making money, taxes add significant complexity to the investing process. Perhaps more than any other factor, the presence of taxes means your investment strategy must be tailored to your personal circumstances. There are few simple rules of thumb in taxable investing that work well in all situations. The influence of taxes on your investment decisions will depend on your personal tax rates, the types of investments and accounts available to you, accumulated losses and gains, your time horizon, and the nature of your investment goals. However, there are some basic concepts that can help you create more tax-efficient investment strategies. This chapter will demonstrate how taxes affect good investment decisions and provide some intuition on how to maximize your after-tax returns.

It is pretty hard to write about taxes and their impact on investing in a way that doesn't result in glazed eyes and prolonged bouts of yawning. Let's face it: taxes are one of the unpleasant realities of life that no one really gets excited about (unless you happen to be a tax attorney). But that does not take away from the fact that taxes are an important consideration for individual investors. Bad investment decisions that ignore the effects of taxes can make a real dent in your financial future. And interestingly, taxes make the process of investing a very personalized affair. Among other things, your optimal investment decisions depend on your income, where you live, how long you have held certain investments, and the prices you paid for them. Cookie-cutter advice and rules of thumb will not get you very far when building taxable investment strategies, and often lead to demonstrably foolish recommendations. Two investors of the same age and with the same goals may need to pursue markedly different investment strategies depending on their personal tax rates and financial circumstances. As an informed investor, you need to have a basic understanding of how taxes affect investment decisions, and how to avoid mistakes that might cost you a lot of money in the future.

Until relatively recently, the whole idea of *tax-efficient investing* was pretty much limited to those with a lot of trailing zeros on the end of their balance statement. Tax-efficient investing means pursuing strategies that maximize your *after-tax* wealth accumulation. Structuring investment portfolios and elaborate estate plans to minimize taxes for the wealthy keeps a veritable army of financial and legal professionals employed at large accounting firms, private banks, law firms, registered investment advisors, and wealth management companies. A great deal of the advice proffered by such organizations focuses on helping wealthy families minimize the taxes associated with transferring wealth to future generations through complex trust structures. If you happen to be a high net-worth investor, then it makes sense to seek the advice of such experts to avoid financial planning mistakes that could be very costly down the road. The complexity of financial plans for wealthy investors with wide-ranging financial holdings can be staggering.

Rather than attempting to cover the many intricacies of structuring your financial affairs to minimize taxes associated with intergenerational wealth transfers and complex investment partnerships, I will instead focus on the basic issues that are important to taxable investors of all income levels. There are plenty of other resources out there if protecting great wealth from the IRS is your primary concern (what my father likes to call a "high-class problem" to have). But taxes also influence the investment decisions of investors who do not attract the attention of an army of wealth and tax specialists. A great many investors in the middle to upper income range would benefit from more tax-efficient investment strategies. If you earn more than about $50,000 in annual income, tax-efficient investing is something you should be thinking about.

It has only been in the last decade or so that typical individual investors have had access to high-quality investment advice on how to build and manage tax-efficient investment portfolios. The issue is that providing tax-efficient investment advice is complex and requires a good bit of expertise and analysis. Prior to the rise of the Internet and cheap computational resources, it was simply not cost effective for advisors to offer good taxable investment advice to people unless they had a lot of money. If anyone even tried, the advice was usually based on simple rules of thumb.

However, in recent years it has become more fashionable in the financial services industry to recognize and address the impacts of taxes on investment decisions. As part of this trend, Financial Engines began offering tax-efficient investment advice to its customers in 2001, thereby opening up a new level of sophisticated advice for investors with modest net worth. Other firms also offer taxable investment advice with varying degrees of sophistication. This chapter introduces the basic concepts involved in tax-efficient investing and demonstrates the effects of taxes on good investing practice. It also provides a grounding on the types of questions you should ask your investment advisor, if you choose to use one, when putting together your overall investment strategy.

WHY YOU DON'T WANT TO MINIMIZE TAXES

First we need to start off by addressing a prevalent myth among many individual investors. *The goal with investing is not to minimize taxes.* Instead, the intelligent investor should strive to *maximize after-tax returns.* These are two very different objectives. You can easily minimize your taxes by simply losing money. With no capital gains or dividend income to report, you don't have to pay any taxes. But this is a counterproductive strategy that does not lend itself to successful financial outcomes. Would you rather have no money and owe no taxes, or have lots of money but have to pay taxes on a portion of it? Though many of us gripe about having to pay taxes, few of us would choose to be poor in order to minimize taxes. What you really want to do is maximize the after-tax returns of your investments and thereby accumulate more wealth that can be spent. All other things being equal, an investment with a higher after-tax return will be preferable, even if its performance before taxes was inferior.

One of the things that makes tax-efficient investing difficult is that your decisions depend on many different factors. Some of these factors are household related, such as your income tax bracket, state of residence, and marital status. Others are related to the characteristics of your investments, for instance how frequently a mutual fund distributes capital gains or the investment style of your portfolio. Still other considerations include the types of accounts in which you hold your assets and whether positions have accumulated gains or losses. Putting all this information together to come up with the right decision can be daunting and quite complex. But tax considerations can have a big impact on the optimal investment decisions and so it makes sense to consider the impact of taxes carefully.

Can you implement tax-efficient investment strategies on your own? Sure. By following some basic guidelines you can significantly improve the tax efficiency of your investing strategy. But given the number of issues to think about, particularly if a large portion of your investable assets are held in taxable accounts, it will generally make sense to enlist the help of a qualified investment advisor or tax expert to help structure your investment portfolio and financial plans. Of course, such expertise typically does not come cheap. In considering the use of such experts, you have to weigh the costs versus the potential benefits. The Financial Engines *Personal Online Advisor* service can be very helpful in providing cost-effective recommendations on how to tax-efficiently allocate your assets, though it will not substitute for the services of a comprehensive tax advisor, particularly if your needs are complex. Luckily, there are a few basic concepts that, once you understand them, can be very helpful in making more tax-efficient investment decisions.

HOW TAXES IMPACT INVESTMENT RETURNS

In the United States, there are two basic kinds of taxes that impact investment returns. *Capital gains* taxes are applied to the profit from selling an asset, such as a stock or bond mutual fund, defined by the difference between the purchase price and the sale price. Current tax law makes a distinction between short- and long-term capital gains. *Short-term capital gains* are defined as appreciation on assets held less than one year, while *long-term capital gains* rates apply to assets held longer than one year. As of this writing, long-term capital gains are taxed by the federal government at a rate of either 5 percent or 15 percent, depending on the level of your income. For the vast majority of investors, the higher 15 percent capital gains tax rate will apply. In contrast, short-term capital gains are taxed at the marginal income tax rate for the individual, which is typically much higher than 15 percent. Finally, most states also tax capital gains in addition to the taxes levied by the federal government. This additional state tax burden increases the overall tax rate applied to the gains from an investment portfolio. In most cases, states do not have separate capital gains taxes, but tax the gains at the effective state income tax rate (if any), which depends on your income and state of residence. Currently, the following states do not charge any state capital gains taxes: Alaska, Florida, Nevada, New Hampshire, South Dakota, Tennessee, Texas, Washington, and Wyoming. Some other states have certain discounts for state capital gains taxes that may apply in certain situations. The majority of states do tax capital gains, which results in a higher effective tax rate for investors.

The federal and most state governments also tax dividends received from holding stocks and the income received from holding bonds or interest-bearing accounts. There are two general kinds of dividend income: *qualified dividends* from holding stocks, and *interest income* from holding bonds and other interest-bearing accounts. Under current tax law (of which certain provisions may expire in 2010 and 2011), qualified dividends are taxed at a rate of 15 percent. For low-income investors, these rates can drop to 5 percent or even 0 percent. Qualified dividends include those paid on common stock and certain types of preferred stock, subject to the stock being held for at least 60 days. Interest and dividends that do not meet the qualified dividend definition are taxed at the *marginal income tax* rate of the investor. The more income you have, the higher your marginal income tax rate. For most people, the marginal income tax rate (state plus federal) is substantially higher than the tax rate for long-term capital gains and qualified dividend income. For higher-income individuals in high income tax states, the combined marginal income tax rate can be 45 percent or more. Note that most dividend income from Real Estate Investment Trusts (REITs) is not considered qualified dividend income, and thus is not subject to the lower-qualified dividend tax rates. The difference between the lower tax rates for long-term capital gains and qualified dividends, and the higher rates for short-term capital gains and interest income is one of the factors that drive tax-efficient investing. You would rather pay the lower tax rates than the higher rates if possible.

While taxes have many implications for smart investing, there are two basic principles that govern how to invest tax efficiently:

- It is better to pay taxes in the future rather than today.
- Paying lower tax rates is generally better than paying higher marginal income taxes.

The first principle stems immediately from the fact that a dollar today is worth more than a dollar in the future. Consequently, you would rather pay a dollar in the future than have to come up with the dollar now. You can reduce the cost of paying the future dollar by investing a smaller amount today that will cover the cost of paying off the future dollar. If you can, you want to defer the payment of taxes into the future, as it will cost you less to meet the liability.

The second point is also relatively straightforward. It will usually make sense to pay the lower tax rates on long-term capital gains and qualified dividends than to pay the potentially much higher marginal income tax rate if you can. This means that in accounts where you have to pay taxes, you will have a preference for receiving investment returns in the form of long-term capital gains and qualified dividends, rather than in the form of short-term capital gains or interest income. By paying the lower tax rates, you will be able to hold onto a greater proportion of your pretax returns. As we will see, this simple principle will have significant implications for the types of investments you will prefer to hold in both taxable and tax-deferred accounts (e.g., your 401(k)).

Taxes affect the net after-tax rate of return that you earn from investing in different kinds of assets. In effect, with taxes, the government shares in a portion of the gains you earn from your investments. What you earn through capital gains and income is not all yours to keep, as the government gets a cut. The higher your tax rates, the bigger the government's share. In addition, the government also participates in the losses that you may experience from holding investments. When you report a capital loss from the sale of a security, you are able to offset that loss against comparable reported capital gains and only pay taxes on the net difference. The government only charges on your overall *net* capital gains reported (gains minus losses). If you have no capital gains in the year you report a capital loss, then you are able to deduct up to $3,000 per year from your taxable income (and you can generally carry over unused losses from previous years).

Since taxes take money out of your pocket, they reduce your after-tax returns (the money that goes in your pocket). When you invest in taxable accounts, you have to save more to achieve the same level of wealth than if you did not have to pay any taxes. Interestingly, the presence of taxes also reduces the volatility of after tax returns relative to pretax returns. Why? When you sell an asset with a large capital gain in a taxable account, you must pay a portion of that gain to the government, reducing the overall size of the net return. The presence of taxes makes the gains lower, reducing the overall volatility of returns. Similarly, if the asset goes down in value and you sell it, the government participates in the loss, which also helps to reduce the overall volatility. So taxes alter both the mean return and the volatility of returns for investments held in taxable accounts.

THE IMPACT OF PERSONAL TAX RATES

Not surprisingly, the more income you make, the bigger the impact of taxes on your investment strategy. In the United States, federal and state income tax rates are based on the amount of taxable income you report that year. High-income investors need to be quite concerned about the tax implications of their investment choices, while low-income individuals will have less to worry about. Under current tax law, as of the time of this writing, the federal marginal income tax rates range from a low of 10 percent to a high of 35 percent of taxable income. In addition, most states charge income tax as well, which increases the overall marginal tax rate. Income tax rates vary significantly across states.

Of course, the total taxes you pay in a year is typically less than your marginal tax rate due to the presence of personal exclusions, deductible expenses like home mortgage interest and medical expenses, and the fact that you pay lower rates on the income earned up to the cutoff for each tax bracket. Economists call this average tax rate actually paid by individuals or households the *effective tax rate*. Based on survey data and analyses of 2006 U.S. tax returns, these effective tax rates—taking into account both state and federal taxes and varying income levels—ranged from 2.3 percent to 39.7 percent of taxable reported income.

Increasing the marginal tax rate increases the taxes paid on bond interest income dividends and short-term capital gains distributions from equity funds. This means that these types of investments, when held in taxable accounts, become less attractive to investors with high marginal tax rates.

As an example, let's look at a simulation for a mutual fund held in a taxable brokerage account for two different individuals: Tom, a high-income resident of California earning $150,000 per year, and Jerry, a low-income resident of Nevada (which has no state income tax) earning $30,000 per year. To highlight the differences, I will choose a relatively tax-inefficient mutual fund, the DWS High Income Plus Fund/S (symbol: SGHSX) from the DWS fund family. This fund has poor tax efficiency due to its propensity to generate a lot of taxable income from the high proportion of taxable bonds held in its portfolio. Let's take a look at the simulation results for Tom's and Jerry's portfolios when they invest $100,000 in after-tax dollars in the DWS fund for 25 years in a taxable brokerage account. To keep things simple we will assume that both Tom and Jerry are single. Remember that all portfolio outcomes are after tax, adjusted for inflation, assume dividends are reinvested, and are expressed in today's dollars. Table 11.1 shows the simulation results for Tom, the high-income resident of California.

TABLE 11.1 Simulation Results for a $100,000 Investment in a Taxable Brokerage Account for a High-Income California Resident

	Value of $100,000 Initial Investment in the DWS High Income Plus Fund (in today's dollars)
	After 25 Years
Upside	$219,000
Median	$106,000
Downside	$45,800

Source: Financial Engines.

As you can see, the median after-tax forecast for Tom's investment is only $106,000 after adjusting for the impact of inflation and taxes. The problem here is that Tom faces high marginal income tax rates due to his high income and state of residence. This makes the interest income from the DWS High Income Plus Fund particularly tax inefficient. In effect, he is giving up a large portion of the return of the fund to taxes, which dramatically lowers his rate of wealth accumulation. Notice that the gap between the upside outcome and the downside outcome is about $173,000.

Now let's examine the same forecast for Jerry, a low-income resident of Nevada, a state that does not charge any income tax. Table 11.2 shows the results of the same simulation for Jerry.

Notice the dramatic difference in the median portfolio outcome for Jerry relative to the result we saw for Tom. Because Jerry faces much lower marginal income tax rates than Tom, the tax inefficiency of the DWS High

TABLE 11.2 Simulation Results for a $100,000 Investment in a Taxable Brokerage Account for a Low-Income Nevada Resident

	Value of $100,000 Initial Investment in the DWS High Income Plus Fund (in today's dollars)
	After 25 Years
Upside	$343,000
Median	$168,000
Downside	$72,900

Source: Financial Engines.

Income Plus Fund is substantially mitigated. With Jerry's tax rates, the projected median after-tax value is $168,000, a result nearly 60 percent higher than the simulation results for Tom! Clearly, tax rates can make a big difference in after-tax wealth accumulation.[1]

While Jerry's lower tax rates makes a big difference in the median forecast for the DWS fund, they also change the overall volatility of the fund from his perspective. In Table 11.2 the gap between the upside outcome and the downside outcome grows to about $273,000, nearly $100,000 greater than the observed spread for Tom. Even though they hold the same investment, the higher taxes paid by Tom reduces the volatility of the fund relative to what Jerry experiences. For Jerry, the range of possible portfolio outcomes is significantly wider than was the case for Tom. However, Jerry also benefits from a higher mean after-tax return, which significantly increases his portfolio outcomes.

The bottom line with this example is that higher-income investors need to pay particular attention to the effects of taxes on wealth accumulation. What is reasonable for one investor may be highly inappropriate for another once you take into account the impact of personal tax rates. Holding tax-inefficient assets in a taxable account can be a major drain on your portfolio growth rate, particularly if your income level is high.

TAX EFFICIENCY OF ASSET CLASSES

As was alluded to in the previous example, some types of assets are inherently more tax efficient than others. A tax-efficient investment generates returns in a manner that minimizes the portion of returns that must be paid out in taxes for a particular investor. Generally, this implies assets that avoid large distributions of dividends or income, or the realization of short-term capital gains that are taxed at higher marginal income tax rates. Instead, a tax-efficient investment will generally accumulate a larger proportion of its returns in the form of unrealized long-term capital gains that are taxed only when the asset is sold. This improves after-tax returns in two ways: the tax rates applied to the gains are lower, and the payment of taxes can be delayed into the future. Both effects serve to improve net after-tax returns.

Note that the relative tax efficiency of a security inherently depends on the tax rates of the person holding it. This means that some securities have higher or lower levels of tax efficiency, depending on the investor. Some assets are highly tax inefficient for higher-income investors, but not so inefficient for investors with lower levels of income. However, an investment that minimizes taxes for high-income investors will generally do a good job of minimizing taxes for lower-income investors as well. The only difference will be the relative proportion of returns lost to taxes. Keep in mind that just because an investment is not tax efficient does not mean it is undesirable in a well-designed investment portfolio. It is perfectly reasonable to hold tax-inefficient assets, but you want to hold them in an account that shields you from having to pay the taxes on accumulations, such as a 401(k) or IRA account.

At the asset class level, equities are generally more tax-efficient investments than bonds. Bonds tend to generate most of their returns in the form of interest income, which is usually taxed at the higher marginal income tax rate. Different types of bonds differ in how their interest payments are taxed. Interest payments from corporate bonds are taxed by both the federal and state government, while Treasury bond interest payments are taxed by the federal government and exempt from state and local taxes.

There is a special class of bonds whose interest payments are exempt from federal taxation and, in many cases, state income tax as well. Such bonds are called *municipal bonds*. Municipal bonds may be issued by cities, counties, school districts, or other local governmental entities. Unlike normal bonds, municipal bond interest does not result in taxable income for holders of the bond.

For equities, most of the return comes in the form of capital gains and qualified dividends. If the equity securities are held for at least a year, the capital gains are taxed at the lower long-term capital gains rates. In addition, when stocks pay dividends, under current tax law these payments are considered qualified dividends that are taxed at a rate of no more than 15 percent. Only the short-term capital gains from selling equities with holding periods of less than a year are taxed at the higher marginal income tax rates. Furthermore, when your total returns come in the form of capital gains, you have some flexibility in the timing of when the gains are recognized. If you hold on to the equity positions, you don't recognize any capital gains until the positions are eventually sold. This allows for taxes to be deferred into the future.

However, keep in mind that with equity mutual funds, the timing of stock sales is up to the manager of the fund, not you. Short- and long-term capital gains recognized from sales of securities in the fund's portfolio are distributed to fund shareholders on a periodic basis. So if your fund manager is trading frequently, he or she is more likely to be generating short- and long-term capital gains distributions that impact how much tax you owe in the year, even if you do not sell the fund. As we will see in later examples, even among equity funds with similar investment styles, the level of tax efficiency can vary dramatically across managers. One advantage of exchange-traded funds, relative to mutual funds, is that their structure allows managers to avoid having to always sell securities to rebalance the portfolio, which reduces the capital gains distributions to fund shareholders. Such funds can be more tax efficient for investors in some situations, making them popular choices for high-income investors holding assets in taxable accounts.

Real estate investment trust funds are particularly tax-inefficient assets when held in taxable accounts. First, they tend to pay very high dividend rates from the income-generating properties in their portfolios, which reduces the after-tax growth rate of the funds. Moreover, these dividends generally do not count as qualified dividends under current tax law, meaning they are taxed at marginal income tax rates, not the lower-qualified dividend tax rate. This means that to the extent you wish to invest in REIT funds, you really don't want to hold them in your taxable brokerage account if you can avoid it.

Figure 11.1 shows the ranking of different asset classes by relative tax efficiency. Of course, individual funds can differ dramatically in their tax efficiency based on the management style and trading activity. The rankings should be considered approximate based on the average tax efficiency of each asset class.

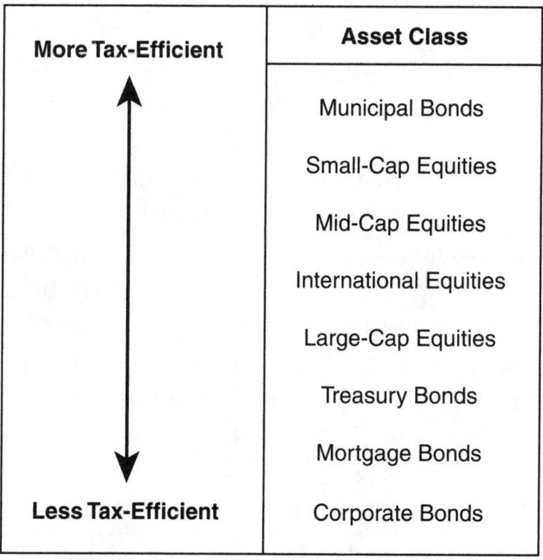

FIGURE 11.1 Relative Tax-efficiency of Different Asset Classes

Tax-efficient asset classes are those that generate fewer taxable distributions, and those that are generated result in long-term capital gains and qualified dividends that are taxed at a lower rate. The key distinction between the tax efficiency of asset classes is the amount of taxable interest income or non-qualified dividends generated by the asset. Taxable bonds will always have lower tax efficiency than equities because they generate most of their return in the form of taxable interest payments. The more your asset holdings allow you to defer the realization of taxes into the future, the more tax efficient your investment strategy will be.

ASSET PLACEMENT

From the previous discussion, it should be obvious that there are significant advantages to structuring your portfolio to maximize the tax-efficiency of your assets. One way to accomplish this objective is by holding the most tax-efficient investments in your taxable brokerage account, and placing the least tax-efficient holdings in accounts that protect them from generating taxable distributions, such as a 401(k) account or IRA. Moving assets into the most tax-efficient locations is called *asset placement*.

Let's examine a very simple example to see how asset placement can improve the performance of your portfolio. Diane is a 40-year-old employee at a telecommunications company. She has accumulated a nest egg for her retirement of $300,000, half in a 401(k) account and half in a taxable brokerage account. Her retirement time horizon in 25 years. Diane makes $125,000 per year and lives in California, giving her a total marginal income tax rate equal to 37.4 percent.

Diane has placed 100 percent of each account into a single fund. For the 401(k) plan, Diane has selected the Oakmark Equity & Income II Fund (symbol: OARBX), a balanced fund with a mix of equity and fixed-income exposures. This fund happens to be a relatively tax-efficient mutual fund for its style. In her brokerage account, Diane has chosen the Columbia High Income Fund/Z (symbol: NYPAX), a high-yield bond fund that generates a large amount of taxable distributions. High-yield bond funds invest in bonds with lower credit ratings and higher yields. These types of investments generate a large percentage of their return in the form of taxable interest. The overall risk level of this household portfolio is approximately 0.80, or about 80 percent of the volatility of the market portoflio.

TABLE 11.3 Diane's Initial Household Portfolio Allocation and Forecast at a 25-Year Horizon ($150,000 Initial Balance in Each Account)

Diane's 401(k) Account		Total Portfolio Forecast at 25 Years	
Oakmark Equity & Income II	100%	Upside	$1,030,000
Columbia High Income/Z	0%	Median	$513,000
		Downside	$222,000
Diane's Brokerage Account			
Oakmark Equity & Income II	0%		
Columbia High Income/Z	100%		

Source: Financial Engines.

Table 11.3 shows the initial fund allocation in her 401(k) and brokerage accounts, along with a forecast of what the total portfolio may be worth in the future (assuming no additional contributions). The portfolio values are shown as pretax amounts and are adjusted for inflation.

As you can see in Table 11.3, with this allocation of her $300,000 nest egg, Diane is looking at a pretax portfolio value of between $222,000 on the downside, and $1,030,000 on the upside after 25 years, with a median value of $513,000. But from an asset-placement perspective, this fund allocation leaves something to be desired. The tax-inefficient fund, the Columbia High Income fund, is being held in the taxable brokerage account, where it generates lots of taxable distributions, while the more tax-efficient holding is held in her 401(k) account. Diane could do better by simply swapping where the funds are held to maximize her net returns.

Table 11.4 shows the result of moving her money to the Columbia High Income fund in her 401(k) and the balance of her brokerage account into the Oakmark Equity & Income II fund.

With this new asset placement, Diane's portfolio forecast has improved without significantly changing the overall risk or asset allocation of the household portfolio.[1] She still has $150,000 invested in each fund, but the combination is now generating a portfolio forecast that is 6.8 percent to 13.5 percent higher than the less tax-efficient allocation she started with. By simply paying attention to the tax efficiency of the funds in selecting where to hold them, Diane has improved her household portfolio forecast significantly.

TABLE 11.4 Diane's Initial Household Portfolio Allocation and Forecast at a 25-Year Horizon ($150,000 Initial Balance in Each Account)

Diane's 401(k) Account		Total Portfolio Forecast at 25 Years	
Oakmark Equity & Income II	0%	Upside	$1,100,000
Columbia High Income/Z	100%	Median	$565,000
		Downside	$252,000
Diane's Brokerage Account			
Oakmark Equity & Income II	100%		
Columbia High Income/Z	0%		

Source: Financial Engines.

Admittedly, this was a stylized example. In the real world, the issues of proper asset placement are typcially not as simple, as you may not have access to exactly the same types of funds in your taxable and tax-deferred accounts. However, the basic principle will generally hold: *it is better to hold tax-inefficient funds like taxable bond funds in your tax-deferred accounts, and hold more tax-efficient securities in your taxable accounts.* In some situations, you may be forced to hold tax-inefficient investments in your taxable account, if your risk target and available fund choices make more efficient allocation infeasible. In these situations, you usually want to try to minimize the holdings of the least tax-efficient funds in your taxable account. However, you need to consider the overall desirability of funds in addition to their tax efficiency. A tax-efficient fund with a high expense ratio may actually be worse than a lower-cost fund that is less tax efficient. In most real-world examples, there will be several factors to consider to determine the most appropriate asset placement.

MUTUAL FUND TAX EFFICIENCY

As we saw in the previous section, some asset classes are inherently more tax efficient than others. In particular, taxable bonds tend to generate higher tax liabilities than equities due to their larger distribution of taxable income as a proportion of total return. But even among mutual funds of the same investment style and asset allocation, there are substantial differences in tax efficiency due to fund-specific characteristics. For an investor earning $100,000 per year, the annual tax burden for many funds can easily subtract

2 percent to 4 percent of total returns on an annual basis. Even the most tax-efficient equity funds routinely lose 0.25 percent to 0.50 percent per year of their total return to taxes. As we saw in the previous discussion on the impact of fees, this is a big deal in terms of your future wealth. Reducing the effects of taxes on your investment returns can make a big difference in your bottom line. If you happen to be investing only in tax-deferred accounts like a 401(k) plan or an IRA, then you do not need to spend any time evaluating the tax efficiency of your mutual fund investments. But if you are investing in mutual funds or exchange-traded funds in a taxable brokerage account, or a combination of taxable and tax-deferred accounts, then tax efficiency is a big factor that should be considered in making informed portfolio decisions.

Specifically, the tax efficiency of a mutual fund depends on its propensity to distribute taxable capital gains, interest income, and dividends to its shareholders. Two things matter: The overall size of the distributions and the specific kinds of distributions that are made. Since different types of distributions are taxed at different rates, the tax efficiency of funds will vary depending on the type and mix of taxable distributions. Current tax law generally regards mutual fund shareholders as owning a proportional share of the underlying assets in the fund. This means that any realized capital gains or income distributions are taxed to the shareholders. For instance, when a mutual fund sells a stock position in its portfolio, the fund manager must distribute the realized net capital gains, if any, to the shareholders of the fund on a periodic basis. In fact, the tax law governing mutual funds requires fund managers to distribute almost all of the income and realized capital gains to shareholders each year in order for the fund itself to avoid taxes.

Mutual fund distributions can be in the form of ordinary income (short-term capital gains and interest income) or long-term capital gains and qualified distributions. Each type is taxed at different rates depending on the tax bracket of the fund investor. Whether a capital gains distribution is short- or long-term depends on how long the stock positions were held by the fund manager, not how long you owned the mutual fund. Of course, when you sell your mutual fund shares, you must also report the capital gains on the profits from the sale. The same rules apply to capital gains on mutual fund shares as for holding individual stocks. The profit on mutual fund positions that are sold after being held less than 12 months must be reported as short-term capital gains.

Tax-efficient mutual funds are those that distribute a smaller proportion of their returns as taxable distributions and in particular avoid short-term capital gains and interest income distributions, which are taxed at higher rates. Obviously taxable bond funds are at a big disadvantage in taxable account, as they generate large amounts of taxable income. However, some equity mutual funds can be very tax inefficient as well. If a mutual fund generates lots of dividend distributions, this lowers the tax efficiency of the fund, since it means having to paying some taxes now, as opposed to paying them in the future when you sell the fund. In general, value-oriented equity funds tend to invest in the stocks of companies with higher dividend yields. This means that value-oriented funds are more likely to make taxable dividend distributions than funds that invest primarily in growth stocks (which tend to pay fewer dividends). While the current tax rate on qualified dividends is relatively low under current tax law, large dividend distributions can still significantly impact the tax efficiency of a fund over time when held in a taxable account. Also, larger stocks tend to pay higher dividends than smaller stocks, which implies that large-cap equity funds tend to distribute more taxable dividends to shareholders than do small-cap equity funds.

A fund that generates the majority of its total return in the form of unrealized long-term capital gains is the most tax-efficient choice, since it means that you can defer paying most of the accrued taxes as long as you hold the fund. If an equity fund manager trades very actively, turning over the portfolio on a frequent basis, then he or she will tend to generate more capital gains as securities in the portfolio are sold, some of which may be short-term gains, depending on how long the positions were held. These capital gains are distributed to shareholders even if they just hold the fund and do not trade. When a mutual fund manager trades frequently he or she is taking away one of the most important sources of flexibility in holding equities—the ability to defer taxes into the future by not realizing capital gains. Since a mutual fund is forced to distribute any capital gains from sales of its positions, a highly active manager will generate lots of sales and lots of taxable distributions. It does not matter if you hold on to the fund for years without trading: you will still have significant tax liability from the fund's periodic distributions. Also keep in mind that even if you choose to reinvest dividends back into the fund, you will still be taxed on the dividend distributions.

How do you spot more tax-efficient funds? More tax-efficient funds will tend to have lower rates of turnover in their portfolio, and thus generate fewer taxable distributions to their shareholders. As we know from previous chapters, index funds have much lower rates of turnover than most actively managed mutual funds. This is yet another reason why index funds are compelling investments, particularly when held in a taxable account. An index fund only has to trade when new stocks are added to the index, or old stocks are replaced in the index, which tends to happen infrequently. The low turnover makes equity index funds particularly tax efficient. In contrast, many actively managed funds engage in high levels of trading as stocks are moved in and out of the portfolio.

The mix of distributions matters as well as the size of the distributions. If a fund manager only sells stocks after holding them for one year or more, then the resulting capital gains distributions will be long-term capital gains, which are taxed at the lower rate of 15 percent (or even lower if your income is small). However, if the manager sells positions after holding them for less than a year, the resulting short-term capital gains distribution counts as taxable income, which can be a much higher rate, depending on your income. Even though qualified dividends are taxed at the lower 15 percent rate under current law, at the time of this writing, the distribution of dividends also creates a tax liability for fund shareholders. To reduce the taxable distributions, you would prefer to hold equities that pay lower-dividend yields, which in general means smaller companies and growth-oriented stocks. Of course, the degree of tax inefficiency for a given fund depends on the personal tax rates of the investor.

Keep in mind that the trading behavior of the fund manager can trump the underlying tax efficiency of the assets in the fund. For instance, a small-cap manager who trades very frequently might generate a large number of short-term capital gains distributions, even if the underlying stocks in the portfolio have little or no dividend payments. Such a mutual fund would be very tax inefficient, even though the asset class exposures are relatively tax efficient. When selecting funds, you need to consider both the investment style and the trading strategy of the manager.

One final note of caution. Many mutual funds pay out their distributions at the end of the year (often in late December). As an investor, you want to be cautious about investing in a fund just prior to it making a distribution to shareholders. Why? You receive your distribution in cash, which can then be reinvested. But the distribution is a taxable event, which means you will owe taxes on the distribution even if your net position in the fund did not change. If possible, you would be better off to wait until just after the fund made its distribution in order to avoid generating the taxable event until later the following year. Remember that paying taxes later is usually a good idea.

Table 11.5 provides some guidelines for identifying tax-efficient mutual funds. While the specific characteristics of tax-efficient funds can vary, the factors listed in Table 11.5 are usually predictive of the tax efficiency of a fund.

TABLE 11.5 Characteristics of Tax-Efficient Mutual Funds

Fund Characteristics Related to Higher Tax Efficiency	Fund Characteristics Related to Lower Tax Efficiency
High-equity allocations	High bond allocations (except for municipal bonds)
Invests in stocks with low dividend yields (smaller companies, growth stocks)	Invests in stocks with high-dividend yields (larger companies, value stocks, REITs)
Low portfolio turnover	High portfolio turnover
Low historical short-term capital gains distributions	High historical short-term capital gains distributions
Index funds	Very actively managed funds

Source: Financial Engines.

These factors are intended to provide general guidance in identifying tax-efficient funds. However, they do not represent an exhaustive list of the factors that might impact a particular fund. But remember, your personal tax rates are a major factor in determining how tax efficient a given fund will be as a part of your household portfolio.

The Financial Engines *Personal Online Advisor* can help with identifying tax-efficient funds for your personal situation. When providing recommendations for taxable accounts, the *Personal Online Advisor* service takes into consideration your personal tax rates in addition to detailed estimates of the relative tax efficiency of the funds available to you. These estimates include predicted dividend, interest, short-term capital gains, and long-term capital gains distributions. Given the large number of factors that can influence such recommendations, I recommend that you consult the *Personal Online Advisor* or a qualified investment advisor with experience in tax-efficient investing to determine which investments make the most sense for your needs. However, the preceding guidelines can be helpful in understanding the general types of funds that may be appropriate for your taxable investment accounts.

MUNICIPAL BONDS

A special class of assets for taxable accounts is municipal bonds. Municipal bonds are issued by various state, city, or local governments. Unlike typical bonds, municipal bond interest payments are generally exempt from federal, and in some cases, state and local income taxes. Generally speaking, municipal bonds issued by an entity in your state of residence will be free from state and local income taxes, though there are some exceptions to this rule. In contrasts to normal bonds, municipal bonds usually do not generate interest distributions that are subject to income taxes. Interest received from municipal bonds is generally tax free. However, in some cases, the interest from municipal bonds may be subject to the *alternative minimum tax* rate.

For higher-income investors—those with high marginal tax rates—the tax-free property of the interest from municipal bonds can be a major benefit. This is particularly true if you desire to hold bonds in a taxable account. Since traditional bonds are highly tax inefficient when held in a taxable account, municipal bonds play an important role for those investors paying higher marginal income tax rates. If you compare a corporate bond and a municipal bond with the same pretax yield, the municipal bond will have a higher after-tax yield due to its tax-exempt status. When you receive interest from the corporate bond, you owe taxes on that income, which reduces the after-tax yield. Since most municipal bonds are exempt from such taxes, the pretax yield is equal to the after-tax yield. Of course, the value of the tax benefit depends on the income tax bracket of the investor. The higher the income, the more valuable the tax benefits.

Note that the tax exemption for municipal bonds at the state level usually depends on your state of residence and the state in which the bonds were issued. For instance, a California resident would not have to pay state income tax on interest income from a bond issued by a local government in the state of California. Also, some municipal bond interest may be subject to *alternative minimum tax* rates. To understand the specific tax implications of a municipal bond or bond fund you should consult the fund prospectus.

Municipal bonds sound like a great deal for all investors, right? Who wouldn't prefer to avoid paying income taxes? There is a catch, however. Because of their special tax status, municipal bonds are priced in the market to pay lower yields than otherwise similar traditional bonds. Why? Because certain investors are willing to accept lower interest payments given that they are exempt from federal and state taxation. This bids the price of the bonds up, and the yields are driven down. Because of the demand for tax-free interest by higher-income investors, the yields on municipal bonds are lower than other types of bonds. In effect, municipal bonds are priced with an implied tax rate that lowers their yield.

How much lower? Studies indicate that municipal bonds have yields that are approximately 20 percent lower than comparable taxable bonds with similar risk and maturity characteristics. For a specific bond, the difference in yields depends on many factors. What this means is that higher-income investors paying higher marginal tax rates will prefer to hold municipal bonds over taxable bonds in a taxable account. If your income is low and you are in a lower tax bracket, the tax benefit to you is too small to make up for the lower yield of municipal bonds compared to normal taxable bonds. *Therefore, municipal bonds are only attractive to those investors whose tax rates are high enough so that the tax benefit outweighs the lower interest rate paid by the bonds.* High-income investors will have a clear preference for holding municipal bonds since the tax benefit is worth more than the roughly 20 percent lower yield they get from such bonds. If your income tax rates are low, you would be better off holding traditional bonds whose interest payments are taxable, rather than accept the lower interest rates offered by municipal bonds. Lower-income investors should just pay the income taxes on the interest received from taxable bonds rather than take the lower interest rates from comparable municipal bonds.

What this means in practical terms is that higher-income investors will desire to hold municipal bonds to the extent that they need to hold bond exposure in taxable account, while lower-income investors will prefer to hold taxable bonds with the higher pretax yields. If your federal income tax bracket is 25 percent or more, then it is highly likely that you would benefit from holding municipal bonds for any desired fixed-income exposure in a taxable account. However, if your federal bracket is 15 percent or less, then you would be better off seeking the higher yields of taxable bonds for your fixed-income needs. Remember that to get the full tax advantages, the municipal bonds must typically be issued from your state of residence. For instance, if you live in the state of California, you will most likely want to purchase municipal bonds issued by entities in California.

As an example, consider a single investor named Stephanie, who has a taxable brokerage account at T. Rowe Price, makes $150,000 per year, and resides in the state of California. Her brokerage account has $200,000 in total assets and is targeted to have a risk level of 1.0. Table 11.6 shows the recommended allocation for Stephanie to maximize her after-tax returns at a risk level of 1.0.

The recommended portfolio for Stephanie consists of a mix of tax-efficient bond and equity funds. Since she faces high marginal tax rates, the recommended bond funds to achieve the desired risk level are municipal funds from California issuers. These funds allow her to attain a significant fixed income allocation (25 percent) while avoiding the tax inefficiency of taxable bonds.

TABLE 11.6 Recommended Allocation for Stephanie's Taxable Brokerage Account with Risk 1.0 (High Income)

Mutual Funds	Allocation (Risk = 1.0)
T Rowe Price California Tax-Free Bond Fund (PRXCX)	19%
American Century California Long-Term Tax-Free Fund (BCLTX)	16%
T Rowe Price International Growth & Income Fund (TRIGX)	26%
Northern Stock Index Fund (NOSIX)	30%
T Rowe Price Extended Equity Market Index Fund (PEXMX)	9%

Source: Financial Engines.

But what if Stephanie was in a lower tax bracket, with an annual income of only $30,000 per year? How would her recommended portfolio change? Table 11.7 shows the results of the new optimization for Stephanie, assuming the lower income tax bracket associated with an income of $30,000.

Now Stephanie's recommended allocation does not include any municipal bonds, instead relying on a taxable bond index fund. Because someone with income of $30,000 is in the 15 percent marginal tax bracket, it does not make sense for her to hold municipal bonds, since the value of the tax benefit is less than the reduction in yields offered by municipal bonds. She is better off going with a traditional bond fund and paying the income tax on the interest distributions to maximize her after-tax returns.

TABLE 11.7 Recommended Allocation for Stephanie's Taxable Brokerage Account with Risk 1.0 (Low Income)

Mutual Funds	Allocation (Risk = 1.0)
Dreyfus Bond Market Index Fund; Basic (DBIRX)	33%
T Rowe Price International Growth & Income Fund (TRIGX)	27%
Northern Stock Index Fund (NOSIX)	27%
Dreyfus SmallCap Stock Index Fund (DISSX)	13%

Source: Financial Engines.

As you can see from this example, the personal tax rates of the investor are of significant importance in determining the proper investment strategy for a taxable account. Note that the tax-efficiency advantages of municipal bonds are meaningless for all investors if the bonds are held in a tax-deferred account. Accordingly, you would never want to accept the lower yields from municipal bonds in a 401(k), IRA, or other tax-deferred accounts.

CAPITAL GAINS AND LOSSES

Another consideration in tax-efficient investing is the impact of accumulated losses or gains in the positions that you already hold in your portfolio. When you purchase a stock, bond, or mutual fund in a taxable account, the purchase price of the security defines a *cost basis* for your position. The cost basis is the value that the IRS uses to determine the capital gains taxes you will owe when you sell the position. The taxes owed are a percentage of the difference between the sale price and the cost basis of the position.

The cost basis of your portfolio positions can be calculated in several ways. The simplest is to calculate an average cost basis based on the average price paid for the shares of the security that you hold. If you made multiple purchases over time, the prices you paid would be averaged to arrive at an average cost basis. A more sophisticated approach is to track the different purchases of a security separately in different subaccounts. For instance, if I purchased 100 shares of a mutual fund at $15.00 per share and then subsequently purchased 50 more shares a month later at $15.75 per share, then I would have 100 shares with a cost basis of $15.00, and 50 shares with a basis of $15.75. By keeping track of each purchase separately, I can better defer the payment of capital gains taxes by selling my highest-cost basis shares first. To continue our example, if I sold 50 shares of my mutual fund at $16.00 per share, I could specify the shares with the $15.75 cost basis as those that were sold to minimize my current tax liability, putting off the sale of the lower basis shares for a future point in time. In many cases, only the average cost basis of your positions will be tracked by your financial services firm, though some firms provide an option to track individual purchases with different cost basis if desired.

Why does the cost basis matter for investment advice? Because if you have a position with a low cost basis relative to its current value, then there is a tax liability associated with selling it since you would have to pay capital gains taxes on the profits from the sale. To maximize your after-tax returns, you might want to avoid creating a taxable event by selling positions with accumulated capital gains, particularly if the position has been held for less than a year. As long as you hold on to the position, you don't have to pay taxes on the unrealized gain. But as soon as you sell the position, you give up the ability to defer the taxes on the capital gain into the future. Similarly, a position with an accumulated loss has a tax benefit if it is sold, since the loss can be subtracted from any capital gains you reported in the same tax year. Even if you have no other capital gains to report, a tax loss on a position can result in deductions of up to $3,000 against current income. This makes it desirable to report losses sooner, since it allows you to avoid higher current taxes.

When trying to maximize after-tax returns by optimizing a taxable portfolio, it is important to take into consideration the impact of any positions with unrealized gains or losses relative to their current value. Values whose cost basis is lower than the current value will tend to be sticky. That is, you want to avoid selling such positions unless the benefits of making the change outweigh the cost of recognizing the capital gains taxes earlier. Remember that you will have to pay the taxes eventually, so the question is how long can you defer the taxable event into the future. Similarly, it will often be beneficial to sell positons with unrealized losses, particularly if they can be used to offset reported capital gains in the same period.

Let's look at a simple optimization example to make the point more clear. Our example is based on an investor named Richard, who lives in the state of Connecticut and is in a high marginal tax bracket. Richard has a brokerage account at Schwab with a number of mutual fund positions totalling $250,000. He is interested in lowering the risk of his portfolio from 1.3 to 1.0 while maximizing his after-tax expected returns. First, let's see how the portfolio should be adjusted if we assume that each of Richard's existing positions have a cost basis equal to their current value. When the current value equals the cost basis, there is no penalty or benefit from selling the position, as there is no taxable event. To keep things simple, we will assume that there are no transaction fees for any of the funds in his portfolio.

Table 11.8 shows Richard's initial portfolio and recommended changes for moving from a risk level of 1.3 to a lower level of 1.0.

In order to move to the new lower-risk level, the optimization suggests increasing exposure to the American Century Tax Free Bond Fund, and decreasing the allocation to the four stock index funds (three Dreyfus and one Schwab fund) to lower the overall risk of the fund. In particular, the optimization suggests reducing the exposure to the Dreyfus Midcap Stock

TABLE 11.8 Recommended Changes to Move Richard's Brokerage Portfolio from Risk 1.3 to Risk 1.0

Brokerage Account	Current (Risk = 1.3)	New (Risk = 1.0)	Change
American Century: Tax Free Bond/Inv.	0%	26%	26%
Permanent Portfolio	6%	6%	0%
UMB Scout International	14%	14%	0%
Dreyfus International Stock Index	22%	20%	−2%
Schwab S&P 500 Index/Inv.	35%	28%	−7%
Dreyfus Midcap Stock Index	17%	6%	−11%
Dreyfus SmallCap Stock Index	6%	0%	−6%

Source: Financial Engines.

Index fund from $42,500 to $15,000. To get the overall portfolio risk down to 1.0, it is necessary to reduce the overall equity exposure of the portfolio.

But what if Richard had already accumulated capital gains of 20 percent in the Dreyfus Midcap Stock Index fund and the Schwab S&P 500 Index fund? That is, what if the cost basis of these two funds in his initial portofolio were equal to 80 percent of their current values. How would the recommendations change to take into consideration the cost of realizing capital gains on the sale of positions? Table 11.9 shows the results of this analysis.

Not surprisingly, it now makes sense to hold on to the Dreyfus Midcap Stock Index fund position, since selling it would trigger capital gains taxes.

TABLE 11.9 Recommended Changes to Move Richard's Brokerage Portfolio from Risk 1.3 to Risk 1.0 with Selected Accumulated Capital Gains

Brokerage Account	Current (Risk = 1.3)	New (Risk = 1.0)	Change
American Century: Tax Free Bond/Inv.	0%	28%	28%
Permanent Portfolio	6%	6%	0%
UMB Scout International	14%	14%	0%
Dreyfus International Stock Index	22%	10%	−12%
Schwab S&P 500 Index/Inv.	35%	25%	−10%
Dreyfus Midcap Stock Index	17%	17%	0%
Dreyfus SmallCap Stock Index	6%	0%	−6%

Source: Financial Engines.

However, the risk level of the portfolio still needs to be reduced. This is accomplished by increasing the allocation to the American Century Tax Free Bond fund to 28 percent of the portfolio, and decreasing the allocation to the Schwab S&P 500 Stock Index fund by 10 percent, and the Dreyfus International Stock Index fund by 12 percent. Note the bigger decrease in the Dreyfus International Stock Index fund is making up for the smaller reduction in the S&P 500 index fund (which had the lower cost basis). But because the Schwab fund also has a cost basis that is 20 percent below the current price, the sale of the position creates estimated capital gains of \$5,000 (\$87,500 – \$62,500 × 20 percent = \$5,000). However, this is still less than the capital gains generated if we had applied the allocation changes in Table 11.8 to the portfolio with the accumulated gains for the Dreyfus Midcap and Schwab S&P 500 funds. Had we sold the Dreyfus Midcap and Schwab S&P 500 funds in the proportions shown in Table 11.8, we would have generated \$9,000 in capital gains instead of \$5,000. By adjusting the portfolio to avoid the sale of all the Dreyfus Midcap fund, the optimizer could reduce the capital gains taxes that must be paid while achieving an efficient portfolio mix of risk 1.0.

PUTTING IT ALL TOGETHER

As much as I would like to say otherwise, taxes are complicated. There are probably more experts out there earning a living by helping people with tax considerations in their personal finances than in any other area. This chapter has provided only an overview of the factors that influence portfolio decisions in the presence of taxes. Given the large number of variables that can influence investment decisions, it is impossible to illustrate all the possible scenarios you might face in building high-quality portfolios. Instead, my intent was to arm you with the necessary intuition to understand how taxes impact your investment returns and how to maximize your after-tax wealth accumulation. If your situation is complex, or a large fraction of your investable assets are in taxable brokerage accounts, then strongly consider seeking expert help to build a tax-efficient strategy. Certainly investors with more than \$100,000 invested in a brokerage account should pay close attention to the impact of taxes on their investment strategy. The gains to a more tax-efficient strategy can be quite significant, particularly if your time horizon is more than 10 years. Remember that the Financial Engines *Personal Online Advisor* service can provide a great start to understanding how to maximize your after-tax returns in your personal investment portfolio.

Building a tax-efficient investment strategy means minimizing the impact of taxes on after-tax returns, avoiding paying high tax rates on taxable distributions where possible, being smart about where to hold different kinds of assets, trying to defer the payment of taxes into the future, and understanding the impact of your personal tax rates on investment selection. Alas, there is no silver bullet for maximizing after-tax returns, but by paying attention to a few key factors, you can make a big difference in your financial outcomes.

TAKE-AWAYS

- The goal with tax-efficient investing is to maximize after-tax returns, not minimize taxes. This is achieved by paying lower tax rates and deferring taxes into the future where possible.
- Tax efficiency only matters if you are investing in at least one taxable account.
- The higher your income tax rate, the more concerned you should be about the tax efficiency of investments in your taxable accounts.
- Equity funds are generally more tax efficient than bond funds (except for municipal bonds).
- Hold less tax-efficient assets (e.g., taxable bonds) in a tax-deferred account and more tax-efficient assets in your taxable account. Asset placement can make a significant difference in your total after-tax portfolio returns.
- Avoid equity mutual funds with large short-term capital gains distributions. Equity funds with high turnover (more than 100 percent per year) are particularly likely to distribute short-term capital gains. Index funds are typically much more tax efficient.
- If you are in a high-income tax bracket, you should likely consider municipal bonds for your fixed income holdings in taxable accounts. But never hold municipal bonds in a tax-deferred account like an IRA. Low-income investors should generally avoid municipal bonds entirely.
- Remember that tax efficiency is only one factor in selecting funds. You also need to consider investment style, fees, and manager performance.

CHAPTER 12

Wrapping it Up

Live long and prosper.
—Mr. Spock (2230–), *Star Trek* (Vulcan and Jewish benediction)

The last eleven chapters have provided valuable insights into how to become a more informed and ultimately more successful investor. Of course, there was a lot of ground to cover along the way. If you are like me, you might be challenged to remember all of the most important concepts covered in the preceding pages. To assist with making things "stick" a little better, I have distilled the most important lessons of *The Intelligent Portfolio* into a short summary, which I now present for your reading enjoyment and benefit. And remember that life is what happens along the path toward your future goals. Don't forget to enjoy the journey!

CHAPTER 1: NOW IT'S PERSONAL

- **Take control of your future.** Be realistic about your ability and interest in managing your investments on your own. Decide whether you are willing to spend the time to educate yourself on how to be a savvy investor, or find a qualified and fee-only (no commissions) advisor to help you at a reasonable fee. But most importantly, don't make the mistake of just sitting there and procrastinating.
- **Always maintain a skeptical attitude about your investments.** Don't be led astray by unrealistic performance claims and sloppy analysis. There is a lot of foolish advice out there. Think critically about your investments at all times.
- **Take advantage of institutional tools of the trade.** Simulation and optimization techniques like those available in the Financial Engines *Personal Online Advisor* service can be very helpful in building

high-quality investment portfolios. Be a more informed investor by taking advantage of these tools, just like the big institutional investors do.

CHAPTER 2: NO FREE LUNCH

- **There is no free lunch.** Risk and returns are always related. You won't find higher investment returns without assuming higher risk. Moreover, risk has a way of catching up with you whether you anticipate it or not.
- **Not all risk comes with expected reward.** In general, only risks correlated with the overall market are compensated with higher expected returns. Risks that are easily diversified away generally do not result in higher expected returns.
- **Not all risk is visible in historical returns.** Be careful about investment strategies with small probabilities of very negative outcomes (doing very badly in bad times). With such strategies, the historical record can be a poor guide to the future risks. Hedge funds are notorious for having such risks.
- **Use realistic investment simulations to understand your range of possible portfolio outcomes.** Sophisticated investment simulation models can provide a realistic view of your future outcomes and help you make better decisions. Don't pay too much attention to the expected outcome—chances are you will experiences something different.
- **Bonds are more risky than cash, and equities are more risky than bonds.** But with this risk comes higher expected returns. The higher the risk, the greater the range of possible portfolio outcomes. Over a five-year holding period, bonds have a range of outcomes that is more than **three** times bigger than cash (adjusted for inflation), while equities have a range that is over **eight** times larger. These ratios go up even more with longer time horizons. Make sure you understand the range of possible outcomes when you invest.

CHAPTER 3: HISTORY IS BUNK

- **Don't fall into the trap of picking the portfolio with the highest historical return.** Always take into consideration the risk of future returns.
- **Past performance is a poor guide for future expected returns.** This is true for both assets classes and investment funds. Just because

a manager did well in the past does not mean that such performance will be repeated. Past returns hold little information about the future.

- **History is only one observation from a wide range of possible but unseen outcomes.** Most of what is possible in investment performance is never actually observed. Don't get too fixated on what happened historically, as the future will almost certainly be different.
- **Don't be misled by a strong historical track record.** There are many reasons why historical track records may not be representative of the future. Be skeptical, especially about newer investment funds with limited histories.
- **Manager performance is only a weak predictor of future performance.** The predictive value of manager track records is weak. Even great track records may be due to good luck as much as investment skill. Don't make big bets on managers being able to repeat their historical performance.

CHAPTER 4: THE WISDOM OF THE MARKET

- **The market is very difficult to consistently beat.** This does not mean that it is impossible to beat, but consistently outperforming the market is highly challenging, even for the most experienced and sophisticated investors. Don't base your financial plan on being able to beat the market.
- **The market portfolio is a good benchmark for the average investor.** It is also an excellent source of information about future expected returns.
- **Don't try to time the market.** Market timing assumes that large numbers of other investors in the market are making a big mistake—a costly assumption if you are wrong. You are much better off sticking with a consistent diversified investment strategy over time.
- **Avoid investment strategies that rebalance to fixed proportions.** They are actually contrarian bets against the market. You should use strategies that adjust with the market portfolio to avoid market timing bets.
- **Higher expected return asset classes have more market risk.** To get higher expected returns, you need to be willing to take more market risk. Equities have higher expected returns than bonds.
- **International assets are a desirable part of your portfolio.** Their relatively low correlations with the rest of your portfolio make them desirable holdings in a diversified strategy.

CHAPTER 5: GETTING THE RISK RIGHT

- **Risk means different things to different people.** Make sure you focus on the risks that are most important to you. Evaluate the trade-offs between short-term and long-term risks.
- **The most important factors in selecting an appropriate risk level are time horizon and your tolerance for downside outcomes, both short and long term.** Make sure your investment allocation is consistent with your time horizon.
- **There is a trade-off between long-term expected returns and short-term volatility.** Higher median portfolio outcomes come with more short-term volatility. In order to achieve higher expected returns, you must be willing to endure more volatility in the short-term.
- **Don't make the mistake of investing very conservatively for long periods of time.** You give up substantial expected growth over longer horizons by investing in very conservative assets like money market or stable value funds.
- **Even with relatively short horizons, it will often make sense to have significant equity exposure.** If your horizon is more than 10 years, consider having at least 60 percent of your assets devoted to diversified equities. Longer-term investors should consider placing 80 percent of more of their assets into equities. Remember that your retirement horizon is generally not the date when you will need to liquedate your assets.

CHAPTER 6: AN UNNECESSARY GAMBLE

- **Investing in individual stocks is an unnecessary gamble.** You can do better, on average, by using more diversified instruments like mutual funds or exchange-traded funds for your core investments.
- **Individual stocks have much higher volatility than funds.** The risk of individual stocks varies significantly across industries and companies, but downside values for stocks are typically much lower than the values for equity funds. Companies can easily go bankrupt, but mutual funds do not.
- **The higher volatility of individual stocks implies much lower expected growth rates.** For many individual stocks, the expected growth rate is zero or even negative for multiyear horizons. Higher volatility is a major drag of portfolio growth rates.

- **When you invest in a diversified portfolio instead of a single stock, you give up a small probability of doing very well, but your overall chances of coming out ahead improve dramatically.** The performance of a broad-based equity index will exceed the returns of a single-stock strategy about 60 percent to 75 percent of the time over a multiyear period. Don't bet the farm on a stock doing much better than expected.
- **The costs of trading a stock portfolio are much higher than most mutual funds.** The costs associated with even moderate levels of stock trading can be a substantial drag on your expected returns, particularly in a taxable account. Don't succumb to the siren song of the active stock trader.
- **Never make the critical mistake of being too concentrated in your employer's stock.** If your company gets into trouble, you could lose your job *and* your retirement savings if you are too concentrated. Do not put more than 20 percent of your retirement portfolio into your employer's stock, and most investors should consider an even lower percentage.

CHAPTER 7: HOW FEES EAT YOUR LUNCH

- **The average index fund outperforms the average active fund.** Only a subset of actively managed funds can beat their benchmark, and this subset changes from year to year. The average dollar invested in an index fund is mathematically guaranteed to beat the average dollar invested in an actively managed fund.
- **Don't buy funds with high expenses.** Avoid equity funds with expense ratios above 1.00 percent per year. For bond funds, avoid expense ratios above 0.75 percent and for money market funds, never pay expense ratios greater than 0.50 percent per year. For index funds, you should not be paying more than 0.40 percent per year in fund expenses.
- **Avoid equity funds with high turnover (more than 150 percent per year).** The high turnover increases the total costs of the fund through brokerage commissions and trading costs. Fund turnover ratios are readily available from several online sources, including the Financial Engines *Personal Online Advisor*.
- **Don't purchase funds with front-end or back-end investment loads.** Particularly if you don't plan to hold the fund for at least

10 years, you are generally better off selecting comparable no-load funds. Try to invest in low-cost no-load funds when possible.

- **Don't pay your advisor with loads or commissions.** Instead, look for an advisor that charges an explicit hourly or asset-based investment advisory fee for advice or investment management. This allows you to avoid conflicts of interest that can compromise the quality of advice that you receive.
- **Take advantage of institutionally priced products if you can get them through your employer retirement plan.** Many large companies offer very attractively priced funds in their defined contribution plans that often represent an excellent value relative to retail mutual funds.
- **Try to avoid purchases of transaction-fee funds.** For small transactions, these fees can be a crushing burden to your returns.

CHAPTER 8: SMART DIVERSIFICATION

- **Diversification is important, but it does not get rid of market risk.** A diversified portfolio may still have considerable risk, depending on the amount of exposure to the overall market. A properly diversified portfolio means only taking risks for which you are likely to be rewarded. A diversified portfolio is still risky.
- **Evaluate diversification at the household level, not at the individual account level.** Consider the impact of all your assets on your overall investment allocation. Make sure your overall household portfolio is properly diversified.
- **Asset class diversification has significant but finite economic value.** The cost of not being able to invest in a single asset class is typically less than 0.50 percent on a forward-looking basis. Asset allocation explains much of the variation in returns for a portfolio, but may not explain much about the mean level of returns.
- **Don't overpay for asset class diversification.** If it costs you more than about 1.0 percent in additional fees to get exposure to a given asset class, you will usually be better off dropping it from your allocation so as to maximize your portfolio expected return.
- **Keep alternative investments to a small part of your portfolio.** If you do choose to invest in alternative investments like real estate, commodities, or hedge funds, keep the allocations to a small part of your portfolio and be very wary of high fees and unobserved risks.

CHAPTER 9: PICKING THE GOOD ONES

- **Fund expenses are important predictors of future investment performance.** These expenses include annual expense ratios, loads, and costs due to portfolio turnover.
- **Stick with low-cost investments.** Generally, you should avoid bond funds with expense ratios above 0.75 percent, large-cap equity funds with expense ratios above 0.75 percent, and small/mid-cap and international equity funds with expense ratios above 1.0 percent.
- **Compare the performance of funds against peers with similar investment styles.** Bond funds should be evaluated against other bonds funds and equity funds should be evaluated against similar equity funds. The Financial Engines fund scorecards on the *Personal Online Advisor* service provide these types of evaluations based on peer group rankings.
- **Managers with good historical performance are not guaranteed to repeat such results.** You should significantly discount history when predicting future investment performance. Even good managers have bad runs of performance.
- **Picking good active funds is difficult.** Identifying high-quality active fund managers is difficult and time consuming. Unless you are willing to invest the time and effort required, you should consider index funds as the most appropriate holdings for your core assets.

CHAPTER 10: FUNDING THE FUTURE

- **Get started early.** Time is your friend when funding future goals. The earlier you start, the less you will have to save.
- **Realistically estimate your retirement income needs.** Most people will need retirement income equal to 60 percent to 80 percent of the annual income they earn in the year prior to retirement to maintain their standard of living. In addition, women need to take into consideration the fact that they are likely to live longer than men, which means they will need higher retirement savings.
- **Determine your odds of success.** Use investment simulation models like that in the *Personal Online Advisor* service to see if you are on track to reach your goal. If not, adjust your strategy until you have a good chance of success.

- **Confidence costs money.** If you want to be very confident of reaching a goal, you will need to save more of your current income and invest more conservatively.
- **Adjust your risk level to be consistent with your time horizon.** For longer investment horizons, it will usually make more sense to invest in portfolios with higher allocations to equities to maximize your chances of reaching a goal.
- **The more flexible your goal is, the more risk you can assume in your investment strategy.** If a financial goal can be delayed or reduced in size if markets perform poorly, then you have more flexibility with your investment risk level.
- **Take full advantage of your retirement plan employer match.** This is free money—take as much as you can get.
- **Revisit your savings plan periodically.** Life changes, so be sure your savings plan changes with it. You may need to change your savings rate over time to stay on track.

CHAPTER 11: INVESTING AND UNCLE SAM

- **Focus on maximizing after-tax returns rather than minimizing taxes.** Your goal should be to maximize your after-tax wealth, not to avoid taxes at all costs.
- **Tax-efficient investing means paying lower tax rates and deferring taxes into the future where possible.** You can't avoid taxes altogether, but you can minimize their impact. Try to avoid higher tax rate distributions like short-term capital gains and interest income from your investments in taxable accounts.
- **The higher your income tax rate, the more important tax-efficiency is to your investment success.** Higher-income investors have more to gain with tax-efficient investment strategies. Anyone making more than about $50,000 per year should be considering the tax-efficiency of their investment strategy.
- **Equity funds are generally more tax efficient than bond funds.** Except for municipal bonds, bond funds tend to generate large amounts of taxable interest income, making them tax-inefficient when held in a taxable account.
- **Hold less tax-efficient assets (e.g., taxable bonds) in a tax-deferred account and more tax-efficient assets in your taxable account.**

Asset placement can make a significant difference in overall after-tax portfolio returns.

- **Index funds are generally more tax-efficient than actively managed funds.** Because they tend to trade less frequently, index funds generate fewer capital gains distributions making them more tax-efficient.
- **Avoid equity mutual funds with large short-term capital gains distributions.** Active equity funds with high turnover (more than 100% per year) are particularly likely to distribute short-term capital gains.
- **High-income investors should consider municipal bonds for bond exposure in taxable accounts.** If you are in a high income tax bracket, you should consider municipal bonds for your fixed income holdings in taxable accounts. However, never hold municipal bonds in a tax-deferred account like an IRA, as you are just giving up expected return.
- **Remember that tax-efficiency is only one factor in selecting funds.** You also need to consider investment style, fees, and manager performance to build good portfolios.
- **Finally, use your common sense.** If something sounds too good to be true. It almost certainly is. Don't be suckered in by a slick sales pitch if the promises don't make sense.

Appendix

The Personal Online Advisor

To assist with applying the investment concepts contained in this book to your personal investment portfolio, Financial Engines has agreed to provide purchasers of this book with a fee waiver for a one-year term subscription to the *Personal Online Advisor* investment advisory service. Developed over a period of 10 years by a team of financial experts and talented software developers, the *Personal Online Advisor* provides investors with the ability to realistically simulate investments and receive personalized investment advice on any number of retirement and taxable investment accounts in a household portfolio.

The service is very easy to use and provides a first-use experience that walks you through the required information step by step. There are a few things that are helpful to keep in mind in taking advantage of this subscription offer for the *Personal Online Advisor*:

- Upon proof of purchase and acceptance of applicable legal agreements, including the Financial Engines Advisers L.L.C.'s Investor Services Agreement and Terms of Service, you may access the *Personal Online Advisor* service, with Total Portfolio Advice without charge for one year. After your one-year subscription expires, you have the option to continue your account at the then current fee rate if you desire.
- Financial Engines does not receive any compensation based on the products it recommends and is an independent provider of investment advice and portfolio management services.
- All information entered into the *Personal Online Advisor* service is strictly confidential and protected against unauthorized access. Financial Engines will not sell, reveal, or share your personal information except as authorized or required by law or with your permission.
- You are responsible for correctly entering your information to get accurate results. For the service to provide high-quality advice, you need

to enter accurate, complete, and up-to-date information about your investments and personal circumstances.

- The service models approximately 26,000 traded mutual funds and individual stocks at the time of this writing. The service does not currently provide modeling of closed-end mutual funds, commodities, or individual bond positions. However, you can proxy most unmodeled assets by using one of the provided generic investment types.
- Financial Engines does not guarantee future results.
- Financial Engines offers e-mail and phone support for the *Personal Online Advisor*. If you have any questions, you can contact the customer support group for help.
- This offer is subject to change or revocation at Financial Engines' sole discretion at any time. Offer is not valid where prohibited and is non-transferrable.

The user interface for the service has been designed with two primary paths, one for first-time users and one for repeat visitors. On the first-time use, the service will walk you through a series of screens to enter your assets, present you with a forecast, and ultimately provide specific investment advice. On subsequent sessions, the interface switches to a more open-ended experience that allows the user to more easily explore various areas of the service.

The *Personal Online Advisor* service is designed to provide investors with personalized advice and analysis. The service delivers two important pieces of information:

- A forecast of estimated retirement income based on your investment holdings and savings
- Specific actionable investment advice for your household accounts

The forecast uses Financial Engines' sophisticated simulation methodology to provide a realistic view of the possible range of outcomes for your household portfolio, taking into consideration the specific characteristics of the actual mutual funds and stocks in your portfolio. You can establish one or more investment goals and assign different accounts to each goal. Using complex optimization techniques, the service will recommend portfolio allocations to help you best achieve investment goals. The most innovative portion of the service is its ability to interactively explore the impact of different decisions for risk, savings, time horizon, and investment goals to develop an investment strategy that has a high probability of success. By moving sliders for each decision, you can see in real time how your forecast changes and how your portfolio outcomes are affected.

To get started, open your browser and go to: http://www.financial engines.com/intelligentportfolio and follow the directions on the screen. To access your account you will need the authorization code found on the card in the back of your copy of *The Intelligent Portfolio*. Once you have entered your authorization code, you will be asked to complete some personal contact information and select a user ID and password.

After you have established your account, you will be requested to provide some basic information about yourself and your investment accounts. You will have the opportunity to provide information on holdings in one or more retirement accounts, including any contributions going into the accounts. The *Personal Online Advisor* models a variety of taxable and tax-deferred accounts, including IRA, 401(k), 403(b), brokerage, and other account types. For each account you will need to specify the funds and stocks you hold and the value of your positions. An important feature of the *Personal Online Advisor* is the ability to electronically link your accounts with other financial institutions so that your account data is automatically updated when you log in. To receive advice on your accounts, you will also need to specify the investment alternatives available to you in each account. This process is simplified with a simple search tool for finding the mutual funds in your account. If you prefer, you can also specify alternatives by fund family or by popular fund supermarkets.

At the conclusion of these steps, you will be presented with a retirement forecast based on the assets you have entered. The forecast is an estimate of the range of alternatives you might experience based on your current investment strategy. The simulation will illustrate the range of possible portfolio outcomes based on your investment horizon. The next step is setting up a retirement income goal for your household. We recommend setting up two goals—a desired level of spending in retirement, and a goal for a minimum acceptable level of spending. The *Personal Online Advisor* will help you construct an investment strategy that yields at least a 50 percent chance of reaching your desired goal and a 95 percent or better chance of attaining your minimum spending goal. With the specification of these goals, the service will estimate the probability of reaching your desired income goal based on your current investment strategy.

Finally, the service will take you through a series of decisions to determine how you can improve your forecast by increasing your savings, changing your risk level, improving the efficiency of your investment allocation, and perhaps changing your retirement date. The objective is to help you develop an investment strategy has with a high probability of success. Once you have developed a strategy that meets your needs, you can generate an advice action kit that provides detailed instructions on how to implement the recommendations.

There is much more functionality in the *Personal Online Advisor* service than I have described here. However, this brief introduction should get you started on applying institutional-quality financial techniques to your personal investment portfolio.

Notes

CHAPTER 1

1. *Source: EBRI Databook on Employee Benefits*, January 2007, Chapter 7.
2. *Source:* U.S. Census Bureau, Population Division/International Programs Center, August 2006.
3. See *Federal Reserve Statistical Release, Flow of Funds Accounts of the United States, Flows and Outstandings,* Second Quarter 2007. Board of Governors of the Federal Reserve System, Washington DC.
4. *Source:* SpectrumGroup, *Retirement Market Insights 2007,* Chicago, Illinois. 2007.
5. Those who are familiar with statistics will recognize this simple simulation experiment as modeling a binomial distribution. We can, in fact, analytically calculate the probability of each number of observed heads exactly without resorting to simulation. Of course in more complex situations, it can quickly become untenable to analytically calculate the probabilities of events without using simulation techniques.
6. As of January 2007, the Financial Engines simulation model incorporated 15 assets classes: cash, U.S. intermediate government bonds, U.S. long-term government bonds, corporate bonds, mortgage bonds, international bonds, U.S. large-capitalization growth equities, U.S. large-capitalization value equities, U.S. medium-capitalization growth equities, U.S. medium-capitalization value equities, U.S. small-capitalization growth equities, U.S. small-capitalization value equities, developed Pacific Rim equities (including Japan), developed European equities, and emerging markets equities. Investments simulated by the model may have exposures to one or more of these asset class factors.
7. Sharpe, William F., "Determining a Fund's Effective Asset Mix," *Investment Management Review,* November/December 1988, pp. 59–69.
8. Upon proof of purchase and acceptance of Financial Engines Advisers L.L.C.'s Investor Services Agreement and Terms of Service, you may

access the *Personal Online Advisor* service, with Total Portfolio Advice without charge for one year. Financial Engines does not guarantee future results.

CHAPTER 2

1. For those who seek to better understand such market dynamics and are willing to delve deeper into the concepts, I highly recommend that you read *Investors and Markets: Portfolio Choices, Asset Prices, and Investment Advice,* by William F. Sharpe. This recent book provides an excellent introduction to the concepts in modern asset pricing theory and is relatively light in the use of advanced mathematics.
2. The average or expected value of the bond asset is $5,000. Similarly, the average payoffs of the safety net and bonus assets is also $5,000 since $0 × 0.5 + $10,000 × 0.5 = $5,000.
3. All simulation results are based on Financial Engines' estimates of expected returns and volatilities from January 2007. As these estimates are updated with new information on a monthly basis (including current market conditions), the forecast outcomes can vary slightly from time period to time period.
4. Note that the range between the downside and upside values represents the outcomes that we would expect to see in 90 percent of the portfolio scenarios. Only 10 percent of the time would we expect to see outcomes that would fall outside of this range, with 5 percent being lower than the downside and 5 percent being higher than the upside.
5. It should be reiterated that the downside and upside values (representing the 5th and 95th percentiles of the distribution of outcomes, respectively) do not represent the best and worst case scenarios. A significant difference between the stock and bond distributions is the width of the extreme tails of the distributions. For stocks, the extreme tails of the distribution (e.g., the 1st percentile) are much more severe than those of bonds, even if the 5th percentile values may be comparable. With stocks you have a substantially higher chance of experiencing severe outcomes in very bad times. This can become an important consideration in determining your tolerance for risk.

CHAPTER 3

1. See, for instance, Sirri, Erik R., and Peter Tufano, 1998, "Costly Search and Mutual Fund Flows," *Journal of Finance,* 53, pp. 1589–1622.

2. In this example, assuming that my volatility estimate of 1 percent was correct, I could be 95 percent confident that the historical average estimate was within 1 percent of the true expected return with only four years of observations if returns were assumed to independent and approximately normally distributed.
3. However, unlike the estimate of the expected return, we *can* get reasonable estimates of the volatility of stock returns and the correlations of stock returns with other assets by looking at history. The reason volatility and correlations are more reliably estimated from fewer observed values is that the precision of the volatility estimate depends on the number of observations, while the precision of the average estimate depends on the length of the historical sample (see Merton, Robert, "On Estimating the Expected Return on the Market: An Exploratory Investigation," *Journal of Financial Economics* 8 (1980) 323–361.) Thus, the volatility and correlations can be more precisely estimated using higher-frequency data (e.g., monthly or daily), while estimating the average requires a longer sample period (a larger number of years). If you are interested in the basic intuition for why splitting up the data does not improve your estimate of the average, suppose that you have 12 months of data and calculate the average return. If you then split the data into 52 weekly observations and take the average, and then convert in back into a monthly estimate by multiplying by 52/12, you get the same estimate of the average. Your estimate of the average does not depend on the number of observations, but only on the total length of the period. In general, the uncertainty about the true long-run estimate of the average goes down with the square root of the length of the historical sample period. This implies that it takes four times as much data to reduce the error in the average estimate by half.
4. For those with some math and statistics background who are interested in a more detailed description of the calculation, I include it here for reference. For a set of observations$\{x_i\}$, the expected value of the sample arithmetic mean is:

$$E\left(\overline{\mathrm{X}}\right) = \frac{1}{N}\sum_{i=1}^{N} x_i = \mu$$

Where μ is the mean of the true underlying distribution, and N is the number of observations (years) in the sample.

With enough data, the estimate of the sample mean (measured over historical observations) will converge to the underlying population mean μ. However, with a limited sample of data, there will be sampling error around the estimate of μ. The variance of the sample mean is given by (assuming returns are independent):

$$Var\left(\overline{X}\right) = Var\left(\frac{1}{N}\sum_{i=1}^{N} x_i\right) = \frac{1}{N^2} Var\left(\sum_{i=1}^{N} x_i\right) = \frac{1}{N^2}\sum_{i=1}^{N} Var\left(x_i\right)$$

$$= \left(\frac{1}{N^2}\right)\sum_{i=1}^{N}\sigma^2 = \frac{\sigma^2}{N}$$

Taking the square root of both sides, we have the standard deviation of the sample mean:

$$\text{Stdev}\left(\overline{X}\right) = \frac{\sigma}{\sqrt{N}}$$

Hence, the potential error in the estimate of μ goes down with the square root of N, the number of years in the sample. If we want the estimate of μ to be within plus or minus 1 percent of the actual expected return with a 95 percent confidence interval, this implies:

$$\frac{1.96\sigma}{\sqrt{N}} = 0.01 \text{ or } N = [196(0.20)]^2 \cong 1{,}500\, years.$$

5. This sensitivity has been documented in many statistical studies of equity returns. In one such study, Bekaert and Grenadier (2001) find the historical (log) equity premium (the expected return of stocks minus the expected return on risk-free bonds) to have an average value of 6.14 percent, but a standard error of 2.4 percent. This implies that the actual risk premium may easily fall within a confidence interval of two standard deviations yielding a range of 1.3 percent to 10.9 percent. Thus, we would expect the true risk premium for stocks over bonds to be in the range of 1.3 percent to 10.9 percent approximately 95 percent of the time. Of course this range is so wide that it is effectively useless for forecasting. Accordingly, available historical data does not provide much precision on estimating the risk premium.
6. *Source:* Yahoo! Finance, Consumer Price Index, and author calculations. Calculation period is from August 1967 to July 2007.
7. The expected real rate of return (arithmetic average) for the simulations of the S&P 500 portfolio was 7.3 percent. This yields an average growth rate (cumulative return) of 4.9 percent for the 10,000 scenarios. The growth rate, or cumulative return estimate, represents the median outcome of the distribution and declines with volatility.

8. If markets are efficient, then stock prices are going to follow what economists call a *random walk*. The price movement in each period will be uncorrelated with the price movements in previous periods. This means that the price will be about as likely to increase in a given period as it is to decrease. In reality, there is a positive bias to overall stock prices as the market has a positive expected return. However, over the timescale of a month, the change in price for a random stock is about as likely to increase as it is to decrease. Another common variation of this example has the newsletter author picking the direction of the stock market as a whole each month.
9. See Wisen, Craig H., *The bias associated with new mutual fund returns,* Kelley School of Business, Indiana University, January 2002, http://papers.ssrn.com/abstract=290463. Also see Evans, Richard. *Mutual Fund Incubation,* Carroll School of Management, Boston College, Boston, MA., http://www.isenberg.umass.edu/finopmgt/uploads/basicContentWidget/15822/Incubation_13Mar2007.pdf
10. See "Do low hemlines spell bad news for the market?" September 7, 2007, Reuters, http://today.reuters.com/news/
11. This calculation is fairly straightforward. The probability of a single person flipping eight heads in a row is $(0.5)^8 = 1/256$. The probability of no one in a group of N coin flippers getting eight heads in a row is the product of the probabilities of each coin flipper failing to get eight heads in a row. Since the probability of a single coin flipper failing is $(1-1/256) = 255/256$, the probability of N coin flippers failing to get eight heads in a row is $(255/256)^N$. The only way that no one out of N coin flippers gets eight heads in a row is that they all fail, so the probability that at least one person succeeds is simply one minus the chance that no one gets eight heads in a row, or $[1-(255/256)^N]$. For a group of 100 coin flippers (N=100), this probability equals 32 percent. If we had a 1,000 coin flippers, the probability increases to 98 percent.
12. For an example of the type of coverage the fund has received in the popular press, see "The Man Who's Beaten the Market 15 Years Running," Andy Serwer, *Fortune Magazine,* November 27, 2006, Vol. 154 (11), pg 212–222.
13. *Source:* Count of unique articles or press releases mentioning Legg Mason Value Trust fund on Lexis/Nexis over the period 2001–2006. The search covered 33 different publications, including: *US News & World Report, NY Times, Washington Post, AP and Reuters Wire Stories, Business Week, Business Wire, Chicago Tribune, Financial Times, LA Times, Forbes, Fortune, PR Newswire,* and *USA Today.*

14. *Source:* Legg Mason Capital Management, Legg Mason Value Trust mutual fund fact sheet, 2007: http://www.leggmason.com/funds/ourfunds/factsheets/value_trust.asp
15. Mauboussin, Michael. *More Than You Know: Finding Financial Wisdom in Unconventional Places,* New York, Columbia University Press, pp. 44–45.
16. It should be noted that the error range on the frequency of such an event is high for a sample of 10,000 scenarios. We would need considerably more scenarios to accurately estimate the incidence of such a rare event. However, the fact that one of these scenarios was observed in only 10,000 scenarios indicates that the probability is much greater than one in 2.3 million.
17. *Source:* Financial Engines and author calculations. The probability of beating the S&P 500 in a year is based on the estimated investment style, expenses, turnover, and fund-specific risk characteristics using the Financial Engines simulation model.

CHAPTER 4

1. *DALBAR Study of Investor Behavior, 2004.* Accessed at http://dalbarinc.com/
2. In reality, the math behind these calculations is a bit more complex, as you need to identify the overall difference between the returns on stocks and those on bonds in order to calculate the relative differences in expected returns for each asset class. There are a variety of methods of running the required calculations. If you are interested in playing around with such an algorithm, William Sharpe makes an interactive worksheet on reverse optimization available on his web site at http://www.stanford.edu/~wfsharpe/ws/wksheets.htm. By experimenting with different inputs you can develop some intuition into how expected returns are reflected in different market proportions.
3. There is an argument that value stocks have additional risk that is not fully captured by the volatility of returns. Value stocks tend to reflect companies that have lower market values relative to their accounting values (often companies in distress), and hence may be more subject to financial dislocations (bankruptcy) if conditions suddenly worsen. Such securities may do proportionately worse in very bad times than more healthy companies. This type of "peso problem" risk may not show up often in historical returns, but it may be anticipated and priced by the market and hence impact expected returns. Such an argument hinges

on the correlations for value stocks with the market being higher when times are very bad (e.g., a depression).

4. The estimate of 5.5 percent is expressed as an arithmetic average real return (adjusted for inflation). Global market portfolio weights are adjusted for the impact of the estimated U.S. home country bias.
5. Actually, for longer horizons and risky assets, the distribution looks like a traditional bell curve that is peaked and stretched to the right. See Figure 6.2 in Chapter 6 for an example diagram of a portfolio wealth distribution with a risky asset.

CHAPTER 5

1. For those readers interested in a more thorough exploration of how our brains think about risk and make financial decisions I recommend reading Jason Zweig's recent book *Your Money and Your Brain: How the New Science of Neuroeconomics Can Help Make You Rich,* from Simon & Schuster, 2007.
2. These estimates are based on highly diversified portfolios. Investments with concentrated positions in a small number of stocks, or actively managed mutual funds can have significantly higher potential short-term losses.
3. The value of 20 percent is slightly higher than the estimated loss potential from the short-term loss metric due to inflation risk. The short-term risk measure looks at potential losses without adjusting for inflation, while the portfolio value estimates are adjusted for inflation and reported in today's dollars. Even though a cash portfolio is unlikely to lose money in nominal terms, unexpected inflation can cause a loss in real terms due to the interest earned being offset by inflation.

CHAPTER 6

1. Technically this is only true if the investment returns are identically and independently distributed. However, in practice this approximation is fairly accurate.

CHAPTER 7

1. To be fair, not everything that is high quality costs more. For instance, mass-produced products often have lower defect rates than more prestigious hand-built products. As an example, certain Japanese automobiles

have demonstrated significantly lower defect rates than many hand-built automobiles costing many times more.

2. For simplicity, we leave aside the discussion of financial products whose primary goal is the provision of insurance benefits. Examples of such products include annuities, life insurance, and long-term care polices.
3. Based on the funds modeled by Financial Engines as of January 2007. Multiple share classes of equity, bond, and money market funds are included in the sample.
4. For one interpretation of this paradox, see Gruber, M. J. (1996), "Presidential Address: Another Puzzle: The Growth in Actively Managed Mutual Funds," *Journal of Finance,* July, pp. 783–810.
5. Investment Company Institute, *Research Fundamentals: Fees and Expenses of Mutual Funds, 2006*. June 2007, Volume 6, no. 2.
6. William F. Sharpe provides a nice exposition of this argument in his paper "The Arithmetic of Active Management," *The Financial Analysts' Journal,* Vol. 47, no. 1, January/February 1991, pp. 7–9.
7. In the U.S. market, about 90 percent of mutual fund assets are invested in active funds. According to the Investment Company Institute, by year-end 2006, total assets in registered exchange traded funds (baskets of stocks tied to certain indexes) and index mutual funds were approximately $1.1 trillion, accounting for about 10 percent of the total assets managed by all registered investment companies (mutual funds).
8. Now this simple calculation has some caveats associated with it. First, the sample of 22,472 open ended mutual funds only includes those that were in existence between January 1993 and May 2007. Funds that went out of business in previous time periods are not counted. And since funds that went out of business were likely to have demonstrated worse performance than those that are currently operating, this creates a potential bias in the sample (called a survivor bias). If we took the time to carefully account for this bias, we would expect to see even worse results. Also, funds with assets of less than $1 million at the time of their last trade were excluded. Note that the sample includes funds with varying lengths of trading history, though it is not obvious whether this would bias the results in one way or the other. Finally, I used Financial Engines' estimates of the investment style of each fund to create the appropriate index benchmark. Your results would vary if you used a different methodology to estimate the asset class benchmark.
9. This quantity can be calculated by comparing the size of the historical alpha to the total expected return of the underlying asset class benchmark. A fund with a positive alpha will add to the underlying

benchmark returns, while a fund with a negative alpha will subtract from it. Across the sample of 22,472 funds analyzed, the average fund gave up 22 percent of the total return from the underlying investment style based on the historical alpha. Since the expected returns of fixed income assets are lower, bond funds gave up a higher proportion of expected returns to fees than equity funds.

10. For additional reading on this subject see John M. R. Chalmers, Roger M. Edelen, and Gregory B. Kadlec, *Mutual fund trading costs,* The Rodney L. White Center for Financial Research, pp. 27–99.
11. One potential complication is taxes. If you are in a high tax bracket, you may be better off investing in a municipal money market fund that pays tax-exempt interest. More on this subject in Chapter 11. However, even in the case of tax-exempt money market funds, expenses have a huge impact on net expected returns.
12. The sample is constructed of funds that have at least 80 percent U.S. equity exposure, have at least 50 percent exposure to large-capitalization stocks, have less than 3 percent cash exposure, moderate to low fund-specific risk, and at least 120 months of trading history.

CHAPTER 8

1. As the proportions in the market portfolio change over time, these efficient allocations will become out of date. To get up-to-date information on recommended portfolio allocations, consult the *Personal Online Advisor* service from Financial Engines.
2. The Financial Engines asset class model consists of 15 different asset classes: Cash, Intermediate-Term Government Bonds, Long-Term Government Bonds, Mortgage Bonds, Corporate Bonds, Foreign Bonds, Large-Cap Value U.S. Equities, Large-Cap Growth U.S. Equities, Mid-Cap Value U.S. Equities, Mid-Cap Growth U.S. Equities, Small-Cap Value U.S. Equities, Small-Cap Growth U.S. Equities, European Equities, Pacific Rim Equities, and Emerging Markets Equities.
3. The 401(k) plan fund options in this example are hypothetical and do not reflect the actual Genentech 401(k) plan lineup.
4. Upon proof of purchase and acceptance of Financial Engines Advisors L.L.C.'s Investor Services Agreement, Terms of Service, and other legal agreements you may access the *Personal Online Advisor* service, with Total Portfolio Advice without charge for one year. Financial Engines does not guarantee future results.

CHAPTER 9

1. Financial Engines uses an exponential weighting scheme that places half of the weight on the most recent five years of fund returns history in calculating manager alphas. The purpose of this weighting process is to place more emphasis of the more recent trading history, but still make use of all the available data.
2. It is worth noting that some studies place the costs of turnover even higher, particularly for funds that primarily trade in smaller-sized companies. The specific costs for a given fund are likely to vary depending on the type of trading, use of electronic crossing networks, custodial arrangements, and other details.
3. At the time of this writing, this fund was closed to new investors.
4. Based on the sample of no-load mutual funds from the Financial Engines database with at least 36 months of trading history, and a minimum of $25 million in fund assets as of May 2007.

CHAPTER 10

1. There are some additional differences between the account types that may have an impact on your preference. As of this writing, Roth IRAs have fewer restrictions on the types of withdrawals that may be made. In particular, Roth IRAs are not subject to minimum distribution requirements after age 70 and a half, and so can be used as vehicles for accumulating wealth for future generations (this is not true for a Roth 401(k) plan). Earnings from the Roth IRA can be withdrawn from the account tax free beginning in the tax year that the investor turns 59 and a half, as long as the account has been in place at least five years. Consult your tax advisor if you have specific questions regarding your situation.
2. There is a school of thought that suggests that people's income needs drop as they approach the later stages of retirement. Generally, the older you get, the less money you spend on travel and other discretionary purchases. However, depending on your circumstances, increasing health care costs could offset this decline in discretionary spending.
3. A couple of caveats are needed in these calculations. First, the inflation-adjusted annuity values reflect some additional costs to compensate the insurance company for the administrative costs of pooling the mortality risk of the annuity holders. Second, if you are married, then you need income for as long as both you and your spouse live. In the

Personal Online Advisor service, we assume for married couples that you purchase two annuities of equal size, one for each spouse, so that if one spouse dies, the other will continue to receive half of the previous household income level for as long as they live. In reality, it will generally be more efficient to not fully annuitize your wealth, but to consider annuities as one part of an overall retirement income strategy. Also, annuity rates are dependent on prevailing interest rates at the time that you annuitize. These estimates are based on long-term estimates of real interest rates.

4. For more reading on this subject, see Scott, Jason S., "The Longevity Annuity: An Annuity For Everyone?" *Financial Analysts Journal,* Vol. 63, no. 6 (January/February 2008).

CHAPTER 11

1. Those of you who are well-versed in tax-efficient investment methodology will note that the asset allocation of the combined accounts is actually somewhat different in the two examples, even though you have the same number of account dollars in each fund. The reason is that the dollars in the taxable account are worth more at liquidation since you have already paid the taxes, while the 401(k) account dollars are worth less since you still owe income taxes on the balance. This means that the two accounts are not of equal size in after-tax wealth, with the taxable account being larger than the 401(k). However, this effect is small in this example since the two funds have similar investment styles and risk characteristics. The majority of the forecast differences are due to the asset placement benefits of putting the less tax-efficient fund in the tax-deferred 401(k) account.

Glossary

401(k) An individual defined contribution retirement savings account, typically setup by employers. Both employees and employers can make contributions to the plan, which is invested at the direction of the employee (though employers may specify a default investment if the employee fails to choose one). Contributions and earnings from the investments are usually free from Federal and state taxation until the employee begins to make distributions from the account.

529 Plans State-sponsored savings accounts designed to help fund the education costs of a student. Anyone can contribute to a 529 plan regardless of income. Distributions are taxed at the child's income tax rate.

Alpha For an investment fund, a measure of the return of the fund adjusted for its risk and investment style. Alternatively, alpha is the difference between the return of the fund and an index investment with the same investment style. Alpha is often used as a measure of investment manager performance.

Alternative Minimum Tax Alternative Minimum Tax (AMT) is an alternative method for calculating income taxes. Alternative Minimum Tax calculations do not allow for standard and personal exemptions, as well as many types of itemized deductions (i.e., mortgage interest payments) and thus may result in a higher tax liability than standard income tax rules. U.S. taxpayers are required to pay the *maximum* of their AMT or normal income tax obligation under current tax law.

Arbitrage An investment strategy that requires no risk, but has a positive expected profit. Formally, this means a strategy that requires no net investment, cannot lose money, and has a positive probability of making a profit. Arbitrage opportunities should generally not exist in an efficient market.

Asset Class A category of investments such as stocks, bonds, or cash that share similar risk-and-return characteristics.

Asset Placement The process of positioning investments like a bond, stock, or a mutual fund in either taxable or tax-deferred accounts so as to maximize after-tax investment returns.

Asset-Liability Study An analysis of the ability of a pension plan, foundation, or endowment to meet future liabilities based on projected returns from a portfolio of investment assets.

Baby Boomer A term generally referring to persons born between the years 1946 and 1964. During this period of time in the United States, there was a significant increase in the birthrate that created a large number of people in this age group. Sometimes shortened to "Boomers" in popular usage.

Backtested Results based on the hypothetical performance of how an investment strategy would have performed in previous time periods, had it been implemented. Such performance results are prone to an upward bias since the data was known beforehand as the strategy was being developed.

Benchmark An investment performance standard that reflects the objectives and investment style of a manager in order to determine relative performance. For instance, managers of large-cap U.S. equity funds often use the S&P 500 index as their benchmark for measuring performance. A benchmark generally reflects the average performance for that investment style or objective.

Capital Gains The amount by which an investment's sale price exceeds its purchase price. A capital gain is the amount of profit realized by selling an asset at a higher price than it was purchased for. A *capital loss* is realized if the sale price was lower than the purchase price.

Caveat Emptor A Latin phrase meaning "let the buyer beware." In modern usage, the phrase is used to imply a lack of warranty from the seller, or for the buyer to use caution when deciding to purchase.

Contrarian In investing usage, an investor who makes decisions in opposition to the prevailing opinion. For instance, an investor who sells equities when they increase in price and buys more when they drop in price. A contrarian investor is the opposite of a momentum investor, who follows prevailing trends.

Cost Basis The cost of an investment used to determine tax liabilities. The cost basis of an investment typically reflects the purchase price, including commissions, accrued interest, and other expenses.

Defined Benefit A defined benefit plan is a retirement plan that pays the employee a specific benefit amount, usually based on salary and years of service. In a defined benefit plan, the employer or plan sponsor bears the investment risk and provides guaranteed payments to the employee.

Defined Contribution A defined contribution plan is a retirement plan where the employee bears investment risk and has discretion over how the assets are allocated. The employer or plan sponsor is responsible for making contributions into the plan, but does not bear any investment risk. The benefits received by the employee depend on the investment performance of the account.

Deterministic The property of events or models that have no uncertainty, but instead are based on fixed assumptions that progress will occur in a predictable fashion. A deterministic model will always return the same result given the same inputs.

Discount Rate A factor that determines the value of money in the future versus money today, usually expressed as a rate of interest. For instance, a discount rate of 10 percent per year, implies that a dollar one year in the future is worth $1/(1+10 percent) = $0.91 today.

Distribution Dividend, interest, or capital gains payments made to the shareholders of an investment. Distributions can be one-time or recurring based on a periodic schedule.

Dividends Payments made to the shareholders of a company in the form of cash or additional shares of stock in proportion to the numbers of shares held.

Effective Tax Rate The average tax rate as a proportion of total income after taking into consideration personal exemptions, capital gains and losses, itemized deductions, and other adjustments. The effective tax rate is typically lower than the marginal income tax rate for a tax payer or household.

Employee Stock Purchase Plan (ESPP) A program that allows employees to purchase shares of common stock in the company at a discount to the current market price (often 15 percent).

Equilibrium A situation where the forces of demand and supply are in balance with each other. For instance, the price of a stock is created by the equilibrium between those who wish to purchase the stock and those who wish to sell it. The market price of the stock balances these two desires.

Equities Another word for shares of stock in a corporation.

Exchange-traded fund (ETF) A fund, comprised of a basket of stocks that trades on a public stock exchange that can be traded at any time during the day. Exchange-traded funds are similar to mutual funds, except that they trade throughout the day like an individual stock. Exchange-traded funds can also be sold short, like a stock. Most exchange-traded funds are designed to track a specific index.

Expected Return The arithmetic average of future possible rates of return on an investment, weighted by their probability of occurrence.

Expense Ratio The operating expenses of a mutual fund including management fees, distribution fees, and other expenses expressed as a percentage of assets in the fund. For instance, an expense ratio of 0.75 percent implies that 0.75 percent of the total amount invested in the fund is paid out in fees. The expense ratio does not include transaction fees or brokerage commissions.

Factor Model A model that seeks to relate the movements of an investment to common relationships with one or more economic factors or variables (e.g., interest rates, inflation, equity returns).

Fixed Income Investments that yield regular fixed payments over time, often expressed in the form of an interest rate. Common fixed income investments can include bonds, money market funds, CDs, stable value funds, and in some cases preferred stock.

Fund Incubation A process by which a number of small funds are created to test managers or investment strategies, but only those that do well are turned into publicly available products. Those funds that perform poorly are terminated or merged into existing funds, with the net effect being a positive bias in the historical returns of new mutual funds.

Fund-Specific Risk The portion of a fund's volatility that is not related to the average investment style. Fund-specific risk can come from active portfolio management decisions, style rotation, or concentration in specific securities. Funds with higher fund-specific risk are more risky than index funds with the same investment style. The more volatile a manager's performance is relative to the investment style of the fund, the higher the fund-specific risk.

Futures Contracts A standardized contract that requires delivery of a specified commodity, such as oil, wheat, foreign currency, at a date in the future. Such contracts trade throughout the day and are listed on various exchanges. Using future contracts, it is possible to establish highly leveraged positions in a given commodity.

Health Savings Account (HSA) A savings account that allows for pre-tax dollars to be set aside for current and future qualified health care expenses.

Hedge Fund A type of investment fund intended for institutional and high net-worth investors with greater flexibility in investment strategies than mutual funds. Hedge funds may employ a wide variety of strategies including the use of leverage, short-selling, and options.

Histogram A chart showing the relative frequency of data values. Histograms are used to illustrate the shape of the distribution of observations for a dataset.

Home Country Bias The propensity for investors to prefer domestic investments over foreign investments. In the United States, the observed home country bias of institutional investors has been steadily declining over time.

Individual Retirement Accounts (IRA) A tax-deferred savings account that allows pretax money to be set aside for retirement and accumulate returns without taxation until the money is withdrawn after age 59 1/2. Individual Retirement Accounts may be invested in a wide range of financial securities, including stocks and bonds. Certain income limits restrict the ability of higher income investors to make pretax contributions into an IRA.

Inefficient Market A condition in which the market values of traded securities do not reflect their true values. In an inefficient market, there may be overvalued or undervalued securities available for sale or purchase. This is the opposite of an efficient market, where the market values of securities reflect their true values.

Institutional Funds Investment funds that are intended for institutional investors rather than retail investors. Institutional funds typically have lower expense ratios and higher initial minimum investment requirements than funds marketed to individual investors. Institutional funds are often found in pension plans and employer defined contribution plans (where minimum investment requirements are often waived).

Loads Sales charges levied on the purchase or sale of mutual funds. Loads are typically used to compensate brokers who sell and market the mutual fund. Load charges are generally expressed as a percentage of the total purchase or sale amount and typically range from 3 percent to 6 percent. A front-end load is charged to an investor who purchases a mutual fund, while a back-end load is charged upon the sale of a fund.

Longevity Risk The risk associated with outliving your assets in retirement. Longevity risk comes from the uncertainty in how long you will live.

Long-Term Capital Gains The amount of profit realized by selling an asset held for one year or longer at a higher price than it was purchased for. Long-term capital gains are taxed at a lower rate than short-term capital gains (assets held less than one year).

Macroconsistent An investment strategy that is consistent with the observed market holdings of all assets. A macroconsistent strategy implemented by all investors would result in holdings that match the observed market value of all investments (the market portfolio). Macroconsistent investment strategies are special in that all investors can implement them at the same time.

Manager Alpha Another term for the alpha of an actively managed fund (see Alpha). A measure of the value added (or subtracted) by a fund manager due to security selection and active management decisions.

Marginal Income Tax The amount of tax that must be paid on an incremental dollar of income. The marginal income tax rate is higher than the average tax rate defined by the total taxes paid divided by total income. In the United States, marginal income tax rates increase with income.

Market Efficiency A condition in which the market values of traded securities accurately reflect their true values. In an efficient market, there are no overvalued or undervalued securities available for sale or purchase.

Market Portfolio A portfolio defined by holding all traded financial assets in proportion to their market values. The market portfolio represents the holdings of the average investor.

Market Timing An investment strategy based on predicting when certain sectors of the market will do better than others (e.g., stocks performing better than bonds and moving in and out of various sectors in an attempt to increase returns). Market timing strategies usually require higher levels of trading and often create more risk than more consistent investment strategies.

Median The middle value of a distribution. The median is the value such that half the observations fall above and half fall below.

Modern Portfolio Theory An investment theory pioneered by Harry Markowitz that describes how investors can build portfolios to maximize expected returns for a given level of volatility. Modern portfolio theory is widely used by institutional investors to construct portfolios.

Money Market Fund An investment fund that invests in low-risk, short-term debt securities such as certificates of deposit and Treasury notes. The net asset value of a money market fund is always set to $1.00 by convention.

Monte Carlo A statistical technique in which many simulations of an uncertain quantity are run to model the distribution of possible outcomes. Monte Carlo simulation is widely used in investment management.

Municipal Bonds Bonds issued by state, city, and local government entities. Municipal bond interest is typically exempt from federal and state taxation.

Mutual Fund An open-ended investment fund that is registered for sale to the public. Mutual funds invest in equities and fixed income and sell proportional shares in the portfolio to investors. Mutual funds are heavily regulated by the Securities and Exchange Commission (SEC).

Outcomes-Based Investing An interactive investment approach relying on observing simulated portfolio outcomes to make appropriate decisions for savings, investment risk, and time horizon.

Portfolio Optimization A mathematical technique used to construct portfolios that have desirable risk-and-return characteristics. The most popular form of portfolio optimization strives to maximize expected returns for a given level of expected portfolio volatility.

Qualified Dividends Dividends paid by a U.S. or qualified foreign company that are taxed at the long-term capital gains tax rate rather than the higher income tax rate.

Real Estate Investment Trust A trust that invests in income real estate properties or mortgage loans and is traded on a major exchange. Real Estate

Investment Trust interest typically does not qualify for the lower capital gains tax rate when held in a taxable account.

Returns-Based Style Analysis A modeling technique, developed by William Sharpe in the late 1980s, for determining the investment style of a fund based on an analysis of historical returns. Returns-based style analysis is widely used in investment management to analyze funds and manager performance.

Reverse Optimization A technique used to estimate asset class expected returns that are consistent with the observed market portfolio. The term comes from reversing the standard portfolio optimization algorithm to solve for expected returns given an efficient market portfolio mix.

Risk Averse An investor who prefers less risky investments to those with more risk. The degree of risk aversion determines, in part, what types of investments will be attractive to a given investor.

Risk Premium The incremental expected return required for investors to desire to hold risky assets over riskless assets. Generally, the risk premium is expressed as the incremental expected return of domestic equities over short-term Treasury bills.

Roth Roth IRAs and Roth 401(k) plans allow investors to make after-tax contributions that accumulate tax free and provide for tax-free qualified distributions after age 59 1/2.

Selection Bias A bias built into an experiment due to an unrepresentative or nonrandom sample. Selection bias problems due to poor sample selection can have a great impact on experimental or analytical results.

Short-Term Capital Gains The amount of profit realized by selling an asset held for less than one year at a higher price than it was purchased for. Short-term capital gains are taxed at the marginal income tax rate of the investor.

Skewed A distribution of outcomes that is asymmetric in shape relative to its mean value. Positive skewness means that the distribution has a longer right-hand tail and more of the mass of the distribution on the left. A distribution with positive skewness (common for financial returns) will have a median value that is lower than the mean.

Social Security A federal government program based on the Social Security Act, which provides workers and their dependents with retirement and disability income. The program is funded by Social Security taxes deducted from the payroll of U.S. workers.

Stable Value Investments in fixed income and certain investment contracts with the objective of capital preservation and interest income. Stable value funds employ a crediting rate algorithm that tends to reduce the short-term volatility of returns, but does not affect long-term volatility. Stable value funds are often found in defined contribution plans like 401(k)s.

Standard Deviation A common statistical measure of how spread out a collection of data values are. The standard deviation measures the spread of the data around the mean value.

Stochastic The property of events or models that include a random element or indeterminate value. A stochastic model will return different results for the same input assumptions depending on how random variables in the model turn out.

Tax Efficient An investment strategy that maximizes after-tax returns by deferring taxes, paying lower tax rates, and placing assets in the most advantageous account types.

Transaction Fee A fee that applies to a transaction to purchase or sell a security. Transaction fees are often applied to transactions in mutual funds and individual stocks.

Zero-Sum Game An economic concept that states that one person's gains must be balanced by another person's losses. Active money management is a zero-sum game in that for one manager to beat the market, someone on the other side of the transactions must underperform the market. Not all managers can be winners.

About the Author

Christopher L. Jones (Palo Alto, CA) is Chief Investment Officer and Executive Vice President of Investment Management for Financial Engines, a leading provider of independent personalized investment advice and portfolio management services in the workplace. Working closely with cofounder William F. Sharpe, Jones built and led the team of experts in finance, economics, and mathematics that developed the financial methodology for Financial Engines' personalized investment advice and portfolio management services. Jones has led the Investment Management team at Financial Engines for more than 11 years, after joining the firm as the third employee in 1996. Jones has frequently appeared in articles for the *New York Times, Wall Street Journal, BusinessWeek, Newsweek, Fortune, LA Times, SF Chronicle,* and other national publications, and regularly speaks at industry conferences and events. Jones holds an MS in business technology, an MS in engineering-economic systems, and a BA in quantitative economics, all from Stanford University. Jones lives in the Bay Area with his wife and two children and a couple of old Abyssinian cats. When not doing finance stuff, he spends his time traveling, hiking, playing basketball, and dabbling in music composition.

About the Author

Index

The Intelligent Portfolio
Christopher L. Jones

SPECIAL VALUE

To assist with applying the investment concepts contained in this book to your personal investment portfolio, Financial Engines has agreed to provide purchasers of this book with a fee waiver for a one-year term subscription to the *Personal Online Advisor* investment advisory service.

For details on this offer, see page 333 in the Appendix. To take advantage of this offer, you will need the unique promotion code printed below.

0520A2505Y

This offer is subject to change or revocation at Financial Engines' sole discretion at any time. Offer is not valid where prohibited and is non-transferable.

To access the *Personal Online Advisor*, please visit www.financialengines.com/intelligentportfolio and enter the code printed above.

ISBN: 978-0-470-22804-3

WILEY
John Wiley & Sons, Inc.